The Dyslexic Adult

The Dyslexic Adult

Interventions and Outcomes – An Evidence-based Approach

Second Edition

David McLoughlin
Independent Dyslexia Consultants, London and Department of Psychology, University of Buckingham

Carol Leather
Independent Dyslexia Consultants, London

BPS BLACKWELL

The British Psychological Society

This edition first published 2013 by the British Psychological Society and John Wiley & Sons, Ltd.
© 2013 John Wiley & Sons, Ltd

Edition history: Whurr Publishers Ltd. (1e, 2002)

BPS Blackwell is an imprint of John Wiley & Sons, formed by the merger of Wiley's global Scientific, Technical and Medical business with Blackwell Publishing.

Registered Office
John Wiley & Sons Ltd, The Atrium, Southern Gate, Chichester, West Sussex, PO19 8SQ, UK

Editorial Offices
350 Main Street, Malden, MA 02148-5020, USA
9600 Garsington Road, Oxford, OX4 2DQ, UK
The Atrium, Southern Gate, Chichester, West Sussex, PO19 8SQ, UK

For details of our global editorial offices, for customer services, and for information about how to apply for permission to reuse the copyright material in this book please see our website at www.wiley.com/wiley-blackwell.

The right of David McLoughlin and Carol Leather to be identified as the authors of this work has been asserted in accordance with the UK Copyright, Designs and Patents Act 1988.

Library of Congress Cataloging-in-Publication Data

McLoughlin, David, 1948–
    The dyslexic adult : interventions and outcomes : an evidence-based approach / David McLoughlin, Carol Leather. – Second edition, revised and expanded.
        p.   cm.
    First edition, London : Whurr, 2002.
    Includes bibliographical references and index.
    ISBN 978-1-119-97394-2 (cloth : alk. paper) – ISBN 978-1-119-97393-5 (pbk. : alk. paper)
1. Dyslexia.   2. Dyslexics.   I. Leather, Carol.
    RC394.W6M43 2012
    616.85′53–dc23
                                                                2012045249

A catalogue record for this book is available from the British Library.

Cover design by Design Deluxe

Set in 10/12pt Minion by Aptara Inc., New Delhi, India

The British Psychological Society's free Research Digest e-mail service rounds up the latest research and relates it to your syllabus in a user-friendly way. To subscribe go to www.researchdigest.org.uk or send a blank e-mail to subscribe-red@lists.bps.org.uk.

Printed in Malaysia by Ho Printing (M) Sdn Bhd

1   2013

To our families – who matter most

Contents

Preface to the Second Edition   xv

Preface to the First Edition   xvii

Acknowledgements   xix

Prologue   xxi

1   **Dyslexia in the Adult Years**   1
    Introduction   1
    History   5
    Terminology   6
    Defining Dyslexia   6
    Evidence-based Practice   8
    The Nature of Dyslexia: Behavioural Characteristics   10
    Observable Behavioural Characteristics   11
    Affective Characteristics   12
    Positive Characteristics   13
    Behavioural Characteristics: Empirical Evidence   15
    Explaining Characteristics   15
    Biology and Neurology   15
    Cognition   17
    Dyslexia: A Working Memory Model   19
    Explaining Positive Characteristics   23
    Explaining Affective Characteristics   26
    A Working Definition   28
    Dyslexia and Other Syndromes   28
    Dyspraxia   29
    Dyscalculia   30
    Attention Deficit Disorder/Attention Deficit Hyperactivity Disorder   31
    Asperger's Syndrome   31
    Visual Stress   32
    Degrees of Dyslexia   32
    The Prevalence of Dyslexia   33
    Summary   34

2 Interventions 35
Introduction 35
Psychological Development in the Adult Years 35
Transitions 37
Successful Adjustment 38
   Risk and Resilience 38
Learning in Adulthood 40
Types of Intervention 41
The Role of the Tutor/Coach 44
   Key Skills 44
The Development of Metacognitive Skills 46
Skill Development, Compensation and Accommodation:
An Integrated Framework for Development 47
Alternative Interventions 49
Summary 51

3 Identification and Assessment 52
Introduction 52
Information Gathering 53
Interviews 54
Screening 57
Checklists 57
Computer-based Tests 58
   LADS – Plus Version 58
   StudyScan and QuickScan 58
Individually Administered Tests 59
   York Adult Assessment Battery 59
   Dyslexia Adult Screening Test (DAST) 60
   Scholastic Abilities Test for Adults (SATA) 60
Formal Diagnosis 61
Testing Intelligence 62
WAIS-IV 63
   Verbal Tests 64
   Working Memory Tests 64
   Perceptual Reasoning Tests 64
   Processing Speed 64
   The Global Composite – Full Scale IQ 64
   The Specific Composite – Index Scores 65
   The Sub-test – Level WAIS-IV as an Ipsative Test 65
   The Item Level and Task Cognitive Capacities 66
Abbreviated Scales 67
Tests for Teachers 68
Further Psychological Testing 68
   Phonological Processing and Naming Speed 68
   Memory Ability 69
   Executive Functioning 70

Achievements in Literacy and Numeracy 71
   Reading 71
   Reading Levels 71
The Components of a Reading Assessment 73
Decoding 73
Comprehension 74
Listening Comprehension 75
Speed of Reading 75
The Assessment of Metacognition in Reading 76
The Assessment of Reading Skills and Information Technology 77
Writing and Spelling 77
Numeracy 79
Measuring Affective Characteristics 80
Self-Esteem 80
Anxiety 80
Re-assessment 81
Diagnosis and English as an Additional Language 81
Diagnosis and Other Syndromes 83
   Dyspraxia/DCD 84
   Dyscalculia 84
   ADD/ADHD 85
   Asperger's Syndrome 85
   Visual Stress 85
Pretending to Have a Learning Difficulty 86
Feedback to Client 86
Report Writing 87
Summary 88
Appendix A: Sample Report 95
Appendix B: A Guide through the Maze of Assessments 97

4 Counselling **100**
Introduction 100
Aims of Counselling 101
Issues in Counselling Dyslexic People 101
Approaches to Counselling 102
Couple Counselling 110
Referring On 110
Summary 111

5 Personal Development **112**
Introduction 112
Self-understanding 112
The Nature of the Difficulty 113
Interpreting Dyslexia 113
Abilities and Strengths 116
Metacognition 123

The Importance of Metacognition to Learning and Working 124
A Metacognitive Technique 127
Issues in Personal Development 128
   Self Advocacy 129
   Personal Organisation 129
   Goal Setting 130
   Prioritisation 130
   Memory Skills 132
   Social Skills 133
A Dyslexic Person's Perspective 135
A Case History – C 138
Summary 140

6   Literacy for Living   141
Introduction 141
   Prose Literacy 142
   Document Literacy 142
   Quantitative Literacy 142
Lifelong Learning 142
Planning a Programme 144
Information Processing and Literacy 145
Improving Levels of Literacy 147
Improving Reading Accuracy 147
Improving Reading Comprehension 151
   The Pass Reading Strategy 151
Improving Spelling 153
Improving Writing 154
Improving Quantative Literacy 156
A Dyslexic Person's Perspective 158
Coaches Comment 160
Summary 160

7   Academic and Professional Learning Skills   162
Introduction 162
The Keys to Success in Higher and Professional Education 164
The Importance of Metacognition 164
Self-understanding and Self-reflection 164
Self Reflection Attribution and Self Efficacy 165
Learning and Working Styles 166
Cognitive Learning Differences 166
Behavioural Learning Styles 166
Time Management 167
Organisation of Work 167
Reading 168
Critical Reading Skills 170
Comprehending Diagrammatic and Tabular Formats 171

Essay Writing   172
   Understanding the Task – Question Analysis and Process Words   173
Proofreading   174
Grammar and Punctuation   175
Spelling   175
Listening Comprehension   176
Note Taking   177
Note Making   179
Revision and Memory Skills   180
Examinations   182
Statistics   184
Presentations   185
Working in a Group   186
Tutorials   187
   The Role of the Tutor   188
   The Role of the Student   189
The Keys to Success   189
The Responsibilities of Colleges and Universities   190
Study Skills Course Outline   190
A Dyslexic Person's Perspective   192
Sample Assessment Report   193
Summary   201

8   Career Development and Guidance   203
Introduction   203
Approaches to Counselling and Development   204
Career Guidance: A Decision Making Model   205
Career Guidance and the Dyslexic: A Model   206
Case Example   214
Career Development   215
A Dyslexic's Perspective: Dyslexia and Journalism   216
Summary   218

9   Dyslexia At Work   219
Introduction   219
The Whole Organisation: Awareness Training   220
Disclosure: To Tell or Not To Tell   224
Goodness of Fit   224
Recruitment and Selection   225
   Recruitment   225
   Selection   226
The Workplace Assessment/Consultation   226
The Manager's Role   227
Challenges Facing Dyslexic People   228
Metacognitive Skills at Work   230
Transfer of Skills   230

Evaluation and Reflection 230
Changes and Transitions at Work 230
Support in the Workplace 231
   Tutoring Training, Coaching and Mentoring 231
   A Coaching Example 232
Programme Length 233
Mentoring 234
Addressing Challenges 234
Organisation 234
Time Management and Work Prioritisation 235
Organisation of Work and the Work Space 236
Memory 237
Reading at Work 237
   Reading for Information 238
   Reading Complex Material 238
Specific Visual Difficulties 239
Performance Issues 239
Written Work in the Office 240
Record Keeping 240
Report Writing 241
Numeracy 242
Proofreading and Checking 243
Listening Skills at Work 243
Minute and Note Taking 244
Meetings 244
Working in a Team 245
Interviews 247
A Note on the Use of Technology 248
Workplace Consultancy Report 248
A Coaching Course Outline 254
Summary 256

10 Advocacy **257**
Introduction 257
The Legislative Framework 259
   Dyslexia as a Mental Impairment 259
   Adverse Effects which are Substantial 260
   Long-Term Substantial Effects 260
   Normal Day-to-Day Effects 260
Reasonable Adjustments 261
   Individual Needs 262
   Integrated Experience 262
   Essential Requirements of the Job/Course 263
   An Undue Financial or Administrative Burden 263
Adjustments in Recruitment, Selection and Promotion 263
Types of Test Accommodations/Adjustments 264

Disclosing Dyslexia 267
   When to Say Something 268
   Whom to Tell 268
   What to Say 268
Policy and Practice in Employment 270
Legislation in Education and Training 270
Policy in Higher Education 270
Self-Help and Self-Help Groups 271
Dyslexia and Criminal Law 272
Summary 272

Epilogue 274

Appendix A Sample Interview Schedule 275

Appendix B Useful Contact Addresses 278

References 280

Index 305

Preface to the Second Edition

There has been an international move in the health professions towards evidence-based practice. Our commitment to this is reflected in the amended title. Nevertheless, the first edition of this book was published in 2002, so most of the research cited and the theoretical perspectives were based on work conducted prior to that date. The past decade has seen an increasing interest in dyslexia as it affects adults, with a consequent rise in the amount of research devoted to its impact in training, education and employment. We have, therefore, perceived a need for a second edition and have revised and added to the original book, to reflect developments in the scientific understanding of dyslexia in assessment methodologies and changing practice in education, the workplace and legal settings.

We have again placed dyslexia in the context of life span development, as it is at times of the normal transitions in life that it becomes most evident. Moving from one level of education to the next, entering the work force, undergoing professional education and being promoted all present dyslexic people with new challenges to which they do not adapt automatically. It is at those times that effective interventions are most important, but too much of the existing literature fails to address this, the assumption being that once an individual has learned a skill or strategy the problem being addressed will disappear. Further, although practice has improved, there is still too much generalisation of interventions adopted by those working with children to adulthood.

Evidence for good practice should be current and relevant. Wherever possible we have relied on primary sources published within the past decade, but have also drawn inferences from these for broader areas of functioning to underpin our recommendations for assessment, counselling, coaching, training and teaching. In so doing we hope that we contribute to improved practice, thereby rewarding all those dyslexic people from whom we have learned so much and who have enriched our professional lives.

David McLoughlin and Carol Leather

Preface to the First Edition

In 1993 we established the Adult Dyslexia and Skills Development Centre in response to a perceived need to provide a specialist service for dyslexic adults. We believed that they needed to be treated as a distinct group and that a particular approach is required to assessment, counselling, teaching and training. Since opening the Centre thousands of people have come through our doors. There has been an increased interest in dyslexia during the adult years. Practice has improved but there are still those who 'get it wrong', including ourselves. This book is an opportunity to pass on to others what we think we have learned. We have addressed conceptual issues and relied on evidence from systematic studies but, in the main, we have relied on our experience of working with dyslexic people on a daily basis.

Scientific research continues to focus on certain aspects of dyslexia but fails to provide a complete picture. We are constantly impressed by our clients' experiences; the anguish they have endured, the fortitude they have shown, their persistence and determination.

We have taken a lifespan approach as dyslexia is much more than an educational matter. Dyslexic people will seek advice from medical practitioners, counsellors, human resource specialists, teachers, tutors, their employers and volunteers. We hope that we have dealt with the important issues in such a way as to be of help to all these groups, and therefore to dyslexic people themselves. As we have aimed at a wide audience a number of the chapters have been written with 'selective readers' in mind. There is, therefore, a certain amount of repetition as the same solutions apply in different settings.

Acknowledgements

Our thanks to Kellie Bolger for her invaluable assistance in preparing the manuscript.

We would also like to express our gratitude to the Trustees of Independent Dyslexia Consultants Carol May and Trevor Hobbs, who give their time freely to help us keep on track, and especially to Pat Stringer who has been a loyal and supportive colleague, as well as friend for more than twenty years, and who contributed to the first edition of this book.

Prologue

Professionals who wish to develop an understanding of learning and performance difficulties and their manifestation in personal, social and work settings must develop an understanding of their impact on the lives of real people. In doing so, it will become evident that even apparently mild problems can have considerable impact on employment, education, relationships and daily living (Getzel and Gergerty, 1996).

While preparing the first edition of this book we wrote to our clients, both former and current, asking them if they could comment either verbally or in writing on their experience of being dyslexic. Some of their responses, as well comments from more recent clients, are recorded throughout the text. The ensuing is from a former client and is reproduced in its entirety as it encapsulates the journey too many dyslexic people have to undertake before gaining contentment in their lives.

The earliest memory I have of the impact of being dyslexic was when I was about seven. My teacher asked the class to write a story about an imaginary land. I remember writing this really long and imaginary story, no holds barred. I put all that I could into it. I handed it in and eagerly awaited its return. The teacher's reaction to something that I was so proud of was not what I had expected. She was really annoyed, she said I had put no effect into it and it was a terrible piece of work. She was blind to the substance, for she could only see the structure. I would take nearly twenty years before I would be so bold as to write so freely.

The next major impact dyslexia had on my life was when I was fourteen, I had to be assessed for my reading and writing. This was to see if I should be aloud to remain in the main stream and work towards my exams. The assessment was some what of a narrow-minded affair, I had to read and then spell, lists of words. An approach that is hardly the best way to determine any ones ability, let alone a dyslexic. In the real world of a classroom, I had long since employed methods and techniques, to enhance my ability, so evident in my successes in my other subjects. But based on this elaborate test I was informed that I had the reading age of a seven-year-old and I was not going to be put forward.

The head of English conclusions were clear. I was stupid, dim, a waste of time. The Education system fails a lot of people it a production line unable or unwilling to accommodate anyone who can't keep up. But it was its willingness to disregard me so readily and it failure to see beyond my bad English, without taking account of my success in other subject, was how it failed for me. This failure had such a negative impact on me. My school, may not have heard of dyslexia or worse chose not to, But that gave them no excuse and me no defence.

My biology teacher who could see my potential did succeed in changing the schools minds. She may not of have a better understanding of the problem then anyone else at my school, but she could easily see that I was not stupid nor a waste of time. With her and my mothers support, I left school with enough qualifications to secure an apprenticeship but school and education have proven to be a dreadful and very painful experience. One that would so soon start all over again.

After leaving school my approach to the problem, was to hid it, to avoid any situation where it would be exposed. I became very good at this. Some of my own family were unaware of the full extent of the problem. What else could I do? This approach worked well at first. I did not have to experience the humiliations that I had suffered at school but it came at a cost. I found myself in my mid-twenties, with limited expectations, a poor, dead end job, with no mental stimulation. This approach of hiding in the shadows, never daring to venture out, may have been safe but very limiting.

My teacher was right. I'm not stupid. So by the time I was twenty-five, I was very frustrated and unhappy, something had to change. Around this time I had started to hear about dyslexia and started to use the word about myself. I once told someone that I was dyslexic, who reply was "why don't you do something about it?" This was a revaluation, it had never dawned on me that I could. It had been such a isolating experience till then. I did not tell anyone, so no one knew and those who had in the past, had acted so negatively. So who was there to help, who was there to understand. The ideal of change scared me but I started to think that maybe something could be done.

The turning point came when I met my future wife. She wanted to go travelling around the world. This would mean I would have to leave my safe little job. It was to be a work holiday so I would have to find work, not long-term but still in another country. On my return home I would also have to find a new job. To put it simply, all the demons were let loose. But just like when I had learnt to drive, something I had put off and put off, then bought a car, so I had to learn. I left my job and went travelling. This was the point of no return. I knew that things would then have to then change. Fear is a very powerful thing but nothing compared to love.

When I come back home, I got a new job in a scientific research group, talk about the deep end. I went to the Centre and met someone who could help and understand. This was a big turning point. With her I learnt many things, like how I can best learn. But the biggest thing was that I as person came out of the shadows to feel the warm glow of the sun without fear and limitation.

It has just occurred to me that until this moment I have never thought about what if? What if I was not dyslexic. This may sound surprising, but I am dyslexic. Just like I am a man. I have always concerned myself with no what I can't do, but with what I can do. I cannot change being dyslexic but I can change the effect it has. I think this realistic approach to dyslexia and life is one of the positive side to it. Another is the feeling that comes with success and achievement, such as to be able to participate in one of man kinds greatest achievement, the written word. The ability to pass knowledge and experiences from one generation to another. This, many may take for granted, as I would take walking. A simple and at times dull activity. But what joy and wonder one would feel, if achieved, when previously perceived as impossible. Every time I read a book and learn and remember the knowledge that is within, I achieve something that I once perceived as impossible.

So where am I now? I am 36 and have long since come out of the dyslexic closet. I also wrote what you are now reading, which is far in a way the best description of where I am and what I can achieve.

The client who wrote the above has been in touch with us recently as he brought his children to be assessed. Both are dyslexic but it seems unlikely that they will endure the same experience, as early identification and intervention as well as parental support should minimise the impact on their skills and their emotional development.

1

Dyslexia in the Adult Years

Synopsis. *This chapter describes the characteristics of dyslexia in the adult years, and the current scientific and theoretical explanations for these. A pragmatic model based on interactions within the working memory system is proposed as a way of understanding dyslexia as it affects people during the adult years.*

Introduction

Dyslexic people seeking the advice, guidance and support of professionals usually want the answers to the fundamental questions, 'Why do I find certain tasks difficult?' and 'What can I do about it?' Alternatively, those referring people for evaluation and advice are asking, 'Why is this person not learning or performing in the way we expect?' and 'What can be done about it?' The subject of this book is the interventions that address these questions and enable dyslexic people to work towards becoming successful in education, employment and life generally.

In the first edition of this book we wrote that 'the past decade has seen a greater interest in dyslexic adults' (McLoughlin et al., 2002: 1). There has been an even greater interest in the subsequent decade. This has been prompted, at least in part, by disability discrimination legislation. Nevertheless, this still does not mean that adults have been recognised as a distinct population, with needs that are quite different from their younger counterparts. There has been more research, but the majority of studies focus on students in third tier education and the population ranging in age from 18 to 25 years of age, a period that has become known as 'emerging adulthood' (Arnett, 2004). In terms of practice there are many more individual professionals as well as organisations providing services for dyslexic adults, but a greater number of 'experts' does not necessarily mean that there is more expertise. Often the practices adopted when working with children are inappropriately generalised to work with adults, who as Patton and Polloway pointed out twenty years ago 'are not and should not be regarded as children with a learning

The Dyslexic Adult: Interventions and Outcomes – An Evidence-based Approach, Second Edition.
David McLoughlin and Carol Leather.
© 2013 John Wiley & Sons, Ltd. Published 2013 by John Wiley & Sons, Ltd.

disability grown up' (Patton & Polloway, 1992: 411). Nevertheless, most interventions from assessment through to tutoring and accommodation are directed to the adult population who are still in education, and methodologies based on models developed for work with children. Even dyslexic people themselves perceive it as an educational issue, this being advanced as one of the reasons for the failure to disclose it to employers (Martin & McLoughlin, 2012). There is still a need for a fundamental shift in thinking on behalf of professionals, researchers, and all the organisations concerned with providing for dyslexic people. That this is the case is reflected by two reports published in the United Kingdom within the last decade: Rice and Brooks (2004) and Rose (2009).

On its release the former, *Developmental dyslexia in adults: a research review,* proved sufficiently controversial for Advocacy and Self-Advocacy groups representing dyslexic adults to call for its withdrawal. Although undoubtedly pleased that this population was being regarded seriously enough to warrant the commissioning of a report of this kind, they were disappointed both by the conclusions and the foundations on which they were based. The authors failed to acknowledge that dyslexia is still an evolving concept, as is the case for all the specific learning difficulties, and that there has been a fundamental paradigm shift, dyslexia having come to mean much more than a reading problem to such groups, as well as practitioners. There is now a better understanding of dyslexia at a cognitive level, and this has broad implications for everyday performance. Reading and spelling difficulties are skill deficits that can occur for many reasons, including lack of education.

In the Executive Summary the authors write: 'dyslexia has been interpreted widely, to embrace most if not all of the ways in which the term has been used by scientists and educationalists' (Rice & Brooks, 2004: 11). It wasn't as Part One begins with the question 'Why do some people find it so difficult to learn how to read, write and spell?' They should have also asked: Why do some learn to read but continue to find spelling difficult? Why do some people achieve good accuracy, but find it hard to retain what they read? Why do people who master skills they found difficult to acquire, such as reading and spelling, report problems in domains such as organisation and time management? It is only by asking the right questions in the first place that we can evaluate definitions and explanations. Suggesting that if the word 'dyslexic' were to disappear 'science and the world of literacy teaching and learning might be no poorer' (Rice & Brooks, 2004: 87), is unhelpful and suggests a bias that undermines the credibility of the report.

Further, whilst the authors make much of the notion that poor readers and/or dyslexics do not constitute a homogeneous group they assume that adults do. Adulthood is the longest stage of human development. There is an enormous difference between the challenges faced by an 18-year-old and those facing a 45-year-old. Learning difficulties need to be understood in contexts, one of them being the stages of development. Dyslexic adults are more than 'grown up children' (Price & Patton, 2002: 38). In a review of the Rice Report, Siegel and Smythe (2006) comment that it 'fails to fulfil its intent by providing an incomplete literature review which ignores critical definitional issues and important studies of the basic cognitive processes, as well as failing to include much of the research on appropriate interventions and accommodations for adult dyslexics, pivotal in understanding the literacy needs of the adult dyslexic' (p. 69). One might add an understanding of all their needs.

In the Rose Report, *Identifying and Teaching Children and Young People with Dyslexia and Literacy Difficulties*, dyslexia is defined as follows:

- Dyslexia is a learning difficulty that primarily affects the skills involved in accurate and fluent word reading and spelling.
- Characteristic features of dyslexia are difficulties in phonological awareness, verbal memory and verbal processing speed.
- Co-occurring difficulties may be seen in aspects of language, motor co-ordination and mental calculation.

On the positive side, authors of the report accept that dyslexia exists and the definition goes beyond reading and spelling, acknowledging that there can be co-occurring difficulties in language, organisation and aspects of maths. The focus of the report was 'children and young people'; but despite this the above is being promoted as a new definition of dyslexia that applies across the board.

It is always difficult to make international comparisons as there are differences in terminology. Nevertheless, in the *Learning to Achieve* report considering learning disabilities, including dyslexia, prepared by the American National Institute for Literacy (Taymans, 2009) it was concluded that:

1. The concept of specific learning disabilities is valid and is supported by strong converging evidence.
2. Learning disabilities are neurologically based and intrinsic to the individual.
3. Individuals with learning disabilities show intra-individual differences in skills and abilities.
4. Learning disabilities present across the life span, though manifestations and intensity may vary as a function of developmental stage and environmental demands.
5. Learning disabilities may occur in combination with other disabling conditions, but they are not due to other conditions such as mental retardation, behavioural disturbance, lack of opportunities to learn, primary sensory deficits or multilingualism.
6. Learning disabilities are evidenced across ethnic, cultural, language and economic groups.

In summary, this report is to be commended as it clearly acknowledges that 'specific' in specific learning disabilities such as dyslexia refers to neurological and, therefore, cognitively based causes that are independent of general intelligence and other potential causal factors, and have an impact on performance throughout the life span. It addresses homogeneity, heterogeneity and co-occurrence, but acknowledges the influence of environmental factors, including transitions, on outcomes for people who have a specific learning difficulty.

Although there have been more studies considering the problems facing and the needs of adults, there is no real research agenda, small projects being undertaken by particular individuals or groups. Conducting empirical studies with adults where they are not a captive audience is difficult, finding samples that represent specific populations being a particular problem, as is establishing control groups. Volunteers are likely to be the 'most needy', others being reluctant to participate, sometimes because they want to be left alone to get on with their lives. From a research perspective and for whatever reason, in the main dyslexia has remained an educational issue, rather than one which affects daily living, including employment. Outcome research on the effects of interventions during the adult years, including the impact of disability legislation, is much needed but is in short supply (Gerber et al., 2011).

In Western society the majority of the population is over 16 years of age, and 'the majority of the dyslexic population are adults' (Eden et al., 2004: 412). Nevertheless, the needs of this group have been given far less attention than those of children still at school. Whilst this makes sense if one assumes that early intervention will minimise the impact of dyslexia on people's lives, it is unfortunate. Considering the nature of dyslexia as it is manifested across the life span should lead to a greater understanding of the needs of dyslexic children. It is only by taking a long-term view that we will develop a complete understanding of the nature of dyslexia and how it affects people, and provide appropriately. Furthermore, the persistence of dyslexia in the adult years raises important issues about definition, with consequent implications for practice. It demonstrates more clearly than anything else that the focus should be underlying processing abilities rather than observable behaviours (Vellutino et al., 2004).

To take advantage of the provisions of disability discrimination legislation both in the United Kingdom and in the United States, for example, a dyslexic person must establish that their difficulties constitute a mental impairment that has significant day to day effects (UK) or substantially limits one or more major life functions (USA). A narrow view based on the experiences of children and focused on literacy or education will not protect dyslexic people from discrimination, nor will it allow them to access important resources. This is best illustrated by a United Kingdom Employment Tribunal decision in which it was determined that an individual should not be considered to be disabled within the meaning of the Disability Discrimination Act, 1995. The decision was based in part on the claimant's educational background. He was educated to degree level, and had received positive appraisals about his report writing at work. This was, however, someone whose processing abilities were within the bottom 1 per cent of the population, and who had significant problems with silent reading speed and comprehension, as well as writing speed. He had allowed himself four hours travelling time to keep an appointment, a journey that would take most people an hour. There was reference to his ability to drive, but not to the fact that he had taken the test more than ten times before passing, and that he no longer drove because, having informed companies of his difficulties, the insurance premiums he was quoted were prohibitive. The 'day-to-day effects' or 'substantial limitations' were patent, but the Tribunal could not see beyond dyslexia being a reading and spelling issue. In commenting on a young dyslexic woman's personal account of the difficulties she experienced Wehman (1996) wrote 'that "dyslexia" does not do justice to the complexity of the experience, the effort required to compensate and cope, or the many other aspects of life that are affected' (p. 347).

Establishing a large body of quantitative data might be an unachievable goal so we must rely on the small scale studies which exist, as well as the individual experiences of dyslexic people and those working with them to underpin interventions. The latter provides only qualitative data, but it can contribute to understanding, as well as inform theory and practice (Everatt, 2007). There are also several factors that should influence good practice in assessment, coaching, teaching, training and employment, including:

i. the nature of dyslexia in adulthood
ii. psychological development across the life span
iii. the principles underlying education and training in the adult years
iv. the factors research has shown to contribute to the success of dyslexic people
v. the educational and legal context.

The first of these is described in this chapter. Chapter 2 describes ii to iv and the last is discussed in Chapter 10.

History

The notion that people can have specific difficulties with reading despite being able to perform effectively in other areas has been around for a very long time (see Miles & Miles, 1999). Nevertheless, dyslexia is one of the specific learning difficulties and the real thrust in understanding these came in the 1960s. In particular, Kirk (1992) proposed a causal model that assumed the concept applied to individuals with average or better than average intelligence, but who experience difficulties at one of four levels:

- Input – from the senses.
- Integration – the brain interpreting this information.
- Memory – the information being stored and retrieved.
- Output – behaviour including reading, writing and language.

The last of these is the result of difficulties at one or more of the first three, although the emphasis in understanding specific learning difficulties is now on integration and memory process, rather than perception. Letter reversals, for example, were originally interpreted as being associated with the latter, but would now be attributed to cognitive/linguistic processes. This model is still relevant today, but too much of the literature still focuses on output or observable behaviour. Historically, the notion that we are addressing a population with average or better than average intelligence has been central to the concept of specific learning difficulties. Even those definitions that focus on specific deficits in the cognitive processes related to reading, such as phonological processing, refer to them as being 'unexpected in relation to other cognitive abilities' (Lyon, 2003: 2). The American Individuals with Learning Disabilities Act (IDEA), 2004 defines a specific learning disability as 'a disorder in one or more of the basic psychological processes involved in understanding or in using language, spoken or written, which may manifest itself in the imperfect ability to listen, think, speak, read, spell or do mathematical calculations' (Flanagan & Alfonso, 2011: 5). It excludes general learning disabilities.

There has been considerable academic debate about the relevance of intelligence and IQ in particular to the definition and identification of dyslexia, as well as specific learning difficulties generally (Siegel, 2003). Much of this is spurious, as it is the content of tests that make up IQ scales that is important rather than the Intelligence Quotient itself. In its historical context and in our view statements such as 'dyslexia occurs across the range of intellectual abilities' (Rose, 2009: 10) contradict the original conceptual understanding of specific learning difficulties and are unhelpful. They raise false expectations amongst individuals who have trouble with literacy, but whose difficulties are much more complex than this. Telling someone whose cognitive abilities are consistently at the sixteenth percentile that they are dyslexic, implying that their difficulties are specific rather than general, leads them to attempt educational programmes and seek occupations that will only cause them frustration. Having a general learning disability and being dyslexic are mutually exclusive, even though there might be similar behavioural characteristics.

Terminology

As dyslexia has been and continues to be regarded as an educational issue, much of the language surrounding it belongs to the world of education, particularly special education, and we find it very hard to get away from it. Viewed from the adult perspective a good deal of the terminology is inappropriate. One should not, for example, suggest that the manager seeking to improve his report writing skills is in need of 'remedial help'. Many professionals prefer the term 'specific learning difficulty', using the term synonymously with dyslexia. The latter is a specific learning difficulty but only one of a number, including dyspraxia, dyscalculia and attention deficit disorder, sometimes referred to as 'hidden disabilities'.

The generic term 'learning difficulty' is inappropriate for many dyslexic adults. It places the emphasis on education and many have learned very well, albeit differently, but continue to have a 'performance or life skill difficulty'. We are using the word 'dyslexia' here in its very broadest sense, that is as 'a family of lifelong manifestations that show themselves in many other ways than poor reading' (Miles, Haslum & Wheeler, 1998). Dyslexic people can find learning difficult, but in the adult years their ability to 'perform' in social, family and work settings is of greater concern. The term 'compensated dyslexic' is often used to describe those individuals who have mastered reading and writing. Literate dyslexics is better, as it implies that people are still dyslexic even if they can read and write.

Further, it has been suggested that it is preferable to refer to 'people with' or 'people who have' dyslexia. We continue to use phrases such as 'dyslexic people' or the word 'dyslexic', having met few, if any, who have described themselves as 'an adult with dyslexia'. Some of our clients have specifically disregarded phrases such as 'a person with dyslexia' because of their medical connotations.

Defining Dyslexia

Defining dyslexia has remained an elusive business. There are many definitions formu-lated by advocacy groups, practitioners and researchers (see Rice & Brooks, 2004).

Gigorenko (2001) has written that the 'quilt of definitions covering the body of developmental dyslexia is a subject for research on its own' (p. 93). The discrepancy between ability and attainment in literacy, particularly reading, has been the focus but should now be considered unsatisfactory for a variety of reasons (Siegel & Smythe, 2008). Discrepancy definitions are entirely behavioural (Ramus et al., 2003), and there have been suggestions for some years that we need to move away from them (Frith, 1999). There are those, however, who still maintain that we should focus on symptoms rather than causes (Uppstad & Tønnessen, 2007). Definitions should reflect knowledge at a particular time. We now know a great deal about the cognitive abilities that correlate with learning and performance, including the development of literacy and numeracy skills. The focus should be on cognitive processes rather than observable behaviour.

Nevertheless discrepancy definitions persist and the proposed revision to the American Psychiatric Association's Diagnostic and Statistical Manual (DSM 5) will include dyslexia rather than just reading disorder, but the suggested criteria for diagnosis are similar to those in DSM IV. That is:

(A) Difficulties in accuracy or fluency of reading that are not consistent with the person's chronological age, educational opportunities, or intellectual abilities.

(B) The disturbance in criterion A, without accommodations, significantly interferes with academic achievement or activities of daily living that require these reading skills.

Discrepancy definitions are particularly inappropriate for adults who have been able to develop their literacy skills to a level at which the discrepancy is no longer obvious. Some individuals can 'achieve typical and even superior levels of reading performance in adulthood' (Grigorenko, 2001: 84). According to a discrepancy definition, such people would no longer be dyslexic, despite clearly continuing to experience difficulties that stem from the same cognitive deficit responsible for their slower acquisition of literacy skills. Attempting to apply a discrepancy definition to adults who are no longer in formal education illustrates both the flaw in such a definition, and the failure to address dyslexia in the context of adulthood. As adults we need the skills we need, not those reflected by test norms.

In a critique of the British Psychological Society's Division of Educational and Child Psychology (DECP) working definition, 'Dyslexia is evident when accurate and fluent word reading and/or spelling develops very incompletely or with great difficulty' (BPS, 1999: 5), Cooke (2001) quite correctly wrote that the definition 'will cause serious concern to dyslexic adults – particularly those who are sometimes (inappropriately) called 'compensated' dyslexics – those who have few problems with reading but have all kinds of other problems' (Cooke, 2001: 49). The emphasis on observable accuracy and fluency, whilst occurring in many definitions, fails to take into account the purpose of reading: that is, being able to access and understand information. What is needed is a definition that addresses dyslexia as it impacts on people across the life span, or at the very least one that is specific to the adult years.

Evidence-based Practice

Much practice with dyslexic adults remains what has been termed 'nomothetic': that is, a 'one size fits all' approach that assumes dyslexic people form a homogeneous group and interventions involve the best approach for an average person. Dyslexic people form a heterogeneous group; they have things in common but their needs vary considerably. What is required is an 'idiographic' approach where decision making and solutions are for individuals.

In the health and allied professions there has been an international move towards evidence-based practice, described as the 'conscientious, explicit and judicious use of current best evidence in making decisions' (Bauer, 2007: 685). 'Evidence-based practice in psychology is the integration of the best available research with clinical expertise in the context of patient characteristics, culture and preferences' (APA, 2009; cited in Spring, 2007).

What have been described as the three pillars of evidence-based practice are shown in Figure 1.1.

Given that the concept has evolved in the health professions, the terminology surrounding evidence-based practice has a medical connotation but the three pillars are:

(a) The best evidence guiding a decision – research.
(b) The expertise of the healthcare professional to diagnose and treat the Client's problems – clinical judgment.
(c) The unique preferences, concerns and expectations that the individual brings to the health care setting.

(Spring, 2007: 613)

A simple example of how this might apply when working with dyslexic adults is making recommendations about accommodations or adjustments in a test setting. It

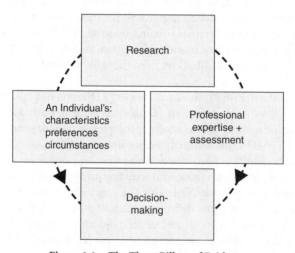

Figure 1.1   The Three Pillars of Evidence

has become standard practice to recommend a 25 per cent extra time in test settings. Allowing extra time has been shown to 'level the playing field' (see Chapter 10), but the figure of 25 per cent is entirely arbitrary and not research based. The adjustment is, therefore, nomothetic. An idiographic approach would be:

(a) Research – there is evidence to show that allowing extra time to complete examinations ensures that dyslexic people are less disadvantaged by their reading disability, but non-dyslexic people are not advantaged (Lesaux, Lipka & Siegel, 2006).

(b) Assessment expertise – proper assessment will demonstrate the extent to which the individual is disadvantaged, so a specific recommendation can be made about the amount of time needed.

(c) Individual preference – the individual should be comfortable with the recommendations made. They might, for example, wish to compete on exactly the same basis as others, or find excessive amounts of time taxing.

An idiographic evidence-based approach is essential if specific needs are to be met and 'the effectiveness of an accommodation in enhancing an individual's performance is dependent upon a professional's knowledge of the specific cognitive, affective and language processes that influence different types of learning demands' (Gregg, 2009: 19).

Evidence-based practice can also contribute to establishing equity, both real and perceived. Media attention has been given to suggestions that dyslexic people are advantaged by adjustments such as being allowed extra time to complete examinations, and research has demonstrated that adjustments such as giving more time to a person with a disability, particularly where the disability is dyslexia, lead to perceptions of unfairness (Paetzold et al., 2008).

Evidence is provided by a variety of different approaches to research, some considered to be much better than others. There are several schemas that allow the grading of the strength of evidence based on research design (see West et al., 2002). There are four levels, summarised in Table 1.1.

The research evidence for dyslexia is provided by all of the above, but a great deal of the literature on adults is based on Grade IV evidence. There are, however, studies that consider cognitive differences which would meet Grade I criteria. We would have preferred to only rely on the research that has been based on adult populations but,

Table 1.1 Schema for Grading Strength of Evidence in Research

Grade	Criteria
I	Evidence from studies of strong design; results are free from serious doubts about generalisability, bias, and flaws in research design.
II	Evidence from studies of strong design but there is some uncertainty about generalisability, bias, research design flaws, or sample size.
III	Evidence from a limited number of studies of weaker design.
IV	Support solely from informed commentators based on practical experience.

as there is evidence from longitudinal studies that suggests that 'deficits in underlying cognitive processes' persist well into adulthood (Maughan et al., 2009: 898) reference to some of the studies of child populations is legitimate.

Frith (1995, 1999) described a framework that provides a useful way of organising what we do know, as follows:

Biological Differences	(Genetics and neurology)
	↓
Cognitive Differences	(Information processing)
	↓
Behavioural Differences	(Primary behavioural characteristics, e.g. reading)

These differences interact with each other, as well as the environment. The latter can include very particular factors such as orthography. There is a substantial literature on the impact of the same cognitive processes on particular languages and writing systems when individuals are learning to read. More general factors include educational and life experience, language and culture. In order to understand dyslexia in its broadest context as it can be manifested and is reported during the adult years we begin with the last.

The Nature of Dyslexia: Behavioural Characteristics

Although in many countries dyslexia is still viewed as a reading difficulty, there does seem to be some agreement that the problems experienced by dyslexic people extend beyond literacy skills. In countries where the term 'learning disability' is used to include dyslexia there is greater recognition of this. There has yet to be a large scale systematic survey of dyslexia in the adult population that attempts to identify the incidence, and more specifically its nature.

The understanding we have of dyslexia is based in our professional training and background, but has been influenced enormously by what we learn from the dyslexic people we work with on a daily basis. Our experience is their experience, and this will have been shared by other practitioners. Reiff et al. (1993) wrote that:

> First hand experience is vital for helping professionals in the field of learning disabilities to understand and appreciate the realities of living with learning disabilities. Such information provides a useful yardstick for measuring current conceptualisations, for one criterion of a definition's validity must be the ability to reflect or correlate with the experiences of those who receive a label based on that definition. Furthermore, those insider's perspectives may provide a foundation for formulating a new definition that blends current theoretical constructs with first hand experience. (Reiff et al., 1993: 116)

The insider perspective is only level IV evidence but 'the relationship between science and practice should be a two way street, with each informing the other' (Pennington, 2009: 39). Often practice is well ahead of science, the latter providing a post-hoc rationale for the former, and scientists sometimes have insufficient exposure to those they are researching and writing about. We cannot say how often they occur exclusively amongst the population of dyslexic adults but, in our experience, those seeking advice and support manifest a number of observable behavioural and affective characteristics. These are listed below, and illustrated by comments from dyslexic people.

Observable Behavioural Characteristics

The primary behavioural characteristics that constitute dyslexia include:

Organisation – including personal organisation, as well as organisation for work and learning. Included here is time management and time keeping.

Organising my life is an arduous task.

Literacy – including word recognition, reading fluency and comprehension, spelling, written expression and writing fluency.

Spelling and numeracy problems are still predominant but I now have strategies to cope with them – on the whole. Knowing left from right and reading the time prove to be problematic (because they tend to have to be performed quickly, removing the opportunity for using strategies). I am incapable of reading aloud and this is a problem when I try to read to my daughter.

Numeracy – this is not a conceptual difficulty but a problem with the procedural aspects, including symbol recognition, calculations and remembering the order in which operations should be undertaken. There can also be a problem with the language of maths. Some dyslexic people become very good mathematicians, but continue to experience problems in areas such as mental arithmetic and have never been able to learn times tables. Poor reading comprehension can also be an issue when maths is presented in written problem form.

Spoken language skills – some dyslexic people do seem to experience problems with spoken language, such as word finding and word order. These are often not well understood in adulthood but, as well as undermining performance in educational and work contexts, they can contribute to social difficulties by interfering with communication and being the source of embarrassment.

You open your mouth to say something and then silence – only a blank space in your head.

Memory – Dyslexic people will often refer to problems they experience with memory, particularly short-term memory, without realising that this is a core issue. They perceive it as a separate problem, complaining of difficulty recalling instructions, people's names, telephone numbers and general information.

Affective Characteristics

The observed and reported affective characteristics are:

Lack of confidence – although many dyslexic people are very able, they do not perceive themselves in this way. Their achievements have often been below their own expectations and this has undermined their confidence in their abilities.

> Dyslexia affects people in different ways, personally it affected my self-confidence I was always made to feel lazy, stupid, ugly and sometimes even worthless. When I was diagnosed as dyslexic it was more a relief than anything else, so this is why my handwriting is like this and that's why I have problems with essays (putting information under the right section), that's why my maths is so bad that's why I always have problems with numbers, I remember once when I was at school someone asked me for my telephone number but I just got more confused and frustrated and couldn't remember it so I felt stupid.

Low self-esteem – dyslexic people often have a low opinion of themselves generally. They do not value their abilities or their achievements and can be inclined to apologise too much, having become used to getting things wrong.

> It's never being sure you are right.

Anger and frustration – this can include anger about the way they have been treated in the past, as well as their current situation.

> I have a lot of anger still about all the failed tasks and why none of the professionals who taught me stopped to ask what was wrong with this child who couldn't produce the written work equal to her other skills. I wish they had.

Anxiety – including general anxiety, as well as a particular reaction to learning, including learning how to use IT, as well as examinations and testing.

> I feel completely out of control and unable to function. Others may tell me that I am not out of control, but that does not alter how I feel: I feel disorientated, I keep forgetting things – my short-term and working memories are terrible, I mislay things all the time – I can't concentrate for more than a few seconds – I can't make even the simplest decision about anything – silly little decisions hold me up for hours – I feel worn out and as if on another planet much of the time – terribly stressed and at the point of collapse – only I never do collapse! I just carry on laughing it off and covering it up – trying even harder to cope when I can't.
>
> Can you imagine the feeling of anxiety building up every time you pick up a pencil, the feeling of despair every time someone asks you to read something with them present; or even worse the dreaded 'reading out loud'. The annoyance and embarrassment every time someone corrects your pronunciation or spelling. The feeling of frustration at being unable to read or write at the same speed as others. The thought that although you might have spent enormous time and effort in completing a piece of work, the chance is that it still has mistakes. The fear that you are always wrong, and pure frustration that what is in your head leaves your hands and mouth distorted.

Social interaction – academic, learning and performance difficulties can lead to poor self-concept, rejection or isolation from peers, or other negative consequences that interfere with the development of social skills.

Being dyslexic obviously creates problems with study within 'normal' systems, as the majority of schooling and higher education is based entirely on the written word. So this alone leads to stress and frustration, but for me the secondary factors of being dyslexic, anxiety and lack of self confidence have had more of an impact on me. It was not until I started to research dyslexia for this learning profile, that I realised how closely related they are.

Affective characteristics are no less important than the primary ones, and are often more difficult to resolve. It can be easier to teach someone to read than it is to improve their confidence. Even highly successful dyslexic people express doubts about their ability. Their confidence always remains fragile and setbacks can be enormous. There is often an incorrect assumption that success in some areas of life will generalise to all aspects. Wolf (2008) quotes from a speech made by former world champion racing driver Sir Jackie Stewart in which he said 'you will never understand what it feels like to be dyslexic. No matter how long you have worked in this area, no matter if your own children are dyslexic, you will never understand what it feels like to be humiliated your entire childhood and taught every day to believe that you will never succeed at anything' (Wolf, 2008: 166). Further, there is a two-way interaction between behavioural and affective factors, and this influences performance from day to day.

On a good day, I imagine that I am a highly creative and intelligent (an original thinker), with amusing and endearing quirks. Work goes better than ever, I feel I'm moving forward in strides and that I am appreciated!

On a bad day, however, I feel overwhelmed, confused and worried about my ability to cope. If I have a lot of work or something I find difficult to do, trying to organise a plan or schedule can send me into a panic. Just the mental act of keeping numerous dates, names and important information in my head is tricky. I feel I'm moving at a snail's pace and at times like these my workroom can begin to resemble the chaos in my mind, with papers spread higgledy piggledy. If I am cold calling people for work/research, I have to do several mini rehearsals first, otherwise I risk sounding tongue tied.

Often I am unable to hold on to the thoughts for long enough for me to form a sentence – either written or spoken. Using a computer helps, in that I can wipe out bits as I go along and keep the text neat and tidy. Handwritten notes always end up in a terrible mess these days – although it used not to be so. But even when using a computer, it is still difficult and of course my eyes feel strained.

Positive Characteristics

The problem with labels is that they refer to only one aspect of a person's life. Dyslexia refers to what people can't do, the risk being that what dyslexic people can do is overlooked.

Dyslexics are usually very creative people they have to be to overcome some of the difficulties they are faced with. Because we think in pictures, dyslexics are usually artistic. They are lateral thinkers and overcome problems by thinking laterally. I would also say that people with dyslexia are more articulate they say things verbally better than maybe in writing. Of course if you are speaking you don't need to bother with logical ordering or handwriting or spelling. To overcome dyslexia you need to be efficient and more organised than if it did not affect you.

Amongst positive characteristics reported are:

- entrepreneurship;
- strategic thinking;
- artistic ability, particularly where good visual-spatial skills are required;
- innovative thinking skills;
- a holistic approach to problem solving;
- empathy.

I think dyslexia forces one to have a more individual viewpoint on life because evidence suggests we think more holistically. Numerous artists, musicians and actors are / have been dyslexic, as well as famous scientists / inventors and so on. I would hope I am better able to empathise with people who experience difficulties in learning or life in general. I also hope I am more open to different learning approaches, even different philosophies, trends, and so on. Some think that dyslexia can 'give you the edge' on your chosen field because you have to be more thorough in your study / practice by necessity.

Much of the so called evidence for the above is based on anecdotes and speculation about an ever growing list of creative and gifted people, such as Einstein, but is sometimes reflected in simpler activities.

I can see the finished design of the cakes I produce before I even start. I can also assemble items very quickly. I also consider myself to be a good leader and others are happy to follow.

The talents of dyslexic people are promoted by advocacy and self-advocacy groups, as well as individuals themselves, although this is not always the case.

I'd like to say yes there are loads of positive things about being dyslexic, unfortunately, I just see it as a pain in the arse. The way I tend to look at my situation is: it could be worse I could be stupid and there is no way back from that. To the best of my knowledge there isn't an operation that cures stupid. I'm fortunate, I have 'brains', it was just not immediately apparent, to the education system, nor myself, how to utilise them.

In our experience dyslexic people can also be very:

- persistent;
- determined;
- hard working;
- resilient.

Not enough attention is paid to those dyslexic people who have demonstrated such qualities and worked effectively in fairly ordinary jobs. They have needed to be in order to be successful. The perseverance many dyslexic people have shown is impressive. This is supported by the risk and reliance research described in Chapter 2.

Behavioural Characteristics: Empirical Evidence

There are a number of systematic studies that have shown how some of the behavioural and affective characteristics described above persist into adult years. These include problems with all aspects of literacy, numeracy and academic performance generally. There are also studies that have considered occupational outcomes, as well as emotional development (see Gerber, 2012 for a review).

Not enough research has been conducted and many studies are based on samples of individuals in emerging adulthood. Nevertheless, Maughan et al. (2009) were able to follow up middle-aged individuals who had been identified as poor readers in childhood and found that on the basis of testing the majority continued to experience difficulties with all aspects of literacy including spelling, and they also reported difficulties in activities such as letter writing and filling in forms.

Few studies have addressed broader issues, but in an on-line study of graduates who had received accommodations whilst at university a significant number reported difficulties in areas such as time management and organisation. They also reported strengths in big picture thinking, empathy, persistence and determination (Martin & McLoughlin, 2012).

Explaining Characteristics

One of the underlying themes in this book is understanding. Philosopher of science Peter Lipton wrote that understanding 'is not some sort of super-knowledge, but simply more knowledge: knowledge of causes' (Lipton, 2004: 30). Most academic research is based in the logical positivist tradition and the focus is on the likeliest explanation: that is, the one most warranted by the evidence. Academic researchers, perhaps correctly, rarely go beyond this. Given the dearth of empirical studies dedicated to dyslexia in the adult years this would provide a very limited picture. We need to rely on the empirical evidence and the theory it has informed and draw inferences from the latter to provide what Lipton referred to as 'the loveliest explanation': that is, 'the one which would provide the most understanding' (Lipton, 2004: 207). This is best provided by combining all levels of evidence. We cannot just rely on anecdotal accounts and self-report, although these provide richness and reality.

Biology and Neurology

There is strong evidence for heritable factors being the initial cause of dyslexia and 'it is well established that dyslexia is a neurological disorder with a genetic origin' (Ramus, 2003: 841). This is derived from family studies, where the relatives of children with reading problems perform less well on reading tasks than those whose children do not have such difficulties, and more convincing evidence comes from twin studies (Pennington, 1990; De Fries, 1991; De Fries, Alarcon & Olson, 1997; Pennington & Olson, 2005). The process of transmission is not fully understood, and multiple genetic factors are thought to be involved (see Pennington, 2009; Grigorenko, 2001; Wolf, 2008 for an overview). The experience of interviewing dyslexic people provides much evidence of a family history of dyslexic type difficulties, although this is by no means universal. Further, it is not the behavioural characteristics such as a reading or spelling difficulty that are inherited, but the neurological and cognitive difference.

It has been established that dyslexics show significant neural organisation differences to non-dyslexic people. These differences persist throughout the life span, and are regarded as the fundamental cause of the characteristics manifested by dyslexic people at a behavioural level (Bigler, 1996). That is, they are dyslexic essentially because of their neurological make-up. The evidence comes from structural neuro-anatomic and imaging studies, as well as functional imaging studies.

Neuro anatomic studies have shown that whereas non-dyslexic people have an asymmetrical brain, the left being larger than the right, dyslexic people show symmetry, particularly in the planum temporale (Best et al., 1999). Further, nests (or clusters) of neurones which reflect 'altered prenatal neuronal migration' to the cortex have been identified where they do not exist in non-dyslexic people. As these develop prenatally, they cannot be attributed to environmental influences. Galaburda et al. (1985) hypothesised that 'the affected cortex is different in terms of its cellular and connectional architecture, hence its functional architecture' (p. 127). Galaburda (1999) has described dyslexia as a multi-level syndrome with areas of the brain connected with perceptual processing, as well as those involved in meta-cognitive tasks being anatomically affected, inferring that dyslexia represents a complex interaction of both low level and high level processing deficits.

The emphasis on 'interaction' is important as too much is made of the left/right or verbal/visual brain dichotomy. 'The brain is made up of anatomically distinct regions, but these regions are not autonomous mini brains; rather they constitute a cohesive and integrated system' (Greenfield, 1997: 39). Skills such as reading rely on the interaction between visual, auditory and motor centres. Stein and Talcott (1999) have argued that the magnocellular pathways in the brain, particularly those which link the parts involved in reading and spelling, differ in dyslexic people. They suggest that dyslexia results from 'patchily abnormal development in magnocellular neurones' throughout the whole brain contributing to visual instability and, like Fawcett et al. (1999) who have identified differences in the cerebellum, associated this with reduced phonological skills and motor problems. The role of the cerebellum in dyslexia is not well understood, but increasingly it is thought to play a part in a range of cognitive processes, including language (Schmahmann & Caplan, 2006).

Brain imaging techniques such as magnetic resonance imaging (MRI) and positron emission tomography scans, combined with blood flow techniques, have allowed the further exploration of structural and functional differences in the brains of dyslexic people. The former have confirmed some of the structural differences, notably those relating to symmetry, identified by autopsy studies. PET and fMRI scans have provided support for functional differences (Hynd & Heimenz, 1997; Shaywitz, et al., 2003, Shaywitz & Shaywitz, 2004). Consistent with structural studies differences are mainly seen in areas relating to language skills (Zeffiro & Eden, 2000; Paulesu et al., 2001; Shaywitz et al. 2003; Shaywitz & Shaywitz, 2005), dyslexic people experiencing more right hemisphere processing in reading. Nevertheless, this is not universal and it has also been suggested that several brain regions are involved.

Other neuroimaging studies have led to researchers describing the 'asynchrony phenomenon' which suggests that dyslexia, when understood in terms of reading accuracy, is caused by a speed of processing gap within and between the components of the brain involved in word decoding, particularly visual and auditory processes. Specifically, there is a timing delay when transferring information from one hemisphere to another through the corpus callosum. Studies conducted by Breznitz and her colleagues have shown initial activation in the right hemisphere amongst dyslexic people before left hemisphere activation, whereas the reverse is the case with non-dyslexic people. The former process has been shown to be slower (Breznitz & Misra, 2003; Breznitz, 2008). In general, poor connectivity amongst areas of the brain associated with reading considered to underlie dyslexia, and this is thought to be the case across different languages (Silani et al., 2005).

There are methodological concerns with functional imaging studies, the brain having been described as both a dependent and independent variable. That is, it provides access to learning but is also influenced by it (Beringer & Richards, 2002; Johansson, 2006). This raises the question of whether dyslexic people manifest problems with reading because of brain organisation, or whether the latter has been influenced by reading problems. Intervention research has suggested that the former is the case, targeted teaching leading to improved performance, correlating with normalisation of brain activation patterns (Shaywitz et al., 2004; Simos et al., 2002). This does, however, only seem to apply to the process underlying reading accuracy, not other aspects such as fluency and comprehension (Eden et al., 2004).

Cognition

To explain why the observed neurological differences are important in leading to behavioural differences, their effects on cognitive processing have been considered. Cognitive processes are hypothetical constructs that can be tested as possible explanations for the differences between dyslexic and non-dyslexic people. There have been three main scientific approaches:

1. Dyslexic people experience problems with phonological processing (Stanovich, 1996; Shaywitz, 1996; Snowling, 2001; Frith, 1999; Vellutino et al., 2004).
2. Dyslexia is a problem with visual processing, including orthographical dyslexia, where there are specific deficits in the visual system or visual memory (Goulandris & Snowling, 1991; Roberts & Mather, 1997; Skottun & Parke, 1999; Stein & Talcott, 1999; Stein, 2008).
3. Dyslexic people fail to develop a number of skills to an automatic level (Nicolson & Fawcett, 1995: 2001), now known as cerebellar theory.

The first of these has been a dominant approach internationally and there is considerable evidence to support the notion that problems in phonological processing undermine the development of reading skills. These deficits are thought to persist into the adult years, even amongst people who have reached age appropriate levels in reading (Wilson & Lesaux, 2001). Although they can co-occur with other problems such as motor and visual deficits, the majority of dyslexic adults present with a phonological processing deficit (Ramus et al., 2003; Reid et al., 2006).

Phonological skills include:

- Phonological awareness – the ability to identify the sounds of a language and manipulate them.
- Phonological memory – the ability to remember sounds, including new words and their order.
- Rapid automatic naming – the ability to retrieve sounds and words from long-term memory.

Weaknesses in any of the above can contribute to reading and spelling difficulties, as well as with language processing generally. Individuals who have problems with all three are likely to find learning to read particularly challenging, but it has been suggested that poor rapid naming ability is one of the best predictors of reading performance across languages (Wolf, 2010). It has been associated with reading fluency and comprehension (Daniels, 2008). Phonological awareness and phonological memory are often subsumed under the heading of phonological deficit. The latter is combined with poor rapid automatic naming to form the double deficit hypothesis, although evidence supporting this in adults has been variable (Vukovic et al., 2004; Cirino et al., 2005; Fink, 2003). Poor rapid naming can often be the source of language problems, including 'tip of the tongue memory' (Faust, Dimitrovsky & Shact, 2003). Price et al. (2006) consider that, at a cognitive level, there are multiple and competing phonological codes involved in reading and speech production, and at a neuronal level this suggests there is a difference in the way in which areas of the brain interact. It has been suggested that there may be a common neurological basis for word reading and rapid naming deficits (McCrory et al., 2005), but studies of young children suggest that, unlike phonological processing, rapid naming is less amenable to intervention such as direct teaching. It influences reading accuracy, but improvement in the latter does not lead to better rapid naming ability (Lervag & Hulme, 2009). This is perhaps why fluency and comprehension do not improve through the direct teaching of phonological awareness in the adult years, rapid naming being associated with those skills (Eden et al., 2004).

This is not to say that the other approaches to understanding are irrelevant. Visual processing is clearly involved in reading (Stein, 2001; Stein, 2008; Mellard & Patterson, 2008), and it has been suggested that there is a 'common linkage between reading comprehension, visual attention and magnocellular processing' (Solan et al., 2007: 270). Nevertheless, the empirical evidence for the relationship between dyslexia and magnocellular deficits is not strong (Ramus et al., 2003; Skottun & Skoyles, 2007). Further, visual processing deficits are unlikely to be associated with the problems in broader areas of functioning noted earlier. Research into automaticity (Nicolson & Fawcett, 1994,

1995, Fawcett & Nicolson, 2008) has focused on the apparent failure of dyslexic people to develop a number of skills to an automatic level, including working memory, motor skills and literacy, thus taking a wider perspective. Whilst acknowledging its significance Nicolson and Fawcett suggest that dyslexia is more than a phonological processing difficulty. Again the role of the cerebellum in dyslexia is not well understood, but the concept of automaticity would seem relevant to many of the tasks dyslexic people seem to find difficult. Nevertheless, it has been suggested that both cerebellar and visual processing deficits might be correlational rather than causal (Daniels, 2008).

Dyslexia: A Working Memory Model

Enabling dyslexic people to deal effectively with the difficulties they face begins with promoting understanding, including self-understanding and that of tutors, coaches and employers. There is a need for a sensible and comprehensive model that:

(a) explains all their primary difficulties;
(b) allows them to anticipate what might be difficult in the future;
(c) enables them to see the relevance of specific strategies.

Swanson and Siegel (2001) proposed that learning disabilities result from an impairment in working memory, and Demonet et al. (2004) have described most explanations for dyslexia as being placed within the context of multiple memory systems. Our practice in assessment, counselling teaching and training has for some years been based on the assumption that all the behavioural difficulties experienced by dyslexic people stem from an inefficiency in working memory (McLoughlin et al., 1994; McLoughlin et al., 2002). This view is based on the scientific literature, but also on our practical experience. It is reinforced by the feedback provided by our clients. We have refined the model we use according to the experiences dyslexic people report, both in terms of the problems they encounter and the solutions they find helpful. A number of studies have considered dyslexia within the context of working memory, including its involvement in literacy and numeracy as well as everyday functioning, dyslexic people reporting more 'cognitive failures' than non-dyslexic people (Swanson, 1999; Smith-Spark et al., 2004; Smith-Spark et al., 2007).

Most human activities involve working memory at some level (Logie, 1999), and most major information processing models of skill acquisition and learning include working memory as a component (Swanson, 1994). 'It is agreed by virtually all cognitive psychologists that the processes attributed to working memory are essential in human cognition. One must keep information in mind while processing it to function intellectually and socially' (Ricker et al., 2010: 573). In evolutionary terms working memory is considered to be a tool genetically adapted to cope with ever increasingly complex environments (Klingberg, 2009).

Working memory is a system fundamental to effective performance in learning and work settings. It is not identical with general intelligence but the two are highly related (Conway et al., 2003), and it has been found to be an important mechanism of general cognitive ability (Baddeley, 2007, Cowan, 2005). There are essentially two different models of working memory: the Multiple Component Model (Baddeley, 1986, 2004) and the Embedded Process Model (Cowan, 2005). Here we elaborate on the former in which working memory is described as a dynamic system responsible for:

1. Holding on to information provided by the senses in the very short term.
2. Entering information for effective storage and retrieval in long-term memory.
3. Enabling the finding of information from long-term memory on demand.
4. Allowing all three of the above to happen at the same time.

In the original model of working memory proposed by Baddeley and Hitch (1974), and revised by Baddeley (1986; 2004), it was conceptualised as being made up of three subsystems:

1. The Central Executive: This controls what we attend to, and in this way determines what information is processed. It directs the ability to focus and switch attention, and combines information arriving via two temporary storage or 'slave' systems, which have larger memory capacities.
2. The Visual-spatial Sketchpad: This is responsible for remembering visual images and spatial position.
3. The Phonological Loop: This deals with words in the broadest sense, remembering letters, words and numbers.

Brain imaging studies have found that these three components 'are echoed precisely in the activity seen when people carry out cognitive tasks' (Carter, 1998: 189). Their approximate cortical location is shown in Figure 1.2. An overview of imaging studies of the components of working memory is provided by Baddeley (2007).

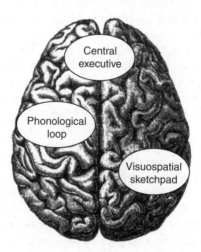

Figure 1.2   Approximate Cortical Location of Components of Working Memory

Research has also indicated that working memory capacity and its components are genetic in origin. Phonological storage has, for example, been shown to be heritable. (Rijsdijk et al., 2002; Ando et al., 2002), as has visual-spatial ability (Hansell et al., 2001) and executive functions (Ando et al., 2002; Coolidge et al., 2000).

The functions of the central executive have been described as 'a set of behavioural competencies which include planning, sequencing, the ability to sustain attention, resistance to interference, utilisation of feedback, the ability to co-ordinate simultaneous activity, the ability to change set, and more generally the ability to deal with novelty' (Crawford, 1998: 209). On the basis of our professional experience we are in no doubt that dyslexic adults manifest difficulties with aspects of executive functioning, including planning, attention and 'changing set'. A good example of the last is the approaches to reading comprehension adopted by dyslexic people. Often, having developed good reading accuracy skills, they will use the same strategy, regardless of the purpose of reading. Ask them to read a poem and they will, appropriately, read all the words carefully. They will do the same with a novel, as well as with a reading comprehension task. In other words, they do not adopt a more suitable strategy. Likewise, they might well be organised in some aspects of their life but do not apply the techniques and strategies they use to other areas.

Executive functions is a highly complex concept, and an understanding of them is still emerging. The term is sometimes used interchangeably with meta-cognition. The former belongs to neuropsychology and the latter to developmental psychology. Meta-cognition has been defined as awareness over one's own cognition, thinking and learning processes (Fernandez-Duque, Baird & Posner, 2000). Dyslexic people do not seem to develop meta-cognitive skills automatically. In particular, they have difficulty with the generalisation of newly acquired skills and strategies. It is not clear whether this reflects a specific deficit in the central executive, but there has been increasing interest in exploring this. Brosnan et al. (2002) found dyslexic individuals to show deficiencies in executive functions relating to inhibition of distractions and the sequencing of events. Smith-Spark et al., (2003) have also identified central executive deficits including those related to planning, problem solving and acting under novel situations. It seems, however, that it is only when there is a heavy task load that these are evident, and the central executive becomes involved in activities such as updating. There might, therefore, be an interactive rather than an intrinsic impairment in executive functioning.

The visual spatial sketchpad processes visual imagery and spatial information, receiving both from visual perception or retrieval from long-term memory in the form of images. It is less well understood than the phonological loop, but is thought to store images of the visual appearance of objects and scenes. It has been suggested that, like the phonological loop, it might contain two systems: a visual cache and a spatial scribe. Although a general deficit in visual spatial ability in dyslexia has been rejected (Brosnan et al., 2002; Bacon & Handley, 2010) this has been based on studies involving static tasks, and it has been suggested that there can be some impairment under taxing conditions (Smith-Spark et al., 2003).

Although it is in the phonological loop component that dyslexic people manifest evidence of a weakness, it would be naive to assume that this will only impact on the specific cognitive domains with which it has been associated. If, as Frith (1999) suggests, 'a phonological processing deficit is persistent and universal', we should be endeavouring to explain its impact on the areas of functioning other than literacy with which dyslexic people commonly report difficulties. That is, we should be asking whether such a deficit can account for the fact that dyslexic adults report difficulties with organisation, including planning and time keeping, concentration and dealing with distractions, as well as with all aspects of literacy and some features of numeracy.

The phonological loop has two components; the articulatory control system, which can hold information by articulating it sub-vocally; and the phonological store which holds speech-based information. Both components use phonological coding. The relationship between the phonological loop and the literacy difficulties experienced by dyslexic people has clearly been established, with Thomson (2001) suggesting that it is indistinguishable from 'phonological deficits'. Its function is not to remember familiar words, but to facilitate the acquisition of new words. It is also thought to be involved in syntax. A low capacity will undermine the formation of permanent representations. In an Italian study polyglots were shown to have a better phonological memory than monoglots, reflecting its importance in language learning. It is mainly in the phonological loop component that dyslexic people manifest a weakness (Ramus et al., 2003; Reid et al., 2006), and a phonological processing deficit is the dominant explanation for literacy difficulties. It is also thought to play a part in dealing with the procedural aspects of maths.

Research (Venneri, 2000; Vandierendoncke et al., 2000) has also suggested a link between the phonological loop and temporal processing as well as time perception, which might explain why some dyslexic people have trouble with time management and time keeping. It would also account for some of the difficulties they have with social interaction, when word finding and word order are an issue. A problem with the phonological loop can therefore explain some but not all of the problems they have with organisation and planning.

The brain consists of about one hundred billion neurones which are connected together in 'circuits of almost baffling complexity' (Bentall, 2010: 75). Its efficiency is determined by these connections. It has been suggested that 'the components of memory interact either positively or competitively during learning processes' (Demonet et al., 2004: 1452) and that when storage demands exceed storage capacity in one of the specific store systems some central executive capacity must be devoted to storage with the result that fewer resources are available for alternative activities (Swanson et al., 1998; Pennington et al., 1996).

It has been hypothesised that the patterns of interaction in working memory are such that, because dyslexic people have a weakness with low order processing in the phonological loop, when there is a heavy demand on speech and language, higher level processing such as executive functioning is disrupted (McLoughlin et al., 2002). This is consistent with neuroanatomic studies (Galaburda, 1999) and the neuropsychological perspective that understands dyslexia in terms of 'constraints in multi-level internal and external systems that interact in a bidirectional way' (Beringer, 2004: 91). It would explain why dyslexic people do report problems with some of the behavioural competencies described as features of executive functions. This is thought to be bidirectional in that if the central executive is overburdened, lower level processing is less efficient. One of the phenomena reported by dyslexic people is 'good days/ bad days', the latter reflected in an exacerbation of memory and literacy difficulties (Freeman, 2003). An overload on either the phonological loop or the central executive might account for this. When there are 'too many words' to deal with it is hard to organise and plan written work. When there is too much planning and organisation to be done it is hard to find the words. That is, working memory is compromised by task loads and central executive resources have to be shared. This might also apply to some visual tasks (Smith-Spark et al., 2003).

Further, it has been suggested 'working memory system processes appear to be involved in a host of mechanisms that may promote successful self-regulation. Specifically, 'working memory may be involved in directing and maintaining attention to goal directed processing, in flexibly updating goal representations in accordance with changing states of the environment, and the inhibition of interfering thoughts and emotions, as well as the inhibition of prepotent behavioural tendencies' (Hofmann et al., 2011: 212). Self-determination and control of one's actions have been described as *the* adult hallmarks of normal human development, and 'the salient feature of this cognitive and behavioural control is the capacity to direct one's thinking and action towards achieving future goals' (Wolf & Kaplan, 2008: 220). Working memory is thought to be fundamental to people's everyday attempts at self-regulation. The tasks involved include self-awareness, self-monitoring, choice of goals and prioritising.

The working memory system's role in executive functions has been of particular interest in understanding self-regulation. These have been described as 'aspects of cognition that can be key contributors to self-regulation of behaviour' (Blair & Ursache, 2011: 304). The concept of executive functions has developed to include its association with social, emotional and self-orientated processes and overall mental regulation (Wolf & Kaplan, 2008). Research has suggested a specific link with temporal processing, as well as time perception (Barkley, 2006). As with cognition the relationship between executive functions and self-regulation, as well as emotion, is thought to be bidirectional, operating in an interactive manner. One component of the working memory being inefficient will have an impact on the central executive and all its functions can be affected.

Explaining Positive Characteristics

It has been argued that the neurological organisation of a dyslexic person's brain leads to them having stronger functioning in some areas (Galaburda, 1993; Davis, 1997; West, 1997; Stein, 2001), and that dyslexic people have a different 'cognitive style' (Morgan & Klein, 2000). Much of the evidence for this is based on anecdotes, as well as speculation about creative and gifted people, many living and some deceased. The latter include Einstein, Leonardo da Vinci and Antonio Gaudi (Wolf, M., 2008). This practice, because it can raise false expectations, is considered by some to be undesirable, as there is little evidence for such claims (Adelman & Adelman, 1987; Thomas, 2000; Kihl et al., 2000). There are many living actors, writers and artists who have been identified as dyslexic, and there are disproportionate numbers of dyslexic students in art colleges (Wolff &

Lundberg, 2002). There are also a disproportionate number of entrepreneurs who are dyslexic (Logan, 2009). Whether this reflects innate abilities or a reaction to experience is open to question, and there is a false logic in assuming that the success of scientists, artists, architects and entrepreneurs is attributable to them being dyslexic. Studies of successful entrepreneurs, for example, have identified factors such as a high need for achievement, a strong inner locus of control and an ability to delegate (Rauch & Frese, 2000; Logan, 2009).

There are some systematic studies that have explored the notion that dyslexic people have visual strengths but these have 'met with limited success' (Alexander-Passe, 2010: 3) and the results have often been contradictory. Shaywitz (1996) has written that dyslexia is 'an encapsulated deficit, often surrounded by significant strengths in reasoning, problem solving, concept formation, critical thinking and vocabulary, an unexpected weakness in a sea of strengths' (p. 104). She identified more activity in the right hemisphere of the brain amongst dyslexic readers, particularly in areas associated with visual processing. Likewise, Von Karolyi et al. (2003) noted increased right hemisphere functioning associated with rapid holistic inspection amongst dyslexics, concluding that they have superior global visual spatial processing ability. There is, therefore, some evidence for the holistic thinking, strengths in visualisation and creative thinking observed amongst and reported by dyslexic people. The right hemisphere has also been associated with empathy (Baron-Cohen, 2003).

In contrast, Everatt et al. (1999) established evidence of stronger creative abilities consistent with anecdotal reports, but were not able to attribute this to enhanced right hemisphere functioning. Winner et al. (2000) found little support for the view of dyslexia as a deficit associated with 'compensatory visual-spatial talents', and suggested that the disproportionate number of dyslexic people in jobs requiring good spatial skills might be the result of them having chosen an occupation by default. That is, they have been channelled into it because of their difficulties with written language. It is perhaps inevitable that they thrive on courses and in jobs where there are fewer demands on language-based activities. It has also been suggested that dyslexics might deliberately choose creative courses and occupations as a way of avoiding reading and writing (Alexander-Passe, 2006; Wolf & Lundberg, 2002).

Having reviewed a number of studies Bacon and Handley (2010) concluded that the evidence for enhanced visual spatial ability amongst dyslexics is equivocal, but pointed out that there is also little evidence for a visual spatial deficit. This is consistent with other studies (Brosnan et al., 2002). Bacon and Handley suggest that the difference might be the way in which dyslexic people deploy the abilities they have. The dynamics of the working memory system might, therefore, provide an explanation as to why it seems some dyslexic people make a success of careers in occupations that rely on good visual spatial skills. If they do not have a deficit in the visual spatial sketchpad, perhaps when they are able to rely more on visual imagery than on verbal or written language, there is no interference with executive functioning, making tasks such as planning and organisation less arduous, particularly if they employ visual strategies. This interpretation would explain why dyslexic people sometimes thrive in occupations that tap visual abilities. It can also explain why in general, dyslexic people can recognise faces but not recall names, are effective at finding their way about using landmarks rather than verbal directions and use strategies such as mind mapping to good effect. Those who gravitate towards careers in art and design, even if it is because they find others too difficult, will be less disadvantaged as training courses will include portfolio work rather than written examinations.

In summary, if we understand the core issue in dyslexia to be a problem with a component of working memory, its nature is such that dyslexic people, especially during the adult years, are likely to experience problems with literacy and language tasks. As higher order processing interferes with lower order processing and vice versa, multi-tasking with words will be particularly problematic and this can have an impact on the following:

- Social communication – word finding and word order.
- Writing – especially organising ideas.
- Spelling – particularly in context.
- Reading – including speed and comprehension.
- Proofreading – especially one's own work.
- Maths – the procedures, including mental arithmetic.

Other behaviours that are likely to be undermined include:

- Goal setting;
- Coping with distractions;
- Self-regulation;
- Prioritisation;
- Organisation;
- Time management and estimation.

Not only should this provide a better understanding of the nature of dyslexia, but when it is interpreted in this way it allows the anticipation of what might be difficult in the future. It also provides a rationale for intervention and strategy development. A working memory model can explain the difficulties but also underpins the strategies it is assumed work for dyslexic people. In a review of the theoretical and empirical support for the use of graphic organisers which include charts, graphs, diagrams and mind maps Dexter (2010) concludes that they:

- Reduce the load on working memory.
- Tap visual spatial abilities.
- Demonstrate relationships without overloading working memory.
- Can serve as memory aids.
- Guide thinking that facilitates problem solving.

Specifically a working memory model can explain why people adopt strategies such as:

1. Preferring to try recognising faces rather than remember names.
2. Relying on landmarks rather than labels such as north and south, or left and right.

3. Word finding difficulties and problems with verbal fluency, which lead to saying the wrong thing, for example, 'an Indian winter' and 'let's not beat the bush around', are addressed through planning, preparation and practice.
4. In general, 'seeing what one has to do', rather than remembering through the use of low-tech aids such as whiteboards. The link between an intact visual spatial sketchpad has implications for career and course choice.
5. The 'good days, bad days' phenomenon can be explained as a result of the impact of a 'heavily loaded' central executive. This allows for planning the use of time in appropriate ways. Knowing that, on days when there are many demands on the behaviours influenced by executive functioning it will be very difficult to write, allows them to consciously decide to leave the report or essay to another day.
6. Relying on past experience to find suitable strategies for dealing with tasks.
7. Planning what one might say in a telephone conversation and having notes.
8. Finding quiet places in which to work to control distractions.
9. Using structure and routine to help with organisation.
10. Endeavouring to make skills automatic by analysing the task and mastering each aspect one at a time.
11. Rehearsal for examinations and presentations.

In subsequent chapters we describe the process of meta-cognition and its relevance to learning and working. Essentially, a working memory model provides a rationale for the development of meta-cognitive skills.

Explaining Affective Characteristics

At a common sense level the origins of affective characteristics are easy to understand; being put down, misunderstood and years of under-achievement do little to enhance confidence or promote positive self-esteem. People whose parents and teachers have held low expectations of them or who have jumped to obvious conclusions about the reasons for their under-performance will have low expectations and jump to obvious conclusions about themselves. They will believe what they have been told, even when this is inconsistent with their achievements. Dyslexics whose academic and occupational status indicate that they are far from idle will, for example, describe themselves as 'lazy'. There are dyslexic people who are 'victims of a poor education'; those whose difficulties were obvious but who received little in the way of support, even if they were identified as dyslexic. There are also 'victims of a good education'; those who have been taught well, worked hard and whose problems were less obvious and were attributed to factors such as attitude, and who are left wondering why they are less efficient in learning and work settings than they would like to be.

We don't know how many dyslexic people experience social and emotional problems but there is a burgeoning literature supporting the existence of affective characteristics such as stress (Miles, 2004), low confidence and self-esteem (Riddick et al., 1999;

Burden, 2008a, 2008b; Tanner, 2009; Humphrey, 2002; Alexander-Passe, 2006), anxiety (Nelson, 2011; Nalavany et al., 2011), and depression (Alexander-Passe, 2008). One of the strongest arguments for early identification and appropriate intervention is the mitigating effect on socio-emotional development (Shaywitz & Shaywitz, 2006; Nalavany et al., 2011).

Affective factors are no less important than the literacy difficulties experienced by dyslexic people, and are often more difficult to resolve. We reiterate that it can be easier to teach someone to read or find a way around it by using text to speech software than it is to improve their confidence. Even highly successful dyslexic people express doubts about their ability. Their confidence always remains fragile and setbacks can be enormous. Problems at a behavioural level cause embarrassment, leading to anxiety, lack of confidence and low self-esteem. There is still a stigma associated with literacy difficulties. Further, cognitive failure makes a person vulnerable to the effects of stress, rather than the other way around (Mahoney et al., 1998).

Although in the past models of working memory have mainly been advanced to understand and explain problems with learning and performance, Baddeley (2007) has added components to his original model, including the episodic buffer which facilitates access to long-term memory and binds together the other components. It is thought to be controlled by the central executive and assumed to play a role in episodic retrieval. Access to long-term memory, including positive and negative episodes, might therefore be impaired when the central executive is overloaded.

Baddeley has also added the hedonic detector, a system that is capable of picking up positive or negative associations from an object or representation within the episodic component of working memory. He has considered the relationship between working memory, stress and depression. The hedonic detector is part of an evaluation system, its function being to evaluate the environment, including past experiences and future plans. When these are negative the signal is negative, leading to rumination and a search for a solution. Baddeley has suggested that, if a solution is not apparent, depressive passivity might develop, and that the detector system will look for an internal explanation, 'leading to self-blame and retrieval of negative rather than positive self-schemata leading to further depression' (Baddeley, 2007: 292). This is consistent with the attribution theory described in Chapter 4. As with cognition the relationship between executive functions and emotion is thought to be bidirectional, operating in an interactive manner. An imbalance in the working memory system and accessing negative episodes might, therefore, put dyslexic people more at risk of experiencing depression.

The elaboration of working memory as a system responsible for much more than effective learning and performance implies that dyslexic people could also be more at risk of experiencing emotional problems, including stress, anxiety and depression, because of their cognitive makeup. This does not mean that past experience will be insignificant and, if we follow Baddeley's argument, dyslexic people are more likely to access negative episodes. Further, difficulties with affect are not part of the common understanding of dyslexia and are more likely to be attributable to attitude and application. Nevertheless, it seems that there might be intrinsic factors which make dyslexic people even more vulnerable to these.

A Working Definition

As described above a working memory model can provide an explanation for all the difficulties experienced by dyslexic people. It can also allow them to anticipate what might be difficult in future and guide them to the best solutions.

Tonnessen (1997) has suggested that proposed definitions of dyslexia should all be formulated and treated as hypotheses. In the first edition of this book we proposed the following definition:

> Developmental dyslexia is a genetically inherited and neurologically determined ineffi-
> ciency in working memory, the information processing system fundamental to learning
> and performance in conventional educational and work settings. It has a particular impact
> on verbal and written communication as well as organisation, time management, planning
> and adaptation to change.

The developments in the understanding of dyslexia over the past decade would suggest that this is still appropriate. The working memory explanation we have outlined here should facilitate the process by providing the 'most understanding', and a rationale for the development of skills and strategies, alternative solutions as well as adjustments. On the basis of an integration of the existing evidence it is the 'loveliest' and forms the basis for the recommendations described in the ensuing chapters.

Dyslexia and Other Syndromes

Specific learning difficulties are not necessarily unitary and there is considerable over-lap. Portwood (2010) has suggested that this is the rule rather than the exception. This is sometimes inappropriately known as comorbidity. The preferred term should be co-occurrence as the overlap is at a behavioural rather than an aetiological level. Descriptions of all the hidden disabilities include at least some of those listed earlier. Nicolson and Fawcett's (1999) observation that whatever one's interest in human behaviour and performance, dyslexics will show interesting abnormalities in that behaviour could be applied to all those who have specific learning difficulties. Interventions designed to assist dyslexic people will have much in common with those directed to people with other specific learning difficulties, and many of the skills, compensations and accommodations outlined in subsequent chapters of this book will be relevant to all the syndromes. 'The label' sometimes gets in the way, and it important to adopt an idiographic approach, focusing on specific needs and solutions. At the same time, professionals must recognise that labels allow people to identify with and learn from others through their shared experience. Individual professionals will have a particular expertise, and will often interpret behaviour and the results of an assessment within that, being susceptible to the availability heuristic. That is, they will be more likely to prefer diagnoses they most often encounter (Groopman, 2007).

It is possible to be dyslexic and dyspraxic and have Attention Deficit Disorder. We do, however, need to be cautious about over ascribing labels, particularly on the basis of scant evidence. One is often sufficient if it leads to appropriate skill development and adjustments. Nevertheless, it is important to understand that observable behavioural characteristics are the result of different neurological and cognitive processing problems. The verbal communication difficulties experienced by someone who is dyslexic might appear to be similar to those manifested by someone who has Asperger's Syndrome, but if their origin is not the same the intervention might need to be different. A multi-sensory approach to learning and working is recommended for dyslexic people but some dyspraxic people find this leads to sensory overload. Outlined below are some brief descriptions of the key features of other hidden disabilities.

Dyspraxia

Dyspraxia is a very good example of an evolving concept. Otherwise known as Developmental Coordination Disorder the criteria for diagnosis in schemata such as DSM IV and the revised DSM 5 focus on motor performance manifested as coordination problems, poor balance, clumsiness, dropping or bumping into things. Traditionally, it has been understood as being characterised by problems with the planning, coordination and execution of tasks involving visual-spatial and motor skills, but has come to mean much more to practitioners and advocacy groups.

Dyspraxia is less well understood at a neurological and cognitive level than is the case for dyslexia. It is thought to be heritable and neurological research has suggested that there is poor connectivity amongst neurones in brain regions associated with coordination and planning. Although originally thought of as a childhood disorder there is now greater recognition that it persists into adulthood (Kirby et al., 2008; Kirby et al., 2011), having an impact on academic and work performance, as well as daily living skills such as driving (Cousins & Smyth, 2003; Kirby et al., 2011). Dyspraxic individuals report difficulties with organisation, time estimation and time management, interpreted as evidence of a problem with executive functions (Kirby et al., 2011), although the question of whether there is an intrinsic deficit in frontal lobe functions has not been addressed.

To account for the latter a useful distinction has been drawn between Ideational and Ideomotor dyspraxia (Benich, 2010). Ideational relates to the conceptual organisation of actions and can affect planning, organisation, including personal organisation, time management and estimation, as well as the organisation of ideas both verbally and in writing. Ideational dyspraxia is likely to be reflected by poor performance in tests involving planning and spatial ability, not necessarily in tests involving motor skills.

Ideomotor dyspraxia relates to the execution of actions, and can have an impact on motor skills, both gross and fine, reflected in clumsiness and skills such as writing. The two can overlap but both will have a considerable impact on performance in educational settings. Ideomotor dyspraxia is likely to be reflected in slow and untidy handwriting, as well as poor performance on tests involving motor speed and coordination.

Dyscalculia

Dyscalculia has been described as an inability to conceptualise numbers, number relationships and the outcome of numerical operations. Diagnostic criteria focus on 'difficulties in production or comprehension of quantities, numerical symbols, or basic arithmetic operations that are not consistent with the person's chronological age, educational opportunities, or intellectual abilities... that significantly interferes with academic achievement or activities of daily living that require these numerical skills' (DSM IV).

There are many reasons as to why people find maths difficult. Chinn (2009) lists some of them as being problems with:

- mathematical memory;
- speed of working;
- reading and writing;
- thinking skills;
- short-term and working memory.

It should be clear from this list that it can be difficult to distinguish between the mathematical problems experienced by those who have dyscalculia and those who have dyslexia. As we have seen earlier dyslexic people will have trouble with the procedural aspects of maths, particularly those which are dependent upon working memory and, when maths is presented in written problem form their performance will be further impaired by literacy difficulties, particularly in reading comprehension.

Again, dyscalculia is thought to be heritable and neurological investigations using fMRI techniques have suggested that the fundamental cause of dyscalculia can be linked to the parietal lobe (Kadosh et al., 2007). It has been described as a lack of numerosity or a feeling for numbers (Butterworth, 1999), and Chinn (2006) suggests that a lack of understanding of maths is the key characteristic. Price (2010) draws a useful distinction between 'dyslexia with mathematical difficulties' and 'dyscalculia'. She suggests that individuals who are dyscalculic only have trouble with maths, not with literacy. In adulthood, especially in the workplace, Price suggests that this will have an impact on:

- mental arithmetic and estimation
- sequences in mathematical operations
- making quotations for jobs
- accurate counting or calculating
- difficulty dealing with change when shopping

(Price, 2010: 97)

Distinguishing between those who have genuine dyscalculia and those who have mathematical difficulties because they are dyslexic is essential in determining appropriate intervention. A 'lack of feeling for numbers' will not be addressed by improved reading strategies, memory techniques or the use of an electronic calculator.

Attention Deficit Disorder/Attention Deficit Hyperactivity Disorder

Diagnostic Criteria for Attention Disorders focus on inattention, hyperactivity and impulsivity. The former includes behaviours such as attention to detail, sustaining attention, not appearing to listen and follow through on instructions, as well as difficulty organizing tasks and activities. The latter includes restlessness, talking excessively, interrupting others and acting without thinking.

As with the other hidden disabilities it is thought to be genetic in origin and neurological studies have shown that, at a structural level, people with ADD/ADHD manifest differences in the prefrontal cortex which relates to attention and the caudate nucleus which relates to self-control. These have been reflected in fMRI studies showing different activation levels in a number of cortical areas. Klingberg (2009) wrote that 'most scientists agree that there is no one cause of ADHD – no one gene, no one neurotransmitter, no one brain area' (p. 108).

The overlap with other syndromes is best highlighted by the fact that some authors have suggested that many of the behavioural problems associated with ADD/ADHD can be attributed to deficiencies in working memory (Barkley, 1997). It would, however, appear that it is the central executive component that is impaired as adults with the syndrome have been shown not to have significant deficits in phonological processing. This is an important distinction as it is because of the latter and the impact on the central executive that dyslexic people have problems with attention, but they are task specific. Further, like dyslexic people those with ADD/ADHD experience problems with self-regulation, planning and organisation. Nevertheless, these are thought to be directly related to executive functioning deficits (Barkley, 2011).

Asperger's Syndrome

There is some debate as to whether disorders on the autistic spectrum such as Asperger's Syndrome should be included under the heading of specific learning difficulties. It is undoubtedly a disability that impairs social interaction, having an impact on eye contact, facial expression and gestures. Some people with Asperger's Syndrome also have verbal communication problems, interpreting and using language literally.

The syndrome is thought to be genetic in origin and that a prenatal abnormal migration of cells affects the structure and connectivity of the brain. This has an impact on the development of the mirror neurone system which allows for imitation. Cognitive theories have explained it in terms of poor theory of mind and empathising-systematising theory (Baron-Cohen, 2003).

It can be easy to misinterpret some of the characteristics of dyslexia as being due to Asperger's Syndrome. Dyslexic people, for example, sometimes avoid eye contact but as a way of controlling information input. Pragmatic language impairment is often associated with Asperger's Syndrome, but this has also been correlated with dyslexia (Griffiths, 2007).

Visual Stress

There are also syndromes which are not usually regarded as specific cognitive difficulties but can affect skills such as reading. One example is the visual difficulties experienced by some people when reading (Wilkins, 1995), given much publicity as one of the solutions is the use of coloured glasses or overlays. It has been known by many names, including visual discomfort, scotopic sensitivity and Meares-Irlen Syndrome. Visual stress is the current preferred term, and it is thought to lead to distortions such as blurring, eyestrain and headaches. It has received both good and bad press, coloured lenses having been hailed as a cure for dyslexia but such claims have also undermined its credibility. It has, however, been investigated systematically in recent years, but results are contradictory. Some studies suggest that coloured lenses improve reading (Evans, 2001; Wilkins, 2002; Ray et al., 2005), others have indicated that they do not (Skottun & Skoyles, 2007). At an anecdotal level they do seem to make a difference to some people. Nevertheless, although more prevalent amongst dyslexic people (Kriss & Evans, 2005), visual stress should not be confused with dyslexia, as it is only concerned with reading, and can occur amongst people who do not manifest other characteristics such as poor spelling.

Degrees of Dyslexia

A common question asked by dyslexic people is, 'How dyslexic am I?'. In the Rose Report it is suggested that dyslexia should be thought of as a continuum, not a distinct category, and that there are no clear cut off points. This is not, however, as straightforward as it may seem despite the existence of much used schemata for ratings of 'degrees' (see Turner, 1997). Do we consider the difficulties with literacy or the processing problem? Further, adults only need the literacy skills that they need. Someone could have fairly basic literacy skills, but it does not present them with a significant problem in terms of their daily and working lives. Another person might have few problems with literacy and processing, but be struggling to cope with the considerable demands upon them. If we understand dyslexia at a cognitive level, the 'degree' should be based on the processing problem not the literacy difficulty, but we should really consider the extent of the disadvantage, especially as transitions in life are particularly challenging for dyslexic people. Adults 'must succeed in a range of new, and often more complex, settings and with new sets of criteria' (Price & Patton, 2001: 12).The emphasis in disability legislation is on day to day effects, but even then it is sometimes because people have been successful that they seek advice. They gain promotion, for example, and suddenly there are increased demands for which they need to learn new skills and strategies quickly. Changes in circumstances at work can also have this effect. One man, for example, had resolved many of his difficulties with written expression by making good use of technological aids, such as a word processor. A new director of the firm he worked for was very keen on the use of information technology; inter- and intra-office communication came through email. The system in his office did not allow him to spell check documents easily, and despite it being good practice as most of us read what we think we have written, he was not allowed to delegate proof reading. He was also used to being able to read using a highlighter pen. Technology had provided him with solutions but had also created new difficulties. His dyslexia had not been a problem until it became a problem!

There are people who have been told they can't be dyslexic, or are not dyslexic enough to be covered by legislation, because they have been successful at degree level, but educational and professional achievement does not tell the whole story. The notion of degrees of dyslexia is a misnomer, as the extent to which being dyslexic affects a person is the result of a complex interaction between cognitive, behavioural and affective characteristics, as well as cultural factors. For some people dyslexia is just a *difference*; they learn to work with it and find solutions, although they sometimes hide the extent of their difficulties by doing so.

Being dyslexic can certainly be a *disadvantage*, particularly in situations when there is a heavy demand on the tasks that tap their cognitive inefficiency, but these can be accommodated and the purpose of the latter is to lessen the disadvantage. Sometimes, however, the problems experienced are such that an individual is unable to perform at an expected level without considerable adjustment being made and without a high level of support.

We work within the parameters of current policy and legislation and, if people are to be afforded equal opportunities and equity through this, dyslexia has to be regarded as a *disability*.

The Prevalence of Dyslexia

Estimates of the prevalence of dyslexia have varied enormously over the years, and are usually based on the child population. In a recent report it was estimated that dyslexia may significantly affect between 4 to 8 per cent of children (Snowling, 2008: cited in Rose, 2009). As people do not 'grow out of it', even if we compromise on a figure of around 5 per cent, it can be concluded that a significant minority of the adult population is affected to some extent.

For many years it was believed that dyslexia was more prevalent amongst males than females, and this is still advanced by the authors of some review studies (Liederman et al., 2005), but has been contradicted by others (Siegel & Smythe, 2005). Estimates of prevalence are often based on referred child samples and Pennington (2009) has argued that more boys are referred for assessment because they also manifest comorbid externalising disorders such as ADHD so their behaviour causes concern, whereas girls are more likely to internalise feelings and withdraw rather than act out. Further, gender differences have been noted during the early school years, but have been found to be less evident in later years. It has also been suggested that fewer females are identified in childhood because they tend more often than men to compensate as a result of essential differences in the neurological processing of language, so that less observable difficulties in areas such as reading comprehension are not manifested until later in life (Shaywitz, 1996).

Summary

1. The study of and provision for dyslexic adults presents a number of challenges, including issues surrounding definition and terminology.
2. The characteristics manifested by dyslexics during the adult years are such that existing attempts to explain their difficulties have been too narrow to provide a complete understanding.
3. Neurological and cognitive studies point to a phonological deficit as being the primary cause of reading problems but, when phonological processing is interpreted as being a component of working memory, they also suggest that patterns of interaction within that system will have an impact on broader areas of functioning, both positive and negative, including affect. This can help dyslexic people understand their current difficulties, predict what might be difficult in the future, as well as see the relevance of the development of specific skills and strategies.
4. Dyslexia can overlap with other hidden disabilities, and interventions will have something in common. It is, however, important to adopt an idiographic approach, based on an understanding of the aetiology of different syndromes to ensure that skills, strategies and accommodations are the most effective.
5. Determining the impact of dyslexia in the adult years requires consideration of a complex interaction between neurological, cognitive, behavioural and affective factors, as well as the demands on the individual. The concept of degrees of dyslexia is a misnomer.

2

Interventions

Synopsis: *In this chapter dyslexia is considered within the context of life-span development, particularly the challenges dyslexic people face. The interventions that can assist them develop their skills, as well as the fundamental principles underlying working with them, are described.*

Introduction

Interventions designed to assist dyslexic people fulfil their potential can be categorised as those that facilitate self understanding, and those which enable people to function more effectively in learning, work and social settings. There is inevitably some overlap. The professional activities involved in the former are:

- assessment;
- mentoring, coaching and counselling.

    The activities involved in the second group are:

- skill development;
- compensation;
- adjustments and accommodations.

    Before describing these in detail, however, it is important to consider them in the context of life-span developmental psychology, the factors research has shown to contribute to the success of dyslexic people, as well as the principles underlying education and training in the adult years.

Psychological Development in the Adult Years

Although adulthood is the longest stage of development, it is the least studied and, therefore, not particularly well understood. Nevertheless, it has been suggested that placing

The Dyslexic Adult: Interventions and Outcomes – An Evidence-based Approach, Second Edition.
David McLoughlin and Carol Leather.
© 2013 John Wiley & Sons, Ltd. Published 2013 by John Wiley & Sons, Ltd.

dyslexia within a life-span developmental perspective will provide a foundation for an understanding of the adjustment challenges faced by adults, and make the knowledge gained from research more meaningful (Gerber, 1994; Patton & Polloway, 1992; Price & Patton, 2002).

Two overriding concepts are important when placing dyslexia within a life-span perspective. The first is the basic assumptions of development, which have been identified as:

1. Development is an active lifelong process; the young adult is not the finished product. We do not just get older but continue to change, development being a process of gains and losses. As we get older, for example, we might become slower at particular tasks, but maturity, experience and expertise can make up for this (Horn & Blankson, 2005).
2. Development is the expression of biological and socialisation processes. That is, maturation involves meeting biological and social needs, including the need to reproduce and be part of a close social network.
3. Development in adulthood is multi-directional, the changes that occur involve a number of aspects, including intellectual, physical and social.

(Baltes, Reese & Lipsitt, 1980)

The second essential concept is that of the mediating factors which influence development. Patton and Polloway (1996) describe four main variables:

1. Biological and intellectual.
2. Personal and social.
3. Past experience.
4. Feeling of control over life events.

The last two of these are particularly important when considering dyslexic people, as previous successes and failures have an enormous impact on them. Many will consider that they have not been successful in the past and will not have felt 'in charge'. Their experiences, positive and negative, will remain in the episodic buffer component of working memory, and this can have a major impact on their response to interventions.

There are several theories concerning life-span development, but there are common themes to them all, summarised by Smith (1996) as:

- There is a fundamental universality to human development; everyone passes through the life stages in basically the same manner.
- There is a basic sequentiality to the human experience, everyone passing through the life stages in the same order. For example, most people leave school, secure a job, find a partner and start a family.
- The life sequence leads towards a goal; we all work towards goals, whether these be in academic achievement, job satisfaction, career development, or personal happiness.
- There are adaptive, or positive, ways and maladaptive, or negative, ways of passing through the sequence of life stages.

(Smith, 1996)

To those working with dyslexic people an awareness of the last of these is particularly important.

Transitions

Everyone faces a series of transitions: that is, life changes to which we have to adjust. A transition is 'a process of change over time – whether the change is conceptualised as being in contexts for learning or in learners' (Colley, 2007: 428). The transition from school to further or higher education, or directly into work, is one that educationalists and teachers generally recognise. There is not, however, enough acknowledgement as to how demanding this can be for the dyslexic person. For anyone the need for independent learning skills that allow them to deal with a great deal of new information, in different environments and in changing formats, is considerable. The challenge is even greater for the dyslexic student who may feel that having left school they have put their problems behind them. Moving on to a university environment, often out of the family home where there is an inherent structure, and supportive parents who provide reminders (and clean clothes!), makes demands on independent living skills. Furthermore, there are changing demands in the learning environment, long lectures, group work, infrequent contact with tutors and different assessment methodologies. All of these require good organisational skills and confidence. It has been suggested that we need to understand transitions within the context of 'life course' rather than 'life cycle', the former acknowledging that life and career trajectories have become less linear and more fragmented, and avoiding the perception of those who do not fit into staged models as being deficient (Colley, 2007). This would certainly seem relevant to dyslexic people, as some do not follow typical educational and career paths, their development being less sequentially linear than it is for others.

After leaving formal education the transition to the workplace is another that all people face. Again the demand for independent learning skills, confidence and the ability to absorb new information and understand job tasks, work culture and procedures is considerable. Dealing with constant change is a key aspect of any job these days: for example, in-service training, job redefinition, promotion to higher levels of a job, and movement from one department to another, from job to job, from employment back to unemployment, from young adulthood to mid-life, and then to old age. All of these can be challenging, and they demand energy that enables coping and adaptation and can be stressful. It is not surprising, therefore, to learn that many people with learning difficulties report that their problems have become worse (Gerber et al., 1990).

Assisting individuals to cope with present demands at any one stage is not enough. It is as important to prepare them for what is ahead of them (Garnett, 1985) as they may not have developed the executive functioning skills referred to in Chapter 1. As Smith-Spark and Fisk (2007) have suggested, 'working memory deficits will have a significant impact on planning, problem solving, acting under novel situations, and learning. Appropriate support must, therefore, be provided across a range of modalities for adults with dyslexia to achieve their full potential in both educational and employment settings' (2007: 51). There is a strong case to be made for the preparation of informal or formal transition plans that predict and address needs throughout the life course. These would enable educators, special needs advisors, trainers and human resource personnel to recognise the challenges that dyslexic people may face, predict what might be difficult and provide solutions.

Transitions can be demanding for anyone, but are particularly galling for dyslexic people, as they might not have the skills necessary to effect a positive adaptation, and often these do not develop automatically. They may need coaching, teaching or training intermittently across all the developmental stages. Dyslexic people can be very successful in all aspects of their lives, but as they confront new demands, and discover that previously developed skills and strategies need adjustment for different situations they might seek assistance.

Ironically it is often at times of transition, as a result of having been successful, that many dyslexic people seek an explanation for the problems they unexpectedly face and present for an initial assessment, as well as seek help with the development of their skills. They have not suddenly become dyslexic. Promotion, for example, can place increased demands on organisational skills as well as written language tasks such as report writing. Adults face increasingly complex tasks, especially at work and in their social lives. It is perhaps unsurprising, therefore, that to some their difficulties seem to get worse (Gerber et al., 1990; White, 1992; Price & Patton, 2002).

Successful Adjustment

Risk and Resilience

Although most research has been devoted to identifying the factors that make life difficult for dyslexic people, in order to understand the successful adjustment of people with specific learning difficulties researchers have adopted a 'risk and resilience' framework. Having a learning difficulty such as dyslexia is regarded as a risk factor: that is, something that might impact negatively on their life. People who have dyslexia can be at risk of failure in academic and employment settings, as well as experiencing social and emotional problems. Resilience refers to 'a class of phenomena characterised by good outcomes in spite of serious threats to adaptation or development. Research on resilience aims to understand the processes that account for these good outcomes' (Masten, 2001: 228). Failure does not always have negative consequences as sometimes 'it can have an impact on one's resilience and motivation and provide a positive challenge' (Tanner, 2009: 796). People with learning difficulties such as dyslexia have been found to be resilient. They have needed to be, to become successful.

Research into resilience has considered the multiple factors, both internal and external, that influence the outcome for people who have learning difficulties (Gregg, 2009). It has focused on success which is not easily defined, but in strict psychological terms this is goal achievement. Individual goals will inevitably be determined by expectations, including personal, familial and social demands. Researchers who have focused on the success of people with learning difficulties, rather than the reasons they fail, have defined it narrowly in terms of educational, occupational and financial status. Nevertheless, it has identified variables that contribute to resilience and success. (Gerber, Ginsberg & Reiff, 1992; Goldberg et al., 2003; Madaus et al., 2010).

Goldberg et al. (2003) identified six attributes common to adults with specific learning difficulties who experience a successful adult life. These include:

1. Self-awareness and an ability to define oneself as more than one's disability.
2. Social, economic and political engagement in the world.
3. Perseverance and flexibility to pursue alternate courses of action.
4. Concrete, realistic, attainable goals with strategies to reach them.
5. A support system of relationships.
6. Emotional stability and coping strategies.

Their findings are consistent with those of studies reported a decade earlier, particularly the importance of self-awareness, perseverance, goal setting, strategy development and supportive relationships (Gerber, Ginsberg & Reiff, 1992; Spekman, Goldberg & Herman, 1992). In an empirical study of successful adults Gerber and his colleagues found the overriding factor to be the extent to which they had been able to take control of their lives or felt in charge. Control was seen to involve two sets of distinct but interrelated and interacting factors:

• internal decisions: that is, conscious decisions about taking control of one's life; and
• external manifestations: that is, being able to adapt and shape oneself in order to be able to move ahead.

Internal factors   Internal factors identified by Gerber and his colleagues were:

• a desire to succeed;
• goal orientation;
• a process of re-framing.

Desire is often manifested in dyslexic people and is the reason they approach professionals for advice and guidance. The motivation to succeed is often very impressive. Many dyslexic people present as being highly motivated and this is often intrinsic rather than extrinsic. It will however sometimes have developed in response to the disappointing experiences of the past.

Goal setting is very important; dyslexic people need long-term and short-term goals. One of the roles of the professional is to assist in helping people establish clear and achievable goals. A long-term goal could be to enter a particular profession, a short-term goal to gain the necessary qualifications. It is important, however, to set even shorter-term goals, such as developing the literacy, learning and technological skills appropriate to a course of training. Addressing the short-term goals makes it easier to achieve the long-term goal. One of the main disadvantages of not being diagnosed and not understanding one's difficulties is that it is impossible to set the correct goals. When deciding on both short- and long-term goals it should be ensured that they are specific, realistic, measurable and have time limits so that they provide a focus

(Nathan & Hill,1992). Goals should also be 'approaching' and 'learning'. The former focus on the demonstration of competencies and the latter on the mastering of tasks (Latham, 2007).

Re-framing refers to the process of self-understanding but is more than this. It involves recognising that there are difficulties, accepting that these exist and developing an understanding of their nature. It also refers to the process of re-interpreting dyslexia in more productive and positive ways. It is, for example, being able to say 'I do it this way', without apologising.

External factors   External factors identified by Gerber and his colleagues are:

• persistence;
• learned creativity;
• goodness of fit;
• social ecologies.

Persistence refers to the quality of determination, often identified amongst dyslexic adults. Again this is very impressive. They are people who have experienced setbacks but have seen these as an opportunity for learning and got on with life.

Learned creativity refers to strategy development. In particular, it is important that dyslexic people become better at information processing, developing appropriate learning, memory and metacognitive skills. They also need to find alternative ways of dealing with tasks, and the use of technology can be a significant factor.

Goodness of fit is a reference to the notion of being in an environment where one is comfortable with the demands. A simple example would be undertaking a course of training or study where assessment is on the basis of coursework, produced on a word processor throughout the year rather than final examinations. It is being on the right course, at the right college or in the right job. It is here that being able to understand and therefore explain to others the nature of dyslexia and how it affects a particular individual is very important. Being able to say, 'I am dyslexic, which means that I like to use my own lap top computer because I am familiar with the software', can only improve understanding.

Social ecologies refers to the support systems people are able to take advantage of, including parents, partners, supervisors and colleagues. It is, for example, having someone who will proofread pieces of work prepared by a dyslexic without being overly critical.

Learning in Adulthood

Learning continues throughout the life span, informally in social or family contexts or more formally in education and work settings. Learning in adulthood is very different from childhood learning. It is important to have some underpinning knowledge of adult learning theory when working with dyslexic people. There are several approaches: an educational perspective (Knowles, 1990; Kolb, 1984); a social constructivist approach (Bandura, 1993, 1997); cognitive psychology (Sternberg, 2004; Swanson, 1998; Zimmerman, 2002); and coaching psychology (Gray, 2006; Passmore, 2007).

The theme common to all adult learning theory is that the learner should be independent and in control of their own learning. As we have seen above, control is a key success factor. This is especially relevant for dyslexic adults as, because of the difficulties they may have experienced with learning, they are likely to be dependent learners. They will try to learn what they are asked to and adopt practices that are less effective for them because that is what they were told to do at school. They are often 'apprentices' regarding their learning behaviour rather than 'masters' of the process (Gardener, 2007).

Knowles (1990) first introduced the concept of androgogy to adult learning. In an androgogical learning environment the individual takes responsibility for their learning. The learner becomes autonomous and self directed as they move away from the pedagogical approaches of school years, where the teacher is in charge and the curriculum governs the whole process. Price and Shaw (2000) consider that 'androgogy' provides 'both a theoretical base and practical guidance regarding instruction for adults with learning disabilities' (Price & Shaw, 2000: 23).

Knowles outlines six fundamental assumptions that underlie the teaching and training of adults and these are of direct relevance to dyslexic individuals: the need to know, the learner's self concept, the role of experience, readiness to learn, orientation to learn and motivation. These are elaborated upon in Chapter 5.

Eventually they imply that those working with adults need to play more of a facilitative role, engaging in constructive dialogue, utilising individual strengths and capitalising on previous experience. It is here that an understanding of the role of the episodic buffer component in working memory is essential, as accessing it might enable the individual to retrieve positive learning experiences.

Types of Intervention

Interventions address the questions 'Why is it difficult?' and 'What can be done about it?' The specific methodologies are described in subsequent chapters but can be summarised as:

Assessment – The purpose of this is to identify abilities, including strengths and weaknesses. The interpretation of results of an assessment should provide an explanation as to why an individual is finding certain tasks difficult and promote self understanding. The assessment process is described in Chapter 3.

> The diagnosis brought about some sort of identity crisis I guess as I am now still unsure where my personality ends and where the dyslexia begins … What I believe to be characteristics of my personality are not actually my own, but coping mechanisms (e.g. keeping lists, the need for tidiness) – it feels like I am not sure who I am anymore sometimes. Overall, though, I feel relieved: at least there is a reason for the difficulties that I am experiencing, and other 'peripheral' issues are now more understandable (e.g. difficulties in translations, remembering names). Hopefully I will be able to work around these difficulties in time, and discover some positive aspects too!

Counselling – the counselling we refer to here is specific to the nature of dyslexia and its impact on the individual; it is the logical extension of the assessment process. The

emphasis should be on the development of understanding, and further explanations as to why a person works or learns in particular ways. Self-awareness and self-
understanding have consistently been identified as key factors in achieving success.

> The only thing I believe that has helped me is getting the long awaited help that I should
> have had as a child. Being told your dyslexic is one thing, but doing nothing to help you and
> explain what it is just leaving you for years thinking you were thick and stupid, and having no
> confidence at all. Is so very wrong. I know that I am not the only person who feels like this,
> which has helped me. I can read, write, but not as good as others. I am luckier than some.
> But the mental block I have is unbelievable at times, and when you do something wrong like
> make a mistake at work, you can feel the whole world falling around your feet, that's the bit I
> still find hard to deal with. I can smile more, I even at times can make myself feel 'better than
> you' because I am gifted. I can learn in al different way from the 'norms' I am different, but I
> am not bad or stupid, thick, lazy. I am me. I feel I can control better, and I think with age it will
> get better with time.

Contextualising problems, in the sense of placing them in perspective, is important,
as is helping people establish realistic and achievable goals. The issues regarding
counselling and suitable approaches are described in Chapter 4.

Training, coaching and mentoring – There are various levels of intervention. What is
appropriate depends on the individual, their circumstances and the nature of their
difficulties. Recommendations for the frequency and level of support, as well as its
content, should come from an appropriately qualified professional who has received
training regarding the nature and impact of dyslexia on an individual, within the
context of their learning and working environment. At present in the United Kingdom
this is carried out by a variety of service providers who do not have a background in
adult learning, psychology or specific learning difficulties. This is discussed further
in Chapters 7 and 9. There is often too heavy a reliance on assessment reports or
the individual themselves, and neither may provide sufficient information as to allow
decisions about recommendations and solutions.

There is much confusion and some conceptual overlap in the terminology of the
different types of intervention. Nevertheless, they do differ in what they provide, not
only in content but also in cost and duration, as well as who is qualified to provide them.

1. **Advice, consultancy, professional guidance** – this largely involves making general
   suggestions about the options available. It can also involve outlining procedures or
   policies of organisations, and the way in which they can move towards supporting
   the dyslexic individual.
2. **Teaching and training** – these activities are both primarily focused on helping an
   individual gain competency in specific areas. Frequently it is curriculum based or
   has a structured format, and it is often provided in groups. Even on a one-to-one
   basis it will be similar as it involves learning information, and new procedures. It is
   a pedagogical, authoritarian approach where the teacher/trainer is in control of the
   format and delivery. As we have suggested above this is not an effective process when
   working with adults.

3. **Coaching** – this is a partnership and a more androgogical approach, in which the learner ultimately takes control of their own learning and progression. The aim is to help and increase the individual's awareness of what they need to do to improve their performance or develop a particular skill. It is usually conducted on a one-to-one basis, and the focus is on specific goal setting, development and personal fulfilment (Hawkins & Smith, 2006; Brook, 2009).

4. **Mentoring** – this is often confused with coaching. It is, however, a very different activity. In theory it involves shaping an individual's beliefs and values in a positive way through discussion with someone who has experience in a particular field.

5. **Professional counselling** – this intervention should be provided by someone who has an appropriate professional counselling training. It usually involves exploring psychosocial issues to gain some resolution, and enable an individual to improve their performance. This is conducted on a one-to-one basis and does not involve any other party.

The essential differences between mentoring, coaching and counselling are shown in Table 2.1.

Table 2.1   Mentoring, Coaching and Counselling

	Mentoring	*Coaching*	*Counselling*
Focus	Aimed at career development	Aimed at personal development but emphasis on improving performance at work	Aimed at improving self understanding and performance
Agenda setting	Agenda decided by mentee	Agenda agreed by individual and organisation and coach	Agenda set based on the difficulties individual is experiencing
Content	Broad view of performance	Specific goals set to improve performance	Broad view but great depth on specific issues
Professional training	Mentor is experienced in the field of knowledge/often senior/not necessarily trained to impart knowledge about two on the own experiences	Should have coaching or professional Spld qualifications. More skill-based and experiential-uses reflective and attributional practice	Professional training in psychosocial issues. Can involve a wide range of theoretical applications
Duration	Ongoing/can be long term	Usually short term/set deadlines	Can vary, usually short term
Timing	Informal as and when	More structured	Regular meetings

The 'coaching' intervention is the one that is usually required by dyslexic people in the workplace. This is because its focus is the professional and performance development of the individual in their job role. The individual has the expertise in their job and the coach provides the specialist knowledge to assist the client and the organisation to address the impact of dyslexia on the individual in their job role and in their relationships with colleagues, clients and customers (Leather & Kirwan, 2012; McLoughlin & Kirwan, 2007).

Coaching is clearly 'a relationship-based intervention' (Passmore, 2007: 10). In order for coaching to be effective the person being coached needs to be involved in defining the overall aims and the specific goals needed to attain them. In a collaborative working relationship the focus is on individual strengths as a way of increasing self-efficacy, creating specific action plans, monitoring and evaluating the coachee's progress, and following implementation and feedback, modifying action plans (Grant et al., 2010; Hawkins & Smith, 2006).

The Role of the Tutor/Coach

Key Skills

Dyslexic people seeking help from a tutor or trainer during adulthood are lacking the skills they need to deal with the tasks before them. Assuming that they have spent the usual amount of time in formal education, it is clear that conventional teaching has not worked for them. Difficulties with executive functioning necessitate an approach to teaching which focuses on the process of learning, particularly the development of meta-cognitive skills. To address this, when working with dyslexic people, coaches, tutors and trainers need to:

Observe	body language, gestures, mannerisms, facial expressions and speech.
Listen to	what is said and how it is said.
Use	what is learned from behaviour, both verbal and non-verbal.
Be aware	of their need to 'unload'. If one can't help or is not seen to be helping, clients can become angry.
Question	are expectations realistic? Are the strategies right? Is the programme suitable?

As well as the above it is essential that a coach or tutor working with a dyslexic person has the following skills:

- The expertise to understand and interpret assessment reports so that they can provide an explanation for the difficulties and discuss the skills an individual needs.
- A knowledge of and ability to administer measures of attainment for supplementary testing.
- Knowledge of how to plan a programme based on the evidence provided in an assessment report and utilising the individual learning strengths.
- A wide knowledge of task specific, multi-sensory, memory and organisational strategies.

- Knowledge of the task demands of college, university and training courses: for example, developing critical thinking skills for writing assignments, or providing strategies for answering multiple choice questions in examinations.
- The ability to be able to analyse the tasks of a job role and provide solution-focused strategy training, including literacy-based tasks.
- Effective communication skills, both listening and speaking.
- Report and letter writing skills.
- The ability to deal with anger and distress.

It is important to be able to relate to and empathise with each individual, developing a knowledge of how they process information. Making use of that is more important than knowing subject matter. As has been suggested previously it is important that the coach or tutor understands the impact of dyslexia in the context within which their client is working. A very detailed knowledge of the client's job or the topic they are studying is not essential, as the emphasis should be on process rather than content. This addresses executive functioning and provides 'an important key to improved adaptation as students learn to structure and organise their behaviour and cognitive resources' (Eslinger, 1996: 368).

Gerber (2012) has suggested that there is a dearth of systematic research on the outcome of instructional practices for adults. Nevertheless, Hock (2012) conducted a systematic survey on the studies available. He concluded that when working with the adult population who have specific learning difficulties such as dyslexia, the following should be included:

- Explicit instruction – teachers providing students with clear statements of process, modelling target behaviours, guided practice, independent practice, corrective feedback and post testing.
- Direct strategy instruction, for example, in metacognitive and self regulation techniques.

Swanson (2012) reviewed the literature on intervention with adults and identified successful models as including:

- Teaching a few concepts and strategies in depth rather than superficially.
- Teaching students to monitor their performance.
- Teaching when and where to use strategies to enhance generalisation.
- Providing teaching that includes supervised practice and feedback.

He concluded that 'only a few components from a broad array of activities were found to enhance treatment outcomes' (p. 27). The most important were explicit practice, including regular reviews and the use of advanced organisers, including directing students to focus on specific information and task concepts prior to teaching.

Hock also concludes that instruction delivered in a one-to-one or small group format over an extended period of time is the most effective in producing significant literacy gains. He wrote that 'instructional arrangements to support explicit instruction and provide intensive, ongoing instruction are seen to be likely to produce results in learning gains' (Hock, 2012: 74), but also suggested that instructional practices and interventions require well-planned, continuous professional development, practitioners needing intensive support as they themselves adopt new skills.

The Development of Metacognitive Skills

Working with a dyslexic person is not just a matter of 'teaching strategies'. In fact, pure skills-based teaching has been found to be less effective in the long term than strategy-based instruction (Gray, 2006). It should be a partnership in learning, and an interactive process that draws out the individual's learning skills. The client will refer to a task they find difficult, and provide clues as to how they deal with it as well as other related tasks. The tutor or coach should then question why the individual thinks they work in that way, asking them to reflect. The coach may then provide an explanation of the underlying processes involved, offering suggestions and solutions that have a rationale and specific relevance to the individual. This exploratory approach increases the self knowledge of the individual's own processing skills. That is, they begin to develop their metacognitive thinking.

In Chapter 1 we referred to the description of metacognition as the conscious awareness over one's own cognition, own thinking and learning processes (Fernandez et al., 2000; Flavell, 1979; Kuhn, 2000; Nelson et al., 1999). It has been acknowledged that good metacognitive skills improve performance in learning and working situations (Swanson, 1990; Schraw, 1997; Ruban, 2003; Schmidt, 2003), and that metacognition is especially important in novel and problem-solving situations as it enables the individual to draw on previous experience (Swanson, 1990; Schmidt, 2003). There is, however, evidence to indicate that dyslexic people do not develop these skills automatically (Wong, 1994; Butler, 1996), possibly because metacognition develops over time from positive learning situations, and many dyslexic people will not have had good educational experiences.

Metacognition is also related to self regulation. Zimmerman (1989) defined the latter 'as the degree to which individuals metacognitively, motivationally and behaviourally are active participants in their learning process' (p. 329). Zimmerman's construct had considerable impact on educationally-focused research and the development of self-regulation programmes (Ellis, 1996; Butler, 1994). It has been considered to be particularly important by researchers in the field of learning difficulties, especially in the United States of America.

Zimmerman (2002) refined his construct, identifying three phases: the forethought phase; the performance phase; and the self-reflection phase.

The forethought phase involved two levels: task analysis, goal setting and strategic planning. The second level he titled self motivation beliefs; these included feelings of self-efficacy, expectations of outcome, interest and learning goal orientations. Self-efficacy is thought to mediate all forms of cognitive motivation (Ponton et al., 2005). The performance phase also had two levels. The first was self-control, under which he listed imagery, self-instruction, attention focusing and task strategies. The second level was self observation. This involves self recording and self experimentation. The final phase is self-reflection; the two levels here are firstly self-judgement, self-evaluation and causal attribution; and secondly self-reaction, self-satisfaction evaluation, and adaptive or defensive action. This was described as a circular ongoing process which leads to improved performance.

The importance and effectiveness of self-regulated learning particularly for dyslexic learners has been documented (Zimmerman, 2002; Swanson, 1990; Goldberg et al., 2003). Implicit in the work of Gerber is that good metacognitive skills are one of the keys to success. Developing metacognitive skills from a self-regulatory perspective should, therefore, be an integral part of any coaching programme.

Skill Development, Compensation and Accommodation: An Integrated Framework for Development

The interventions that address the question 'What can be done about it?' are skill development, compensatory strategies and accommodation or adjustment. These need to be understood within the context of development across the life span, which is an adaptive process and is both proactive and reactive. That is, individuals can actively effect change, but also react to changes such as physical and intellectual maturation, as well as different circumstances. There is a maxim in developmental psychology that states 'there is no gain without loss and no loss without gain'. Successful adaptation to developmental changes has been described as involving *selection, optimisation and compensation* (Marsiske et al., 1995; Baltes & Freund, 2003).

Selection refers to the choice of areas for continued development. It can be specialising in a particular academic subject or job, as well as acquiring specific skills that allow one to pursue these. Selection is concerned with (a) creating and giving direction to development, and (b) managing the fundamental resource limitations inherent in all living systems. Selection acts to focus development and make the number of challenges and demands facing an individual manageable.

Optimisation reflects the view that development is the internally and externally regulated search for higher levels of functioning, leading to an increase in 'adaptive fitness'. It means that individual competencies are acquired and maintained at desirable levels. Optimisation is aimed at enhancing the strategies used in achieving goals.

Compensation results from internal and external limits. It relates only to those processes whereby new means are acquired or old means are reconstructed and used to counterbalance functional limits or losses. That is, compensation is an adjustment process by which the impact of internal and external limits is minimised through relying on other means. It is however insufficient on its own; just working harder, for example, can lead to negative consequences such as being too exhausted to do anything else (Marsiske et al., 1995).

Skill Development This is an exercise in selection and optimisation. It is the process of the dyslexic person setting goals and developing the literacy, numeracy, learning, memory and technological skills necessary to achieve these. Skill is co-ordinated activity to achieve a goal, in terms of fluency, accuracy and speed. It involves knowing how to carry out a task, a key aspect being adaptability to new situations and changing task requirements (Chimel, 1998). It is more than just developing skills, but includes self-efficacy or the belief an individual holds in their ability. Self-efficacy correlates with the achievements of dyslexic people, influencing 'choice of activity, task perseverance, level of effort expended and ultimately the degree of success achieved' (Klassen, 2002: 88).

> As time goes on, I get better at dealing with situations, largely because I'm that much more practised. Also faith in myself and my ability to get through grows. The first time one approaches something new one can put up a log of unconscious resistance due to fear. Once that hurdle is over things get easier. However, it is also good to acknowledge when you need help or feedback from people and not be afraid to seek it. Also, generally the more anal one can become (in terms of making notes, developing filing systems etc) the better.

Compensatory Strategies and Solutions   The term 'compensation' is sometimes used in a negative way, and often suggests 'covering up'. Compensation should in fact be seen as a positive and deliberate approach to finding and applying immediate and alternative solutions. Examples would include the use of diaries and other aids such as a Filofax or an electronic device to assist with organisation. The idea of compensation must be conveyed positively to dyslexic people as it can easily be perceived as 'cheating'. That is, if they listened to a recording rather than read the book they feel they have cheated.

Working harder and investing more time or effort is regarded as compensation (Blackman & Dixon, 1992). It is, however, an affective factor related to the individual's personality. Often dyslexic people work far too hard because they are reluctant to find other ways of dealing with tasks or simply because this has not occurred to them. The term 'compensation' is used here to describe deliberate efforts to find alternative and more efficient ways of dealing with tasks.

An example of a compensatory strategy is the use of technology. This can:

I. augment an individual's strengths so that his or her abilities counter balance the effects of any disabilities;

II. provide an alternative mode of performing a task so that the disabilities are compensated for or bypassed entirely.   (Lewis, 1993)

Cavalier et al. (1994) have written that 'technology can act as a cognitive prosthesis replacing an ability that is missing or impaired, or as a cognitive scaffold, providing support needed to accomplish a task'. Wanderman (cited in Lewis, 1993) distinguishes between 'low tech' and 'high tech' aids. The former include Post-it notes, flags and highlighter pens. They also include digital and talking clocks, wrist watches, recorders and organisers. High tech compensatory aids include the use of computers. Voice recognition software can compensate for writing and spelling difficulties; Text to Speech software can compensate for reading comprehension difficulties. Planning software can assist with the organisation of ideas on paper, as well as with note-taking, and specialist spell check packages can compensate for continuing problems with spelling, especially difficulties with irregular words and homophones. Technology can provide immediate as well as

Table 2.2   Skill Development v Compensation

Skill Development	Compensation
Teach	Offset
Learn	Substitute
Train	Work around

long-term solutions. It has been described as motivating for adults, but not sufficient without related instruction on how to use the tools (Hock, 2012).

The essential difference between skill development and compensation can be illustrated through action verbs (Howard & Howard, 2000). Some examples are shown in Table 2.2.

Accommodations and adjustments   These involve the adjustments made by others in work and learning settings. They include support from colleagues, supervisors, teachers and tutors, as well as provision which can be made in situations such as examinations and adjustments to work tasks and settings. For many dyslexic people, however, they should only be interim measures. Skills can be improved and this leads to greater autonomy in learning and work settings. Being flexible about achieving targets in performance appraisals might, for example, allow an individual time to develop new skills or learn how to use a particular piece of software.

Dyslexic people should be encouraged to ask three questions: What can I do or what skills can I develop? What else can I do or what compensations are there? and What can others do for me or what accommodations might be available? Some of the answers are shown in Table 2.3. They reflect a three strand approach, and involve evidence-based decisions made by the individual and the specialist. Accommodations will, however, require collaboration with friends, family and colleagues. They will also necessitate flexibility within organisations.

The distinction between skill development, compensation and accommodation allows individuals to realise that they have a choice. They can improve their proofreading skills or delegate. They can learn to spell or use voice recognition software. The choice is theirs and a solution should not be imposed upon them.

Alternative Interventions

The difficulties dyslexic people experience can make them vulnerable and at risk of being tempted by 'easy solutions'. As is the case for most learning difficulties dyslexia has attracted many 'alternative interventions' (see Fawcett & Reid, 2008; Pennington, 2009 for reviews). In commenting on the search for 'cures' Gardner (2000) wrote:

> The popular literature of recent decades is littered with premature claims that dyslexia –
> or autism or depression – can be cured by a single intervention, a single treatment, a
> single drug. Perhaps reading disorders have an intimate relation with colours or shapes or
> elongated sounds or patterns of crawling, but perhaps they do not. While the misleading
> media personality suffers no penalties for having "hyped" the cure prematurely, the student

and her family often do suffer. Most disorders, be they physical or cognitive, are complex, and most do not lend themselves to an instant cure. Caution should be the order of the day, particularly where another person's welfare is concerned. (Gardner, p. xiv)

Table 2.3   Skills, Compensation and Accommodation

Task	Skills	Compensation	Accommodation
Spelling	Over-learn key words Memory strategies Learn rules	Make lists of key words Use technology - word processor - portable spell checker	Ask for someone to proofread
Prioritising workload	Develop concept of time and estimation	Use alarms and timers Use software	Seek assistance of supervisor or secretary
Filing	Sequencing skills	Colour code and use highlighters Use technology	Delegate or seek administrative assistance
Proof reading	Develop systematic strategy	Use text to speech software, Spellchecker and grammar checker	Delegate
Improving attention	Develop self-awareness Task analysis	Use timer and other electronic aids	Seek distraction-free environment
Telephone work	Develop listening and note taking skills Learn to control conversation	Use recording device such as answering machine Use personalised proforma	Ask employer to provide equipment such as electronic aids and memo pads

There is no doubt that individuals and employers often seek simple solutions, expecting and hoping that brief and inexpensive interventions will 'cure' the problem. The field of learning difficulties has had more than its share of what have been described as controversial therapies (Jackson, Foxx & Mulick, 2005), ranging from auditory, visual and motor treatments, to dietary treatments. Some of these have been subject to systematic study, but their efficacy has not been proven. Others have not been evaluated at all but are promoted by enthusiasts despite this. None of them addresses the very specific difficulties experienced by dyslexic people in the workplace. There is no evidence, for example, to show that better diet, balance exercises or listening to relaxing music will improve a skill such as proofreading. Specific difficulties require specific solutions.

Smith (2005) has suggested controversial therapies are characterised by:

- the promise of a cure;
- being discrepant with the scientific understanding of the disorder it is supposed to treat;

- claiming benefits for many different disorders;
- the use of sophisticated technology in applications that have not been validated;
- criticism of validated treatments;
- support from testimonials and anecdotes;
- appeal to the popularity or longevity of the treatment.

There is often reference to neuroscience to support therapies that makes them appear to be legitimate and adds to the attraction (Weisberg et al., 2008). Pennington remarked that 'if something looks too good to be true then it probably is' (Pennington, 2009: 266). The promotion of controversial therapies detracts from the credibility of the science of specific learning difficulties. There are already a sufficient number of people, including professionals, academics, bureaucrats and politicians, whose 'scientific illiteracy' leads them to portray syndromes such as dyslexia as being mythical (Barkley, 2006). Most importantly, 'the extent of the damage caused by claims for a treatment of dubious validity should not be underestimated – not only the waste of effort and money but the damage done to dyslexics and their families when yet another proffered treatment turns out to be ineffective' (Miles, 2007: 254).

The promise of cures raises expectations and even conventional practitioners can contribute to this by recommending IT solutions as a panacea, and set periods of training and general memory courses that will guarantee improvement, despite their manner of delivery being based in administrative and economic expedience, and entirely contrary to good learning principles. When these do not produce the results promised it is often the credibility of the dyslexic person that is undermined, the assumption being that they have failed to make the best of the intervention.

Summary

1. Successful development across the life span involves adapting to transitions. It is a process of gains and losses. Transitions are particularly challenging for dyslexic people and it is at such times that they will need support and guidance.
2. Successful adjustment starts with the dyslexic person feeling in control and this involves internal and external factors.
3. Interventions designed to assist dyslexic people should promote self-understanding and provide them with the meta-cognitive and practical skills they need to adapt.
4. Tutors, trainers and coaches working with dyslexic people should be guided by the fundamental principles that underlie successful adult learning, particularly as these transfer control to the student/client.
5. A three strand evidence-based approach involving skill development, compensation and accommodation promotes autonomy by allowing dyslexic individuals a choice with regard to the way forward.
6. There are no easy solutions and alternative approaches that promise cures but are not validated can cause more harm than good.

3

Identification and Assessment

Synopsis. *This chapter outlines the process involved in the identification of dyslexia, from the initial interview, through screening to formal assessment. Appropriate measures of cognitive ability and attainment are described. The issue of reporting, both verbal and written, is addressed. A sample assessment report is provided.*

Introduction

In a sense there is no such thing as a test for dyslexia, and adherence to protocols just designed to determine if someone is dyslexic risks the failure to provide alternative explanations. Identification and assessment address the question 'Why are tasks difficult?' It is a process known as differential diagnosis, as it attempts to isolate aetiological factors associated with a syndrome from other potential explanations for difficulties. Pennington (2009) likens it to testing a hypothesis in scientific research and here we focus on that process. It is not simply administering a collection of recommended tests. He wrote that a good diagnosis of a syndrome 'should be more than just a descriptive relabeling of the data and should contain explicit criteria for ruling it in or out' (Pennington, 2009: 35).

Turner (1997) outlined the criteria for diagnosis dyslexia as being:

- An unexpected underachievement in one or more basic skills areas (reading, spelling, number).
- Positive evidence of inefficiency in the management of information, for instance in short-term memory.

Turner was mainly writing about dyslexia in childhood and the criteria should be broadened to take into account our current understanding of dyslexia, particularly as a life span issue.

The Dyslexic Adult: Interventions and Outcomes – An Evidence-based Approach, Second Edition. David McLoughlin and Carol Leather.
© 2013 John Wiley & Sons, Ltd. Published 2013 by John Wiley & Sons, Ltd.

Table 3.1   Steps in Assessment

STRUCTURED INTERVIEW
↓ + ve

SCREENING
↓ + ve

FORMAL PSYCHOLOGICAL
ASSESSMENT

The underachievement addressed should include:

* Skill areas such as reading accuracy, speed and comprehension, maths, writing speed and spelling, as well as proofreading. Problems with organisation, planning and self-regulation should also be considered. The discrepancy should be in relation to ability, education, culture, family background and employment history.

The inefficiency should be in the cognitive processes shown to be associated with the above, identified by Swanson (2012) as:

* phonological processing;
* verbal memory;
* naming speed.

On the basis of the model described in Chapter 1 we would also want to include measures of executive functions.

In order to meet both criteria differential diagnosis should involve the several stages shown in Table 3.1.

* information gathering – interview including history taking;
* screening – this formally identifies the existence of behavioural characteristics;
* psychological testing – this endeavours to explain the existence of behavioural characteristics.

Information Gathering

Dyslexic people display inconsistencies in their performance, the most obvious being when someone appears intelligent and has spent the usual amount of time in school but cannot read and write. There is also an inconsistency in a professionally trained person having difficulty with spelling. It is evidence of such discrepancies which leads to an initial evaluation. Adult dyslexics are often self-referred, recognising inconsistencies in their performance themselves, but it is also friends, tutors or employers who notice these and suggest an assessment.

There are many ways of explaining such discrepancies and they should not automatically lead one to conclude that a person is dyslexic. They should not be dismissed either; one of the reasons so many dyslexic people have not been identified during their school years is that someone has jumped to an obvious and incorrect conclusion. Information should be gathered in a systematic way through interviews, screening and formal psychological evaluation.

The purpose of assessment is ultimately to explain why there are discrepancies in an individual's performance, not just to label them as being dyslexic. To be effective an assessment should be rigorous. It should distinguish between:

1. People whose cognitive and language skills are adequate, but whose educational experience has been such that they leave school without having developed appropriate skills. There are also many intelligent people who, because of inadequate education, have poor literacy skills or who have underachieved in life generally.
2. People whose overall level of cognitive and language functioning is such as to predispose them towards finding the acquisition of literacy, numeracy, learning and work-related skills difficult. Many people of low general ability, for example, exhibit behaviours, such as difficulties with literacy and working memory, which have typically been associated with dyslexia.
3. People whose cognitive and language functioning is at an average or better than average level, but who have specific areas of weakness which undermine their acquisition of skills. Dyslexic people, for example, come into this category.

Before the process begins it is essential to establish that an individual is ready to accept the conclusion to which it might lead. Some people are just content to know that they 'might' be dyslexic, and they should never be pressed into pursuing the matter beyond a level they are comfortable with.

My plan was to exclude dyslexia-related difficulties as I was about to embark on a PG course as a mature student (which was terribly scary in itself . . .). What I was hoping for was reassurance: excluding dyslexia, I was hoping to gain more confidence in building up my writing skills! The results of the assessment came as a real shock to me, especially as the dyslexia was clearly recognised before looking at my written work! The assessor was really tactful and supportive, and stressed the positive results highlighted by the tests and the creative potential of the 'diversity'. Still, it was such a shock as I never really believed I could be dyslexic – with my love of reading and of the written word!. . . . The diagnosis brought about some sort of identity crisis I guess as I am now still unsure where my personality ends and where the dyslexia begins.

Interviews

The assessment process should begin with an interview. The information of significance includes that relating to education, qualifications, work experience, present occupation and family history, including details of the incidence of dyslexia within the family, as well as health. This information is best collected using a structured interview. Interview schedules should be designed for specific educational and work settings. One of the fundamental differences between the assessment of children and adults is that the latter are better able to provide their own perspectives on their difficulties, but there are particular issues which should be raised. These include:

1. ***Reason for referral***   There will be a reason as to why an explanation for difficulties experienced is important at a particular point in time. Knowing this will help establish a client's level of motivation. Those who are self-referred are likely to be more motivated to understand and address their difficulties than those who have been persuaded by others, for example, friends, relatives or employers, to seek advice.
2. ***Goals***   A client might have difficulty identifying their goals and might talk in general terms. Helping them to be more specific can influence the assessment process, particularly the advice given on follow up. It may transpire, for example, that they are required to work with numbers, to write reports quickly and under pressure, to use filing systems, to undertake tasks in certain sequences or to carry out instructions given verbally, all of which place heavy demands on working memory. Specific information such as this can lead to them being provided with a satisfactory explanation for all their difficulties, as well as advice on appropriate skills, compensations and accommodations.
3. ***Understanding of dyslexia***   What people understand about their difficulties is helpful in determining the level of explanation they will require. Many will focus on behavioural characteristics such as poor spelling, without seeing the relevance of other factors such as memory. They perceive the latter as being unrelated to literacy.
4. ***Educational experience***   The client's achievements, failures and preferences for particular subjects should be explored in detail. Absence through illness or difficult family circumstances may offer an explanation for lack of academic success. More useful information can be gleaned from their answers to questions about specific difficulties they encountered and whether these were addressed by teachers. Inconsistencies in performance are especially relevant. 'My class work was good but I had trouble with examinations' is a common remark. Their own explanations for poor performance at school are also important as they can reveal something about their attributions and self-concept. 'I didn't do very well but then I am lazy' comes up time and time again. They have come to believe it because it is what their teachers and school reports said. Difficulties reported should always be understood within the context of transitions, as they are not always evident until the demands on skills increase. This does not have to be a different level of education or work. It could include changes in the assessment process during a course, and increased pressures with regard to reading and writing, including the expectations of a new manager.
5. ***Experience of learning and training***   Training or other learning situations that the client has been exposed to since leaving school should be explored. This enables one to determine if strategies for coping with learning have been developed. It also provides further insights into how they perceive themselves in learning contexts. It could be that they have low expectations of themselves or become resigned to failure.

Alternatively, they may be overcompensating by being very persistent and working much harder than others.

6. **Medical information**   As well as general health any history of neurological disorder and/or head injury is of significance as one might be dealing with acquired dyslexia. The student born with hydrocephalus, for example, did not see that this might be relevant to her learning difficulties. Sensory impairments may also have a bearing; impairments in hearing or vision can, for example, undermine the development of the perceptual processes that underlie literacy skills. Glue ear has, for example, been seen as a contributing factor (Peer, 2009). If there is any doubt concerning the integrity of hearing and vision then an investigation by an appropriately qualified person should be recommended.

7. **Language background**   An increasing number of individuals whose first language is not English present for assessment. In an ideal world they would be tested in their native language, as even non-verbal tests can have a language aspect. Nevertheless, during the course of an interview there are specific questions that can be asked which will facilitate interpretation. These include those concerning their competence in their first language, the age at which they were introduced to English and the amount of tuition they have received. A guide to their automatic use of English will be whether they revert to their first language when with family and friends.

While conducting an interview it is important to note how clients answer questions and communicate information generally. A tendency to talk excessively, for example, may be a strategy for limiting the flow of information received. Alternatively, a reluctance to speak may be a way of hiding an inability to keep track of what is said. Word finding difficulties will often be in evidence. Further, it is not enough to simply ask an individual if they are well organised or if they have difficulty with remembering telephone numbers. They might have developed strategies for overcoming such difficulties and not really be aware of the fact that they are 'different' in the way they deal with such things. It is more important to ask 'how' they deal with tasks.

The information gathered in an interview is critical to identification. It might be sufficient to suggest that someone should not pursue the matter further, but it is more likely that it will indicate that further investigation is warranted and a screening evaluation can be recommended.

Whether conducting a screening evaluation or a full psychological assessment there are several considerations those administering tests should take into account:

As I suppose you may have gathered, I was very nervous and apprehensive about the day and really expected the whole thing to be a much more difficult and traumatic experience than in the end it turned out to be. After the assessment, I felt a little 'mixed up', well, for want of a better phrase, I really found it difficult to explain exactly how I felt. As I explained to you, part of me felt relieved because at last there was a legitimate label to explain why, yes, I may make mistakes, but this doesn't mean that I'm 'thick'. On the other hand, although part of me had accepted (from the original assessment that I told you about) that I was dyslexic, another part had always hope that if I worked hard enough and tried hard enough, the problem would somehow magically disappear. Coming to see you and taking part in the assessment meant letting go of that part of myself. I locked myself away in my room for a few days afterwards, not because I felt particularly upset, but because I needed to sort things out in my head – but I feel much better now and really feel that coming to see you is probably one of the best and most sensible things that I ever did. This visit, plus becoming registered as a disabled adult, were quite symbolic for me in the sense that for me it's the beginning of facing up to who and what I am, coping with it, and indeed realising that 'this is me' – and there's nothing to be ashamed or embarrassed about. This will make it so much easier, I feel, not only to cope with my dyslexia, but also to work in partnership with my employers so that they can better support me.

Table 3.2   Considerations in Testing

1. Assessment should promote self-understanding and should be a positive rather than a negative experience.
2. Dyslexic people have been humiliated in the past and should be allowed their dignity.
3. Assessments are only as good as the information they yield and should focus on the information required for diagnosis, and the provision of advice.
4. Tests used should have a face validity for the client: that is, they should clearly relate to explanations for difficulties and advice on strategy development.
5. The results of an assessment should always lead to an explanation. 'You are not dyslexic' is insufficient, as it does not address the issue of why the individual sought advice in the first place.
6. Feedback should be provided during the course of the assessment, as this reduces anxiety. Many people worry that the assessment will show them to be lacking intelligence and need reassurance that this is not the case early on in the process.

Screening

One of the biggest improvements in identifying dyslexia during the adult years has been in the development of relevant screening tests so that we no longer need to rely on adapting those devised for use with children. There is no excuse for using inappropriate tests, although the practice continues. There is also no need to administer screening tests as part of a full diagnostic assessment. The purpose of administering them is to systematically establish if behavioural characteristics exist, and determine if further investigation is warranted.

Checklists

Screening instruments include the widely used Adult Checklist, which has had several incarnations and has been reproduced in many publications and on a number of websites. The best version in terms of its research base was developed by Smythe and Everatt (2001). Essentially checklists help organise information in a formal way. They are 'a guide rather than a definitive assessment tool' (Kirk & Reid, 2003: 79).

Computer-based Tests

There are now a number of computer-based packages (see James, 2004 for a review). Some of those in use in the United Kingdom are described below.

LADS – Plus Version

LADS Plus (**L**ucid **A**dult **D**yslexia **S**creening – Plus Version) is a computerised test designed to screen for dyslexia in persons of 15 years and older. LADS Plus comprises of five subtests, which measure:

1. Non-verbal Reasoning.
2. Verbal Reasoning.
3. Word Recognition (lexical decoding involving speeded recognition of real word from non-words).
4. Word Construction (speeded lexical encoding of non-words from syllables).
5. Working Memory (backwards digit span).

The last three of these are thought to be *dyslexia sensitive* measures. The two reasoning tests produce a rough estimate of the person's intellectual ability.

LADS Plus is not a full diagnostic test but it is designed to provide a quick screening for adults in order to indicate if they are likely to have dyslexia. LADS Plus provides ratings for people taking the test into the following groups:

1. Low probability of dyslexia.
2. Borderline.
3. Moderate probability of dyslexia.
4. High probability of dyslexia.

StudyScan and QuickScan

The StudyScan Suite (Zdzienski, 1997, 2008) is a package of computer programmes, including QuickScan, a questionnaire designed for adults who want to find out about the way they learn. QuickScan outlines individual learning preferences and study styles, and produces a printed report on personalised study guidelines. It also indicates whether the student shows any signs of dyslexia and may result in a recommendation to go on to complete the full assessment in StudyScan.

StudyScan is a comprehensive battery of tests that covers most aspects of a full educational assessment. It will give an indication of general levels of attainment and highlight specific areas of strengths and weaknesses. It will automatically analyse the individual performance of students in different tests and produce a printed diagnostic report. StudyScan contains the following tests:

*   memory (auditory and visual) and coding;
*   literacy (including reading and listening comprehension, spelling and punctuation);

- numeracy (including calculations and applications);
- phonological subtests (audio spelling);
- cognitive abilities (including verbal and non-verbal reasoning, as well as vocabulary);
- proficiency tests (speed of reading and speed of copying);
- free writing.

The principle of 'specificity', that is, the notion that dyslexic people have an underlying neurological inefficiency, is central to the assessment process. Even in screening some measurement of general ability as well as specific processes such as working memory is important. Any procedure that fails to incorporate appropriate cognitive tests is likely to produce false positives: that is, the incorrect identification of people who have low intelligence. This can raise their expectations and lead to further frustration. One young woman who had been told she was dyslexic on the basis of a literacy assessment alone was trying to complete university level studies with an IQ of 60. Both StudyScan/Quick Scan and the Dyslexia Adult Screening Test include relevant measures.

Computerised packages can meet the need for quick and low-cost screening and both LADS and StudyScan are being used in the Further and Higher Education sectors. It has been suggested that they have the potential for a wider application, and that one of the advantages of such packages is that it minimises the need for clinical judgement (Reid & Kirk, 2000).

Individually Administered Tests

One of the major flaws of computerised assessment is, however, that it does not allow for behavioural observation and it is often the latter which is crucial in diagnosis. The way in which people do things can be more important than the scores they achieve.

York Adult Assessment Battery

This was designed to provide a low-cost evaluation of a student's strengths and weaknesses as a basis for immediate intervention, as well as for further referral. It includes:

- Measures of phonological processing
  - nonsense passages
  - spoonerisms
- Measure of attainment
  - writing speed based on copying
  - spelling (WRAT)
  - a timed précis
  - proofreading

The norms are based on a small sample of very able undergraduates, so high general intelligence is assumed. Low scores (10th centile) on nonsense passages, reading, spoonerisms, writing speed and spelling are thought to be indicative of dyslexia (Hatcher et al., 2002).

Dyslexia Adult Screening Test (DAST)

The Dyslexia Adult Screening Test (Fawcett & Nicolson, 1998) consists of 11 individual subtests. A description of its development and purpose can be found in Fawcett (2003). The sub-tests include:

- rapid naming;
- one minute reading;
- postural stability;
- phonemic segmentation;
- two minute spelling;
- backwards digit span;
- nonsense passage reading;
- non-verbal reasoning;
- one minute writing;
- verbal fluency;
- semantic fluency.

The DAST is soundly based in the authors' research into automaticity and several of the sub-tests are derived from existing established tests. The DAST provides an 'at risk' score and can be a useful first step in formal identification but it is not without its faults. Gunn (2000) suggests that use of the DAST 'raises underlying issues that cause more problems than it solves' (p. 42). These include the need for a clear distinction between dyslexia and general learning difficulties at the screening stage; the use of psychological tests by non-psychologists, and the need for clarity as to its purpose. Of particular concern has been the use of the Postural Stability Test with disabled people, as well as with adults generally as it involves a degree of physical contact. It has also been suggested that administration of the DAST leads to disproportionate numbers of false negatives and false positives (Jackson, 2004; Harrison & Nichols, 2005). Again the effectiveness with which it distinguishes between dyslexia and general learning difficulties is being questioned (Bodenham, 2000). It is, however, the 'at risk' quotient that contributes to this and the overall score should not be reported without reference to the profile of scores. In our experience, when it is used as a screening rather than a diagnostic test, and administrators are properly trained in its theoretical underpinnings, the DAST is a useful tool in identifying those who need support in education in the workplace. Further, it can be valuable in helping both dyslexic adults and those working with them to understand the processing issues involved.

Scholastic Abilities Test for Adults (SATA)

Another test worthy of mention here is the Scholastic Abilities Test for Adults developed in the United States. It is based on the discrepancy model and does not include tests of specific processing abilities, but some of the achievement tests are quite useful for the measurement of attainment.

The SATA (Bryant et al., 1991) is designed to be a general measure of scholastic accomplishment. It can be administered as an individual or group test, and either timed or untimed, although the former is recommended for group testing. The SATA consists of nine subtests. One to three measure aptitudes, and are:

1. Verbal Reasoning.
2. Non-verbal Reasoning.
3. Quantitative Reasoning.

The achievement tests are:

4. Reading Vocabulary.
5. Reading Comprehension (multiple choice).
6. Maths Calculations.
7. Maths Application.
8. Writing Mechanics.
9. Writing Composition.

Formal Diagnosis

It is formal diagnosis which can best answer the question 'why are tasks difficult?' As well as providing an answer to this question, it should identify abilities and strengths. A thorough assessment should show what a dyslexic person can do as well as what they can't do.

Formal diagnosis involves psychological testing, careful observation and clinical judgement. In the main and internationally it is carried out by a psychologist because it requires the interpretation of 'closed tests' which are only available to qualified psychologists, as well as the exercise of judgements that require psychological understanding and knowledge. There are fundamental differences between the skills of psychologists and those of teachers. In particular, the former are trained according to a scientist-practitioner model and this is essential to conducting differential assessment. This does not always mean that they adopt this approach and the professional background of some psychologists means they are ill equipped. Educational psychologists are often only experienced in working in educational contexts and make recommendations appropriate to those, rather than the specific employment issues facing a dyslexic person. Diagnostic assessment is not part of an occupational psychologist's initial training. In both cases further professional development is needed.

In the United Kingdom some appropriately qualified specialist teachers can follow the process using tests available to them. Again most, by definition, will be experienced in working in educational contexts but not the workplace. Professionals should really confine themselves to their area of expertise and not comment on matters for which they have no training. There are of course those who have over the years developed skills, knowledge and understanding out of necessity, but we are well beyond the stage at which people just learn on the job and there is need for all professionals working with dyslexic adults to undergo relevant training.

The content of an assessment should be based in research and a diagnosis on a 'weighing of all the evidence to achieve and integrated formulation' (Pennington, 2009: 38). Experience and clinical judgement are essential components. There are a minimum number of areas that should be evaluated before a conclusion can be drawn. Swanson (2012), on the basis of a meta-analysis of studies of adults with reading disabilities, concluded that measures of verbal IQ, word recognition and reading comprehension, phonological processing, naming speed, vocabulary, spelling and verbal memory are fundamental.

The steps leading to formal diagnosis are shown in Table 3.3.

Table 3.3   Steps in Diagnosis

Fluid and Crystallised Intelligence
Administration of Ability Test
e.g. WAIS-IV, Woodstock-Johnson III
↓
Analysis of Ability Profile
(Index and sub-test scores)
↓
Testing of Specific Cognitive Abilities
(e.g. Verbal memory, Executive functioning,
Naming speed, Phonological processing)
↓
Achievement
Reading
- Accuracy
- Comprehension
- Speed
Spelling
Writing
Numeracy

Testing Intelligence

There has been considerable debate and much disagreement concerning the measurement of intelligence in the identification of dyslexia, the focus being on the relationship between global IQ and reading. Nevertheless, if we take a broader view of specific learning difficulties the issue is quite clear. The concern is to distinguish between the second and third groups of people described earlier:

- People whose overall level of intellectual and language functioning is such as to predispose them towards finding the acquisition of literacy, numeracy, learning and work-related skills difficult: that is, people who have problems learning most things.
- People whose intellectual and language functioning is at an average or better than average level, but who have specific areas of cognitive weakness that undermine their acquisition of some skills.

It is the latter group who constitute the population of people who have specific learning and performance difficulties such as dyslexia.

As a first step in rebuilding my confidence, my assessment to identify if I had any specific cognitive skills and weaknesses has helped a great deal. While the assessment identified that I was dyslexic it also showed that I was far from unintelligent; importantly, the assessment has given me tangible evidence of this fact. Further explanation made me realise that it is something I should now use to constructively develop an awareness of my skills and abilities.

In order to establish potential and eliminate general learning problems, a comprehensive measure of intellectual ability or intelligence is administered. These should measure fluid and crystallised intelligence, as both are important in predicting what people should be able to achieve. The former relates to abilities that are not dependent on acquired knowledge such as non-verbal reasoning, attention, memory capacity and processing speed; it deteriorates with age, although it has been suggested that it can be improved through training in domains such as working memory (Jaeggi et al., 2008). The latter is the problem-solving abilities, vocabulary and information acquired through experience; it is likely to improve across the life course.

There are several comprehensive tests in common use but internationally the Wechsler Adult Intelligence Scale – Fourth Edition (WAIS-IV) is the most popular. Lichtenberger and Kaufman (2009) provide a very comprehensive guide to its administration and interpretation. They suggest that the WAIS-IV can be interpreted at multiple levels:

- Global composite – Full Scale IQ.
- Specific Composite – Index scores.
- Sub-test level.
- Item level.
- Task Cognitive Capacities.

This means it can be used as a normative test, allowing comparison with others of the same age, and an ipsative test allowing comparison of some of an individual's abilities with other abilities.

WAIS-IV

The WAIS-IV consists of 15 subtests, four verbal, five Perceptual Reasoning, three working memory and three processing speed. It provides a full scale IQ and four Index Scores, the latter being based on core sub-tests. The sub-tests and the abilities they purport to measure are:

Verbal Tests

1. *Information:* This measures the ability to access long-term memory by focusing on general knowledge.
2. *Vocabulary:* This sub-test, which requires the examinee to define words, involves word knowledge and the ability to express ideas.
3. *Similarities:* This measures verbal concept formation and verbal reasoning. It requires the individual to consider the relationships between objects and concepts by explaining what they have in common. It is regarded as a good test of general intellectual ability, since it is virtually independent of any memory component and it is not unduly influenced by social and educational background.
4. *Comprehension:* This sub-test is designed to measure 'common sense', and the ability to understand social situations, as well as use practical reasoning.

Working Memory Tests

1. *Arithmetic:* This is a test of mental arithmetic, and requires an understanding of basic mathematical concepts; it also taps memory and attention.
2. *Digit Span:* This sub-test is designed to measure auditory sequential memory. It has three components, digit forwards, digits reversed and digit span sequencing. The first involves short-term memory and attention, but the other two measure working memory and are particularly important in the diagnosis of dyslexia.
3. *Letter Number Sequencing:* This involves the recall of combinations of letters and numbers, and is a measure of working memory.

Perceptual Reasoning Tests

1. *Visual Puzzles:* Measures non-verbal reasoning and the ability to analyse and synthesise abstract visual stimuli.
2. *Block Design:* This measures visuospatial organisation.
3. *Matrix Reasoning:* A measure of non-verbal abstract reasoning ability.
4. *Picture Completion:* This measures visual recognition and discrimination.
5. *Figure Weights:* Measures numerical reasoning ability.

Processing Speed

1. *Coding:* Coding requires the individual to associate an abstract symbol with a number and write it down. It is a strictly timed test that requires speed and accuracy. It can also be administered as a measure of incidental learning that is the extent to which the symbols can be remembered without someone having tried to learn them.
2. *Symbol Search:* A symbol checking task, involving memory and visual motor speed.
3. *Cancellation:* A timed scanning task using coloured shapes.

The Global Composite – Full Scale IQ

Although designed as a measure of intelligence originally defined by Wechsler as the 'capacity of the individual to act purposefully, to think rationally, and to deal effectively with his environment' (1944: 3), in the context of identifying dyslexia the WAIS (IV) is at its least useful as a measure of IQ. It will distinguish between the 'unable' and those who have specific difficulties, but because some of the sub-tests tap the areas of cognitive weakness associated with dyslexia, the overall scores can be an underestimate of potential. Miles (1996) has, for example, questioned the value of calculating a global IQ. By definition dyslexic people will find some of the sub-tests more difficult than others and a Full Scale IQ does not necessarily reflect their intellectual potential. In general and whatever the test used, calculation of an overall IQ score when working with individuals who have a specific learning difficulty should be discouraged.

The Specific Composite – Index Scores

As well as a Full Scale IQ score the WAIS (IV) allows for the calculation of Index Scores; Verbal Comprehension, Perceptual Reasoning, Working Memory and Processing Speed, calculated on the basis of scale scores for:

Verbal Comprehension	*Perceptual Reasoning*
Vocabulary	Visual Puzzles
Similarities	Block Design
Information	Matrix Reasoning
(Supplemental test – Comprehension)	(Supplemental test – Figure Weights)
Working Memory	*Processing Speed*
Arithmetic	Digit Symbol – Coding
Digit Span	Symbol Search
(Supplemental test – Letter Number Sequencing)	(Supplemental test – Cancellation)

The Index scores provide useful diagnostic information, the discrepancies amongst them being regarded as a better guide to evidence of a learning difficulty than the ACID profile (Kaufman & Lichtenberger, 1999). They also provide measures of competencies and this enables an assessor to inform clients of what they can do, as well as explain why some things are difficult for them. Further, whilst the relevance of IQ might be questioned, identifying particular abilities, notably language skills such as vocabulary, verbal reasoning and comprehension, is important as they underlie the development of reading skills. Without an adequate vocabulary, for example, skills such as reading comprehension will be impaired (Swanson, 2012).

Knowing about competencies is helpful in providing academic and career guidance. Individuals who have an average or better than average Perceptual Reasoning Index score are likely to be suited to occupations involving visual perceptual skills. Abilities such as verbal comprehension have been identified as good predictors of success at college (Leonard, 1991) and in making the transition from school to employment (Faas & D'Alonzo, 1990).

The Sub-test – Level WAIS-IV as an Ipsative Test

The WAIS (IV) measures a wide range of abilities and dyslexic people often show an uneven profile, reflecting contrasting strengths and weaknesses. Ipsative testing refers to consideration of the potential implications of such contrasts.

A considerable amount of research has been devoted to identifying 'typical' dyslexic profiles of Wechsler sub-test scores. Bannatyne (1974), for example, proposed four groups of sub-test combinations on which dyslexics and non-dyslexics are presumed to differ. They are Spatial (Picture Completion, Block Design and Object Assembly), Verbal Conceptualisation (Comprehension, Similarities, Vocabulary), Sequential (Digit Span, Arithmetic, Coding or Digit Symbol) and Acquired Knowledge (Information, Arithmetic, Vocabulary). Dyslexics were found to be equal to, or better than, non-dyslexics in spatial ability and conceptual ability but they do less well in sequencing ability and acquired knowledge. A large number of studies identified what is known as the A C I D profile of Wechsler sub-test scores and in the past this has been used as a basis for diagnosing dyslexia. That is, Arithmetic, Coding (Digit Symbol), Information and Digit Span were shown to be the sub-tests on which dyslexics typically scored less well than non-dyslexics (Thomson, 1990). Changes in the Wechsler Scales as they have been developed mean that the acronym no longer applies, and the diagnostic utility of the ACID profile was called into question (Frederickson, 1999). The problem was not with the profile as such, but that it took on a life of its own; the presence of an ACID profile being interpreted as definitive when there might be other explanations for some of the low scores; the absence of an ACID profile leading to dyslexia being dismissed, when behavioural observation suggested that the examinee might have had difficulty with some of the ACID sub-tests. Much of the research involved children but there are several studies which provided support for both Bannatyne's clusters and the ACID profile (Cordoni et al., 1981; Salvia et al., 1988; Katz et al., 1993).

Critics of the reliance on the ACID profile as an indicator failed to adequately address the issue of why it is so often a feature of the performance on the Wechsler tests amongst people who have experienced problems with literacy. One way of interpreting it is that it reflected an inefficiency in working memory, Arithmetic, Coding, Information and Digit Span all tapping this to a greater or lesser extent. Frith (1999) was more specific, regarding the profile as evidence of a phonological deficit. At the very least it should have led to hypotheses about why tasks are difficult which could be explored through further testing.

The Technical and Interpretive Manual for WAIS-IV lists a range of specialist group studies. In this context those most likely to be of interest are those described as Individuals with Learning Disorders, including reading disorders, mathematics disorders and Attention Deficit Hyperactivity Disorder. Classification of the disorders is based on the DSM-IV- TR criteria and, therefore, on a discrepancy model, and the studies are small in terms of their sample size and for limited age groups. Nevertheless, it is worth noting that in general individuals with reading disorders (dyslexia) scored less well on the Working Memory Index than on the other Indices. As the authors point out this finding is consistent with current research. They also add weight to the argument against calculating a Full Scale IQ.

The Item Level and Task Cognitive Capacities

The greater emphasis on processing ability in WAIS-IV is reflected in the provision of *Process Scores*. There is one for Block Design, six for Digit Span and one for Letter Number Sequencing. They are designed to facilitate the qualitative analysis many psychologists already conduct by providing objective scores for the cognitive abilities that can contribute to sub-test performance. They are not, however, a substitute for a sub-test score or used in the calculation of Index scores.

The authors have made recommendations regarding the use of supplemental tests in the calculation of composite score. They have suggested that this be done when the sub-test performance is invalidated by factors such as administration errors, recent exposure to test items and response sets. This is an important consideration when assessing individuals who have specific learning difficulties. One might, for example, use Cancellation rather than Coding when problems with fine motor skills are evident as it does not require the formation of symbols. Further, it is not unusual for adults to have developed strategies that enable them to deal with working memory tasks; 'chunking' when remembering a series of numbers and relying on their fingers to help with mental calculations. These should be regarded as invalidating factors, the intention being to measure ability rather than strategy use. In general, it becomes increasingly difficult to distinguish between ability and strategy as people mature, particularly when anxiety is an additional factor. When working with older adults, for example, it can be better to use Letter Number Sequencing rather than Arithmetic as the former is less influenced by experience, including the humiliation some people have suffered in the past. Mental arithmetic is often the task that reduces grown men and women to tears. Some of the behaviours that should be noted are listed in Table 3.4.

Abbreviated Scales

In situations where a quick measure of intelligence is helpful a four sub-test version of the WAIS (IV) is available. Known as the Wechsler Abbreviated Scale of Intelligence – Second

Table 3.4   What to Look for When Testing

What to look for when testing
1. General confidence and anxiety
2. Verbal tests – problems with 'word finding'
3. WAIS IV – 'dyslexia sensitive' subtests

Information — problems with labels
e.g. names of people

Arithmetic — use of fingers
— subvocalisation
— asking for pen and paper

Digit Span, Digit Span Sequencing and Letter Number Sequencing
— differences between forwards, reversed and reordering
— use of fingers
— subvocalisation
— chunking
— visualisation

Coding, Symbol Search and Cancellation
— use of finger as a guide
— subvocalisation

Edition (WASI –II), it provides measures of crystallised intelligence based on Vocabulary and Similarities, and fluid intelligence based on Block Design and Matrix Reasoning, as well as an estimated Full Scale IQ based on all four. A two sub-test Full Scale IQ can be calculated on the basis of Vocabulary and Matrix Reasoning.

Tests for Teachers

The qualifications required for the use of tests vary from country to country. In the United Kingdom the Wide Range Intelligence Test (WRIT) is used by Specialist Teachers as an alternative to the WAIS. It provides a measure of overall intellectual ability (General IQ), based on four sub-tests, two verbal and two non-verbal or visual. The verbal tests are Vocabulary and Verbal Analogies, the visual tests are Matrices and Diamonds.

An alternative to the WRIT is the Kaufman Brief Intelligence Test – Second Edition (KBIT-2). It provides measures of crystallised and fluid intelligence – that is, verbal and non-verbal ability – and provides a composite IQ. The verbal tests include Verbal Knowledge and Riddles, whereas the non-verbal test is Matrices.

Whilst the Wechsler tests are normed for different populations, the KBIT and WRIT only come with American norms. Some tests do not travel well, verbal tests being of particular concern as they can involve 'local' knowledge and vocabulary. This is when item analysis can be important, noting that culturally biased questions might have depressed a score.

Further Psychological Testing

Administration of a test such as the WAIS (IV) is necessary and will provide insights into cognitive abilities and clues about areas of weaknesses. It is not, however, sufficient, for diagnosis and psychologists, in particular, can be guilty of failing to measure abilities not covered by an intelligence test. These include phonological processing and naming speed.

Phonological Processing and Naming Speed

The most widely used measure of phonological processing and naming speed is the Comprehensive Test of Phonological Processing (CTOPP). It measures:

- Phonological awareness.
- Phonological memory.
- Rapid naming.
- Elision – removing phonological segments from words to form others, e.g. *toothbrush* without *tooth* is *brush.*
- Blending Words – synthesising sounds to form words, e.g. *ham-er* is *hammer.*

- Memory for Digits – repeating numbers forwards, e.g. *1-6* to *4-9-6-7-3-1-6-5.*
- Nonword Repetition – *meb, nigong, shaburiehuvoimush.*
- Rapid Digit Naming, e.g. 4 7 8 5.
- Rapid Letter naming – s t n a k (36 × 6).
- Rapid Colour Naming – (36 × 6).
- Phoneme Reversal – say *ta* backwards (*at), metsis* is *system.*
- Rapid Object Naming – (36 × 6).
- Blending Nonwords, e.g. *mo-tab* is *motab.*
- Segmenting Words – say *pig* one sound at a time *p-i-g.*
- Segmenting Nonwords – *seb* is *s-e-b.*

The CTOPP is only normed for the population up to 24 years and 11 months, but we know enough about the effects of ageing on some of the abilities it measures to allow for a qualitative judgement about the performance of an individual whose age is outside that of the sample population. In normal adults, for example, rapid naming slows on average by ten seconds between ages 15 and 95 (Jacobson et al., 2004). In general the slowing of cognitive speed over the life course is linear and reduces by one second per decade up to age 55, and one second per every seven years beyond that (Wiig et al., 2007). An alternative measure of processing and naming speed is the AQT, A Quick Test of Cognitive Speed (Wiig et al., 2002) which covers the age range up to 95 years.

Memory Ability

The separate measurement of memory abilities can both provide further explanation and suggest strengths on which an individual might capitalise. Psychologists are able to use tests such as the Wechsler Memory Scales – 4th ed (WMS-IV) which provides a very comprehensive measure of memory ability including:

- *Immediate Memory* – auditory and visual. Specific auditory sub-tests are Logical Memory and Paired Associate Learning, whilst the visual sub-tests are Memory for Faces and Family Pictures.
- *General (Delayed) Memory* – auditory and visual. Specific auditory sub-tests include alternative forms of Logical memory and Paired Associates, as well as Auditory Recognition. The visual tests are alternative forms of Memory for faces and Family Pictures.
- *Working Memory* – auditory and visual. The auditory sub-test is the Letter Number Sequencing Test included in the WAIS (IV) and the visual sub-test is Spatial Span, described as a visual equivalent to Digit Span.

Like the WAIS it provides individual sub-test scores as well as Index scores. Both sets of scores are useful diagnostically, as well as in programme planning. Low scores clarify the specific areas of weakness, and average or better than average scores provide clues as to the strategies that might help circumvent these.

The WMS-IV is only available to psychologists but teachers and tutors can use the Wide Range Assessment of Memory and Learning – 2nd ed (WRAML-2) and the Test of Memory and Learning – 2nd ed (TOMAL-2). Both provide norms for adult populations and measures of auditory immediate, short-term and long-term recall, as well as visual equivalents.

Executive Functioning

We have suggested in Chapter 1 that executive functions can have an impact on the academic and work performance of dyslexic people. Separate measurement of these can, therefore, be helpful in explaining and predicting difficulties, as well as pointing to solutions. It has been suggested that reversing digits is a simple measure of executive functions (Hale et al., 2002), but the latter are complex and their measurement has been fraught with conceptual and methodological problems (Miyake et al., 2000). In the past the adequacy of the executive system was measured by transfer or generalisation tests. The most commonly used instrument has been the Wisconsin Card Sort Test (Heaton et al., 1993). It measures the ability to shift cognitive strategies in response to changing environmental contingencies.

A more comprehensive test is the Behavioural Assessment of Dysexecutive Syndrome (BADS). The authors of this test (Wilson et al., 1996) argued that most conventional neuropsychological tests failed to capture the core difficulties faced by someone with executive dysfunction as they are typically highly structured, deal with circumscribed material and the criteria for success are clearly specified.

Executive functioning is often difficult to assess because although the individual components are intact, people may be unable to use these skills. Clients are asked to tackle a single explicit problem, one at a time. In contrast, many everyday activities involving executive abilities require people to organise or plan their behaviour over long time periods, or to set priorities in the face of two or more competing tasks. If the working memory model of dyslexia described in Chapter 1 is correct it is also likely that dyslexic people will not show executive functioning problems unless there are heavy demands on the phonological loop.

The BADS test addresses these issues by addressing several aspects of executive functions and it consists of the following sub-tests:

- *Rule Shift Cards.*
- *Action Programme Test.*
- *Key Search Test.*
- *Temporal Judgement Test.*
- *Zoo Map Test.*
- *Modified Six Elements Test.*
- *Dysexecutive Questionnaire.*

The BADS provides standardised scores which allow ratings from impaired to very superior. Limited experience of using it with dyslexic people suggests that it can be of value, tests such as Temporal Judgement being particularly revealing.

The Hayling and Brixton Tests (Burgess & Shallice, 1997) are published as a package but are two separate tests. The Hayling Test is verbal and involves sentence completion. It has two sections: the first is simple sentence completion, the second involves suppression and yields three measures relating to executive functions: response initiation, response suppression and the efficiency of the latter reflected in speed of response.

The Brixton Test is a rule attainment test akin to the Wisconsin Card Sort Test but also involves spatial anticipation. Among other processing abilities it is thought to tap spatial working memory.

Experience of using these tests is consistent with the theoretical perspective outlined in Chapter 1. Dyslexic people find the suppression section of the Hayling Test difficult, there being a heavy verbal cognitive load, but they have less difficulty with the Brixton Test, visual spatial ability being intact.

Achievements in Literacy and Numeracy

Reading

There has been a great deal of improvement in the availability of tests covering all aspects of reading that are suitable for adult populations, although many are only normed up to the end of emerging adulthood.

There are essentially three aims in assessing an adult's reading skills:

1. Establishing whether the reader has sufficient competence in all aspects of reading as to enable them to deal with the tasks they face on a daily basis, in a particular occupation, or at least the programme of study leading to that occupation.
2. Diagnosing reading difficulties and establishing a starting point for instruction.
3. Measuring progress on reading programmes.

Reading Levels

Where standardised tests have been used to assess reading levels scores have often been expressed as reading ages. This practice must be abandoned when working with adults. It is not helpful for an adult to know they have a reading age of 10 years, for example, and is demoralising as they relate it to their chronological age. Self-esteem can be damaged and there are people who have lost their jobs because employers do not know what it means in real terms. Even standard scores and percentiles are of limited value when working with adults. They allow comparisons and can be useful in the allocation of resources, as well as determining accommodations in educational and assessment settings, but can be meaningless for most adults.

Table 3.5 Levels of Reading

Level	Education Level	Age
Professional	Grades 11–12 and above	Over 16 years
Technical	Secondary/junior high school	13–16 years
Vocational	Primary/elementary school	9–12 years
Functional	Infant school	Up to 9 years

We only need the reading skills we need: that is, those which enable us to deal with the demands placed upon us by our educational, work and social programme. The most enduring and important situation in which adults need reading skills is their work environment. Criteria for establishing levels of attainment amongst adults are, therefore, best derived from work tasks.

There are insufficient criterion referenced tests but adult literacy and numeracy skills can be rated as being at one of four levels. These are professional, technical, vocational and functional. For those who are more familiar with reading in an educational setting, these levels are set out in Table 3.5 with their equivalent educational levels.

Professional reading skills are those required by the upper levels of secondary and high school, as well as university studies and a professional occupation. Someone who has reached this level is capable of independent reading, and has a wide reading vocabulary and the ability to understand sophisticated material.

Individuals who read at the technical level have sufficient competence in decoding and comprehension as to enable them to complete secondary/junior high school courses and a programme of further education. They would be able to work in occupations such as sales, secretarial work and computing. Those who are at vocational level in all aspects of reading would have difficulty completing secondary education, but should be able to understand the fundamental needs of many jobs that require a moderate amount of reading.

Adults who read only at the functional level will show considerable variation but it can be expected that they will find jobs that require even a little reading difficult. Those at the upper end of the functional level may have sufficient reading survival skills as to enable them to deal with jobs which place minimal demands upon reading skills but those at the lower end may not be able to deal with any type of job which requires some reading.

Within these four levels individuals can be identified as being at an independent, instructional or frustrational stage. The first reflects a stage at which the reader demonstrates excellent proficiency and is able to deal with material without assistance. The instructional stage indicates that the reader requires minimal assistance. Performance at this stage suggests that the reader would benefit from tuition to bring up their skills within this level. Once this stage has been established it is assumed someone can be given materials that are written at the particular reading level. Individuals who score at the frustrational stage cannot deal with reading material at that particular level and should be provided with materials at a lower level.

The Components of a Reading Assessment

Reading is a very complex skill, however, for the purpose of assessment, Aaron and Baker (1991) suggested that it can be regarded as having two major components:

1. Decoding – that is, the ability to pronounce the word, either overtly or covertly.
2. Comprehension – that is, the ability to understand the word and the text.

It is important to add to the first of these the ability to correctly pronounce the word covertly at an acceptable rate, as being able to read to oneself quickly is important in the adult years. To the second should be added 'when listening'. Listening comprehension underlies many adult activities including working, learning and socialising.

The assessment of adult reading skills should therefore include measures of decoding, reading and listening comprehension, as well as reading rate. Each sub-skill should be evaluated separately, particularly when the aim of an assessment is to diagnose reading difficulties and plan instruction. Some of the tests that measure the various sub-skills involved in reading are listed below. Selection of appropriate tests should be based on context, as well as the preference of the assessor, but those used should always be the most up to date. Reviews of tests are provided elsewhere, but for a list of those currently considered appropriate readers are referred to the website for the Professional Association of Teachers and Students with Specific Learning Difficulties.

Decoding

Decoding skill has been measured typically by the use of single word reading and prose reading tests. There have been many examples of single word reading tests and they are much the same. They consist of lists of words graded in order of difficulty. Single word reading tests that provide suitable norms include:

- Test of Word Reading Efficiency (TOWRE).
- Spadafore Diagnostic Reading Test (SDRT).
- Wechsler Individual Achievement Test-Second Edition (WIAT – II).
- Wide Range Achievement Test 4 (WRAT 4).
- Woodcock Reading Mastery Tests (WRMT-R).
- Woodcock-Johnson III Tests of Achievement (WJ III).

Although they do have a place in the assessment of decoding skill, single word reading tests are of a limited value. When assessing an adult's reading skills, one is really attempting to determine how well they can function in everyday life, as well as in academic and work settings. Most people have to deal with prose rather than individual words. Prose reading tests usually consist of a set of passages graded in order of difficulty, which the examinee has to read aloud. Tests in use include:

- Adult Reading Test (ART).
- Gray Oral Reading Test – Fourth Edition (GORT-4).

- Gray Oral Reading Test – Fifth Edition (GORT5).
- Spadafore Diagnostic Reading Test (SDRT).

Two other prose reading tasks have become quite widely used in the assessment of adult reading skills. These are Cloze procedure and Miscue Analysis. The former involves passages of a particular readability from which words have been deleted. The person being assessed is expected to supply these. Usually every fifth, seventh or tenth word is replaced by a blank space. Although it can be used as a measure of reading level, and to successfully complete a Cloze task decoding must be involved, the procedure is of limited diagnostic value because it does not separate individual sub-skills.

Miscue Analysis measures how well a reader is able to use language clues, their own expectations and decoding skills to derive meaning. That is, when the reader encounters the printed page they use a variety of language clues or cues, individual expectations about the message, and decoding cues to make rapid guesses about the words. Sometimes a reader makes wrong guesses and reads words different to those in print. These are not counted as errors but miscues. By careful examination of these one is able to draw conclusions about strengths and weaknesses in the reading process. The examiner is looking for indications of how well a reader is interacting with the language. One of the main problems with miscue analysis is that it is an oral reading task and the assumption is made that miscues in the silent reading process are reflected in oral reading. The precise relationship between the two is, in fact, unknown (Quandt, 1977). A further criticism is that when asked to read material which is unfamiliar in content and difficult, even the best readers will make errors that do not fit the context.

Comprehension

Measures of reading comprehension take a number of forms. In general they involve answering questions about material which has been read aloud or silently. Measures of silent reading comprehension are much more important. It is silent reading comprehension which is fundamental to being able to pursue formal education and most occupations. If one were to choose a particular aspect of reading which would predict success in an occupation it would be silent reading comprehension.

Tests of silent reading comprehension usually involve asking individuals to read a passage to themselves within a prescribed time then answer questions about them. Reading comprehension tests include:

- Adult Reading Test (ART).
- Gray Silent Reading Test (GSRT).
- Gray Oral Reading Test 5 (GORT5).
- Nelson – Denny Reading Test (NDRT).
- Scholastic Abilities Test for Adults (SATA).
- Spadafore Diagnostic Reading Test (SDRT).
- Wechsler Individual Achievement Test – Second Edition (WIAT-II).

- Wide Range Achievement Test 4 (WRAT-4).
- Woodcock Reading Mastery Tests (WRMT-R).

The greatest strength of both Cloze procedure and Miscue Analysis lies in the fact that what they do best is measure reading comprehension. It has been suggested that Cloze only measures reading comprehension. Passages can be selected and analysed for readability, relevant to factors such as age and occupation. Miscue Analysis suffers from the same problem as other oral reading tests. That is, the process of reading aloud can interfere with comprehension.

It is important to note that comprehension tests vary in their format. Those selected should approximate to the tasks individuals have to deal with. Students and professionals needing to complete multiple choice tests, for example, should be assessed using comprehension tests designed in that format (see Gregg, 2009 for a review).

Listening Comprehension

Listening comprehension is an important skill. It is the ability to analyse and understand what is presented aurally. A great amount of new knowledge is acquired through listening. Listening comprehension underlies performance in learning situations such as seminars, tutorials and work training programmes, as well as skills such as note-taking. Adults with poor listening comprehension skills can have difficulty functioning in learning and work settings. At the professional level, reading can be more efficient than listening, but below that people are heavily reliant on listening comprehension, even though it involves working memory. Measures of listening comprehension consist mainly of the examiner reading passages to the person being tested and then asking them questions about what they have heard. Examples from the Spadafore Diagnostic Reading Test and the Wechsler Individual Achievement Tests.

Speed of Reading

There are adults who can decode words quite well but do so very slowly. Being able to decode words at the professional level does suggest that an adult might be able to tackle courses of advanced study or undertake a professional occupation, but if the process is very slow there will be limitations. Being able to read quickly is also important to comprehension. Unless a person can read at a good rate they cannot keep the content in memory long enough to comprehend it.

Reading aloud is not a particularly important skill for most adults. The appropriate measure of reading speed or rate is based on silent reading, particularly when reading for meaning. Reading rates tend to increase in predictable increments across the age span. Average expected reading rates for the four levels of reading are set out in Table 3.6.

A number of tests listed above include measures of speed, but those that involve silent reading speed are the most appropriate. Reading rate can also be tested by asking

Table 3.6   Expected Rate of Silent Reading

Reading level	WPM
Functional	100
Vocational	150–175
Technical	200–250
Professional	+250

the examinee to read a passage silently, with a view to answering questions about the material. 'MARK' is called after one minute has elapsed, and the number of words read counted. The average for several passages at the same level of difficulty provides the most reliable measure (Manzo & Manzo, 1993).

The Assessment of Metacognition in Reading

We have referred to the importance of metacognitive skills. When related to reading, metacognition can be described as reading for meaning (comprehension monitoring) and reading for remembering (studying or learning). A good reader possesses meta-cognitive skills in reading, is aware of the purpose of reading and differentiates between task demands. When reading text for a study assignment, for example, or reading a magazine for pleasure, the reader actively seeks to clarify the task demands through self-questioning prior to reading material. This awareness leads to the use of suitable reading strategies. A good reader varies their reading rate and comprehension level as a function of materials being read. The altering of reading rate according to the purpose of reading and the difficulty of the text is flexibility. This can be tested, by calculating and comparing rates of reading for simple and difficult materials (Manzo & Manzo, 1993).

Awareness can also lead readers to monitor their reading comprehension. When a good reader encounters a comprehension difficulty they use 'debugging' strategies. These attempts at problem solving reflect self-regulation. A good reader evaluates their own comprehension of material and this has important consequences. If a reader does not realise that they have not understood a particular part of given material, they will not employ suitable 'debugging' strategies such as back tracking or scanning ahead for possible cues to solve the difficulties. The fluent or mature reader is rarely conscious of his overall comprehension monitoring. When a comprehension failure arises the fluent reader immediately slows down in reading and either reviews the difficult sections or reads on, seeking clues in subsequent text. Metacognition, therefore, does have two components: one is on-line monitoring of comprehension; the other is taking corrective action when encountering difficulty (Wray, 1994). The assessment of metacognition in reading involves investigating two sub-skills:

1.   Whether someone has a reasonably correct estimate of their own abilities.
2.   Whether or not they are comprehending what is read or heard.

Readers should be encouraged to ask questions such as:

1. When I read a book how often do I go back to a passage or sentence and re-read it so as to clarify things?
2. How often do I ask a fellow student or tutor for clarification of ideas?
3. How often am I unable to get the main idea of a passage that I have read?
4. How often after an examination do I feel I have done well but find the results are disappointing?

If the answer is rarely to the first three and often to the last, it might be that the reader is not good at comprehension monitoring (Wong, 1986).

The Assessment of Reading Skills and Information Technology

Although we know a great deal about the skills involved in reading printed matter, we know less about whether the same skills are involved in reading when using information technology. In terms of decoding it has been suggested that the skills involved include the ability to locate information using a search engine, reading the results of such a search and reading web pages quickly to locate the best links. It has been suggested that people with reading difficulties do not know how to use or read search engine results quickly and efficiently. With regard to comprehension the functions involved include identifying important questions, as well as locating, analysing, synthesising and communicating information. Suggested ways of assessing decoding skills include observation, and for comprehension multiple-choice and short-answer questions have been recommended. Research into online reading and its assessment is in its infancy (see Gregg, 2009, for brief overview). It suffices here to say that it should never be assumed that the measurement of reading skills for printed matter is necessarily tapping those required for accessing information online.

Writing and Spelling

Writing is a very complex process. Gregg (2009) cites Luria's reference to the importance of using various task formats in its assessment. Three different tasks are suggested:

- copying;
- dictation;
- spontaneous writing.

Each of the above 'calls upon' distinctive cognitive and linguistic processes, and assessment should separate out higher and lower level abilities. The task set should also be appropriate for the individual. Copying is, for example, the most appropriate for people with very limited literacy skills. It demonstrates basic writing skills such as letter formation and fluency of handwriting.

There appear to be few, if any, standardised tests for dictation, but to consider spontaneous writing skills a sample of the client's writing should also be examined. A simple topic can be suggested or they can choose one of their own. Many dyslexics find this difficult and it is important to suggest something that they do not have to think too much about. Something such as their journey to the assessment centre or a description of hobbies minimises thinking time. The quality of the written work in terms of legibility, structure, syntax and punctuation should be evaluated. Again, one is interested in the contrast between this and verbal ability. Dyslexics will make characteristic errors such as omitting words and they had intended, as well as have difficulty with spelling (see Gregg, 2009). There are structured tests of writing skills which require individuals to write about a specific topic. Others require skills such as summarising or providing a précis, but both of these require higher level processing and specific skills a dyslexic person might not have developed.

Estimates of the average writing speed for particular groups of adults vary, but Hedderly (1996) cites research which showed that the writing rate for an average adult not in education is 20 words per minute but 25 words per minute for an adult in education. Dyslexics can be slow to produce written work. Sterling et al. (1997) found that dyslexic undergraduates wrote significantly shorter essays than their non-dyslexic peers, the difference being approximately 100 words over a half hour period. The mean rate of writing for the dyslexic was 16 words per minute whilst it was 19 words per minute for the non-dyslexics. A measure of writing speed can be established by calculating the number of words produced per minute. It can be difficult to separate out writing and thinking speed but one can make a judgement about the individual's verbal fluency. Structured tests such as the Detailed Assessment of Speed of Handwriting (DASH 17+) provided normative data up to 25 years of age. For many adults, however, writing speed is not particularly important as they will need to type all written work. The speed at which they will need to be able to type is entirely contingent upon the context in which they work.

Administering a single word spelling test can always be helpful. Tests with adult norms in current use include:

- Wechsler Individual Achievement Test – Second Edition (WIAT-II).
- Wide Range Achievement Test – 4th Edition (WRAT-4).

Knowing a spelling age, grade level or standard score can be helpful to a teacher, but these are relatively meaningless to the client and can in fact be depressing. What is often more important is to go through the words on the spelling test with them and point out how close they were to getting a particular word correct. The dyslexic who has benefited from a good education will often make only minor errors but this would still result in a very low score on a spelling test. Further, writing and spelling places a very heavy load on working memory. There are individuals whose score on a standardised spelling test will not be significantly outside average limits. However, their skills can deteriorate markedly when they are writing prose, particularly under pressure. Often these errors

Table 3.7   Spelling Error Analysis

Target Word	Client A	Client B
PICTURE	PITCHER	PITURE
CENTURIES	SENTERIES	CENTRIES
REPLY	REYPLE	REPLIE
ASSISTANT	ASSIENTIANT	ASSISTANT
PRODUCED	PRODUST	PRODUSED

can be construed as carelessness, so it is important to look at their nature. For example, confusion of letter order, omission of letters and phonic spelling or words spelled as they sound are characteristic of dyslexia. Problems with homophones often persist.

The nature of spelling errors has important implications for appropriate solutions, as well as adjustments. Shown in Table 3.7 are some sample misspellings on a standardised test. There is a considerable qualitative difference. Client B's attempts would be high on a list of suggested alternatives when using the spell checker in Microsoft Word, meaning that they would be able to use such a package to good effect. Client A's attempts yield 'no suggestions', meaning that the immediate solution would be in the use of voice recognition software.

It is not just the end result that is important, however, but the automaticity of spelling. Some individuals produce the correct spelling, but take a long time to do so and this will inevitably have an impact on their work rate.

Numeracy

The testing of arithmetic skills can be helpful, particularly when difficulties with these have been raised by a client or an employer. Dyslexic people do not usually have a conceptual problem with mathematics and the specific difficulty known as dyscalculia is rare. This does not, however, mean that dyslexic people find mathematics easy, but that their difficulties are 'manifestations of the same limitations which also affect their reading and spelling' (Miles & Miles, 1992).

Arithmetic tests are usually just measures of attainment and a low overall score might only reflect gaps in knowledge of mathematical operations due to poor teaching. Appropriate tests include:

- Wechsler Individual Achievement Test – Second Edition (WIAT-II).
- Wide Range Achievement Test (WRAT 4).

Both of the above can be of diagnostic value when responses are analysed carefully. That is, an examination of the kinds of error made can determine whether they reflect underlying processing problems or poor learning. Chinn (2000) has produced The

Informal Assessment of Numeracy Skills to be used alongside standardised tests as a way of providing a comprehensive diagnosis.

Measuring Affective Characteristics

The affective characteristics manifested by dyslexic people – that is, problems with confidence, anxiety and self-esteem – will usually be evidenced by their behaviour and verbal responses at interview. Quantification can, however, be valuable in some situations and two examples are given here.

Self-Esteem

Self-esteem refers to the perception an individual has of their own worth. It is a composite of their feelings, hopes, fears, thoughts and views of who they are, what they are, what they have been and what they might become (Battle, 1990). The Culture-Free Self-Esteem Inventories (Battle, 1992) provides a measurement of three dimensions in adults: General, Social and Personal. Clients are asked to provide a yes/no response to questions such as 'Are you as intelligent as most people?' There are 40 such items which can be read by the client administered verbally or using a tape recording. Scores are expressed as centile rankings and the results can be used to identify those people in need of counselling or psychotherapy. The results can also be used to support clinical judgement in a more objective fashion. In a litigation case where an adult was seeking financial compensation from their former Local Education Authority, it allowed the conclusion that 'although X had made up much lost ground in terms of her literacy skills, her self-esteem was so low that it might take years for her to recover'.

Anxiety

The Beck Anxiety Inventory (Beck,1990) provides a quick and easily administered measurement of anxiety levels experienced by individuals. It evaluates both physiological and cognitive symptoms of anxiety. Clients are asked to indicate the extent to which they have been troubled by 21 symptoms (e.g. Unable to Relax), using a four-point scale. Total scores are rated as indicating Normal, Mild to Moderate, Moderate to Severe, or Severe levels of anxiety.

Again this can be useful for planning or recommending further counselling or therapeutic intervention. Another example of its use with a dyslexic adult was in supporting a request for accommodations in examinations. That is, a dyslexic who had developed most of his literacy/learning skills to an advanced level experienced extreme examination anxiety. His 'severe' rating on the Beck Scale successfully supported an application for extra time in examinations.

Re-assessment

There will be times when dyslexic people need a re-assessment. This can be for several purposes including:

- monitoring progress;
- determining need with regard to adjustments and accommodations; and
- determining need with regard to provision.

The purpose of the re-assessment should establish its content. Entire diagnostic assessments should be unnecessary if dyslexia is recognised as a syndrome which is intrinsic to the individual and persists across the life span. One of our clients was forced to undergo three complete diagnostic assessments during the course of her undergraduate studies. Her comment was that each time she thought 'this is where I discover that I am not really dyslexic but just stupid'.

Re-assessments directed towards monitoring progress should include measurement of the skills being taught, and ideally should employ the same tests as were administered initially.

When needs regarding accommodations and provision are being determined it is important to establish what a dyslexic person is able to do, as well as what they can't do. Persisting reading difficulties can be compensated for by the use of CD-Rom based material and Text to Speech software, but their use requires adequate listening comprehension skills. Slow and untidy handwriting can be accommodated by allowing someone to use a word processor. It is, however, necessary to establish that the latter has become the main way in which someone communicates in writing and that their typing skills are automatic. Voice recognition software can be very effective, but requires verbal fluency and experience in its use. Failing to ensure that they have the requisite skills can lead to a dyslexic person being even more disadvantaged.

Diagnosis and English as an Additional Language

An increasing number of adults who do not have English as their first language present for assessment and Schwartz (2006) has suggested that when trying to identify the nature of a learning difficulty experienced by someone for whom English is an additional language, diagnosis is an 'educated guess'. Assessors should, therefore, educate themselves with regard to the factors that underlie the development of both spoken and written language, especially when they are using tests that have been designed for and normed with people for whom English is a first language (see Schwartz, 2009 for a comprehensive review).

Any test given in English is first and foremost a test of English. Even non-verbal tests have a linguistic aspect and can be culturally biased. Those who are apparently competent in terms of their spoken English might need more time to think about the words they use. Cultural factors extend beyond the use of language as there are individuals who will have come from a background where testing is only associated with passing and failing, and where learning difficulties are associated with mental health problems.

There are two levels of language development (Cummins, 1979):

- Basic Interpersonal Communication Skills (BICS) – the initial stages.
- Cognitive Academic Language Proficiency (CALP) – that are needed for study and work. It can take five to seven years of language instruction before this level is reached.

Sometimes the former can be deceptive and individuals can present as having better spoken English skills than is the case. There would seem to be certain fundamentals or universals in the development of literacy levels, including:

- A good foundation of oral language skills is essential to the development of literacy in general.
- The better developed language skills are in the first language the better English skills can be predicted.
- First language reading skills transfer to the second language but the student must have first language literacy skills.
- Vocabulary is an important predictor of reading comprehension, influencing it directly and through listening comprehension.
- Older children acquire a second language at a more rapid rate than younger children, the years 8–12 being the best.
- After puberty it is almost impossible to learn to speak without an accent.

During the course of an interview questions addressing the following can provide an indication of language competence:

- Competence in their first language (verbal and written).
- Age of introduction to English.
- Extent/duration of English tuition.
- Education level in the first language.
- Number of languages spoken and or written.
- The language spoken with friends/siblings/parents?
- Language spoken at school.

Cross-language studies as well as studies of those who are bi-lingual 'provide evidence for a common biological origin and for a universal, neurocognitive and phonological processing deficit in dyslexia across regular and irregular orthographies' (Nergard-Nilssen, 2006: 30). First and second languages are processed by the same networks, and differences in first and second language representations are mainly related to specific demands, which vary according to the age of acquisition, the degree of mastery and the level of exposure to each language. Linguistic and cultural influences related to speech and orthography also play a part (Johansson, 2006).

There is also evidence to support the role of working memory, especially the phonological loop, for acquiring high proficiency in the reading of native and second languages.

Research into second language learning ability and bilingualism links problems in learning a foreign language with reading difficulties that may be present in the native language. It points out cases of second language learners who experience reading problems only in English, but who can read in their native orthographies. These readers actually do experience problems in their native language; however, the reading problems are less severe than in English and reflect what we know about dyslexia in different orthographies. Some languages have been described as being more 'transparent'. That is, there is a greater consistency between the spoken and written form. Spanish and Italian are, for example, easier than English because of their regularity. To some extent therefore the assessment of the reading difficulties experienced by students for whom English is not their first language will mirror those for whom English is a first language. It should include measures of language and reasoning ability, phonological processing and working memory. Additional questions should address:

- Level of reading and writing in first language.
- Nature of script in first language.

The Wechsler Scales are available in many languages and ideally people should always be tested in their first language. This does not, however, mean that it cannot be used to assess those who are working in an English speaking environment but, in a second language. In a study of overseas students attending a university in the United Kingdom, McLoughlin and Beard (2000) found that those experiencing more difficulty than anticipated with the development of their literacy and learning skills gained low scores on the sub-tests associated with working memory. Digit Span, Coding and Symbol search can be regarded as relatively 'culture free'. Provided the language is understood the arithmetic test is also culture free. Information is culturally biased but there are a number of items that can be considered as universals. The main difference between the profiles of students from the United Kingdom and those from overseas was that the latter had more difficulty with the vocabulary sub-test, although there was considerable variation. Similarities and Comprehension posed fewer difficulties, the former requiring only one or two answers and the latter 'common sense' responses.

The additional tests included in an assessment such as phonological memory and rapid naming will also be relevant if the underlying cognitive processes associated with literacy occur across languages. After all, if individuals are attempting to learn to speak, read and write English their competence on such measures in the language will be fundamental. If individuals continue to display poor phonological memory, experience great difficulty despite direct teaching of basic skills and fail to become literate in English despite their first language skills a diagnosis of dyslexia is warranted.

Diagnosis and Other Syndromes

The attempt to explain why someone is finding something difficult should always begin with a cognitive assessment of the kind described earlier in this chapter. When considering syndromes other than dyslexia the process can be enhanced in a number of ways. These include the kinds of questions incorporated in an interview, examining cognitive profiles for specific areas of weakness and the use of checklists and questionnaires specifically designed for a particular syndrome.

Dyspraxia/DCD

Although the manuals for tests such as the Wechsler Adult Intelligence Scale do not provide profiles for individuals who have dyspraxia or developmental coordination disorder, a discrepancy between the Verbal and Perceptual Reasoning Index Scores is often taken as an indicator of a non-verbal learning difficulty such as dyspraxia. It is part of the folklore of learning difficulties, and often misunderstood. Someone who has high verbal ability and only average non-verbal ability is not necessarily dyspraxic. They could just be someone who will make a better lawyer than an engineer. This is particularly the case now that the non-verbal tests focus more on reasoning ability than spatial ability. In Chapter 1 we referred to a distinction between ideational and ideomotor dyspraxia. The former is likely to be reflected by poor performance in tests involving planning and spatial ability, such as the non-verbal tests from the WAIS-IV and WRIT, not necessarily in tests involving motor skills. Ideomotor dyspraxia is likely to be reflected in slow and untidy handwriting, as well as poor performance on tests involving motor speed and coordination, including Digit Symbol Modalities and the processing speed tests from WAIS-IV. Specific tests of motor skills can be helpful in clarifying identification.

In an interview it is essential to take a history, particularly anything that relates to activities involving coordination. This is not always easy, however, as the older individuals become, the less likely it is that they will remember much about their childhood with regard to the achievement of milestones and coordination. After the emerging adult years, clients do not always have access to their parents so that they can gain such information.

When dyspraxia has been raised in an initial interview a checklist such as The Adult Developmental Coordination Disorder/Dyspraxia Checklist for Further and Higher Education (Kirby & Rosenblum, 2008) can be used as a screening instrument. It can also be helpful later in the process as a way of clarifying the picture, when dyspraxia has been hypothesised on the basis of the results of a cognitive assessment and an interview.

Dyscalculia

When dyscalculia has been raised as an issue, a screening test such as DyscalculiUM (http://www.dyscalculia-zone.com) can be included as a precursor to formal assessment. This is an on-line screening test designed for those over sixteen years of age, examining the understanding of number concepts and their application to everyday situations.

One of the important contributions to the development of the WAIS-IV is the inclusion of the Figure Weights Sub-test as this is thought to involve numerical reasoning. When dyscalculia has been raised this sub-test should be included in the assessment process. The arithmetic sub-test also provides a measure of basic mathematical knowledge. Profiles of individuals with mathematics disorders have been shown to score less well on the Working Memory Index when arithmetic has been included, and the Perceptual Reasoning Index particularly when figure weights were included.

ADD/ADHD

Differentiating between those who have intrinsic difficulties and those whose problems with attention are task specific can be facilitated by the administration of checklists such as the Adult ADHD Self-Report Scale (ASRS-v1.1), which consists of 18 items, based on DSM-IV criteria. The Brown ADD Scales are widely used and cover abilities also associated with executive functions including:

- Organising, prioritising and activating to work
- Focusing, sustaining and shifting attention to tasks
- Regulating alertness, sustaining effort and processing speed
- Managing frustration and modulating emotions
- Utilising working memory and accessing recall
- Monitoring and self-regulation action

The cognitive profiles associated with attention deficit disorder on WAIS-IV indicate that those with ADD/ADHD score less well on the working memory and Processing Speed Index scores, thereby overlapping with profiles for dyslexia. Clarification will come from information obtained at interview, as well as the use of checklists and scales such as those referred to above.

Asperger's Syndrome

The WAIS-IV also provides evidence to show that there are specific areas of cognitive weakness associated with Asperger's syndrome. These include lower scores on the processing speed sub-tests and, therefore, the Processing Speed Index.

There are specific scales designed to identify such disorders including the Gilliam Asperger's Disorder Scale. This scale assumes at least average cognitive and language development and is designed for the population age range 3 to 22 years. It is a 32-item scale which includes four sub-scales: social interaction; restricted patterns of behaviour; cognitive patterns and pragmatic skills. There is also a parent interview schedule. Baron-Cohen (2003) developed the Autism Spectrum checklist, a 50-item scale which produces an Autistic Spectrum Quotient (AQ), based on his systematising/empathy theory.

A formal diagnosis should, however, be provided by an appropriately qualified specialist such as a psychiatrist or clinical psychologist.

Visual Stress

That an individual might be experiencing visual stress is often evidenced by the comments they make during the course of an interview, and when asked to complete reading tests. There are screening tests such as the Wilkins Rate of Reading Test (1996) that are designed to identify some of the specific visual difficulties associated with reading. This can be a useful starting point, and one can always experiment with overlays of different colours, as well as fonts and colour backgrounds on a computer. Nevertheless, screening should not be construed as definitive. There can be many reasons for visual stress and sometimes these are to do with quite subtle ocular motor or acuity difficulties that require investigation by a specialist.

Pretending to Have a Learning Difficulty

In our experience most people who are dyslexic would like not to be. They would prefer to compete on the same basis as their non-dyslexic peers, whether this is in education or employment. There can be educational, employment and economic advantages in being 'disabled', such as accommodations in tests and grants for technological aids, and there will always be those who seek to abuse this. They will, however, be in the minority. Shaywitz has written, 'In all my experiences with scores and scores of students, I have yet to encounter a young man or woman who falsely claims to be dyslexic. For those who understand dyslexia and its tremendous costs to the individual, the very idea that someone would willingly seek such a diagnosis is absurd' (Shaywitz, 2003: 164).

Nevertheless, there is a growing literature addressing the issue of feigning or exaggerating characteristics of learning difficulties such as ADHD and dyslexia. This is largely North American and the experience on that continent might be quite different to elsewhere. On the basis of this, however, it has been suggested that the use of 'feigning indexes' can improve diagnostic accuracy (Harrison, Edwards & Parker, 2008). In the interest of fairness this might improve practice, but an experienced and competent assessor will have made observations about the client's effort and performance and should be able to detect faking. If they have taken a proper history and place the results of testing in context, it should be obvious as to whether there are inconsistencies that the latter might explain.

Feedback to Client

Acceptance and understanding have been identified as essential factors in determining whether a dyslexic is able to take control and overcome their difficulties. Providing feedback is therefore the most important part of an assessment. The goal is to enable the individual to understand their difficulties in order that they can take appropriate action. It is through a proper explanation that the client will be able to start developing their awareness and understanding. If, following an assessment, a client leaves without a greater understanding of the nature of their difficulties, whether they are dyslexic or not, and what they can do to overcome them, then it has been a waste of their time.

Too often one meets teenagers and adults who have known that they are dyslexic for years but, when asked what it means, can only describe symptoms such as poor spelling. Professionals conducting assessments should spend time explaining the nature of dyslexia to their clients. It is particularly important for adult dyslexics to know that their main weakness is in phonological processing and working memory, and that their problems with reading and spelling are only signs of this.

Feedback should take two forms: immediately after testing and this should involve a careful explanation of the test results and their implications. A simple operational model, preferably one which is illustrated graphically, can be a useful aid to understanding. The client's strengths and weaknesses should be described and strategies for dealing with the latter outlined. It is important to be positive. Many adult dyslexics will have already developed their own strategies and the way these can be applied constructively to deal with other areas of difficulty can be explained. Practical information about sources of further help, including agencies and appropriate literature, CD-Roms, DVDs and Web addresses should be provided. It can be helpful to include partners, colleagues or employers in the feedback session so that they too develop a better understanding of the client and their needs.

Report Writing

Written reports of assessments are only as good as the information they generate, and reports are useful only to the extent that they convey information clearly to the client, as well as tutors and employers. They are a form of advocacy that should lead to a dyslexic person, as well as those working with them, being better informed than they were, not more confused. When working with adults it essential to remember that reports, although read by professionals working in education who might be familiar with the terminology, often end up in the hands of individuals who have no such background. Formats designed for reporting the results of the assessment of children are inappropriate.

In writing the report the author should consider whether it will help the dyslexic understand and address their difficulties, and whether it will help tutors and employers support the dyslexic person. Essentially the report should reiterate what the client was told at the end of the assessment session. It should be as 'jargon free' as possible, because the language can be misinterpreted. The negative consequences of reporting age scores have been mentioned earlier, but statistical terms such as 'significance' can be confused with real-life significance when it might in fact be of no practical importance. Even 'mean' and 'average' can be misinterpreted. Statistics can support and provide evidence for a diagnosis. They can also mask functional limitations. An average score on a standardised test does not tell the whole story. It does not, for example, reflect the effort required to gain such a score; behavioural observations are therefore essential.

Reports should:

- Be clear and concise.
- Describe abilities and skills.
- Provide an explanation.
- Address the immediate and the future.
- Recommend evidence-based solutions.

Recommendations should be specific enough to address areas of difficulty, but allow for experimentation and the client's own perspective.

Too many assessment reports written about adults are based on the format used by psychologists when describing the assessments of children. It should be remembered that they are being written for quite a different audience. A dyslexic adult should feel comfortable about showing it to people, such as a Personnel Manager, who will not necessarily be trained in test interpretation. Further, managers have no right to some of the information. They do not usually have access to the IQ scores of employees, and there is no reason as to why the dyslexic person should be an exception. The same argument holds for university students as, although academics might have a better understanding of the language in a report, knowing a student's IQ might affect their expectations of them. We have developed a tripartite reporting system, partly in response to comments from employers. The perspective of the latter is best summed up by the question asked by one manager whose organisation has contracted a large provider of assessments: that is, 'who do we go to to help us interpret and understand the reports we receive?'.

Reports should begin with a summary. This can then be followed by recommendations for skill development, compensations and adjustments, particularly as this is all most employers are interested in. There should then be a diagnostic section which provides the evidence for the interventions. It should be descriptive and not include scores. The latter are best summarised in a detachable appendix, so that the client can make them available at their own discretion. A sample report is provided in the appendix to this chapter.

Summary

1. The identification of dyslexia involves three stages; information gathering, screening and psychological testing. The last of these is an exercise in differential diagnosis, which attempts to isolate factors that answer the question 'why are tasks difficult?'
2. The concept of 'specificity' is essential to identification. That is, it should distinguish between those who have trouble learning most things because they are of low general ability, and those who have difficulty learning some things because they have specific cognitive weaknesses. Measurement of general ability is fundamental.
3. There are essential cognitive abilities that should be measured, including phonological memory, rapid naming ability and sometimes executive functions.
4. The assessment of attainments should be comprehensive and include reading accuracy, fluency and comprehension, as well as listening comprehension. Measures of writing fluency, single word spelling, and spelling in context are important. The testing of maths can sometimes be helpful.
5. Affective characteristics can be measured objectively by the use of anxiety and self-esteem scales.
6. The correct reporting of assessment findings is fundamental to the development of self-understanding, as well as accessing resources.

1. Report of Assessment

Name:	**Male Employee**	**Date Seen:**
Address:		**Date of Birth:**

Summary

- This assessment shows Male to be of high average verbal ability and average non-verbal ability, although he has some strengths in both areas.
- Diagnostic testing indicates that Male is dyslexic as he has difficulty processing information in working memory.
- Male's reading accuracy skills are well developed, but he has trouble with silent reading speed and comprehension. His proofreading skills are weak.
- Male writes legibly and his rate of writing is satisfactory. His spelling skills are weak.

Introduction

Male has been quite successful in employment and has developed some of his skills to a good level. He can improve his performance and this involves three processes that can be described as adjustment, skill development and compensation.

Adjustments

Adjustments can be made for Male in assessment, training and work settings. These should be discussed with Male but could include:

1. In assessment the following adjustments should be made for Male:
   i. Male should be allowed extra time to complete examinations so he is less disadvantaged by his slow rate of reading and difficulty with comprehension. As his rate of silent reading is around 60 per cent of that expected, an additional 40 per cent is recommended.
   ii. When completing multiple choice tests male should be allowed to mark his answers on the question booklet as his performance on some cognitive tests suggests he will have trouble locating answer codes on a score sheet quickly.
   iii. In the evaluation of Male's written work, the emphasis should be on content, an allowance being made for his weak spelling.
   iv. Male could be allowed to use a word processor to deal with written work in a test setting, as he has made this the main way in which he communicates in writing.
   v. Male needs to read aloud to help with understanding, so should be able to take tests in a room separate from other candidates.
2. Male can improve his skills and would benefit from receiving assistance from a tutor who specialises in working with dyslexic adults. This should be based on a coaching model and address work specific tasks.

3. Male should be provided with technological aids. These need to be relevant to his job role, but some are suggested below.
4. Expectations with regard to the times at which Male achieves targets in performance appraisals should be modified, especially where written language activities are involved. His performance on some cognitive tests suggests that he will not adapt to changes in demands on written work easily.
5. Male should be able to seek assistance with proofreading as his skills in this area are weak.
6. On request, Male should be given written as well as verbal instructions to accommodate his memory span.
7. Male should be helped to develop his career in such a way as to ensure he is tapping his strengths. Those will be best evidenced by his day to day performance at work.

Skill Development

Considering that Male has been working against a previously unidentified area of cognitive weakness, he has done well to achieve his current level of competence. He can, however, improve his skills and could pay particular attention to:

1. Male needs to change his approach to reading tasks when he is looking for information. He has good visual reasoning ability so is likely to be a big picture thinker. This means he should be using summaries, as well as techniques such as skimming and scanning, to gain an overview before reading to answer specific questions he has formulated.
2. Male should always plan written work as a step by step approach will reduce the cognitive load when he is writing or typing. Planning should also help him focus his reading, as well as organise information as he collects it, when he is preparing written documents. Again his strength in visual reasoning suggests he should find visual strategies helpful.
3. In spelling Male has sufficient competence to enable him to rely on a technological aid, but he would find it helpful to know how to use memory strategies to assist with technical words and homophones.
4. When not in a position to seek assistance with proofreading Male should take a step by step approach, focusing on grammar, punctuation and spelling individually.
5. I do not think Male has an intrinsic problem with concentration, but he does have to work harder at routine tasks than others and this will make him susceptible to distractions. Wherever possible he should deliberately focus for short periods at a time. This will facilitate concentration and when he is learning new material it should enable him to remember more. He could also vary the activities he engages in regularly.
6. When not in a position to seek assistance with proofreading Male should take a step by step approach, focusing on grammar, punctuation and spelling individually.

7. Memory improvement is a matter of developing techniques. There are many of these and Male should experiment so he can choose those he finds the most effective. The strategies he uses should always suit the task, as well as Male himself.
8. Male should be confident in his own way of learning and working. He has developed some of his skills to a good level and been successful in employment. This means he has already developed techniques and strategies he finds effective. He should be trying to identify these so that he can generalise them to other areas.

Compensation

Compensation provides immediate as well as long-term solutions. This is largely a matter of using technological aids. I reiterate that these should be relevant to his job role, but they could include:

1. Planning software would help Male organise his ideas as well as make visual notes and organisational charts.
2. Text to speech software would allow Male to read, as well as proofread by listening.
3. Male could try using voice recognition software, even if this is just selectively, as a way of achieving a better match between his verbal ability and his written work, as well as circumventing his spelling problem.
4. A recording device could be helpful as a back up to note taking, as well as for dealing with general memory tasks.
5. Male will always learn and work best in a multi-sensory way so should make good use of DVD and CD-Rom-based material. This also means he should be reliant on low tech organisational aids such as lists, white boards, calendars and diaries. He needs to see what he has to do rather than remember.

Author of report   **Date**

2. Diagnostic Evaluation

Introduction

I interviewed and assessed Male (aged 40 years) with a view to determining if a specific syndrome such as dyslexia might account for difficulties he is experiencing with written language, as well as with studying and working generally.

Male told me that he has a long standing history of difficulty with written language skills. He had additional help with reading during his primary school years. He needed to re-sit his 16+ examinations, but this did not lead to significant gains in general. He was more successful with a vocational programme in Sports Science. Male worked in a variety of different jobs, but has now been a police officer for 12 years. He found the course at Police College very demanding and received additional support from the training staff.

Male's general health has been sound. His vision and hearing are within normal limits. There appears to be some history of written language difficulties within his extended family.

Behaviour in Test Setting

Male worked well during the course of the assessment, adopting a thorough and systematic approach to all the tasks. He persevered even though he found some of the tests challenging. His spoken language skills are normally developed and he engaged in general conversation easily. Male showed an interest in understanding his difficulties, as well as learning how he might improve his performance.

Cognitive Ability

Administration of the Wechsler Adult Intelligence Scale (Fourth Edition) showed there to be considerable variation amongst Male's cognitive abilities.

On the verbal scale Male gained competent scores for Vocabulary (defining words) and Similarities (verbal reasoning). His score for Information (recalling factual material) was good. His Verbal Comprehension Index score (similar to Verbal IQ) suggests he is someone who ordinarily, in the absence of any specific cognitive weaknesses, could be expected to have quite well developed reading, writing and spelling skills.

On the non-verbal scale Male gained competent scores for two dimensional problem solving (Block Design), as well as Matrix Reasoning. His score for Visual Puzzles (visual reasoning) was good. His Perceptual Reasoning Index score (similar to non-verbal IQ) places him within the average range. This means he has the kinds of conceptual abilities that should ensure he is competent in practical areas, including maths.

Male gained good scores for the two processing speed sub-tests: Symbol Search (a symbol checking task) and Coding (copying symbols at speed). He did, however, gain weak scores for tests of working memory. That is, his scores for Letter Number Sequencing (working memory) and Digit Span (auditory memory) were both weak, placing his Working Memory Index score at a level discrepant with his other Index scores, meaning that the profile of these is consistent with that associated with dyslexia.

Memory and Processing Ability

Auditory/Verbal Memory: Male's performance on Digit Span and Letter Number Sequencing from the Wechsler Scale showed that he has some difficulty with the processing of auditory/verbal information. This was supported by him gaining low scores for tests of Rapid Naming from the Comprehensive Test of Phonological Processing. This test is designed for the population up to 25 years age and rapid naming ability deteriorates with age. Nevertheless, Male's scores were sufficiently low as to indicate that he has a genuine difficulty with rapid automatic naming.

Visual Memory: Male's ability to recall visually presented information was tested by the administration of the Wechsler Memory Scales Spatial Span Test which is the visual equivalent of Digit Span. He gained low scores for all dimensions, suggesting he has some difficulty processing visual information when it is sequential in nature.

Executive Functions: Male's completion of the Hayling Sentence Completion Test indicated that he has difficulty with aspects of executive functions when verbal processing is involved. In contrast, his performance on the more visual Brixton Spatial Anticipation test was competent.

Literacy Skills

Reading: Male's reading skills were tested by the administration of the Spadafore Diagnostic Reading Test. He read prose aloud accurately at the Professional level, the highest level of reading. This means he has sufficient competence in word recognition as to enable him to study and work at an advanced level. In contrast, he scored at the Technical rather than the expected Professional level on a test of silent reading comprehension and his rate of silent reading was around 60 per cent of that expected. He does not assimilate and retain information efficiently through reading, and I noted that he sub-vocalises in an effort to enhance comprehension.

I also administered the proofreading sub-test from the York Adult Assessment Battery. Male identified only 60 per cent of the errors and could find it harder to proofread his own work as he will anticipate, reading what he thinks he has written.

Writing and Spelling: Male writes legibly and his rate of writing is satisfactory. His spelling skills are unreliable. That is, he gained a weak score on the Wide Range Achievement Spelling Test (Fourth Edition). In the main, his errors were only minor in nature and would have been corrected by the use of a technological aid. He does, however, have trouble with homophones so needs to acknowledge that the use of technology is not failsafe. Male reports difficulties with structure and grammar when writing. It can be expected that his spelling skills will deteriorate when he writes prose.

Conclusion

Male has good verbal ability and competent non-verbal ability. His performance in silent reading speed and comprehension, as well as in proof reading and spelling, is inconsistent with this. Diagnostic testing does show that his working memory ability is inefficient. As this would explain the inconsistencies in his performance it is appropriate to describe him as being dyslexic.

Author of report   **Date**

Appendix A: Sample Report

Name:
Date of Birth:
Date Seen:

Underlying Ability
WAIS-IV (Wechsler Adult Intelligence Scale – Fourth Edition)

		I	DSp	V	LNS	S	SS	C	VP	BD	MR	
H	19											19
I	18											18
G	17											17
H	16											16
	15					X						15
	14			X								14
A	13					X	X					13
V	12	X							X			12
E	11									X		11
R	10				X						X	10
A	9											9
G	8		X									8
E	7											7
	6											6
	5											5
	4											4
L	3											3
O	2											2
W	1											1

Index Scores	*Standard Score*	*Centile*
Verbal Comprehension	120	91
Perceptual Reasoning	105	63
Working Memory	95	37
Processing Speed	117	87

Names of Sub-tests and Guide to Scoring

I   *Information (recalling factual material)*

DSp   *Digit Span (auditory memory)*

V   *Vocabulary (defining words)*

LNS   *Letter Number Sequencing (working memory)*

S   *Similarities (verbal reasoning)*

SS   *Symbol Search (symbol checking task)*

C   *Coding (copying symbols)*

VP   *Visual Puzzles (visual memory)*

BD   *Block Design (two dimensional problem solving)*

MR   *Matrix Reasoning (non-verbal reasoning)*

Memory and Processing Ability				*Centile*
Auditory:	WAIS-IV.	Digit Span		25
		Letter Number Sequencing		50
	CTOPP	Rapid Naming (Colours)		25
		Rapid Naming (Objects)		16
		Rapid Naming (Letters)		16
		Rapid Naming (Digits)		9
Visual:	Wechsler Memory Scales (3rd Edition) Spatial Span Test		Forwards	63
			Reversed	75
			Total	75

Literacy Skills

Reading
Spadafore Diagnostic Reading Test:
– Accuracy (Prose Reading)	–	Professional Level
– Comprehension (Silent Reading)	–	Professional Level (Instructional level)
– Speed (Silent Reading)	–	90 wpm
Proofreading (York)	–	Identified 80% of errors

Spelling
WRAT 4 Spelling Test	–	55th centile

Writing
Rate of Writing	–	+ 25 wpm

Appendix B: A Guide through the Maze of Assessments

When someone discloses that they are dyslexic or are experiencing difficulties at work, employers might ask for evidence or suggest an assessment. This is not as straightforward as it should be as there are different types of assessment. The terminology is not always clear and there is often confusion between a **'screening'**, a 'diagnostic' and **'workplace'** assessment.

The following questions and the table below may help to clarify the process. It should also help human resource personnel to evaluate the relevance and usefulness of documentation that is presented to them.

Has it been suggested that they might have a specific learning difficulty before? – When, where, why, what happened?

Have they been assessed previously?
- Do they have reports – what is the date of the last report?
- Were the reports written by teachers or psychologists?
- What were the recommendations – did they have extra help or extra time in examinations?

If the answer is yes:
If the individual has a report of an assessment that was conducted post 16 years old and it makes clear recommendations then the employer can put adjustments in place, such as extra time for training and in examinations. A workplace assessment might, however, allow for specific recommendations for the individual in that workplace. This must be carried out by someone who has a good understanding of dyslexia in occupational settings.

If the answer is yes, but there is no report
It is advisable for the employer to put adjustments in place, such as extra time and support for training, on a temporary basis to see if this helps. If performance does not improve, refer for a diagnostic assessment by an educational/occupational psychologist to determine the impact of dyslexia at this point in time would be appropriate.

If the answer is no and they have never been assessed
It is still advisable for the employer to put some adjustment in place even on a temporary basis to see if this helps.

These are essentially two kinds of assessment: screening which confirms in a systematic way that some of the characteristics associated with dyslexia are present; and diagnostic, a process of implementation.

Type of test	Who administers?	What does it involve?	What it should reveal?	What to watch for
Checklists	Self administered	Paper and pencil Answering a list of questions using a rating scale	The first step in the process: A possible indication of dyslexia	Subjective answers can give false positives or negatives. May satisfy an individual.
Computerised tests 1. Am I dyslexic 2. The Lucid Adult Dyslexia Screening test (LADS)	Self administered Self administered Often used by HR Depts as first screener	Filling in questionnaire and test items on line Recording responses on a p/c. Covers following areas: 1. word recognition 2. spelling 3. non-verbal reasoning 4. working memory items	Will provide a report on performance Rating of level of dyslexia: Provides a profile of strengths and weaknesses	This is only an indicator of dyslexia as there is no objective observation of the person's performance Recommendations for support can be made but will be general
The Dyslexia Adult Screening Test (DAST)	Psychologists/ Dyslexia specialists/ Trainers	1:1 interview Plus administration of test items covering 1. literacy 2. working memory 3. non-verbal reasoning and verbal fluency	At risk quotient/ score for dyslexia Profile of strengths and weaknesses	Recommendations for extra time in test situations Personalised recommendations based on results and interview
Teacher's/ college assessment	SEN/Learning Support Teachers	Testing is often in-house for education or college purpose only Wide variety of reading and spelling tests used	Will give outline of literacy skills	Extra time recommended May not have relevance to work situation Further assessment may be needed
Specialist teacher/ trainer assessment	Qualifications include: Dip Spld. AMBDA/APC	Some assessment of cognitive abilities, tests of phonological processing and working memory, tests of literacy	Overview of skills and abilities An explanation of problems Recommendations for skills training and workplace adjustments	Essential that assessor has experience of working with adults and understands job demands and impact of dyslexia in that workplace Recommendations must be relevant to latter

(*continued*)

Type of test	Who administers?	What does it involve?	What it should reveal?	What to watch for
Psychologists' assessment – Educational, Clinical Occupational psychologists	Chartered Psychologists, Qualifications to look for: HCPC Registered Psychologists C. Psychol	Detailed assessment of intellectual, processing abilities and literacy Highlighting areas of strength and weakness To be strongly recommended	More in depth profile of strengths and weaknesses than above and explanation for why the problems are occurring Recommendations for skill development and adjustments specific to the job role	Essential that assessor has experience of working with adults and understands job demands and impact of dyslexia in the workplace
Workplace assessments	Ideally trainers who have dyslexia specialist knowledge Access to work assessors	Identification of skills and abilities in relation to the demands of the job and the shortfall	Provide practical information about tools and techniques Recommendations regarding adjustments	Important that assessor has experience of working with adults and understands job demands, and impact of dyslexia in that workplace

Inappropriate assessment can be costly in personal and financial terms, but also in loss of productivity. The better understanding that is gained through an appropriate assessment can make all the difference to the individual and the employer. It means that adjustments can be made specific and relevant.

4

Counselling

Synopsis. *This chapter outlines the issues that arise when counselling dyslexic people. Appropriate models for counselling, as well as suitable techniques, are described. The emphasis is on educational and cognitive rather than psychodynamic approaches.*

Introduction

When an adult has been identified as dyslexic and starts to work with an appropriately trained person it is often the first time in their life that they have felt properly understood. It is inevitable, therefore, that the relationship which develops is such that dyslexic people will feel they can unburden themselves. They will wish to talk about their anxieties and frustrations as well as other personal problems.

> It is perhaps easier to tackle the learning difficulties than it is to pursue the emotional back-log which resides in you. I have a lot of anger still about all the failed tasks and why none of the professionals who taught me stopped to ask what was wrong with this child who couldn't produce the written work equal to her other skills. I wish I had been diagnosed as a child and never blamed for what is wrong.

It is not necessary for tutors, psychologists and trainers to become counsellors, but they can engage in what Sanders (1994) has termed 'informed helping', and it is therefore useful for them to understand and adopt some of the fundamental principles and practices of counselling. Likewise, professional counsellors working with dyslexic people need to understand the nature of dyslexia, as well as its manifestations and consequences. Without this inappropriate interpretations and interventions can occur. One psycho-dynamically orientated psychotherapist, for example, interpreted an adolescent's problem with organisation as being 'an over-dependence on his mother'. He was perhaps overly reliant but this was because, being dyslexic, he was so disorganised.

The Dyslexic Adult: Interventions and Outcomes – An Evidence-based Approach, Second Edition.
David McLoughlin and Carol Leather.
© 2013 John Wiley & Sons, Ltd. Published 2013 by John Wiley & Sons, Ltd.

Aims of Counselling

The aims of counselling are:

- that the client will have a greater sense of personal autonomy;
- the client has a greater sense of self understanding;
- to enable the client to live in a more satisfying resourceful way;
- that the client has a greater sense of well being;
- that the above gains should be enduring (Saunders, 1994).

Issues in Counselling Dyslexic People

In meeting the aims described above the issues to be addressed when working with dyslexic people are quite clear. Firstly, counselling or informed helping should be an extension of the assessment process in promoting self understanding including:

- explaining what dyslexia is and how it affects people;
- 'normalising' characteristics: that is, putting them in context, for example, 'we all forget sometimes';
- helping establish long- and short-term goals;
- advising on strategies and sources of help;
- assisting with the process of reframing.

> For me being dyslexic has caused me much upset and still does. I can't seem to function properly, don't understand anything first or third time around. I cry a lot. I don't like myself. I have no confidence and this is very noticeable to others. I hate being dyslexic. I have known since the age of ten. Dyslexia is to me – panic, anxiety, waiting for things to go wrong. When they do you give you such a hard time. Frustration when you can't understand anything, I forget things all the time, I have a bad memory. I don't trust anybody. I can't believe anything I am told, as the trust is not there. I am negative. I have no confidence. I can't understand numbers in my head, they do not mean anything i.e. I can read them for the price of things, but more than one thing, I can't add up or even see the sum my brain goes black inside, and that panic starts up again. I hate maths at school; no one would help me. This made me feel unworthy and so I did not bother going to maths!

The second function of counselling is dealing with affective characteristics. Barton and Fuhrmann (1994) described four issues:

1. Stress and anxiety resulting from being overwhelmed by the complexity of life's demands.
2. Low self-esteem and feelings of incompetence.
3. Grief or a feeling of loss over what might have been.
4. Helplessness, resulting from a limited understanding of learning abilities and disabilities.

> My first session with you last week shattered the way I have been able to live previously. I have always blocked off a great deal. I have always thought I have been unable to do a lot of things. I always knew there was some reason for this but I didn't know what it was. I actually thought I wasn't entitled to anything or to be able to do very much and as long as I believed that, it was all OK, but now, having spoken to you, and seen the graph that you produced, I realise what I could have done and perhaps what I could have achieved and how different things might have been. I don't know what to do with the feelings of loss and anger that I have now. I am also dealing with my mother's guilt. I have found this book that I keep reading wonderful. I have read it over and over again. All the others talk about reading and spelling. This one talks about the memory being part of the problem and it is this that has pervaded the whole of my life. It has been so insidious because I have never understood what it is all about. Now I don't know where to go, what job to do. I can't cope with my present job any more. I feel completely unable to do anything. I hate my job and I seem to be getting less and less confident and more and more dyslexic. Is that possible? My mother's guilt is very difficult. I feel I should try and make it better for her, but she told me that when I told her, she didn't help. I am hurting so much. I don't know how to deal with this. Through my life I have had a lot of therapy and a nervous breakdown, but I now strongly believe that being dyslexic has been the reason and cause of most of it.

To some extent these are addressed by dealing with the behavioural characteristics. Improved skills and performance, greater self-understanding and feeling more in control will diminish anxiety and increase confidence. Sometimes, however, affective characteristics are pervasive and there can be a need for specific counselling.

Approaches to Counselling

There are numerous different theoretical approaches to counselling, Nelson-Jones (1995) lists 13 under six general headings. All these different approaches might have something to offer when working with dyslexic adults but, as they all involve an explanation of behaviour according to a particular theory, some are likely to be more helpful than others. A major review of the outcome of different approaches to counselling or therapy led to the conclusion that there is little evidence to show that one approach is necessarily better than another, non-specific factors such as the relationship between client and counsellor being more important (Roth & Fonagy, 1996; Smith & Glass, 1977; Smith, Glass & Miller, 1980). The difference in outcome appears to be determined by the effectiveness of the therapist rather than the therapy (Wampold, 2001).

One way of defining counselling is in fact to stipulate the central qualities of good helping relationships which are both ***necessary*** in that change will not occur if they are not present, and ***sufficient*** in that, if they exist, change will occur. Rogers (1957) who developed Person Centred Therapy has defined the qualities or core conditions as:

Empathy – seeing the world of another from their point of view.
This involves:
- listening sensitively;
- trying to make sense of what is heard;
- understanding the other person in their own terms;
- checking to see if the meaning, with all the subtleties, has been interpreted properly.

Non-judgemental acceptance – described as 'unconditional positive regard'. This involves accepting the other person as being a worthwhile human being, regardless of their faults and failings.

Genuineness – this involves the helper being open to their own feelings, being fallible, vulnerable and imperfect, not knowing all the answers. It is also known as congruence.

Egan (1994) elaborated on Roger's work, arguing that the core conditions are necessary but not sufficient. In particular he focused on the skills needed by helpers during the different stages in the process of change. Egan identified three stages and the skills required as follows:

Stage 1

Building a relationship and exploration: that is, developing empathy, genuineness and non-judgemental acceptance.

Skills   Developing a trusting relationship:

- making and maintaining contact;
- structuring;
- communicating non-judgemental warmth;
- communicating genuineness;
- active listening and communicating empathy;
- identifying, acknowledging and reflecting thoughts, behaviours and feelings;
- paraphrasing;
- clarifying.

Stage 2

Changing the clients' perceptions of themselves.

Skills   Linking and integrating individual issues and problems into themes:

- showing deeper understanding and empathy;
- helping the client focus on specific issues.

Challenging the client's views:

- offering new perspectives;
- sharing experiences and feelings;
- helping the client move on.

Goal Setting
- helping the client identify what they want to achieve.

Stage 3

Considering ways of acting to help resolve the problem, including risk assessment and possible outcomes.

Skills   Helping the client move on to considering action, as well as developing and choosing action plans.

Developing and choosing action plans:

- brain storming;
- creative thinking;
- problem solving;
- decision making;
- planning.

Evaluating consequences of actions:

- recording events;
- evaluation;
- reviewing plans.

An approach to counselling which seems relevant to working with dyslexic people is known as the Psychoeducation Model (Authier, 1977; Hornby 1990). This adopts the view that the client's problems are skill deficits rather than abnormality (or illness). Illness – Diagnosis – Prescription – Therapy – Cure, is replaced by Dissatisfaction – Goal setting – Skill teaching – Satisfaction (or goal achievement). The model further elaborates on the work of Rogers and Egan, there being a three-stage approach:

Exploration, Intervention, Empowering

The skills required by counsellors at Stage I according to both the Egan and Hornby models are very much the same as those needed by tutors working with dyslexic people. It is the relationship with the tutor that will allow the dyslexic person to disclose the issues that require further intervention. Tutors do, however, need to recognise the limits of their skills and be prepared to refer on when issues are beyond their own expertise.

Central to Stage II is changing self perceptions. It is here that the reframing process identified by Gerber et al. (1992, 1996) as being essential to success is important. Reframing refers to:

Table 4.1   Psycho-Education: The Three Stages

STAGE	EXPLORATION I	INTERVENTION II	EMPOWERING III
AIMS	Relationship building Clarifying concerns/ patterns Assessment	Developing new perspectives Increasing experiential Awareness Developing new behaviours	Consolidating changes Supporting action programmes Enabling self-actualisation
SKILLS	– empathetic responding – respect – genuineness – probing – immediacy – specificity – self-disclosure – linking – circular questioning *ASSESSMENT:* – intrapersonal – interpersonal	PSYCHO-EDUCATION *Focused on: AFFECT:* *for example:* – focusing – evocative responding – active listening **BEHAVIOUR:** *For example:* – teaching life skills: goal setting; communication skills; family living skills; vocational skills, etc. *COGNITION:* *For example:* – active listening – reframing & metaphors – cognitive restructuring – interpretation & confrontation	*For example:* – identifying changes – elaborating action programmes – affirming strengths – developing skill deficit areas – increasing self-esteem & self-control – expanding options – referring on – promoting self-help strategies – developing personal & social responsibility *TERMINATION:* – evaluation – follow-up

(Adapted from Hornby, 1990).

A set of decisions relating to reinterpreting the learning disability experience in a more productive and positive manner. It clearly allows for one to identify strengths and parlay them into successful experiences, while still being aware of weakness that have to be mitigated or bypassed. (Gerber et al., 1996: 98)

I would advise other dyslexics to never let dyslexia hold them back from what they want to achieve. There are always ways of overcoming any difficulties, perhaps by finding the right types of coping strategies that work effectively for that particular individual. People with dyslexia are usually intelligent, creative, thinkers, as they have had to use creativity and innovation to devise alternative methods for dealing with various situations. This creativity should be used positively as strength.

Reframing is a dynamic process, consisting of the four stages shown in Table 4.2.

Table 4.2   Reframing Stages

Stage		
1. Recognition	–	that one is dyslexic
2. Understanding	–	the nature and implications of dyslexia
3. Acceptance	–	that there are issues to be dealt with
4. Action/Plan of Action	–	to achieve goals

In facilitating reframing, 'cognitive restructuring' approaches can be helpful. Rational-Emotive Therapy, developed by Ellis (1962), for example, assumes that maladaptive feelings are caused by irrational beliefs. Ellis argues that through mistaken assumptions people place excessive demands upon themselves. The adult dyslexic who assumes, incorrectly, that most people are very skilled in spelling and who consequently thinks that their own spelling skills are much worse than they really are, is a typical example. Counselling involves challenging such assumptions. Likewise, Beck (1995) considers numerous psychological problems to be the result of the negative ways in which individuals think about themselves. His approach is based in attribution theory, where behaviour is thought to be determined by the causes an individual associates with it. Attributions are made to either internal causes which are self blaming or external causes such as circumstances. An example of a dyslexic person making an internal attribution would be for them to blame their literacy difficulty on lack of intelligence; an external attribution would be for them to blame it on poor schooling. The former would also be regarded as stable, implying that it can't be changed. The latter would be considered unstable, as something can be done to make up for poor educational opportunities. Attributions can also be global: that is, associated with many aspects of life such as dealing with any kind of paperwork: or specific: that is, blaming problems with written work as being because of a particular problem with spelling.

> Dyslexia has really affected my self-esteem and confidence, due to negative experiences at school, such as being placed in the bottom sets for English and being labelled as thick and slow by my peers. I know that these sorts of experiences were encountered a long time ago, but the feelings do stay with you.

Individuals who are inclined towards making global, stable and internal explanations for negative events are vulnerable to depression. When things do not go well they think badly of themselves and their confidence and self-esteem are affected. In contrast, mentally healthy people respond to positive events by making internal, stable and global attributions, and make external, unstable and specific attributions when things do not go well (Mezulis et al., 2004). As we have suggested earlier, because of their inefficient working memory system, dyslexic people might be more susceptible to making internal, self-blaming attributions. These 'will influence their self-perception, expectations concerning the outcome of future events, feelings about the ability to influence these events, as well as learning motivation' (Kominsky, 2003: 271). In education and training these can be addressed through improving meta cognitive skills.

In counselling the approach known as Cognitive Behavioural Therapy (CBT) involves questioning and collaborating with clients so that they can discover for themselves the distortions in their thinking, that is, their inappropriate attributions, and can then make changes that are consistent with reality. It has been extensively researched and applied to a wide variety of mental health issues including anxiety and depression. Positive outcomes have been reported for these areas as well as an improving self-esteem and work motivation (Winspear, 2008). A cognitive-behavioural approach has also been adopted effectively in coaching (Ducharme, 2004; Sherin & Caiger, 2004). It is essentially a meta cognitive activity.

> The sessions have also helped restore my confidence, which has – over the years – been eroded by the fact that I have associated the problems that dyslexia causes me with my being unintelligent and partly lazy. This loss of confidence has been compounded by feelings of inadequacy caused by my modest academic achievements at school and my lack of further education. It has been important for me to address in my development sessions why I failed nearly all my formal school examinations despite being motivated and highly determined to succeed.

A cognitive-behavioural approach attempts to identify the typical distorted cognitive processes of the client. Scott and Dryden (1996) outline Burns' (1980) list of the ten most common self-defeating thought processes, adapted here to apply to dyslexic people, as:

1. **All or nothing thinking** – seeing everything as black and white: for example, 'if I am not in complete control, I will lose all control'.
2. **Over-generalisation** – where it is concluded from one negative event that other negative events are thereby likely: for example, 'I wasn't successful at that and now everything is probably going to fall apart'. 'I forgot to mention some points in my presentation so it must have been really bad'. 'I left something out of the report and forgot to proofread it – it must have been awful'.
3. **Mental filter** – seizing on a negative fragment of a situation and dwelling on it, omitting any consideration of any positive feature: for example, 'The boss didn't like my report, and it was awful'.
4. **Automatic discounting** – sensitivity to absorbing negative information and summarily discounting positive information: for example, 'My boss said my presentation was good, but he always says that'.
5. **Jumping to conclusions** – where a conclusion is inferred from irrelevant evidence: for example, 'I won't get the job because of my poor handwriting'.
6. **Magnification and minimisation** – magnifying imperfections and minimising positive attributes: for example, 'I can't spell so I am hopeless'.
7. **Emotional reasoning** – using feeling as evidence of the truth of a situation: for example, 'I didn't do very well at school so I can't have worked hard enough'.
8. **Should statements** – an overdose of moral imperatives, 'shoulds', 'musts', 'have to's and 'oughts': for example, 'I should be able to spell (remember names etc.) better'.

9. **Labelling and mislabelling** – emotional reactions are in large measure a product of the label a person attaches to a phenomenon. An inappropriate label can produce a distressing reaction: for example, 'I forgot his name so I am stupid'.
10. **Personalisation** – egocentric interpretation of interpersonal events relating to the self: for example, 'Two people laughed and whispered something to each other when I walked by, they were probably talking about me being dyslexic'.

The last of these is particularly important when working with dyslexic people. Writing specifically about counselling and dyslexia Scott (2004) includes:

1. **Dysfunctional schemas** – general beliefs that are at the back of our minds, that provide reference points for choices in our life; 'I am lazy – I would do better if I worked harder, it is what teachers told me at school'. These become ingrained beliefs.
2. **Cognitive distortions** – biased interpretations of external events that lead us to catastrophise; 'My boss found errors in my work and that I am slow with my work; he thinks I am stupid'.
3. **Over generalisations** – taking one event as representative of all others; 'I made a spelling mistake, my spelling is terrible'. 'The presentation didn't go well – I am really bad at it'.
4. **Making internal attributions** – attributing to oneself unwarranted responsibility for all negative events; 'The project wasn't a success, so it must be my fault'.

> I don't think I have ever come across anything positive about being dyslexic. I am a very negative person. I think it is all due to the unnecessary and horrible experiences I have had since a small child to date. It is very hard to be positive when nothing you do is right.

By addressing such distortions dyslexic people can be helped to reframe and move on to find solutions.

This approach to counselling involves questioning clients so that they can discover for themselves the distortions in their thinking and can then make changes that are consistent with reality. Scott (2004) recommends Cognitive Behavioural Therapy as the most powerful and long-term solution to problems with anxiety. She suggests that some of the negative thoughts and beliefs particularly common with dyslexics are:

- Oil Slick thoughts – transferring negative feelings about one aspect of one's life to every aspect. "I forget things so I must be stupid".
- The habit of beating yourself up – self-blaming for causing others inconvenience. "I am always late", "I have to ask others to check my work so I am a nuisance".
- Giving power away to other people – that is, learned helplessness. "My wife deals with all the domestic paperwork and won't let me do it".
- Old behaviour that gets in the way – unlearning bad habits can be harder than developing new skills. "I have to re-read everything before I remember it".
- Separating the truth from the lie – thinking problems are much worse than they really are. "I can't read aloud". "My spelling is dreadful".

(Scott, 2004: 269)

Some of the skills described at Stage 3 of the Psycho-Education Model, especially those that facilitate control, can address the specific issues described by Barton and Fuhrmann (1994). One of these is stress and anxiety. These are factors which can undermine the ability to function effectively in learning and work situations, exacerbating behavioural difficulties. It can therefore be beneficial for dyslexic people to be taught relaxation techniques. These are well documented and include the following:

- Progressive relaxation – focusing on the major muscle groups of the body, group by group.
- Visualisation – producing feelings of calm and well-being by training people to use pictures in their minds of themselves in safe, warm and comforting environments.
- Deep breathing – which stimulates relaxation and reduces stress and anxiety.

There is an extensive literature on the use of hypnotherapeutic techniques to treat anxiety, including specific disorders such as examination anxiety (Hart & Hart, 1996). Such approaches are, however, never enough on their own. Symptom removal without addressing the underlying problem can only lead to short-term gains. This is well illustrated by the college student who was suffering from panic attacks to the extent that she was no longer able to attend classes. She had tried hypnosis with only limited success. It was only when a diagnostic assessment conducted by an educational psychologist revealed poor working memory that the source of her panic was understood. She had been struggling with increased demands on her learning and organisational skills, and this had led to feelings of being out of control. A programme of skill development combined with hypnosis enabled her to deal more effectively with both behavioural and affective issues.

In building up confidence and self-esteem techniques such as assertiveness and social skills training can be useful. Learning to advocate for themselves with tutors, employers and socially is very important for dyslexic adults. They have often not learned to negotiate for their rights and for appropriate accommodations at college or in the workplace. Some, because of their inefficient information processing system, have not intuitively learned appropriate social skills. These need to be directly taught and treatment of problems with social skills has focused on educational rather than therapeutic interventions (Forness & Kavale, 1991). Assertiveness training can also be of value in helping deal with their anger. Many dyslexic people are justifiably angry about the way they have been treated. This should be acknowledged but they must be helped to manage their anger and learn how to respond appropriately when put on the defensive.

> Dyslexia has really affected my self-esteem and confidence, due to negative experiences at school, such as being placed in the bottom sets for English and being labelled as thick and slow by my peers. I know that these sorts of experiences were encountered a long time ago, but the feelings do stay with you.

As we have learned from our dyslexic clients, dyslexic people can learn from each other. There is no doubt that they can benefit from formal and informal support groups. Group therapy has in fact been utilised with college level students. Rosenblum (1987) for example describes a group which was directed towards raising self-esteem. This allowed the members to share:

- past experiences;
- feelings of being misunderstood;
- ideas on the development of strategies.

It was considered that there were direct benefits in terms of the development of skills, but also indirect ones in that the group members were accepting and supportive of one another, providing comfort and strength.

> Being aware of what my own strengths, weaknesses and difficulties are has helped me to understand and to deal with my dyslexia. Also, on my current training programme, my tutor and two other colleagues on my course are dyslexic. We are able to talk quite openly to each other about our dyslexia and I find that this sharing of experiences and difficulties is very useful, as this helps me to cope with my dyslexia, by knowing that I am not alone and not the only one who struggles with certain things that other people find quite straightforward or easy to do.

Labelling oneself as belonging to a particular group and then favouring it helps to maintain one's sense of potency and self-esteem (Rubin & Hewston, 1998). Baron-Jeffrey et al. (2003) describe a self-help programme based on research into resilience and success, adopting a psycho-educational model and cognitive-behavioural principles.

Couple Counselling

As social ecologies are important to success, as well as having better self-understanding dyslexic people need to be understood by others, especially those close to them. It can be helpful to include partners in counselling sessions as this can improve the way they perceive and support the dyslexic person. Living with someone who is disorganised and forgetful, for example, can place stress on a relationship. Understanding that this is 'can't' rather than 'won't' can ease the situation and lead to the non-dyslexic person supporting their partner in constructive ways.

Further, following diagnosis and effective training there can be quite dramatic changes in confidence and motivation. As the dyslexic person becomes more competent they are less dependent and this can change the balance in a relationship, leaving their partner feeling threatened. Including them in counselling can help them understand and adapt to the changes taking place.

Referring On

Professionals working closely with dyslexic people need to be aware of the possibility of their clients becoming more dependent rather than independent. Further, one of the characteristics of a mature professional is knowing when they are out of their depth and other expertise is required. There are dyslexic people whose life experience has been such that they need in-depth counselling. Rogan and Hartman (1990) reported that amongst a sample of 68 adults with learning disabilities, 75 per cent of college graduates and 62 per cent of high school graduates had some type of psychotherapy or counselling in their lives and considered this a significant factor in determining a successful outcome.

Counsellors do not need to be experts in dyslexia, but it is necessary to recognise that a dyslexic person has a constitutional difference that makes certain tasks more difficult for them than they are for people who are not dyslexic. They need to be aware of how these difficulties have operated to produce further complications in a person's life and behaviour. The complex interaction of the psychological difficulties and the constitutional difference must be fully acknowledged if the individual is to make progress. That is, the relationship between behavioural/cognitive and affective difficulties needs to be acknowledged and understood. Further, counsellors need to adapt their approach to take into account the unique processing style of each individual.

Summary

1. Counselling dyslexic people should promote self-understanding, assist in goal setting and include advice on strategy development.
2. Counselling should also address affective factors such as confidence, self-esteem, anxiety and stress.
3. Educational and cognitive models of counselling are the most suitable for dyslexic people.
4. Dyslexic people can help each other through participating in group counselling.
5. Partners of dyslexic people might helpfully be involved in the counselling process so that their understanding of issues that arise is improved.

5

Personal Development

Synopsis. *This chapter addresses the issues facing dyslexic people in their personal development, including memory, organisation, goal setting and social skills. The importance of the development of metacognitive skills is emphasised, as is the role of the professional working in partnership with dyslexic people.*

Introduction

All interventions directed towards assisting dyslexic people, regardless of the issues or skills addressed, should contribute to their personal development. Dyslexic people need to be able to access the expertise of professionals, but they also need to tap and enhance their own experience as a learner and worker. Everyone has their own individual skills and abilities, and enabling the dyslexic individual to capitalise on their strengths allows them to deal more effectively with both behavioural and affective problems.

Self-understanding

One of the keys to becoming a successful dyslexic person is self-understanding. This has several dimensions including understanding:

- the nature of the difficulty;
- what they can do about it;
- their strengths and abilities.

It involves more than just knowing the above. Dyslexic people need to be able to focus on their abilities and what they can do if they are to feel more in charge of every aspect of their lives.

The Dyslexic Adult: Interventions and Outcomes – An Evidence-based Approach, Second Edition.
David McLoughlin and Carol Leather.

The main fear that I had to face was working with and coming to terms with being dyslexic. The revelation that I had to start working with my dyslexia did not appear overnight, more something that went hand in hand with knowing it was time for change. I realised that I had to stop fighting against being dyslexic and start working with it. The critical turning point came for me when I visited a dyslexia centre. Guidance and help was what I was looking for but I left the building knowing that I could achieve anything I want to, for at last someone totally understood me. They were there to point me in all the right directions, give me sound advice to what I was entitled to and where to get it, and also to offer tutoring and counselling. I can clearly remember sitting on the train going home, thinking this is the first day of the rest of my life, I can achieve my goals if I want to, for at last there is the kind of help that I had longed for.

The Nature of the Difficulty

When trying to understand dyslexia there are several facts people should know. These are:

1. It is usually genetic in origin and they are not therefore to blame.
2. It is part of their make up and always will be.
3. It is not an insurmountable barrier to educational or occupational success, provided they have the necessary abilities.
4. They need to acknowledge that it is there and they might need to make more effort than most when faced with new challenges.

Interpreting Dyslexia

Before dyslexic people begin to actively work towards seeking effective solutions they need to understand why tasks are difficult for them. We use a simplified version of the model of working memory described in Chapter 1 as a way of interpreting their difficulties as inefficiency in the processing of information. Working memory is described as a system that allows performance of several tasks at once and illustrated graphically as shown in Figure 5.1.

The way in which specific skills are affected is explained. A problem with reading comprehension, for example, would be described as a result of the overload resulting from recognising words, finding their meaning and making sense of the material simultaneously. Difficulties with written expression are explained as the result of overload which comes from thinking of an idea, finding words to express it, spelling the words correctly and putting them in order, with proper regard for grammar and punctuation. We also go beyond the simple model shown above and explain the relationship between the components of working memory.

Dyslexia affects people in different ways, personally it affected my self-confidence. I was always made to feel lazy, stupid, ugly and sometimes even worthless. When I was diagnosed as dyslexic it was more a relief than anything else. So this is why my handwriting is like this and that is why I have a problem with essays, that's why maths is so bad, that's why I always have problems with numbers.

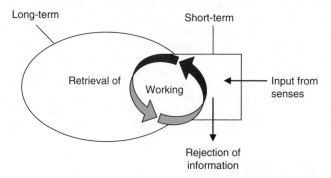

Figure 5.1   A Model of Working Memory

This model is one that we find dyslexic people can identify with. Once they have adopted it, they are provided with a method of interpreting their difficulties themselves. It enables them to make sense of the problems they have experienced in the past, and their current difficulties, and enables them to predict what might be challenging in the future. We encourage them to make it relevant to their situation and some have taken the model further, providing their own analogies. One young man, for example, explained his difficulties in an examination setting as follows:

> The main effect of my dyslexia in the examination setting has been that I read and write more slowly as my word recognition and retrieval is not as automatic (i.e. efficient). I find it takes me longer to assimilate longer questions. To use a computing analogy, if the mind is like a computer running Windows, the working memory is like RAM where the processing is done and the long term memory is like the hard disk. If a computer has more data to process than can be stored in RAM, it stores it temporarily on the hard disk in 'virtual memory' and has to constantly refer to it. This is comparatively much slower than holding it in RAM, thus the task is accomplished, but takes longer than would be achieved by a computer with more RAM. Being dyslexic is like a computer with insufficient RAM, you can accomplish as much but take longer to get there.

A further advantage of this approach is that it enables dyslexic people to explain their difficulties to others in a way that can be understood. They are, therefore, in a better position to advocate for themselves. People do need to know that dyslexia can be recognised as a disability and that this means they might be able to access resources. They already know that being dyslexic is a disadvantage; it is why they are seeking help. In interpreting it to them, however, the emphasis should be on 'difference'. We describe dyslexia as an 'inefficiency', the implication being that people can become more efficient by being confident in their own different way of learning.

> My results prove what you and my parents always told me, and I might just be starting to truly believe, and that is that I can do almost anything if I set my mind on it. What next, I do not know but I plan on setting myself a high standard so that I finish off one level higher than I would have done if I had set no standards at all. Thank you very much for helping me to Believe in myself.

Dyslexic people will of course want to know more and what follows are some common questions asked and suggested responses.

What is it?
Dyslexia is very complex and we still don't know everything about it. It is best described as an information processing difference that affects all aspects of life, including organisation, literacy skills, time keeping and remembering things. It can be described simply as an inefficiency within the working memory system which, when overloaded, crashes. When talking about literacy skills, it is often simplest to say that dyslexia means that you have a problem when 'multi-tasking with words'.

How did I get it?
It is usually genetic so therefore some member of the immediate or extended family must be dyslexic. However, the actual genetic link is, at this stage, unclear. Some families have one dyslexic person, in others all members are dyslexic.

Will my children have it?
It is quite possible – the answer is as above really, but it is important to emphasise that dyslexic children of dyslexic parents are not necessarily going to experience the same learning difficulties as their dyslexic parent. This is partly because they are likely to be identified sooner and partly because each dyslexic person has their own pattern of difficulties.

Why wasn't it found out earlier?
There are often many reasons for this. Sometimes it is due to lack of awareness in schools. There might have been other reasons that have prevented identification, and it may indeed be that the dyslexic person has been 'a victim of their own success'. That is, they have either worked hard and overcome many of the more obvious difficulties, or alternatively they have just worked hard, sat quietly in the classroom and been passed over. Dyslexia is very complex and, therefore, unless the indicators really are quite pronounced during the school years, it quite often does go unnoticed. It could be said that dyslexia is only a problem when it becomes one and it is usually at times of change that it becomes evident.

Is the fact that I muddle up my words because I am dyslexic?
Yes, muddling up words or not being able to find the right word at the right time is one of the characteristics of dyslexia. It occurs as a result of the overload in the working memory system. It is not that the person does not know what the word is. Being unable to tell left from right, for example, is simply being unable to find the label at the right time, as is remembering someone's name. Many of our clients identify with the experience reflected in the picture below.

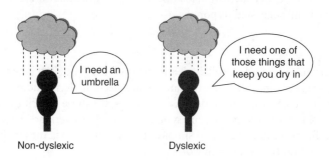

Non-dyslexic   Dyslexic

Why do I forget?
A poor memory is characteristic of dyslexia because again, the working memory system is inefficient. If it is overloaded, the information does not go in effectively, and what is stored is harder to retrieve.

How do I tell people?
To disclose is a difficult matter and it is a very personal one. Some people feel that they don't want to say anything, but if they want to access resources and accommodations, they need to disclose that they are dyslexic. People need to think carefully about what they are going to say. It is better to keep the explanation as simple as possible and to say how it affects them, but it is very important to say what they can do rather than what they can't. The emphasis should be on solutions.

Will I ever be cured?
A person with dyslexia will always be dyslexic, but if they develop the right skills and strategies, this should not prevent them from being successful. They do, however, need to recognise that times of change will be particularly demanding and they might need to make more effort to develop new skills and strategies at that time.

Why is my dyslexia not the same as others?
Dyslexia can be described as a pattern of strengths and weaknesses. It affects each person differently; some people can be very articulate, others have a word-finding difficulty. Some can read well, others always find it hard. Some people can spell and write well, others find these impossible tasks. Educational and family experiences will have an impact on the outcome. This is why understanding the nature of dyslexia and 'self-understanding' are so important. In simple terms people need to be able to interpret it as an information processing difficulty or difference.

Abilities and Strengths

Identifying abilities is as important as understanding the 'disability'. Dyslexic people should be encouraged to be confident in their own way of doing things, as well as the fact that they already have many of the skills, strategies and solutions they need. Often they do not recognise their strengths and do not use them automatically when appropriate. Many will have been actively discouraged from approaching tasks in a way that suits them, and some believe that it is wrong to do so. An example is the man who had employed someone to read material to him when studying, and used the word 'cheating' to describe how he managed to gain a university degree. A common experience is to find that when told that a way of enhancing reading comprehension is to read the questions before the material, a dyslexic person will admit with embarrassment that they already do it that way, despite having been told not to do so when at school. Some have been discouraged from their preferred way of taking notes, such as drawing pictures. They have therefore unsuccessfully attempted to deal with it in a more conventional way.

I had the feeling that knowing would be enough but once you know that you are dyslexic, you want to go back and learn all the things you couldn't learn the first time.

Hopefully a dyslexic will have gained insights into their abilities from their diagnostic assessment. They might, for example, have learned that their memory for images is better than their auditory memory. Further, information about their abilities and learning style can be elicited in a number of ways, mainly asking the right questions. One of the simplest examples is asking a dyslexic person how they find their way about. The usual response is that they rely on landmarks (the pub) rather than labels (left and right or north and south). This is an indication that they process visual information better than auditory information. Appropriate questions can be included during an initial diagnostic interview.

There are systematic approaches to evaluating learning styles, mainly questionnaires (Dunn & Dunn, 1996; Lashley, 1995, Hobson, Ashley & Kibble, 1998). Studyscan (Zdzienski, 1997) referred to in Chapter 3 is a computer-based approach to analysing an individual's learning profile. They are, however, only a starting point and should always be followed up by a discussion about how the individual does things automatically. Do they, for example, talk to or argue with themselves, visualise, or role play? Do they make plans, write lists, draw pictures? Questionnaires have good face validity – that is, they seem like an objective test – but an individual's own insight into how they learn and work can be as revealing.

In Chapter 1 we referred to the literature that focuses on the visual strengths of dyslexic people. It has been suggested that they are more 'right-brained' than 'left-brained'. We have also written that it is misleading to talk about the hemispheres of the brain as independent entities, it being the interactions between them that are important. In general, however, the right hemisphere of the brain has the ability to generate mental maps, to rotate images and to conceptualise visually. It has been suggested that learning is most effective when the two hemispheres work co-operatively, but that the demand on verbal left hemisphere activities is greatest in most academic settings. Those with a strong preference for right hemisphere functioning are therefore at a disadvantage.

A simple model of the abilities associated with the two hemispheres of the brain is shown below.

Hemispheres of the Brain

Left hemisphere		Right hemisphere
• language		➢ pictures
• analysis		➢ music
• time orientation		➢ spatial awareness
• sequencing		➢ dimension
• logic		➢ pattern
• listening		➢ emotion

Dyslexic people need to be encouraged to be comfortable with and confident about the use of visual imagery. This will often have been discouraged during their school years. They can, for example, be encouraged to use visual strategies, such as mind mapping, for the planning of pieces of written work and then translate their ideas into language. These have been shown to be highly effective for people who have learning difficulties (Dexter, 2010). They can also be encouraged to use visual information, such as graphs and pictures, to locate information, as well as rely on symbols rather than words and use colour.

I have managed to find my own coping strategies. For example, each Sunday evening I write out a timetable, putting down a couple of things that I need to do for each day in the week ahead. I also write a To Do list every evening for the next day, usually listing about eight things that I have to do. This really helps to keep me organised and motivated and as I have a very short-term memory, having what I need to do written down somewhere helps me to overcome this. As I don't have a good concept of time, if I am going to an appointment somewhere, I usually work out a couple of days beforehand how long it will take me to get there and then I write down exactly what time I will have to leave home by. I also have a very supportive partner, who after twenty years of being together, knows exactly what is it like to live with someone with dyslexia and so understands ways of how to make my life a lot easier. I am very good at delegating tasks, such as having someone to work out the various timings for me when I am cooking a meal. I also have a Mum who is dyslexic and when we get together we don't take things too seriously, but like to have a good laugh at the various things that we have done, or situations that we have found ourselves in. I think it is important to be able to have someone to identify with and to share experiences.

Personality is also a factor in effective learning and performance. This can be illustrated by analogy through reference to fictional detectives such as Poirot and Sherlock Holmes. They both gather information in order to make sense or find a solution to a specific problem, but they each use a different approach. The same can be said for someone learning. Some are very methodical in the way in which they approach a situation, some are very logical and rational and others are much more intuitive. Some people have leaps of cognition and a variety of ideas, and others absorb the information in a step by step approach. Those people who make 'cognitive leaps' need to be able to track back their thinking process so they can explain it to the more methodical learner. Cottrell (1999) suggests that there are a 'range of approaches to learning' including: 'the diver' who jumps in and has a go working in short bursts of activity; 'the logician' who needs to know the reasons behind things; 'the dreamer' who thinks a lot about a subject and has no idea where times goes; and 'the searchlight' who finds everything interesting and has difficulty selecting what is relevant. This model can be applied to anyone, but it can encourage dyslexic people to realise that there is more than one way in which to learn. Understanding and being confident in the way they think and recognising their learning preference, can lead to people becoming creative problem solvers, allowing them to develop their skills and abilities (Reid & Strnadova, 2008; Mortimer, 2003).

One student brought the following as an example of an essay he had written with great difficulty.

It is illegible as reproduced here but so was the original and the student himself was unable to read it.

During the course of the interview it was noted that he 'doodled' a lot. This was discussed and it was suggested that he tried to use drawings in planning. At the next session he returned with the following which contains some pictures and quite a lot of words.

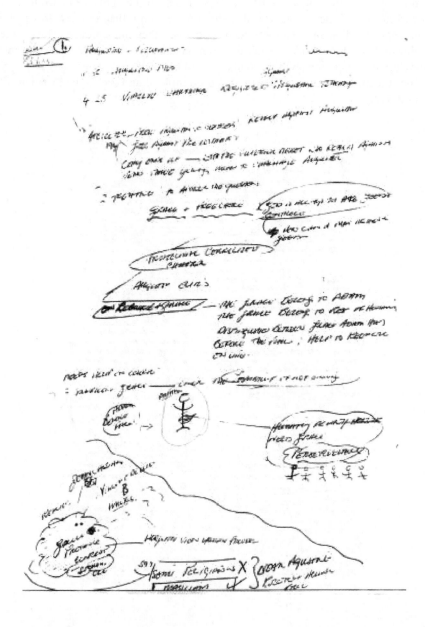

When he returned for another session he demonstrated that he had further developed the skills of note taking and planning through pictures.

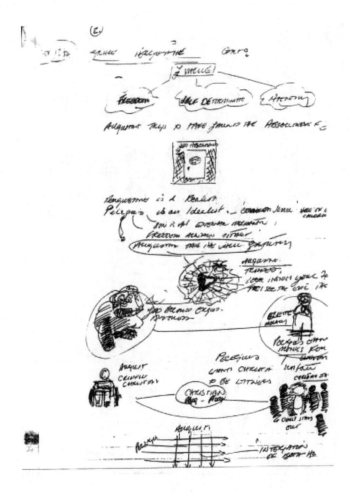

Ultimately he was able to plan and record everything in pictorial form, the following two examples being his notes from separate one and a half hour lectures.

He can still recall most, if not all, of the ideas from both several years later.

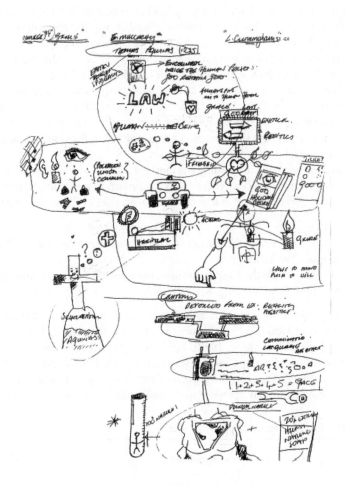

Metacognition

Although adult dyslexics seeking help are presenting with problems they wish to address, they will already have developed their own way of learning and dealing with tasks. Encouraging them to engage in metacognition – that is, 'think about the way they think' – can enable them to be more efficient in the way they learn and work. It is particularly important to encourage them to consider things they do well and endeavour to analyse what they are doing and have done. If they can apply the same processes to tasks they find difficult, they will often find solutions.

The Importance of Metacognition to Learning and Working

The role of metacognition in adult learning has been outlined in Chapter 2 but it bears repetition here. Metacognition allows people to deliberately use the skills that they find most effective. The reflection and evaluation processes encourage positive attribution, as well as the transfer of skills and knowledge to other areas. Furthermore, because of the difficulties they may have experienced with learning, dyslexic adults are likely to be dependent learners and they will try to learn what they are asked to and adopt practices that are less effective for them, as that is what they were told to do at school; learning through repetition and concrete action rather than a more strategic approach. They are often 'apprentices' regarding their learning behaviour rather than mastering the process and becoming independent (Moran & Gardener, 2007).

Metacognition becomes increasingly important and it develops over time. This is demonstrated in Moran and Gardener's (2007) approach to metacognition from a multiple intelligences perspective. It is a developmental model and they outline two broad stages:

- the apprentice stage, where the learner is directed and driven by external factors such as cultural goals. See Table 5.1.
- the master stage, where the learner becomes increasingly self-aware and orchestrates their own thinking and learning. See Table 5.2.

The master stage is one at which individuals have become highly metacognitive in their approach to tasks and there is evidence to suggest that this increases self efficacy (Goldberg et al., 2003; Rashkind, 1999). Feelings of positive self efficacy contribute to success in academic and occupational settings (Bandura, 1997; Zimmerman, 2002). It has been identified as a factor in the success of dyslexic people (Leather et al., 2011). It also increases motivation, competence and confidence as they become agents of their

Table 5.1   Moran and Gardner's Apprentice Stage

Table 5.2 Moran and Gardner's Master Stage

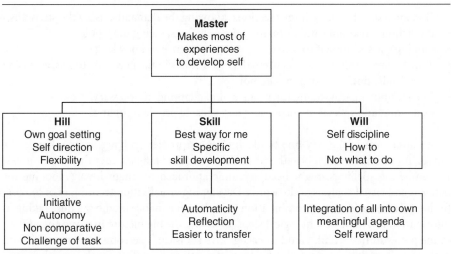

own learning. They attribute their success to themselves rather than extrinsic factors such as luck or a good teacher (Dweck & Elliot, 2007). It enables people to become flexible and develop strategic thinking skills, thereby improving performance. It has also been linked to better self-regulation (Barkley, 2011).

> Developing an awareness of my own skills and abilities has also enabled me to think more practically about strategies which I can adopt to help me learn and work more effectively. By analysing how I currently best carry out difficult tasks I have been able to identify factors which stimulate my memory recall more effectively. For example, I have difficulty recalling from memory even the simplest mathematical formulas. If I use a spreadsheet it makes solving a mathematical formula easier for me because the task becomes visual as well as a memory task. I now believe that strategies that will enhance my learning and working capability should ideally encompass some visual feature.

Metacognition enables people to match their skills to the tasks with the right strategy. It is essential because it gives more control over learning and working processes, and can improve information processing skills, thereby increasing the efficiency of the learning ability and problem solving. Dyslexic people appear not to develop metacognitive skills automatically. Because of the impact of the phonological deficit on executive functioning it is especially important for dyslexic people to become 'more metacognitive' because this can counteract the effect of some of the negative aspects of their schooling, where they may have been taught to learn or work in a way that does not suit their skills and abilities. Many dyslexic people, once they are out of the school situation, become more reliant on their own skills and use them more effectively. Good meta-cognitive skills enhance executive functioning and this is important as the 'development and elaboration of Executive Functions . . . can provide a basis for continuing adaptation, adjustment and achievement throughout the lifespan' (Eslinger, 1996: 392).

The skills involved in metacognition are:

- Task analysis – breaking it into sections, knowing the demands, using the strengths.
- Prediction – planning and estimating the outcomes, seeing the whole.
- Linking – associating it to other activities, experience or knowledge.
- Transferring – using previous strengths or successes in the new task: that is, accessing the episodic buffer in working memory.
- Self-monitoring – assessing the progress and adapting, if necessary.
- Evaluation and reflection encourages task specific problem solving.

An awareness of the way one thinks influences problem solving. Note taking techniques, for example, might be either flow charts or mind maps, rather than linear notes. Remembering spellings might need a phonic approach or might involve looking for patterns and visual analysis of the words. Developing visualisation techniques or looking for logical associations, or a combination of both, can enhance memory skills. Taking in information might be best in logical steps, or seeing the big picture first and then filling in the pieces in fine detail. Good metacognitive skills can overcome weakness or avoid problems altogether, and can also facilitate the setting of realistic goals and, therefore, contribute to success. They enable the dyslexic person to understand and develop his or her talents, as well as flexibility and creativity in the way they learn and work. Furthermore, they allow people to advocate for themselves by making positive meta-cognitive statements. Dyslexic people need to be able to describe their difficulties and ask for what they need in a positive fashion, some suggestions being:

- I read carefully – I highlight the important parts.
- I work at this speed because I take care and pride in my work.
- I am not so good at X but I really know what I'm doing here at Y because . . .
- I get my assistant to check everything. It is the best way to proofread.
- I always do a rough copy so the ideas flow more easily.
- It takes me a while to produce my work, I have so many ideas, I like to be sure I use the best one.
- I do not want to change the design – I just know it is right.

A simple example of a metacognitive exercise is the Performance Improvement Strategy (see Table 5.3) which is essentially a planning technique. It is in fact something both non-dyslexic people and dyslexic people often do automatically, but the latter need to be more deliberate about using it and applying it in all situations. When we go shopping we often plan ahead, and while we are shopping we will often make adjustments to what we put in the basket. When we look back on our shopping trip, we will review whether it was a good time to go and whether we got everything we needed.

Broadly speaking, sportsmen also use this strategy to improve their performance. Before they play a match, players of team sports such as football and rugby know what their aim is and they will predict a result. During the course of the match, especially at half time, they will review the first half and make changes accordingly. They ask themselves

Table 5.3 Performance Improvement Strategy

Think before	*Think during*	*Think back*
What is the aim	**Is this right**	**What was the result**
What is the task	Is this the best way	Was it good
What do I already know	Should I change something	What was bad
How best can I do it	How can I improve it	How long will it take

if they have chosen the right strategy or whether they should change tactics. At the end of the match they will have a post-match debrief, reviewing the whole game, building on their strengths and trying to improve their weaknesses. They will predict how their matches will go in the future. This strategy of 'positive' self-appraisal, and self-evaluation helps develop self-understanding, improves self-confidence and increases motivation.

A Metacognitive Technique

We have, for some time, used a simple metacognitive approach to problem solving and learning generally, which we call the 3M Model. It is based on the notion of dyslexia being an inefficiency in the working memory system, and three simple principles which derive logically from this. These are used to facilitate task analysis and the generation of solutions. The principles are:

Make it Manageable	– analysing the task
	– breaking it into component parts
	– identifying the part that needs the most attention
Make it Multisensory	– increase power of learning
Make use of Memory Aids	– knowledge and deliberate use of strategies

These are used to facilitate task analysis and the generation of solutions.

Making it Manageable   *– reduce the load on working memory*
– avoid dual processing wherever possible

To accommodate their memory capacity, dyslexics need to make any material being learned by recognising the demands and breaking it into a more manageable task, a simple example being that a series of numbers can be made more manageable by reducing them to smaller units: the sequence 5, 9, 8, 3, 6, 2 would become 59, 83, 62. A dyslexic is able to deal better with these three units than the original; this is why most of us reduce seven digit telephone numbers to three numbers followed by four numbers.

This principle has implications for literacy skills; reading comprehension can be made more manageable by focusing on only the important sections; writing is more manageable when planned carefully, and using a computer makes it even more manageable.

Making it Multisensory   *– increase the power of learning by using a variety of stimuli.*

Multisensory teaching/learning enhances the encoding process so that it is easier to get information into long-term memory; the pathways to the memory are the senses. The more one uses at a time, the more direct and powerful the input. Simple examples of this are learning a foreign language in its country of origin, and watching a television programme rather than listening to the radio.

Making Use of Memory Aids   *– to facilitate recall*

To facilitate recall, it is important that a dyslexic learns how to use memory aids such as mnemonics for irregular words and factual material; visual imagery can be particularly powerful.

These principles can be applied to personal, learning and work settings. It is suggested that people consider a task and ask:

'How can I make this manageable?'
'How can I make this multisensory?'
'What memory aids can I use?'

Before considering new tasks, however, it is suggested that they consider things they have done well before. That is, they should access the episodic buffer to look at good aspects of their performance and ask:

'Why is it manageable?'
'In what ways is it multisensory?'
'What memory aids am I using?'

Issues in Personal Development

There are certain very specific areas of personal development which must be addressed if we are to help dyslexic people become successful. These include:

- self advocacy;
- organisation;
- goal setting;
- memory skills;
- social skills.

Self Advocacy

Dyslexic people need to advocate for themselves in a positive and constructive way. They need to be able to explain what being dyslexic means, and offer solutions. Often they have the best understanding of what suits them. Therefore, they need to consider when to disclose, to whom and what they should say. They should be able to identify potential problems and suggest solutions: for example, 'I have trouble with time estimation but set my watch ten minutes early so I am on time'. The ability to advocate for oneself is a recurrent theme in subsequent chapters, particularly in Chapter 10.

Personal Organisation

We have seen in Chapter 1 that the organisation of time, and time management are difficult for dyslexic people. Time is abstract, which is one reason why dyslexic people have trouble with it. It is difficult to estimate and seemingly fixed periods appear variable. One minute sitting down talking to friends, for example, will not seem the same as one minute of hard running.

It is easy to underestimate how difficult personal organisation is for a dyslexic person. Even having the right clothes ready to wear at the right time makes demands on organisational skills. Remembering to put the washing on the night before an important meeting, so having the right clothes to wear, leads to one being able to make a better impression in the business world. Being organised with items such as personal possessions, including keys, mobile phones and wallets, demands attention. Having a particular place to put essential day to day items is one answer, and double checking every time one leaves a room is another. One young man regularly tapped each of his pockets in turn before leaving a room, checking he had his keys, his mobile phone, his wallet and his glasses. A student has three sets of glasses in her various places of work, as well as one in her bag, in case she loses or forgets them.

Skill Development   There are no set rules for the best way to organise time. It starts with being able to estimate how long a certain task will take. Estimation is a skill that needs to be developed. If something is not achieved, it is worth looking at the reasons why this is so. It can help at the end of the day, having only completed 50 per cent of the workload, to review where the time has been spent; often there are valid reasons – interruptions, frustrating phone calls, for example.

Another important factor is for the dyslexic person to know when they work most efficiently – is it morning, afternoon or evening? Different people work best at different times. It is important that a dyslexic person matches the most difficult tasks with the time their concentration is at its height. Tasks will seem less difficult and fewer errors will be made if the individual is not tired. It is also important to look at a task when trying to establish how long concentration can be maintained to see how interesting it is. It can help to think about the best way to work; should, for example, one spend a small amount of time on a variety of tasks or totally immerse themselves in one small job? A quiet environment with few distractions significantly speeds up the production of work for most dyslexic people. Planning time on a daily and weekly basis, reviewing success, building in contingency time, and rewarding oneself with time off lead to increased motivation and greater confidence.

Compensation   The main way in which one can compensate is by using aids, including:

- year planners;
- filofaxes;
- electronic organisers;
- IT software and hardware;
- wallcharts/whiteboards;
- timetables;
- diaries.

It is important that the individual chooses what works for them.

Accommodation   Some examples of the ways in which others can help include providing reminders, providing secretarial support, providing technological aids and having an organised partner.

Goal Setting

All activities demand some organisation and planning. Each day involves knowing what has to be achieved, setting goals and then organising one's time to achieve those goals. A successful or straightforward day would be one when all goals are achieved. Goal setting, planning and prioritising are often difficult for the dyslexic person. Sometimes they set unrealistic goals and are, therefore, disappointed when they don't succeed. Having too many goals can be another problem and lead to some not being reached, as can be a lack of time. Dyslexics can see this as another failure and it is important, therefore, that goals are manageable. Setting realistic deadlines and adding some extra time if possible is essential. Many people use the SMART strategy (Bandura, 1997). Goals should be Specific, Measurable, Achievable, Realistic and Time bound. Reflection is also an important part of the goal setting process, both those achieved and those unachieved, as this can help establish the reason for failure and aid future success.

Effective planning, goal setting, task analysis and organisation can significantly reduce the anxiety dyslexic people experience. It has been identified as one of the keys to success. These are activities that many people would like to be better at. In Table 5.4 there is a checklist which provides a basis for discussion.

Prioritisation

There are various methods for improving prioritisation skills. First of all, looking at all that needs to be done and evaluating the importance for the individual and from the perspective of others. The notion of 'urgent' versus 'important' outlined in Stephen

Table 5.4 Planning and Goal Setting Checklist

Planning	Please can you tick the appropriate number for each question 1 = very often 2 = quite often 3 = occasionally 4 = very rarely 5 = never				
I set myself specific goals	1	2	3	4	5
I organise my time	1	2	3	4	5
I ask myself questions before I begin a task	1	2	3	4	5
I analyse what I have to do	1	2	3	4	5
I have a strategy to prioritise my tasks	1	2	3	4	5
I estimate how long it will take	1	2	3	4	5
I think of several ways to do something before I start	1	2	3	4	5
I check how I am getting on	1	2	3	4	5
I change my plan if it is not going well	1	2	3	4	5
I stop and seek advice if it is not going well	1	2	3	4	5
I reflect on how well the task has been completed	1	2	3	4	5

(Leather et al., 2011).
Persistent ratings above 3 suggest the need for advice and the development of these skills.

Covey's Time Management Matrix (2004) can be very useful in improving prioritisation. It is a form of self regulation and can prevent people becoming distracted by less important tasks and spending too much time on those. Making lists and colour coding or numbering tasks so as to sequence activities according to importance is a practical strategy.

Developing skills in these areas must be individualised. People need to be able to learn how to set goals, as well as achieve levels of organisation that are appropriate to their own situation. Imposing a rigid organisational structure on people is often counter-productive.

Skill Development   The process of goal setting helps people work out what is important. It helps them learn how to use their time more effectively and can increase confidence. Goal setting can be long term, medium, or short term. Successful dyslexic people set a number of goals on a daily basis. It gives them a feeling of being in control. Goals should be measurable in as much as they have a beginning and an end. Some targets, such as keeping an appointment, might be fixed and this would be a priority. Then a plan of action around those goals can be considered. Flexibility is a key part of goal setting. Being able to monitor goal achievement and change plans if they are not working is essential. Some people like a daily list of things to do, others prefer a set of weekly goals. The list of goals could be written on a whiteboard or dictated to recording device. Concentrating on one task at a time reduces the frustration and overload that occurs when too much is attempted at once. Deciding to become 'super organised' will lead to failure. Working towards a simple aspect that can be improved will lead to success.

An effective approach to successful goal achievement is visualisation; visualising oneself in a successful situation rather than looking at the worst scenario. Positive 'self-talk' is powerful. It is unsurprising that dyslexic people tend to participate in more negative than positive 'self-talk', but it is important to encourage them to view things positively. 'Oh well, I always get it wrong', should be 'Well, that is typical and I will try again'. Negative comments include, 'It will be just the same next time'. A confident person says, 'I will do much better next time'. A person who lacks confidence will say, 'It was a fluke', a confident person will say, 'This is what I can do consistently. I will do that again in the future'. Self-talk is determined by belief; phrases like 'I want', 'I will', 'I am going to', 'I like', 'I can do this' should replace 'I ought', 'I may', 'I don't think'. Encouraging and practising making positive statements can enable the dyslexic person to believe in himself more.

Other ways of maintaining motivation and achieving goals are:

- By writing down the long-term goal and tracking the route to it – putting it on the wall and looking at it.
- By writing a list of goals achieved.
- By writing a list of positive motivation statements or having a motivational wall calendar.
- By seeing setbacks as challenges and mistakes as learning experiences.
- By positive self-talk.

Many dyslexic people report that they are frustrated by their apparent 'perfectionist streak', particularly when it comes to presenting written work. This is often the result of years of criticism of their spelling, untidy presentation or handwriting. It is important to reiterate that goals should be realistic. Feelings of competency and self-efficacy come from achieving goals and these lead to increased success (Lock & Latham, 1990).

Memory Skills

It is perhaps problems with memory on a day-to-day basis which affect dyslexic people most. Forgetting can be distressing and embarrassing. Their problems can become exaggerated in their own minds. They can think they are the only people who forget how to spell a word or people's names.

> I honestly thought I had Alzheimer's disease.

Skill Development   Skill development begins with normalising forgetting. We all do it and self-disclosure can help the dyslexic person understand this. The professional will of course then be asked, 'Are you dyslexic yourself?'

Memory improvement is just about the development of strategies. Swanson et al. (1998) sum up the above by describing several major principles that must be considered if the teaching of memory strategies is to be successful. The most important are:

1. Memory strategies serve different purposes – it is important therefore to suggest several, each addressing different tasks.

2. Good memory strategies for non-dyslexic people are not necessarily good strategies for dyslexic people and vice-versa – strategy development needs to be individualised.
3. Effective memory strategies do not necessarily eliminate processing differences – having good strategies doesn't mean having good memory.
4. The effectiveness of memory strategies can be determined by an individual's knowledge base and capacity – the best ones come from an individual's experience.
5. Strategy instruction must operate on the law of parsimony – people only need the strategies they need.

The last of these is particularly important in ensuring that dyslexic people are not taught 'packages' which involve a number of techniques and strategies. Often little is known about which component of a package best predicts performance nor can one determine why the strategy worked. Good strategies are 'composed of the sufficient and necessary process for accomplishing their intended goal, consuming as few intellectual processes as necessary to do so' (Pressley, 1991: 150).

Memory strategies involve similar elements: repetition, multisensory input, the use of logic and links. Swanson et al. (1998) list ten techniques. It is, however, essential that memory strategies are task and person specific. It has been acknowledged that the brain has greater plasticity than was originally thought, but stimulation of one area through strategy development does not generalise. Klingberg (2009) uses the analogy of the impact of physical exercise on the body, pointing out that exercising one set of muscles does not improve all the body's muscles. Likewise developing an area of the brain associated with visual memory will not improve **all memory**. Further, individuals will prefer different strategies, and choosing the right one should be a process of experimentation. In deciding which is the most appropriate task-specific strategy the dyslexic person's own inner resources should be paramount. Often it is a matter of helping them identify strategies they already use.

Compensation Electronic aids such as digital recorders, timers, mobile phones. Some dyslexic people leave messages for themselves on their own voicemail. Sometimes low-tech aids such as lists and whiteboards can be as effective.

Accommodation Asking for reminders and written memos. 'Ring me', 'Leave me a message', 'Put it in writing and I will remember to do it', 'Send me an email'.

Social Skills

Information-processing difficulties experienced by dyslexic people can interfere with social skills, particularly social communication. The problems they experience with language, as well as the processing of auditory and visual stimuli generally, can prevent them from being comfortable in social situations, dealing with arguments, and reading non-verbal cues. One young woman reported that she had been bullied at work by an aggressive colleague and found it difficult to deal with her because she was often lost for words. She certainly had a marked word-finding difficulty and confused the order of words. She said, for example, that she is inclined to say 'beat the bush about', rather than 'beat about the bush'. Other dyslexic people have reported problems in communication when they are not in a position to observe non-verbal cues. Sometimes people can present as being very intense because they work so hard at finding the cues. They can also find it hard to concentrate on tasks that require concentration when there is a lot of background noise.

> When I am in a situation for the first time, I feel so scared inside in case I make a mistake in front of people or I let myself down. I always want to cry and feel like I want to run away. All I have ever wanted was to have more chances than what I have been given, and the so 'wanted' understanding to take the panic away.

Improvements in social communication begin with an explanation as to why such problems arise. They need to be described as part of the processing problem. The 3 Ms can be applied to social communication in the following way:

Making it Manageable
Planning what you are going to say
Having a list of questions or topics to discuss when meeting people

Making it Multisensory
Looking for visual cues
Drawing to aid expression
Using hands and gestures
Rehearsing what one might say

Make use of Memory Aids
Having a small notepad on which issues they wish to clarify or notes they wish to make can be written down.

Perhaps above all dyslexic people need to use humour in social situations. We live in a world where quick responses and good repartee are valued. Those who are not good at these reactions can be made to feel inadequate. At the same time, we all make mistakes, forget names, use the wrong word and make social gaffes. 'Normalising' such experiences can help dyslexic people become more at ease in social situations.

Improvement in social communication begins with self-understanding. In particular, dyslexic people need to know that communication problems can be a result of poor processing skills. Years of misunderstanding can make dyslexic people defensive in certain situations and oversensitive to criticism. This can lead to a more exaggerated reaction, which sets up miscommunication between people. Knowing that they might over-react to certain situations enables dyslexic people to avoid these or be better prepared for them.

Finally some dyslexic people can be very literal in their interpretation of what is said and misunderstanding can arise quickly. This is obviously important at work or with the general public, but also has implications for personal relationships. While many dyslexic people rely heavily on their partners for support and help with some of the things they find difficult, it can cause a problem if the partner is dyslexic. The young man who forgot to put the 'you' on his Valentine's card, leaving the message 'I love', for example, discovered his girlfriend found it a little hard to accept. When a wife decided that, by helping her husband write letters, she was making him lazy and stopping him from learning for himself, this caused him a great deal of anguish and led to tension in the relationship. This was quickly resolved when she understood that she was in fact helping him learn it for himself. The information processing difference can also be a reason for misunderstanding or misinterpreting what is actually being said. Dyslexic people quite often only hear half of what is said or only hear the negative part, and this can lead to a breakdown in communication.

Another area for developing awareness is recognising that certain behaviour can be attributed to having to rely on cues other than the verbal ones: the invading of personal space, for example, because the dyslexic person needs to concentrate fully on what is being said. Staring hard at a person speaking can be disconcerting if the reason for it is not understood. It is often one person who contributes to a dyslexic person's success or downfall. Careless or deliberate remarks can undermine a dyslexic person's confidence very rapidly. Equally, too much support from a partner or friend can lead to stifling an individual's creativity and promote over-dependence. Furthermore, some people, in an effort to help, can be patronising which is also undermining.

Sometimes the diagnosis of dyslexia, subsequent re-framing and personal development can change the nature of relationships between mothers, fathers and their children, as well as between partners. Forgetting birthdays and anniversaries can create conflict. There must be a degree of acceptance that this can happen; alternatively a partner can give very obvious reminders that a big event is about to happen. Forgetting a personal date or event does not detract from a dyslexic person's feeling for another person. Being dyslexic is the reason for the poor memory skills, although not an excuse. As we have suggested in Chapter 4 it can be helpful to involve those close to a dyslexic person in training and counselling.

A Dyslexic Person's Perspective

We reiterate that we can all learn from dyslexic people. What follows are the responses of one of our clients to several questions we asked her.

What it is like to be dyslexic?
- Frustration.
- Feeling stupid or slow.
- Not retaining information (poor memory for some things).

- Takes longer to write things or even get started.
- Inefficient brain.
- Exhausted easily.
- Trouble spelling and constructing written sentences.
- Takes longer to read, understand certain information.
- Trouble completing note taking.
- Have trouble when pronouncing certain words.
- Different tasks produce their own set of problems to overcome.
- Your brain feels like a sponge that has a constant leak.

How has it affected you?
- Lack of confidence to do certain things
- Shy away from political or educational conversation. So not to sound inadequate/incompetent. I tend to stay quiet and listen (hoping I can learn and take in others views, rather than join in).
- Stick to safe jobs and near to understanding people, as their help is invaluable.
- Seeking answers all the time – sometimes never finding the answers.
- Can get quite stressed and anxiety levels increase, when unsure of things.

Any positives of your dyslexia?
- Conscientious in all that I do.
- Organised.
- Seeing things differently.
- Problem solving. Sometimes this happens without realising I'm doing it. As I sometimes have to do things differently I have found that I have solved issues for not just myself but others too.
- More determined – never give up.

What advice would you give to other dyslexics?
- Never give up.

Do you study, work, follow hobbies/interests?
- My interests are more physical, it gives my mind a rest and I find great satisfaction in achievements.
- I like historic cultures, learning and where possible arrange holidays (back packing) to visit what I have read about. This backs up my memory from the sights, smells and sounds for these cultures.
- From getting into the outdoors, new places or visiting events/exhibitions. Despite not retaining the information I still enjoy the experience and always take pride in getting out and taking a chance.
- Taking photos – helps my memory and nice to create scrapbooks.
- I work as a researcher – I enjoy finding the facts and information. Piecing this together to get a whole picture. I look at it as creating a puzzle. I take

this researching strategy into my personal life for example before I go and buy something I will look into the pros/cons etc. Unbeknown to me this is a coping strategy I have developed to calm my nerves and thinking ahead.

What, if anything has helped your dyslexia?
- Having my assessment.
- Having some dyslexia coaching – we met in total for eight one-hourly sessions.
- Meeting other people with dyslexia and trying a few different support groups.
- Not giving up.
- Being open minded to trying new things, involving techniques around being dyslexic.
- Coming to terms with my dyslexia and not giving myself such a hard time at times.

Other Comments

Frustration – pure frustration.

I feel I have a lot of things going on in my head but have difficulty expressing this into words that make sense.

Making my ideas, thoughts and opinions clear and precise without the waffle and limit language. I hear others talk or write and I think that's what I wanted to say or was trying to say. It is like they are mind readers. I wish I had that brain power.

It is the same for written work. I have great admiration for someone who can just turn a blank page into a work of art. I always have to ask, or use designed templates to get me started. Worse still read someone else's work and take notes using some of their style, to produce my writing. This makes me feel like a failure or fraud.

My free text writing often ends up jumbled. I go off on tangents (I do this in speech too). I write and rewrite, never really happy with what I have written, (I always feel there could be more or something better just waiting to escape) until the point where I am exhausted. When I do feel happy with my work after going through this lengthy process I then always ask someone to proofread my work. They tend to always come up with a more superior quality of work. This upsets me but I would never let on – that I feel my best is never good enough and will probably always be that way.

I hear people all the time say that I am a bright girl, lots of confidence, great outlook on life, always busy and you're gonna do so well.

Well inside I'm screaming for a new brain, one that works better as everything is so hard, I'm exhausted and so frustrated.

My head feels like it is filled with a fog and despite sounding the fog horn on one side the other side cannot hear it.

Meeting my dyslexia coach has made a big difference. It feels like she has climbed into the fog and made sense of what causes it. Even better she has provided some answers for my brain to understand so that it can hear the horn through the fog. The fog hasn't completely cleared but it's more of a mist now.

A note from her coach – while this client developed many of her skills for her workplace, it was her confidence that greatly improved. She began to take pride in the way she worked, she always worked carefully to avoid mistakes and her managers accepted that it took her a little longer as the accuracy and depth of her information was very good. She always had to reprocess or make a checklist of the record forms that she had to complete, but she fully understood it then and could train new staff members better than her colleagues. She was recently given an award for developing a new system that helped her whole team.

A Case History – C

How the 3Ms as well skills, compensations and accommodations can be applied is illustrated by the following case study in which a single parent's (C) organisational and memory problems, as well as residual difficulties with written language, were addressed.

Reason for Referral   C sought advice at the suggestion of her friend. She had experienced some difficulties with reading and spelling during her school years, but this had not prevented her from going to college and gaining a degree. A screening assessment during her time at college had suggested that she was dyslexic but it was taken no further. C had an administrative job which did not present her with any particular difficulties, but she was struggling with managing her family life. She said she had difficulty with the following tasks:

- a very messy house;
- never being able to find things;
- trouble getting her children to school on time;
- being late for appointments;
- forgetting to attend school meetings;
- avoiding writing letters as her spelling was so bad;
- reading instructions;
- paying household bills on time;
- helping her children with homework.

Strengths and Weaknesses: C's performance on the Wechsler Adult Intelligence Scale showed there to be considerable variation amongst her abilities. She achieved very high scores for verbal reasoning, vocabulary and comprehension. It is verbal ability which is the best predictor of attainment in reading and writing, and she is someone who could be expected to have very well developed skills in these areas. She also achieved excellent scores on most of the non-verbal tests. C scored less well on mental arithmetic, auditory memory, copying symbols, and she had difficulty with items which involved the labelling process, such as identifying geographical directions on a test of general knowledge. These lower scores rendered the profile of her sub-test scores typical of that of a dyslexic person, reflecting the inefficiency in working memory which characterises the condition. Separate memory testing did, however, show that her memory for meaningful pictorial material was very good.

Self-Understanding Although C has always thought she might be dyslexic she did not know what it meant, seeing it only as a reading and spelling problem. The model of memory described earlier was explained to her, as were the 3Ms.

	Solution			
Problem	*Manageable*	*Multi-sensory*	*Memory aids*	*Outcome*
Organisation				
Documents	Special/important documents box	Colour coded	Keep box in same location	Can find thing more easily
Meals	Weekly timetable plan	Pictures	Pin to wall	
Messy house	Set goals/re-plan one room at a time	Make colour coded plan	Kitchen cork board	
	Keep only one room tidy			
Remembering appointments	Routine daily and weekly check. Plan ahead	Wall design chart	Post-its	Arrive on time
		Colour coded pictures	Electronic aids	

This chart was developed by C as a structured plan to help her find solutions to her organisational problems – she became more organised and less stressed. C still uses it as a tool to help her.

Outcome C was able to return to work with a better understanding of her difficulties, as well as ideas on how to resolve these. She was also encouraged to practise making positive rather than negative statements about her way of working. These included:

'I read slowly' became 'I read thoroughly so need more time'.
'I have a problem with proof reading' became 'Could you check over this?'
'How do you spell "beginning"?' became 'Are there two n's in "beginning"?'
'I forget to do things' became 'Please put it in writing'.

A combination of the 3Ms technique and Personal Improvement Strategy leads people to match their skills to the task with the right strategy, which leads to increased success.

Summary

1. Supporting dyslexic people should begin with improving their self-understanding.
2. Enabling dyslexic people to become successful begins with their personal development, including their organisational, memory, goal setting and social skills.
3. Personal development is not enhanced by teaching skills alone but by ensuring that the dyslexic person has better metacognitive strategies.
4. The role of the professional is that of a partner in helping the dyslexic person understand themselves better.

6

Literacy for Living

Synopsis. *This chapter addresses the issues involved in helping dyslexic people develop the literacy skills they need on a daily basis. The principles underlying teaching the skills should be taught, as well as appropriate compensations and adjustments are described.*

Introduction

Daily living requires a standard of literacy and numeracy beyond the very basic. Raising a family, even being unemployed, leads to having to deal with quite complex literacy and numeracy tasks. Although some dyslexic people leave school completely illiterate and innumerate, many will have developed an ability to get by. Either they are able to read and write simple words and sentences and deal with basic numeracy tasks, such as counting, or else they have a partner or friend who will do it for them. If, at some point, they are unable to deal with these tasks, or the tasks become more complex, they seek help. In modern society, more and more people are being exposed to change and increasingly living and learning is based on basic literacy skills. Technology, for example, has been a boon to dyslexic people in helping them with their writing and spelling difficulties, but to use it requires new learning and places increased demands on reading. 'New literacy', for example, means that people need to develop the skills, strategies and self regulation required to read, write and learn using Internet technologies that prepare them to communicate in a rapidly changing world (Leu, 2002, cited in Hock, 2012).

Literacy has been defined as:

> Using printed and written information to function in society, to achieve one's goals and to develop one's knowledge and potential. (Carey, Low and Hansbro, 1997: 13)

The Dyslexic Adult: Interventions and Outcomes – An Evidence-based Approach, Second Edition.
David McLoughlin and Carol Leather.
© 2013 John Wiley & Sons, Ltd. Published 2013 by John Wiley & Sons, Ltd.

In their survey of adult literacy in Britain, Carey et al. (1997) measured three dimensions of literacy identified in an earlier international survey. Literacy was seen as a broad range of skills required in a variety of contexts. The three dimensions are:

Prose Literacy

The knowledge and skills required to understand and use information from texts such as prose, newspaper articles and passages of fiction.

Document Literacy

The knowledge and skills required to locate and use information contained in various formats such as timetables, graphs, charts and forms.

Quantitative Literacy

The knowledge and skills required to apply arithmetic operations, either alone or sequentially, to numbers embedded in printed materials, such as calculating savings from a sale advertisement, working out the interest required to achieve a desired return on an investment or totalling a bank deposit slip.

One might now add a fourth dimension, technological literacy. For some information technology has provided solutions. For others it has created new barriers.

Lifelong Learning

There are now greater opportunities for adults to participate in education and training, particularly now lifelong learning is being emphasised. The idea of going back into education fills many dyslexic people with trepidation to say the least. But if they have the confidence and can set their own goals regarding achievement, it is the chance to bring their interests and experience to the learning environment, and many have found it an enjoyable experience.

We live in an age of conspicuous achievement, there being an increasing societal expectation that individuals should have qualifications. People need 'qualifications' to get jobs, and those who have been working effectively in a particular job can suddenly find they need to deal with more paperwork or undertake courses. They might also need to take tests and examinations so that they can continue to do the same job or gain promotion. The competent playgroup leader with ten years' experience suddenly finds her job under threat because there is an increased demand on training, record keeping and form filling. The very capable and popular teacher of swimming is not allowed to continue with a formal course of training because she cannot cope with the written demands, including taking tests. There are many examples of similar occurrences in the workplace today. Furthermore, there has been a significant change in office work with the increase in the use of technology, everybody becoming more generalist and having to do their own typing rather than being able to delegate. This has meant that dyslexic people have been less able to avoid written language tasks and become more exposed.

Many dyslexic people have developed their own way of coping with the demands on them, but it is clearly not just in educational and work settings that they can be at a disadvantage. Daily living has become more complicated in terms of the demands on all aspects of literacy, and much more so since the increase in the use of technology. It is easy to underestimate the importance of literacy and numeracy demands in everyday activities, but it is problems in this area which can do the most damage to feelings of competence and confidence. It is humiliating to only be able to order steak or a hamburger in a restaurant because you can't read the menu. It is equally humiliating to order steak in a seafood restaurant or indeed order duck, mangoes and trout instead of duck and mange-tout. Missing the bus because it took so long to recognise the sign on the front is frustrating and time consuming, as is not being able to read timetables. Missing an appointment because you misread am or pm can be devastating. Seeing a child upset because they are taken to school in fancy dress on the wrong day is something a mother is never likely to forget, nor indeed the child. All of these undermine the individual's self-esteem and self-confidence. Some of the demands on literacy and numeracy during the adult years are listed in Table 6.1.

Examples of the specific skills involved in dealing with personal and family tasks are shown below:

Task	Skills required
Management of finances	Basic literacy and numeracy skills plus filing and record keeping. Copying numbers and letters from one place to another. Writing cheques and filling deposit slips. Remembering PIN numbers. Online banking.
Driving	Makes demands on automaticity, visual processing of road signs. Memory (which way to go), following instructions, anticipation, good spatial ability.
Shopping	Prediction, memory, list making, financial planning. Online shopping.
Cooking	Reading, following instructions, gathering information on ingredients, planning, timing and estimating.
Arranging appointments and social activities	Talking on the telephone, processing information quickly, taking down names and times. Listening skills and memory.
Children's education	Basic literacy skills. Ability to express ideas clearly and effectively. Confidence in the education setting (schools are likely to be frightening places for dyslexic adults). Mixtures of fear, anger, aggression, incompetence. Form filling. Memory, time management and planning.

Similar analysis for each area will assist in planning a programme which is relevant and enables people to experience immediate improvement.

Many of the above skills rely on the effective use of information technology. There is, therefore, an increasing need for the development of technological literacy.

Table 6.1 Literacy and Numeracy Tasks in Adulthood

Task

Personal and family	Leisure pursuits	Participating in community life	Legal matters
Management of finances	Travel	Voting	Reporting a crime
Car and home repairs	Reading newspapers	Public transport	Writing statements
Driving	Sports	Telephone	
Shopping and cooking	Entertainment	Following and giving directions	
Arranging appointments and social activities	Hobbies	Emergency services	
Arranging childcare	Dining out		
Children's education	Health		
Social security	Medication		
	Appointments		
	Visits to the doctor		
	Health education		

Planning a Programme

In planning a programme it is important to be guided by the principles which underlie the teaching of adults described in Chapter 2. It should begin with helping people to recognise the skills they need to develop, as well as the compensations and accommodations that are available. To achieve this, they need to know what their skills are, especially those that will transfer from one situation to another. A 'skills audit' can be undertaken to assist in setting goals, priorities and needs. It is important for a dyslexic person who has very weak literacy skills and limited time available to be realistic about what they can achieve, and to reiterate that people only need to develop the skills they require for living and working. Helping set realistic goals is, therefore, essential.

In Chapter 2 we referred to the importance of an andragogical approach (Knowles, 1990). Motivation is a starting point; this can be internal, just for self-esteem or job satisfaction. It can also be prompted by external factors including domestic, work or training demands. It is, however, essential that the student comes to see that achievement is important for them. They need to be able to evaluate their own performance, perceiving mistakes as a learning opportunity and progress as evidence of the fact that they can learn. Only if goals are achieved, is confidence enhanced and persistence fostered. The motivation of a student can be undermined very quickly, and it is therefore essential that the programme is planned in conjunction with the student.

Tutors must take into account the student's self concept, particularly their perception of themselves as a learner. It helps if they have been provided with an explanation for their difficulties, and been advised of ways in which they can build on their abilities and experience. They also need to feel in control of the learning situation as they will have a low opinion of their ability to learn, having been called 'lazy' or 'a daydreamer', or just knowing they found learning so much harder than their peers. They need to be reassured that they can be successful, and this involves careful planning of achievable short-term goals so that confidence is increased.

Utilising their own experience can give dyslexic people more confidence. They often learn best when they can relate their learning to their own context: the footballer whose reading programme was based entirely around football, for example, or the assistant buyer who worked her way up from window dressing, avoiding tests, examinations and written work until she had had ten years of experience. Programmes based on real life situations are likely to be the most effective. Examples of forms, reading material or numerical tasks with which they have difficulty can be the best teaching materials.

Life and work experience are sources of knowledge, as can be an understanding of the strategies people have used to get by; the phone number on the back of the hand, the diagrams in their diary, their use of colour as well as a variety of memory joggers. Although they use such strategies on a daily basis and are often good at learning in practical situations, when they find themselves in an educational setting, dyslexic people tend to revert to old behaviours left over from school days. It is important, therefore, to help change their perception of what learning is about, and encourage them to evaluate their own learning style.

Implicit in the fact that someone has sought teaching is a readiness to learn. They will not, however, know what to expect, and being ready and being prepared are two different things. It is for this reason that the goals set should be relevant and realistic. Success should be cumulative, each session adding to self-understanding and feelings of competence. Ideally the programme should be complete, and not leave the student feeling as though they have reached the edge of a springboard, but do 'not have the energy or support to jump off alone'. An individual's knowledge and experience of teaching should be taken into consideration. IT solutions can be the best option for someone who is very technologically aware but has weak literacy skills. There are an increasing number of readily available downloadable applications available on smart-phones that can provide solutions.

The learning environment is very important. It needs to be friendly, relaxed and unthreatening; professional, but on an informal partnership basis, tutor and student working out an appropriate programme together. It can be helpful to draw up a learning contract such as that shown in Table 6.2. It is metacognitive in its approach and encourages the client to take responsibility for learning, and they can see its relevance.

Information Processing and Literacy

The way a dyslexic person thinks will affect their learning and working. The first part of any programme should therefore be a discussion of how the individual learns and works best, and determine which kind of sensory input is the most effective for them. Do they, for example, use the visual, auditory or kinaesthetic mode predominantly? Is it a combination of all three? In our experience many dyslexic people and learn through visual

Table 6.2   Learning Contract

Personal Development Plan

Name:.. Date................................

<u>GOALS</u> – what do I want to achieve

> Long Term:

> Medium Term:

> Short Term:

1. What skills do I have?

2. What experience do I have? Do I have any transferable skills?

3. What are my interests?

4. What do I need or want to learn?

5. What do I already know?

6. What is the most important priority?

7. Which is the most interesting to me?

8. What are the potential problems?

9. How best can I do it?

Skills – i.e. did I used to do spider grams? – they might help me plan Technology/Compensations. . . . What's on YouTube

10. What resources do I need/have?

Time –

Money –   Motivation –

Help (who) –   Encouragement –

<u>THE ACTION PLAN</u>

	What to do first–Goal	Resources	Achieved
	Next goals	Resources	Achieved

When will it be reviewed?

End result?

or kinaesthetic routes, the auditory channel being the least utilised. This is consistent with the theory outlined in Chapter 1 and has important implications for the way in which they need to process information. Some people, for example, report that in order to understand they have to 'make a film' of the material in their head.

For learners who like to learn visually, the way to remember, take notes, and fill in diaries or wall planners is through symbols and pictures. Knowing this also enables people to ask for information to be provided for them in the appropriate format; asking for landmarks rather than directions, for example. Understanding how they learn and becoming more confident about their own way of doing things will facilitate the development of skills, as well as the use of the compensations listed above. It should also enable them to seek the correct accommodations. We reiterate that the development of metacognitive skills is a key to progress.

Improving Levels of Literacy

It will of course be important to establish current levels of literacy and this can be achieved by administering some of the tests described in Chapter 3, as well as through informal means such as asking them to read from the newspaper dyslexic people often carry. Tasks they need to deal with on a daily basis such as reading a letter or email can be useful.

At the functional level reading, writing and spelling should be taught simultaneously as some people learn to read through spelling. It is essential that the programme is structured, cumulative and multisensory, and that the materials used are relevant to and preferably brought in by the student. It should at first be based on their experience, as this gives them concrete knowledge on which to build the abstract concepts of written symbols.

The skills people can be taught, the compensations they can use and the adjustments which can be made at the various levels of literacy, specifically reading and writing, are listed in the Tables 6.3 to 6.6.

Improving Reading Accuracy

Skill Development   Teaching adults to read from the beginning should start with an explanation of the nature of the reading process. That is, the student should be told that it is complex, but that reading can be made manageable when words are broken down into their component sounds.

It is important that tutors be guided by one of the structured phonetically based programmes designed for dyslexic people. In the main, however, these have been designed for children and will need to be made relevant, incorporating the students' interests, as well as their existing reading skills. Interest-driven reading has been shown to be a key in the development of high literacy skills (Fink, 1998, 2003). The best way of demonstrating how words can be broken into sounds is by focusing on words they can already recognise.

Table 6.3   Literacy at the Functional Level

People at the functional level of reading can only deal with activities and jobs that place minimal demands on literacy.

Reading		
Skill Development	*Compensation*	*Accommodations*
Decoding	Instructions on tape	Someone to read for them
Understanding of sounds and symbol correspondence	Reading pen	Structured reading
Word attack skills	Instructions presented visually	Simplified and annotated diagrams
Sequencing of sounds/blends of letters	Text to speech software	
Using prediction		
Understanding inference		
Building a sight vocabulary		

Writing		
Skill Development	*Compensations*	*Accommodations*
Handwriting skills	Using a proforma	Secretarial support
Sentence building	Speech to text software	College scribe
Grammar	Dictation onto a recorder	
Punctuation	Using symbols or drawings	
Paragraphs		
Planning – who, what, when, where, why		
IT skills – typing etc.		

People whose literacy skills are at the functional level will probably require the longest period of specialist training.

As well as building up word recognition skills, there needs to be an emphasis on language generally: dictionary work, focusing on the derivation and meaning of words, facilitating the process of being able to use contextual clues to facilitate decoding through the application of logic. Contextual guessing strategies are sometimes more reliable than phonological decoding strategies for many dyslexics (Fink, 1998, 2003).

There is a need to include whole word recognition as we do not proceed very far with English before encountering pronunciation that defies the phonetic structure of the word. For most adults, being able to read aloud well is not an important skill. However, to secure feedback on the correct pronunciation of words, it is important that dyslexic people be encouraged to read aloud. This can, because of their experience at school, be painful. Allowing preparation time – that is, letting them look over material first – can facilitate the process. They can also be encouraged to listen to recorded material whilst

Table 6.4   Literacy at Vocational Level

Reading		
Skill Development	*Compensations*	*Accommodations*
Technical sight words	Text to speech & speech to text	Highlight important bits
Overviewing the text	software	Given an overview
Using contextual clues	Reading pen	
Fact/opinion/influence	Text put on a recorder	
Asking questions & predicting answers		
Cloze procedure		
Syllabification/suffixes		
Scanning		
Skimming		
Noting from text		

Writing		
Skill Development	*Compensations*	*Accommodations*
Handwriting skills	Speech to text software	Administrative support
Grammar	Dictation onto a recorder	
Punctuation	Specimen letter on computers	
Sentence building	Providing proformas or copies	
Paragraphs		
Phrases		
Planning & drafting skills		
Using different formats		
Proof reading		
Building a word bank		
IT skills – typing etc.		

following the text, as this allows for the provision of feedback without them having to read aloud.

Compensations   Learning to read can be a lengthy process and for some dyslexic people it will always be hard work. 'People tell me I should read for pleasure, but it isn't', is an often quoted remark. Because they are intelligent and articulate there is often a residual discrepancy between what they would like or need to be able to read and their reading skills. Immediate solutions can come from:

- Listening to recordings of books and podcasts.
- Using DVDS.
- Relying on the radio/TV for the news rather than a newspaper.
- Relying on pictorial rather than written information.

Table 6.5   Literacy at Technical Level

	Reading	
Skill Development	*Compensations*	*Accommodations*
Scanning & skimming	Text to speech and	Text on tape
Identifying the main idea	speech to text software	Given overview or highlight points
Abstracting ideas	Using highlighters	Given previews or summaries
Identifying the organisation	Talking Thesaurus	
of the text	Reading pen	
Using dictionaries and		
Thesaurus		
Understanding inference/		
opinion/bias		

	Writing	
Skill Development	*Compensations*	*Accommodations*
Grammar active/passive	Dictation	Amanuensis
Sentence structure	Speech to text software	
Punctuation	Use writing frames	
Proof reading COPS	Software such as	
Planning strategies	Inspirations	
Mind mapping		
Editing		
Analysis of different styles		

- Scanning material into a computer and using text to speech software.
- Using Directory Enquiries rather than a telephone book.

In suggesting the use of the above, it is always important to let people know that these are legitimate ways of receiving information which non-dyslexic people rely on. It is not unusual for dyslexics to perceive them as 'cheating'.

Table 6.6   Literacy at Professional Level

	Reading	
Skill Development	*Compensations*	*Accommodations*
Review the skills of Technical level	Text to speech software	Highlighted sections
Efficient strategies	On a recorder	Overview – abstract
Scanning & skimming	Mind mapping software	
Monitor comprehension		
Critical reading		
Analytical strategies		
Note making strategies		

Accommodations   Persisting difficulties with reading can be accommodated in domestic, learning and work settings. This can include:

- Relying on a spouse/partner to read material.
- Providing pictorial material such as graphics, drawings and cartoons.
- Having someone record important material.
- Providing a 'reader' in test/examination settings.

Improving Reading Comprehension

Skill Development   Reading comprehension is one of the most important skills. Comprehension generally (Faas & d'Alonzo, 1990) and reading comprehension in particular (Spadafore, 1983) have been described as the best predictors of successful transition from school to employment and should be given particular attention in learning or study skills programmes.

Enhancing reading comprehension begins with helping people to understand the purpose of their reading and therefore to develop the skills they need. Dyslexic people often seem to apply the same technique to every task, usually focusing on recognising all the words accurately. This can be a slow, tedious and ineffective approach. They are often not aware of the different reading skills they possess, and this can be compounded when they have developed a fear of missing something from past experience.

A good reader appears to be automatically aware of the purpose of reading and varies their reading rate and approach to comprehension depending on the material being read. Dyslexic people do not do this automatically, devoting too much attention to decoding, and need to be taught deliberately to use different approaches. They need to enhance their metacognitive skills for reading.

It is assumed here that the development of comprehension skills will be accompanied by language work, specifically on the meaning of words. Good reading comprehension begins with the question 'Why am I reading this?', followed by 'What is the function of the text?' or more specifically, 'What do I need to know? Is it providing information, an explanation, a description or a request?' This enables one to choose the correct technique. One might, for example, scan a guide to what is on television, but skim the football column in a newspaper. Dyslexic people do this except when faced with material they perceive as being important and complex. The PASS Strategy (Ellis, 1993) for reading comprehension is described below.

The Pass Reading Strategy

Preview, Review and Predict

Preview by reading the heading and/or one or two sentences
Review what you already know about this topic
Predict what you think the test will be about.

Ask and Answer Questions

Content-focused questions	Monitoring questions	Problem-solving questions
Who? What? When? *Where? Why? How?* *How does this relate to what I already know?*	*Is my prediction correct?* *How is this different from what I thought it was going to be about?* *Does this make sense?*	*Is it important that it makes sense?* *Do I need to reread part of it?* *Can I visualise the information?* *Can I visualise the information?* *Do I need to read it more slowly?* *Does it have too many unknown words?* *Do I need to pay more attention? Should I get help?*

Summarise

Say what the short passage was about.

Synthesise

Say how the short passage fits in with the whole passage.
Say how what you learned fits with what you know.
Applying the PASS strategy is deliberate, and monitoring and refinement are built in.

Where there is resistance, it can be helpful to point out that they are often applying the fundamental principle of a step by step approach when reading a newspaper or magazine. If that is something they are able to do confidently, the sense of adopting such a systematic approach becomes clear.

Compensations   Compensations for dealing with reading comprehension can include:

- Audio books or the use of text to speech software, the emphasis becoming on listening rather than reading comprehension. Taking away the process of recognising words reduces the load on working memory significantly, and they are better able to focus on content.
- DVDs and CD ROMs can be even more powerful than audio books.
- Using summaries of texts rather than the actual book enables people to just deal with the important content. It can provide the whole picture without becoming bogged down in detail. The obvious example is the study guides provided for classical texts.

Accommodations   Accommodations can include having someone highlight the important parts of a text, providing the reader with a summary and having someone else read the material for them.

Improving Spelling

Poor spelling is one of the obvious signs of dyslexia. It is often the area of weakness which has caused a dyslexic person most embarrassment. It continues to be difficult, rarely becoming an automatic skill. Even dyslexic people who can do well on single word spelling tests find they make errors when writing continuous prose and it is often therefore the area in which they seek to improve. Helping them to establish priorities is therefore very important. It is likely to be very time consuming, will involve a great deal of determination and persistence, and it still might remain an area of weakness. Spelling can be dealt with in a number of ways, and these need to be explained.

Skill Development   The basic approach to teaching spelling is systematic, structured and phonetically based. The multisensory techniques applied to reading are essential, with a particular emphasis on visual approaches which will allow them to analyse words. Understanding about word families, as well as the meaning and derivation of words, can also support basic teaching. There is a need for over-learning and repetition. This approach can be too long for the time available and it can be extremely boring as it focuses on developing the auditory skills that can be an area of significant weakness in dyslexic people. A multifaceted programme is often better and includes the development of strategies for common words using the Look –Say – Cover – Write – Check system, or mnemonics and visual imagery, as well as specific spelling dictionaries for the individual and the words needed for daily living. The other skill that needs to be developed is how to use a Spellchecker effectively. This involves the visual analysis of words, being able to hear the number of syllables in a word, and understanding the importance of vowels and what a suffix is. If the reading skills are good, then correct spellings can be found through using the Thesaurus function.

A spelling programme should include:

- an understanding of the process of spelling – and how the individual approaches it
- an understanding of sound/symbol correspondence and sequencing
- introduction to syllables and suffixing
- some basic spelling rules
- a variety of spelling strategies, e.g. visual analysis, mnemonics, syllabification
- common words vocabulary
- technical spelling needed for work – building up a word bank
- proofreading techniques
- over-learning, patience determination and time.

Compensations   Compensations can include the following:

- Keeping a list of key words to hand.
- Creating a personal dictionary.

- Using memory devices, such as mnemonics and visual imagery, to facilitate recall. It is, however, important that these provide a rationale, rather than just give the dyslexic person something else to remember.
- Using technology, such as portable spellcheckers or the spellcheck package of a word processor.
- Using voice activated software on a word processor or smartphone.
- Using web searches.

Accommodations   These include:

- The provision of technological aids.
- Having someone proofread work for the dyslexic.
- Secretarial support, especially someone who can take dictation and audio-type.

Whether someone can take advantage of the compensations and accommodations described above will depend on their competence in spelling. Conventional word processors and electronic spellcheck devices will only be of use if someone has basic spelling skills. Bizarre attempts will not be identified correctly. Voice activated word processing should be more effective, but even then this, as well as conventional word processors, cannot deal easily with words such as homophones.

Dyslexic people need to feel comfortable about the use of the compensations and accommodations described above. Again, the notion of 'cheating' comes up and needs to be addressed. Often, it can be pointed out that they need to devote more time to other skills rather than engage in a time consuming and perhaps frustrating spelling improvement programme.

Improving Writing

Writing has been described as a juggling act. That is, when writing, one has to remember many things at the same time, including letter formation, grammar, punctuation, spelling, vocabulary and ideas. Putting ideas on paper is perhaps the activity that places the greatest demand on the working memory system. It is a very complex skill.

Skill Development   In our experience most, if not all, adult dyslexics have sufficient competence in letter formation as to be able to write, or at least copy, their own name and address and write simple phrases. Their ability to express more complex ideas is often limited by their spelling skills, as well as a lack of confidence in their ability to put ideas on paper. Very often, this will have to do with unrealistic expectations of what writing involves. At a basic level, writing is essentially communication. It is the expression in symbols of what they can say. It is important that dyslexic people know that writing is just that. Communication is enhanced by clear and simple writing and this should be the first goal.

I have adopted simple good practices when it comes to writing e.g. make sentences no longer than a line. Writing things down exactly as I would say them has also been very useful. I have started to read a lot, in order to familiarise myself with English vocabulary and developed simple techniques to remember how to spell/pronounce words. Word processors with their in-built- spell-checkers are a great help.

The juggling act becomes less threatening when people are able to focus on matching their own inner thoughts with what appears on the paper. Descriptive rather than interpretative writing separates out thinking from putting ideas on paper. Teaching writing should begin with simple dictated sentences, the most effective being those which relate to their own experience. Keeping the work simple also enables them to deal with the beginnings of punctuation. The more this can be related to speech, the better. When conveyed as pauses in conversation, full stops and commas make sense.

Adults are able to match their own verbal communication with their writing by copying or typing ideas they have dictated to someone else. This is a particularly good confidence building activity. The next stage is for them to construct their own sentences and produce longer pieces in the form of simple letters or a diary.

A step by step approach to writing is always important and should begin with planning. Even a simple letter will involve several points which need to be covered, and listing these first means that they do not have to be held in memory whilst other material is being written.

When I went to the centre, we concentrated on sequencing on putting things in order, this helped because people have always commented on how my ideas were out of synch. I've learnt by using my positive skills to overcome some of the problems that I've had. At the centre we concentrated on breaking things down into smaller manageable tasks and then sequencing things under headings. Using a word processor or computer helped as well because I could restructure things and change things at the touch of a button, also by using a computer my handwriting wasn't a problem any more. When I know a system or rules to work by it helps, for instance grammar rules because then I can see how I can construct things in a certain way or order.

Compensation   Compensation when there are writing difficulties mainly involves the use of technology. Using a word processor reduces the load on working memory signif-icantly. That is, there are few concerns about legibility, neatness, letter formation and spelling. Voice activated word processing should allow a direct match between verbal ability and writing skills.

A tape recorder and word processor are both useful for clarifying ideas by listening to oneself talking or seeing ideas printed out on the page. Computers are also invaluable spell checkers. They can help speed up output considerably. Unfortunately it takes time to learn packages and you pray that your computer doesn't break down.

Dyslexic people with poor writing skills can also learn to dictate using a voice-recorder. Even when using technology, however, planning will always be important.

Accommodations   The accommodations include relying on a spouse/partner or employee to deal with writing tasks. A secretary with audio-typing skills would allow someone to deal with writing by dictation.

Giving dictation is the preferred way of many professional people who are not dyslexic and in fact have highly developed literacy skills. It is, however, a quick and efficient way of dealing with correspondence.

Improving Quantative Literacy

Dealing with numeracy or quantative tasks is a feature of everyday life; at work, in education and at home.

> Most individuals are able to generalise the maths they learned in school to the wide variety of real-life situations that require math competence. However, for a significant number of people with learning related problems, this transfer to everyday living remains elusive. (Patton et al., 1997, p. 179)

The problems experienced in numeracy by dyslexic people are threefold. First of all there are those who have a very poor background in the subject and will need to go over basic concepts. Secondly there are people who understand the concepts but, as a result of their poor memory skills, have trouble dealing with symbols, remembering sequences in operations as well as formulae, and dealing with calculations. A third problem which can compound the foregoing is lack of confidence in their ability to deal with maths. We do have to deal with arithmetic in everyday situations and this causes many dyslexic people a great deal of anxiety. Some examples of the comments they make are:

> 'Say the word maths and I get cold sweats, hot sweats and twitching'.
>   'Shopping used to be agony because of writing cheques. Going into a bank would make me feel sick. I thanked God when shops started printing cheques'.
>   'I hate people asking me to work something out in my head. I get flustered and I can't do it. I feel like an idiot'.
>   'Checking totals is a nightmare, especially from paper to screen'.
>   'I work things out differently and people think I'm stupid'.

First and foremost, therefore, assisting dyslexic people to improve their maths needs to start by building up their confidence in their ability. Asking them how they deal with it and approving of their 'alternative' strategy can enhance their confidence.

Skill Development   Dyslexic people whose background in maths is obviously lacking need to be taught the basic concepts. Much of the teaching of maths they have encountered will have been at an abstract level. They need to begin with the concrete, using very practical examples. For many adults the most important aspect of numeracy is in dealing with money, and this can often be used as a basis for teaching mathematical concepts, as well as arithmetic. It is important to establish that they understand the language of maths.

Dyslexic people whose difficulties with maths are procedural – that is, they relate to dealing with symbols, sequences and calculations – need to be taught strategies that circumvent such problems. Strategies can include the use of concrete aids, including fingers, to help check calculations. Sub vocalisation (muttering to oneself) can be helpful in preventing the misinterpretation of symbols. Dyslexic people should be encouraged to look at the symbol first and say it aloud. Memory devices such as mnemonics and visual imagery can be helpful for recalling the sequence in operations, as well as dealing with concepts generally. One woman for example learned to imagine boxes in her mind's eye. Their size was determined by a number of items. One box might equal 1000 for example. If she had to deal with 2000 she would imagine two boxes.

Having identified the particular problems experienced it is important that strategies are 'task specific'. Someone who has trouble dealing with sequences of numbers can be taught to identify patterns, using a grouping technique or involving rhyme and rhythm.

Maintaining the place when dealing with a series of numbers can also be a problem. This can be resolved by encouraging people to use a guide, such as a ruler or pencil. One person who had to deal with quite complex accounts could do the maths, but often transposed numbers incorrectly. It brought her into conflict with the Revenue and Customs over her tax returns.

It is important to reiterate that the underlying problem with maths is often a lack of confidence. In particular, people will have been in situations where they have expected to resolve a mathematical problem immediately. This is unrealistic and they need to give themselves thinking time, as well as be comfortable about their own way of dealing with the task.

Compensation   The most obvious compensation in maths is the efficient use of an electronic calculator. Those that contain a voice-chip so that auditory feedback is provided can be particularly useful.

Other compensations can be compiling a 'ready reckoner', which contains accessible information about weights, measures and conversions. One nurse used this strategy to good effect to help her deal with dispensing medicines. A carpenter had written down his own conversion chart for dealing with measurements.

Accommodations   These can include delegation, reducing demands in this regard and relying on an accountant. Supervisors in employment can prepare some of the aids described in the above section on compensations.

The most important factors for me were realising I had a problem; then telling someone; then seeking advice and specialist help. Seeking advice and specialist help were, ultimately the most advantageous. As a rule I know my own mind and wherever possible I rely on me. With dyslexia I couldn't do this. I found that help had to come from someone who knew what my mind was up to and had empathy for a person in my situation. I am under no illusions, there is no way I could have dealt with this on my own. Once I found people to help me and I found out the knowledge I needed to change and alter my behaviour, I could reduce the affects of dyslexia. Fortunately, it is in my nature to be, in certain situations, obdurate: I was stubborn enough to perceive and effect the necessary changes. Finally, just knowing what is happening and why certain tasks are and always will be harder than they otherwise would be takes a lot of the stress and difficulty out of them.

Developing basic literacy and numeracy skills should enable a dyslexic to move on, but be able to cope with more advanced training they need to develop higher learning skills. The appropriate interventions are described in Chapter 7.

A Dyslexic Person's Perspective

The following account was written by one of our clients. It is a good example of the perseverance shown by many of our dyslexic clients. Peter was referred by his employer for literacy skills training in 2005. At that time he had minimal reading and spelling skills but he was very determined. What he has written is a testament to how much he has achieved. Is it reproduced here with his permission.

This is Peter's Weekes story of how I coped with dyslexia and times when I didn't.

Here are some my first memories of dyslexia, the first was my first day at primary school when all of a sudden I could not spell a single word not even my own name. I have others memories of me always sitting at the back of the class room staring at the black board and doing nothing. But what was even more shocking was that the teacher didn't care. Most days he would drag me into his office by my ear shouting 'Weekesy.' What he said to me I just can't remember but I do recall my mum and dad saying 'No Peter is not backward'. That is when they decided to take me to the hospital to try and find out what was wrong, The hospital said that I was dyslexic. As they didn't know much about dyslexia in those days I was sent to a school for physically and mentally handicapped which was so wrong for me. In a way it had destroyed my self confidence but on the other hand made me a stronger person.

I was there from the age of 8 to 16- these were not the most happy years of my life. I didn't learn at this school because I thought I didn't belong there. There were not a lot of subjects taught at the school because most of the pupils had to have physiotherapy so the lessons were fitted around the physiotherapy sessions which only left time for the basic education.

I coped with being at the school for the first two or three years but by the age of 11 I started to notice a growing anger of being at the school. Was it anger for being at this school? Or was it that other kids took the mickey out of me for being in a handicap school calling me such names as flid? Perhaps it was a bit of both! But to make matters worse my school was right next to a 'normal' Secondary School. I also had bright ginger hair and a stammer and if that was not bad enough I had older parents that would dress me in clothes ten years out of date so I was an easy target for every kid on my Estate. Things got worse and then better around the age of 12 when one day I completely lost the plot and beat up one of the so called hard nuts from my Estate. I had to be pulled off by some of the parents because I couldn't stop hitting him, I suppose a person can only take so much before they flip and I think that's what happen to me.

So as soon as I was old enough to walk to school with my new found friends I did. There use to be around 40 of us that use to hang around together, we often played football and when the teams were picked I was always one of the last to be chosen as my football skills were absolutely useless. I was so bad at the game that whenever the ball was passed to me I would kick it to the right and it was actually meant go to the left!! and because the timing of my tackles were so bad I was known as 'psycho.' But I did bring a lot of humor to the game because of this.

When I was around 15 years old I started boxing at the famous Repton Boys Boxing Club because my dad's mate was a trainer there. I started boxing because my dad had always wanted one of his sons to box. I think he hoped it may help me control my anger and aggression I had around that time in my life. I found boxing a lot harder than I thought it was going to be because it was not like street fighting it was a completely different ball game, its all to do with hand and eye co-ordination, upper body movement and foot work all of which I wasn't any good at! So for almost every night for nearly a year I would spend an hour or so in front of a mirror seeing where I was going wrong and improve on it. I also worked extremely hard when I was in the boxing gym to get it right. I continued boxing until I was 23, altogether I had 45 bouts and won around half of them but the nerves never went I was either sick or felt sick before each fight.

I left school without any qualifications (because I was not capable!) which destroyed my confidence. After I left I went on a Y.T.S scheme which was college based. It was not like your normal Y.T.S scheme because it was designed for people with learning difficulties. There were four trades you could choose from, Car Mechanic, Plumber, Electrician and Chef. But after a month the lecturer had a row with the college over pay and left! So for the rest of the year I was still working under Y.T.S but at a D.I.Y store three days a week and the other two days were spent working at the back of the college breaking wooden pallets and other odd jobs. Then the job centre got me a job in a glass factory cutting the glass. The pay was not good but at least I had a job. I then had several jobs when my brother's father-in-law who worked for the Corporation of London said that there was a job at his place. The job was on the function team setting up functions in The Guildhall. I would help to set up by putting out the tables and chairs, erecting staging and making sure that the Banqueting area was spotless. I did this job for 14 years which took me to the grand age of 34. Then another door opened with great opportunity for a job within the Corporation of London. The job on offer was for a drainage inspector, it was a higher grade than what I was on and for more money. The job entailed going down sewers to survey them to see if the sewer is blocked, damaged or to help a surveyor survey them.

Quite early on in this last job I told them I am dyslexic and my manager suggested I should get some help and improve my literacy skills as I could not really read or write. I have been in this job 7 years now so I have actually been working for the Corporation of London for 21 years now. Since I have been having 1 to 1 sessions on and off over the 6 years (only one hour a month) with a dyslexia specialist. I have learnt more with her than all the time I did at school and I'm truly thankful to her with all her help and support she has given me. I read the paper everyday and am writing this with a little help from my wife. Using a computer has made a huge difference and I use the internet too, I can find information on and send emails. But I do feel that what I have achieved is more down to me being in the right place at the right time. My dyslexia teacher says that it is my determination because not many of her clients have worked as hard as I have to improve my reading and writing. Dyslexia does affect my confidence and my self belief and sometimes I feel very angry about how long it has taken me to get where I am now but I am going to keep on learning because I have to.

To conclude my story so far even though I have struggled through my life with a having stammer and suffering from dyslexia I have managed to hold down a good job, been happily married to my very understanding wife Lee for almost 11 years, have two wonderful boys Luke aged 6 and Jack 3. We have a nice house and I went on to become a boxing coach and still am today (for 18 years in total). I have had my fair share of success with the 3 national champions and a number of semi finalist in various competitions.

Coaches Comment

Peter's skills training was always on a 1:1 basis, originally he came once a week. We worked on basic sound – symbol correspondence and syllabification so that he understood the process of spelling, but he had great difficulty remembering the spelling rules so he worked on the visual analysis of words; he could always recognise if it was wrong and he became frustrated quite quickly when trying to write a simple dictated sentence. When his initial programme finished his employers were so impressed with his determination, they continued to fund his tuition on a monthly basis. He did homework every month. For the next two years Peter read a bit of the paper and would hand write a diary two or three times a week; sometimes it took him over an hour to write two or three lines. He did not have a computer at that time and did not like them; he was aware that he would find remembering the procedures hard. He got close to giving up at times – at the end of a busy day with two small children, it was hard. He got angry at his slow progress but he never gave up. He always attended his sessions. Gradually his reading improved, his confidence continued to grow, and he did get a computer at home and began to produce work he had written and compiled for subjects he researched on the computer.

Summary

1. To function independently on a daily basis dyslexic people need to reach the upper limits of the functional and lower limits of the vocational level in prose, document and quantitative literacy.
2. The skills taught to dyslexic people should be relevant to their needs and draw on their own experience.

3. In helping dyslexic people develop their skills it is imperative that they be encouraged to understand the process of learning. Opportunities for immediate success are essential.

4. As well as developing their literacy skills dyslexic people need to be helped to find alternative solutions through compensation, and to know how to seek relevant accommodations or adjustments.

7

Academic and Professional Learning Skills

Synopsis. *This chapter addresses the issues faced by dyslexic people when they make the transition to higher and professional education. The skills and compensation they need to develop, as well as the accommodations that can be made for them are described.*

Introduction

As we have written earlier, the majority of studies of dyslexic individuals beyond the age of 16 focus on emerging adults, mainly students in third-tier education. In terms of intervention, certainly in the United Kingdom, this population has been well served. Unfortunately this is less so for those on post-16 vocational programmes, particularly as some dyslexics benefit from being able to develop their learning skills and build up confidence in their ability by working towards short-term goals, progressing through alternative routes to gaining higher qualifications. Support for people who have finished formal education, but are training to meet the standards required for a profession through training and examination is patchy.

To function effectively in further, higher and professional education, an individual needs to be able to do the following:

- Organise themselves personally.
- Cope with independent learning and working.
- Manage their time effectively.
- Read and comprehend complex material accurately and fluently.
- Find relevant information from a variety of sources.
- Have good IT research skills, competency and knowledge.
- Think about and critically analyse information to an increasingly complex level.

The Dyslexic Adult: Interventions and Outcomes – An Evidence-based Approach, Second Edition.
David McLoughlin and Carol Leather.

- Plan written work – develop an argument, provide logical structured ideas supported by previous research.
- Express ideas verbally and in writing, completing essays, assignments, reports and dissertations.
- Type quickly.
- Listen, understand and take notes quickly and legibly.
- Revise effectively.
- Demonstrate their knowledge and understanding in exams and assessment settings.

Moving on to higher education represents a major transition for dyslexic people. This is not widely recognised in the United Kingdom, but more formal transition planning is undertaken in countries such as the United States. Much more could be done in terms of preparing dyslexic students for the realities of college life. Moving away from home in itself can present more of a challenge for a dyslexic student as they rely more on the implicit structure and routine of their home life. Combining this with the requirements of academic life, such as independent learning, is very demanding. Further, transitions occur with courses of higher education; the complexity of material increases, the nature of assignments changes, as does the format of examinations. With regard to the latter, for example, there is a big difference between multiple-choice formatted tests and essay type examinations. Post-graduate programmes require different skills from those needed during undergraduate course. Whilst the latter should be a preparation for the former, dyslexic students do not automatically develop the new skills they need and are unaware of the demands likely to be made of them.

My first semester was hell, a nightmare, my worst nightmare. It went wrong from week two. The first week was OK, but the second week we were dropped in the deep end, work was piled onto us. I wouldn't have made it but for the support of one friend at home who pulled me through, she said I could do it.

I lived at home, not on campus, so had to travel to London. The journey only takes forty minutes but as the railways are so bad I often had to change trains or they were late. I tried to leave early so that I would have fifteen minutes to recover, but was always late. Then the lecturers would change the lecture rooms so by the time I got there, I couldn't think straight. I was exhausted and it all flew past me.

I had no friends to ask what was going on, where to find things like the library or a photocopier, and I couldn't remember.

I had difficulty organising my time – it was all down to me, and I had so much freedom it was difficult to control. I had so much to organise and remember – different days meant different buildings. I would check and double check. I had to remember to take different files so I colour coded them for different days.

It was all new – places, people, more to do. It was not just the work, it was everything, but I was also having to work so hard just to survive. Then the lecturer said that if I didn't improve my scores I would be out. He said he didn't think I would make it. I knew what the problems were but couldn't do anything, there seemed to be too many to solve in one go.

I was constantly being asked to fill in forms, which just reminded me that I had a problem. Many of the tutors don't know what dyslexia is.

It is a bit easier now, but I wish the lecturer hadn't said that I wouldn't make it.

The student quoted above eventually gained an upper second class degree despite her lecturer's prediction.

The Keys to Success in Higher and Professional Education

The above are all tasks that dyslexic people find challenging. Some of the skills, compensations and accommodations that can enable them to become more effective are described below. It is at this level that addressing executive functioning is particularly important, and developing metacognitive skills is therefore a recurrent theme. In terms of the development of skills, the general goal is to enable dyslexic people to become good at information processing. Fundamental to this is the notion that the development of strategies is deliberate and requires ongoing experimentation, monitoring, reflection and refinement (Pintrich, 1994; Zimmerman, 2002; Raskind et al., 2004).

The Importance of Metacognition

Success at college and in professional education relies very heavily on independent learning skills. It demands confidence and the ability to deal with a great many things at one time. Borokowski and Muthurkrishna (1992) describe a set of behaviours that might be common to sophisticated learners. These can be divided into *cognitive* and *affective* and are:

Cognitive Behaviours
1. They know a large number of learning strategies.
2. They understand when and why these are important.
3. They select and monitor wisely and are extremely reflective.
4. They adhere to an incremental view regarding the growth of the mind.
5. They deploy effort carefully.
6. They know a great deal about many topics and have rapid access to that knowledge.

Affective Behaviours
1. They are intrinsically motivated and task orientated.
2. They are unafraid of failure, realising that failure is a learning opportunity.
3. They have a history of being supported in all of these characteristics by parents, schools and society at large.

In effect they should have moved from Gardener's apprentice stage outlined in Chapter 6 to the master stage and be in control of their own learning.

Self-understanding and Self-reflection

Understanding that learning at this level requires more independence and that the tutors are often there to present information rather than to 'teach' is important. A dyslexic person's understanding of the nature of their skills and abilities, and of their areas of weakness, is essential. They need to know what skills they have, what skills they must develop, and what compensations and accommodations are available to them.

Dyslexic people already know learning can be difficult for them if information is presented in conventional ways. They might also know it takes them longer to complete work. They have therefore to learn to be much more efficient in their study habits. It is essential they recognise that many people will not understand the nature of their difficulty. There is evidence to suggest that the success of a student can be a reflection of departmental attitudes towards dyslexia, and the extent to which they collaborate with the student and student support services (Scott & Gregg, 2000). Dyslexic people do, therefore, need to be able to explain how dyslexia affects them and be specific about their requirements.

It is rarely lack of ability that causes a dyslexic person to struggle at university. It is more often because they do not understand task demands and have problems with organisation, getting on with and working with their tutors as well as their peers. External factors such as these lead to their downfall rather than just their problems with literacy. Misunderstandings between student and tutor can often exaggerate a dyslexic person's difficulties. Students who know that it will take them a long time to orientate themselves to university life or a course of professional training, and what they need to do to make the process manageable are usually successful. This is particularly important for those who have to balance the demands of a job and further study.

Self Reflection Attribution and Self Efficacy

Part of improving one's performance is the ability to self-reflect, on both positives and negatives. Identifying and recognising strengths and areas for further development is the key. Dyslexic students, because of their past experience, tend to only review negatively, their self-attribution being internal, blaming themselves for past failures.

It can be helpful, therefore, for dyslexic students to keep a record of their achievements in which they reflect or assess their own skills, so they can attribute their success more accurately to themselves, rather than good teaching or good luck. Reflective assignments are an increasing part of some courses. Social science and health service courses, for example, often have a reflective practitioner element. This is aimed at developing reflective practice to improve professional skills. Self-reflection also enables the person to set realistic targets for future development. Perhaps all dyslexic people should adopt this process as a personal development tool. Some students undertake reflection informally in a record or a diary; others are more formal about it and retain a file. Self-reflection should increase self confidence as strengths are understood, short-term goals are achieved and progress is made over a period of time. At university and on professional training courses the goalposts are constantly changing and, therefore, performance is not always seen to be improving despite the fact that it is.

Students should also be encouraged to see feedback as being constructive, valid and helpful as it can be a tool to aid self-review. They need to know that they are entitled to reject criticism if it is not productive. How other people see us and our performance from an objective point of view is important, but dyslexic students must learn to accept comments for what they are, consider them and set new goals. The need to learn independently means that students may have to engage in a variety of activities at any one time. They must control the order and pace of their learning.

Learning and Working Styles

Another aspect of metacognitive processing is the 'knowledge of cognition' (Flavell, 1979) which includes an awareness of the way one processes information best. There are a variety of information processing strategies and the emphasis needs to be on the development of those an individual finds most useful. It is, therefore, a process of experimentation.

Cognitive Learning Differences

Understanding whether one processes information best through visual, auditory or ki-naesthetic sensory input should influence the strategy adopted when learning. According to the model of working memory outlined in Chapter 1 dyslexic people can often deal with images more readily than words. Knowing this should affect the strategy they use. Graphic organisers, including concept maps, have been shown to be highly effective in improving a range of skills (Dexter, 2010).

Behavioural Learning Styles

Honey and Mumford (1986) have described four different types of learner. These are:

Activists   – Activists learn best when working in groups with other people, such as being involved in workshop activities; when they are working to tight deadlines and discussing ideas. Interaction is the key.
Reflectors   – Reflectors learn best when attending lectures, undertaking project or research work. Working on their own, they are thinking back and reflecting on what has happened.
Theorists   – Theorists are most effective when reading and evaluating ideas, questioning theories and discussing theories with other people.
Pragmatist   – Pragmatists prefer to do things, such as be involved in practical problem-solving. They learn best from work experience or taking part in workshops.

While people rarely fit one behavioural or cognitive category in any of the learning and working style profiles, outlining the differences in approaches to learning can be useful as it increases the awareness of the learning process and what it is for the individual. Thinking about the way they learn best, and knowing about the various approaches to learning, enables people to develop more flexibility, and to be more creative, more task specific and, therefore, more effective.

It is also important that individuals know when and where they work best. People prefer to work at different times and for different lengths of time. Some people like to be in the environment of a library, where it is quiet and there are no interruptions. Other people like to be in their own surroundings, and others can work anywhere. Everyone needs to know when, where and how they work best, but it is essential for that dyslexic people acknowledge that struggling through a difficult text when tired or at a bad time of day is ineffective.

Time Management

Being able to organise and manage time is important to anyone, but for a dyslexic student being able to organise time is essential, as working and learning are harder and take longer. Some people prefer a very rigid plan and are able to adhere to it. Others prefer a more flexible overall weekly goal rather than daily ones. As we have seen dyslexic people are not good at estimating how long tasks take and have a poor concept of time generally. Learning support tutors have an important role to play in helping students become aware of where time goes, and how easy it is for it to be unproductive.

Some universities and colleges allow students greater control in planning their own course through the years of study. When drawing up a schedule of work, dyslexic people need to be especially careful that they don't overload themselves with too many demanding courses. Departments sometimes encourage students to undertake complementary courses that require an investment of time, disproportionate to the overall programme. Dyslexic students need to be very selective and make informed decisions if this is the case.

University and college life can also be stressful, which inevitably affects performance, so relaxation is important. It is essential for dyslexic people to be able to relax and unwind. However, for some people, even this is a struggle. One student found social situations such as going to the pub so tiring that she couldn't concentrate in lectures. She had to learn to limit herself to one night a week of social activity so she could face the demands of her university day during her first year. As she settled in she expanded her social life.

> Being at University is like being at the bottom of a waterfall.

Skill Development   Involves being able to assess how long a task takes and knowing when is a good time to work. Realistic goal setting and prioritising are other skills which need to be developed. Making timetables and setting timed tasks can help develop time estimation.

Compensations   Can be a mobile phone, alarm clock, stop watch or electronic aid, as well as wall charts, wall planners, year planners, day planners, diaries, timetables, filofaxes and lists.

Accommodations   Having friends provide reminders; tutors seeing drafts a week to two before the deadline.

Organisation of Work

As we have suggested in Chapter 1 organisation does not come naturally to dyslexic people. They need to work hard at it. Some people like to be very organised, having a good filing system which is kept up to date, for example. Organising notes can be a key to keeping information under control. The 3Ms described earlier can be useful:

Manageable   Breaking the course into sections, course outlines, a reading reference file, lists of lectures, indexes in files and overviews are all essential to making information manageable. Identifying the key, core elements of the course, as well as those that will require the most focus also makes learning more manageable. Developments in technology mean that knowing where to find information that has been previously covered is as important as being able to remember it. Making reading records not only acts as an aide memoire, but also facilitates reference to material later.

Multisensory   The use of coloured files, box files, different coloured files and various papers for courses, makes organisation multisensory.

Memory Aids   Filing is a way of revision but often this means a student has to find time and be disciplined enough to file material on a regular basis. Again lists and files can act as memory aids, as well as making organisation multisensory.

Reading

Dyslexic people, especially in higher education or work settings, often over-read, focusing on word recognition rather than comprehension. They do not automatically develop systematic approaches to reading comprehension, but these can be taught. Sometimes they are using a variety of strategies in different contexts but are not aware of it and so do not use them appropriately. Many dyslexic people, for example, do use scanning and skimming techniques when reading a newspaper, but do not generalise this to their studies. It is important that they know the difference between reading to learn and learning to read. Studying at an advanced level requires someone to be able to recognise sophisticated words quickly, as well as critically analyse, assimilate and retain material.

Skill Development   Before teaching any systematic reading strategy, it is important to ask students questions about their reading, to establish how metacognitive they are in their reading behaviour. There is ample evidence to indicate that good readers use more metacognitive skills when reading (Butler, 1995; Wong, 1986). Fidler and Everatt (2011) argue that good readers utilise metacognitive strategies such as previewing the task, monitoring comprehension, summarising and reflecting to improve comprehension as it enables the reader to structure the information more easily into existing metal maps.

Developing a metacognitive approach to reading begins with questions such as:

- 'What is your reading like?'
- 'What are the problems you associate with your reading?'
- 'Is your main difficulty decoding the long words, reading aloud or comprehension?'

- 'How do you read – aloud, silently, quickly, slowly, or every word?'
- 'Do you miss lines or lose your place?'
- 'Where do you start your reading – at the beginning, and read on?'
- 'Do you read the same way if you are reading different types of material?'
- 'Are you aware of punctuation and the function of paragraphs?'
- 'Are you able to pick out the main idea?'
- 'Prior to reading something – Do you think why you are reading this, what information do you hope to gain?'
- 'Do you check your comprehension?'
- 'Do you reflect back on the effectiveness of the time spent on the text?'

Asking people to think about their reading habits does help them to refine their skills as they become more metacognitive in their behaviour.

Many dyslexic people tend to read in the same fashion, whatever the text. They are often not aware that there is much more to reading than decoding and remembering what is read. They do not realise that using a variety of approaches to reading makes it more efficient. The reading process should be targeted, flexible, active and monitored: targeted in that the reader knows what information they are looking for; flexible in that they may change and use a variety of different reading strategies during the course of one period of reading; and active in that the reader has a response to the text. Reading can be very passive as the emphasis is on decoding, and there is not time to interact with the text, so it is not easily remembered. If the text is very difficult to read then another strategy should be adopted or the question of whether it is essential to read the material at all should be asked. That is, the reading process should be monitored.

Possibly the best knowns of the reading strategies is **SQ3R – Survey, Question, Read, Recite, Recall.** Some dyslexic people do not find this effective if it is not sufficiently structured. Other examples are the **PASS** Strategy described in Chapter 6 and **PARTS** (Ellis, 1993), which is as follows:

Perform goal setting
    Clarify why you are analysing the chapter parts.
    Identify the goal related to this reason.
    Make a positive self-statement.

Analyse little parts (title, headings, etc.)
    Explain the information indicated by the part.
    Predict what the section under the part is about.
    Tie the parts together.

Review big parts (introduction and summary)
    Search for signal words that indicate main ideas.
    Decide what the author thinks is important.
    Relate new information to what you already know.
    Paraphrase the main message.

Think of questions you hope will be answered
Check questions provided by the chapter.
Identify your own questions.

State relationships
How does the chapter relate to the unit being studied?
How does the chapter relate to what you already know?

All these strategies require the student to develop the skills of scanning, skimming and careful analysis. By being more deliberate in their use of these, reading can be made more efficient.

Reading comprehension skills can be further developed through the analysis of the text, determining the author's purpose and recognising the organisation of the passage; whether it is argumentative or comparative, descriptive, evaluative, or discursive; and identifying the key idea of a paragraph and its structure. Using signal words such as 'however', 'similarly' and 'in contrast' can improve clarity of means. Is it introducing a new idea or extending a concept? Knowing the author's intentions and method of organising their ideas can greatly enhance comprehension of a passage. Continued problems with comprehension should be analysed further. One can ask 'Is it that there are too many unfamiliar words or that the author is ambiguous in what he is saying?', for example. It is important for the student to understand that meaning is not always explicit in the text and that each reader brings his own meaning to what he reads, based on what he expects from the text and his previous knowledge. Equally the author may not be clear in the way he is expressing his line of thinking.

Understanding the patterns of organisation improves the processing of information and this can influence the way notes are made from the text. Chronological information can, for example, be noted in flow chart form; comparative material can be organised in tabular form. Descriptive information can be arranged as a mind map. Understanding the task demands does mean the appropriate strategy can be chosen.

Critical Reading Skills

These skills are essential for the successful reader in any academic and many work environments. The struggle to read, comprehend and retain information is so demanding that many dyslexic readers do not apply critical thinking and reading to the texts. Many dyslexic people are not aware that this is part of the process and when questioned they do not believe they can do it. Often further discussion regarding whether they believe all they read in the paper or promotion leaflets usually demonstrates that they can and do read critically at times.

Reasonable scepticism is an important part of critical reading – being able to distinguish between opinion and bias, identifying if there is enough robust and reliable evidence for an argument. That it is not flawed, is logical and well reasoned, and that the conclusion is convincing are all aspects of the reading process that require confidence.

Furthermore, becoming a critical reader often improves the individual's writing style as paying attention to different authors' texts from an objective point of view can affect the quality of their own writing. That is, they should become more sensitive to developing a reasoned and researched line of argument.

Compensations   Can include substituting listening comprehension for reading comprehension by the use of a recording. Highlighting important parts of the text, as well as reading summaries. Using reviewers or other people's notes can also enable the individual to find the time to think and develop their own line of argument. Using a critical reader's check list can help.

Accommodation   Having someone else read to the student directly or to a recording device. Being able to discuss a text or article with a friend or colleague can aid the formation of their ideas.

Comprehending Diagrammatic and Tabular Formats

Reading comprehension is not just a matter of dealing with text. Students have to interpret tables and diagrams. Even though these can sometimes enhance comprehension they can present difficulties.

Skill Development

In terms of the development of skills Ellis (1993) suggests a systematic approach known as SNIPS.

Start with questions
Question to clarify your goals. Why are you analysing the visual aid?
Question to find out what kind of information to look.

Picture	*What is it a picture of?*
Graph/Chart	*What is being **compared**? How?*
Map	*What **key areas** are important to see? Why are they key areas?*
Time line	*Show the **history** of what? From when to when?*

Note what you can learn from the hints
Look for hints that signal answers to your questions (*e.g. Title, Caption, Line Numbers, Colour*).
Activate your knowledge.

Identify what is important
Identify the **main message** of the graphic.
Identify two **facts** from the graphic.

Plug it into the chapter
How does the visual relate to what the chapter or unit is about?

See if you can explain the visual to someone
Find someone to whom you can explain the visual (*explain it to yourself if nobody else is available*).
Tell **what** you think the visual is about and **how** you think it relates to what the chapter is about. Identify what you think are the best clues in the visual and say **why** they are useful.

Compensations   Can include highlighting important parts of diagrammatic information and reformatting.

Accommodations   Talking through the visual representations with someone.

Essay Writing

A problem with essay writing is one of the most common reasons students and people undergoing professional training seek help. Putting ideas on paper is the task that most dyslexic people find difficult as there is a high cognitive demand, involving not just writing skills but also organisation. Difficulties are often exacerbated by a lack of confidence in their ability to write.

Skill Development   The skills required for essay writing include: gathering information on a specific subject; being able to interpret and add original ideas; being able to identify the key points; being able to develop a line of argument; being able to structure and organise thoughts and information in a logical fashion; and being able to cite references accurately and write it all down. The two key skills for producing an insightful piece of writing are understanding the task demands and planning. Essay writing put simply involves the student displaying what they know, how they can use their knowledge, and their own informed ideas on the subject. Bloom's (1956) Cognitive Domain Taxonomy provides the structure and criteria by which most academic essays are marked. This domain has six levels: knowledge, the comprehension of that knowledge, application of the information, analysis of information, the synthesis of information into a new and original form, and the evaluation of information.

- *Knowledge* involves understanding lists of facts and terminology, methods, trends and conventions, as well as principles, theories and descriptions.
- *Comprehension* involves showing that these things can be communicated in other terms or another form. The ideas are not remembered in the way they have been read but in the way the student has made sense of them.
- *Application* involves the student being able to apply the theories to real life situations.
- *Analysis* involves breaking the information into parts and explaining what relationship exists between the whole, and being able to identify cause and effect, as well as make inferences.

- *Synthesis* involves using the acquired knowledge in a new, creative, original way.
- *Evaluation* is making judgements on ideas, methods and information, and being able to justify the reasons for these judgements.

Understanding these six levels of academic writing provides the dyslexic student with a better idea of what they are trying to achieve. It explains the nature of the task, and provides a structure within which they can express their ideas. They can, therefore, be specific in their approach to processing the information, formulating a good plan or structure to work from.

Understanding the Task – Question Analysis and Process Words

It is essential for the student to know what the question is about and why it is being asked, as many dyslexic people can miss the point. Process words are extremely important in question analysis as they give an indication of how the essay should be structured. Words such as 'describe', 'analyse', 'evaluate' and 'outline' are each asking for a different way of presenting information. Understanding this can make it easier for the student to structure the essay correctly. One student was disappointed when for one assignment the question set was 'In your opinion, what are the reasons for the lack of women in top management jobs?' She wrote a very powerful, cogent description of how she felt about the lack of women in top management jobs. She failed, however, to provide the other point of view because she had taken, 'In your opinion . . .' literally. She was awarded a low mark and it was not what she had hoped for or expected.

When the question has been analysed relevant information can be gathered. To improve their results many dyslexic people need to analyse how they write essays and what loses them marks. Some students are not clear in their explanations, others do not justify their statements sufficiently, often because they think the logic is too obvious, or because they lack confidence in their ideas. Dyslexic students have sometimes developed very contracted writing styles and prefer bullet points; others ramble on. Being able to critically analyse one's own work, however painful, can be productive. Applying the same critical reading skills to one's writing as outlined earlier can greatly improve the quality of the end result. For example asking questions such as: have I clearly developed my argument? Is there enough evidence for it?

Compensations   Many dyslexic people are much better verbally than they are at putting ideas on paper. Dictating to tape and writing from the recording can be a useful approach. Developing dictation skills generally, particularly if they can use the services of an audio-typist, enables them to achieve the best match between verbal ability and written work. The use of a word processor means that the cognitive load is reduced because they do not have to concern themselves with legibility, neatness and spelling. They can also reorganise material easily. As technology develops, voice activated word processing is increasingly being seen as the solution for dyslexic people. It is for many but it does require the development of underlying planning skills.

Accommodations   Accommodations include making sure that technical as well as secretarial support is available. It also involves supervisors and tutors facilitating the process of students being able to structure and organise their ideas. They may well need to talk through their ideas to gain a deeper understanding, thus enabling them to commit their ideas to paper more easily. They may need more reassurance and clarification concerning what is expected of them. They require constructive feedback on how they can improve, as well as plenty of time in which to re-draft. Flexibility with regard to deadlines can be appropriate but there is a danger in allowing dyslexic students extra time to complete assignments, as they can often end up with a backlog of assignments.

Proofreading

Proofreading one's own work is difficult. Often one becomes too close to the material to see the errors. It is easy to anticipate what one thinks is on the page, rather than what has actually been written. As a result of difficulties with the printed word for dyslexic people, proofreading can be doubly difficult.

Skill Development   Structured approaches to proofreading can include COPS: Checking **C**apitalisation of letters, and examining the **O**verall appearance, **P**unctuation and **S**pelling (Schumaker et al., 1981). This may seem long-winded, but it is better to break the task of proofreading into small steps rather than trying to do too much at once. Such approaches can be redundant with easy access to computers, but even then running the spell checker where headings are and then reading from the printed copy can be helpful.
   Other aids can include:

- Keeping a list of errors one consistently makes.
- Leaving proofreading for at least 24 hours so that it is looked at afresh. This can allow the identification of errors otherwise missed.
- Reading from right to left can assist, as this prevents anticipation. It enables people to focus on each individual word, and excludes the context.
- Maintaining a sense of why something has been written down can help with the clarity of expression.

Compensations   Compensations for proofreading and checking mainly include the use of technology, such as spellcheckers and grammar checkers. These need to be used carefully as conventional spellcheckers will miss words which are correctly spelled but inappropriately placed and do not correct homophones, for example, and these cause dyslexic people a persisting difficulty. Text to speech software can allow proofreading by listening and many dyslexic people find this very effective.

Accommodations   The most obvious accommodation is to have someone else go over the work. Dyslexic people will often do this with trepidation as they fear criticism. It is important, so they do need to have someone they trust. Someone who will be 'fussy' and overly critical can be demoralising.

Grammar and Punctuation

Sentence structure and punctuation are often areas of difficulty for the dyslexic person.

Skill Development   It is not always feasible to embark on a programme to improve grammar, but some basic principles often improve the structure and expression of ideas. A basic course in punctuation can significantly improve the quality. Understanding the reason for punctuation, in that it adds expression and clarity to a sentence, in itself can make a difference to the writing. In particular, many dyslexic people's sentences are either too long or indeed too short. The sentences that are too long are often phrases that are strung together. The subject may have been lost or the verb omitted. It is usually better to keep writing short and simple, so it is easier to identify that the subject and the verb are present and in agreement. Basic punctuation such as commas, semi-colons and colons often greatly enhance the student's writing.

Compensation   As has been suggested above, dictation and the use of voice recognition software so that there is a match between verbal ability and written work. Many dyslexic people cannot see their own grammatical mistakes when proofreading, but can hear them when they read aloud or when they make use of a Text to Speech package.

Accommodation   Providing a proofreader or secretarial support is the most effective solution.

Spelling

The extent to which spelling remains a problem for dyslexic people is very varied. There are people who have a major spelling difficulty, but who do not see it as a problem and therefore write freely, finding other ways of dealing with spelling. Other people are extremely sensitive about their spelling whatever their level, having been embarrassed by it in the past, and are easily thrown off track when they make a mistake or if someone points out a mistake. It inhibits their thinking and slows down writing. The improvement of spelling demands a considerable amount of time. This is often an unachievable goal during a course, so other solutions should be sought.

Skill Development   The aim of any spelling instruction at this level should be to ensure that the student has enough knowledge as to be able to use a spell checker effectively. Much of the instruction should, therefore, focus on the identification of the number of syllables in a word, learning the blends and suffixing rules, and knowing that there are a variety of vowel combinations.

Other skills involved in spelling include listening for sounds in words and putting them in the right sequence. Once the dyslexic person becomes aware of this they are more likely to approach it systematically. A step by step approach – listening to the syllables and then to the individual sounds, for example, and knowing which sounds or which areas of a word they cannot hear clearly or isolate – enables them to write most of the word they can hear. Then they can focus on the hard parts and use visual skills to check or recall what is missing. Using other memory strategies, such as visual imagery or mnemonics, will also significantly help the spelling of individual words. Many students report that once they understand the process, and once they let go of the stigma attached to poor spelling, they have found their spelling improves.

There are two approaches:

1. A short course on spelling strategies, looking at personal spelling errors and developing their own lists, focusing on common words and specific technical spellings. Using the varied strategies mentioned above, and utilising their own thinking and memory skills to help. Overlearning course and subjected related words.
2. A longer spelling course looking at the key elements of spelling, including a brief history of English orthography. This provides an explanation for why the English spelling system is so complicated. Understanding that some words are derived from Greek, Latin or Anglo Saxon gives a structure that many dyslexic people find useful. Looking at letter patterns, prefixes, suffixes and root words, word derivations and word families can all be targeted effectively to help the dyslexic student analyse the word. It can often lead to improvements in both reading and spelling.

Compensations   These include using a hand held spell checker or one on a computer. The spell checker on a computer often eradicates the majority of difficulties but certain words, such as homophones and the wrong use of words, will not be corrected.

Accommodations   Having someone to proofread the words or asking a friend or colleague are the most effective methods.

Listening Comprehension

Being able to follow training courses, benefit from lectures and presentations, as well as participate in tutorials, means that dyslexic people need to develop good listening comprehension skills. It is a skill that places a heavy demand on working memory.

Skill Development   Previewing is an essential part of good listening comprehension. That is, actively thinking about a lecture before attending. If, for example, one were going to a lecture on existentialist philosophy, looking up a dictionary definition beforehand helps. The many basic guides to complex topics can be a good preparation. It provides a structure and enables students to establish what is relevant. Reading pre-training course hand-outs is very important.

Another way of enhancing listening comprehension is to ask questions and seek clarification. There are appropriate and inappropriate times for the asking of questions. Lecturers and fellow students can be irritated by constant interruptions. Listening can also be enhanced turning in to verbal clues – 'firstly', 'a final point', 'on the other hand'.

Systematic approaches to listening comprehension include PQLR. That is:

P – Preview and tune in to the lecture
Q – Generate questions about the topic for the end of the session
L – Listen for the speaker's position
R – Mentally review the material so that the important points are remembered.

Compensations   In formal learning situations, the most obvious compensation is to take a dictaphone to lectures. This allows one to listen and control information more readily. A variable rate machine and one which has a counting device is useful, so that important parts, or ones which have not been fully understood, can be specifically identified. Mobile phones are now often used to take photographs of key parts of a presentation.

Accommodations   These can include providing an overview of lectures or training sessions so that the participants can preview the information. Many universities do record lectures now and then they are posted on the intranet system for all students. An interactive format can be an effective method of presentation. Students should be encouraged to participate through questions and discussions. Dyslexic people can often deal with visual material effectively, while others prefer a variety of formats, and so the use of diagrams and illustrations can be helpful. Allowing the recording of seminars enables people to listen and focus on understanding the content and also contribute more. However, there is still reluctance in many situations to allow this to happen.

Note Taking

Listening comprehension and taking notes in a learning situation are closely related. Too many people 'take notes at the expense of noting'. It is more important to be able to listen and understand than to be able to write comprehensive notes, particularly as dyslexic people often report that they cannot read what they have written. Note taking is a very complex skill for dyslexic people because it places a very heavy load on working memory. It is affected by a significant number of factors including listening comprehension, attention, processing information, organising and recording notes in a legible and fluent fashion (Boyle, 2005). Other variables include: how much the student already knows about the subject; how familiar they are with it; their personal confidence in their ability to take notes; their spelling skills. In addition note taking is often related to the way material is presented. If a lecturer presents notes in a clear concise fashion, with lots of signal clues (e.g. 'first', 'second'), or provides an overhead showing what is being covered then it is easier. It is a task that causes dyslexic people to panic as they feel that if they don't take notes they will not be able to remember what is being said. Some students feel that if they can't take notes adequately, there is no point in going to the lecture.

At a practical level encompassing visual features into performance-enhancing strategies has improved my effectiveness at taking notes down in meetings and at college lectures. So for example when not taking, I now make greater use – where possible – of diagrams and symbols to supplement key points that I have jotted down. In the past I either avoided not taking altogether or I would attempt to write everything down and give up part of the way through.

Skill Development   The best approach to taking notes is a minimalist one but it does have to be effective. Here a metacognitive approach aids the efficiency of note taking. It is a question of matching the individual skills to the topic with the right strategy. Some people find using visual strategies such as drawing pictures, mind-maps or diagrams extremely helpful. Others prefer to write down headings, bullet points and key words. One skill that should be developed is the use of abbreviations, including one's own specific shorthand for technical words. Some people find it is beneficial to divide the page into four quarters, each representing fifteen minutes of an hour long lecture. This is particularly useful when using a recorder and can avoid the individual having to listen to a whole lecture again if they only missed one part of it.

Before developing an appropriate technique, people need to identify the purpose of taking notes as it may affect the strategy chosen. They need to identify the themes and ideas being presented. This can be done by listening for signal words, such as 'an important theme', 'a key feature', or statements such as 'and now we will move on to . . .'

Visual aids, such as overheads, will often provide a guide to the key words and headings. However dyslexic people find it difficult to copy down the content of the overhead quickly. This is where the use of abbreviations and developing a glossary, particularly for recurring technical words, can be helpful. In addressing the issue of 'self review' of lectures attended, Ellis (1993) suggests the use of the mnemonic CROWN.

C – communicate what you have learnt, the general and the specific things that have been learnt, how different are they and what is new about them.

R – reactions. Surprises, corrections, interests, images, conflicts.

O – offering one sentence to sum up what a whole lecture was about.

W – where are some different places you can use this information or transfer it to?

N – notes. How well did it go today, the best part, the hardest part, and was a personal goal achieved?

As with the Performance Improvement Plan, this is a cognitive strategy for monitoring goal attainment, summarising, prioritising, noting and self-enforcement.

Compensations   The compensation mainly involves the use of a dictaphone as a back-up to a minimalist strategy. It is important to have one which has a counting device. This enables students to index mark when important points have been made, so that when replaying the recording, they can focus on these. When students have good keyboard skills, taking a laptop or notebook computer to lectures and training sessions can be very helpful. Touch typing allows one to be able to focus on visual clues, as well as on the overheads, without having to keep looking back and forth. The notes they have taken will also be legible and can be extended at a later date.

Accommodations   Accommodations can include lecturers and trainers providing handouts which summarise the main points of the lecture, and providing reading lists. Students can also rely on other people's notes. Where difficulties are severe, a note-taker can be engaged, preferably someone who is familiar with the topic as the notes will be clearer.

Note Making

Note making is a different task from taking notes in lectures. The student has considerably more control over the information when making notes from texts, videos, or handouts, or when making notes of their own ideas for an essay. The purpose of the note making is important, and the strategy used should be deliberately chosen: matching skills to the task. Making notes aids concentration and understanding of the subject. They enable the reorganisation and linking of ideas, enabling the student to rewrite material in their own words, and remember it better.

Skill Development   A key skill to develop in note making is being able to identify the key points. Using key words is a skill that many dyslexic people find difficult and this often requires practice. Whenever any notes are taken, it is essential to write down the source of the notes, the date of the lecture or seminar, the book title and reference page. A personal comment on the interest, understanding and importance of the text or lecture also helps recall. Notes should be as personal as possible. As long as they are effective for the student, in that they can decipher them, the way in which they are taken is not an issue, but it is important to remember that they might be needed in the future. Furthermore, reviewing notes shortly after they are made can ensure they are sufficient, as well as provide a starting point for revision. The graphic organiser below in Figure 7.1 is a student's note from a study skills session on reading.

Compensations   These can include talking into a Speech to Text software package; using a dictaphone and having the notes typed up. Using a note making pen scanner enables one to scan quotes from the text and transfer them straight to a computer. Photocopying important texts and highlighting the key words can also be helpful.

Accommodations   As mentioned in the previous section the accommodations are using other people's notes, being given highlighted texts or abstracts, as well as copies of overheads or handouts.

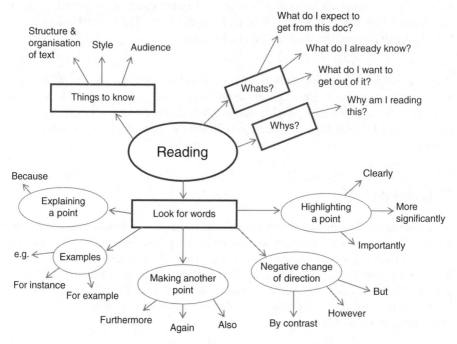

Figure 7.1 Graphic for Note Taking and Reading

Revision and Memory Skills

Applying and using new knowledge involves being able to remember what has been learned and central to this process is being able to revise properly. This is particularly important to dyslexic people as the automatic retrieval of information does not come easily to them. Revision should be an ongoing and active process. It can begin with adding new information to notes taken during the course of a lecture. Ideally revision starts at the beginning of a course of work and training. The 'principle of recency' suggests reviewing material on a regular basis makes it easier to recall. The purpose of revision is usually to reorganise the information that has been given so that it can be recalled clearly and appropriately under timed conditions. Examinations are aimed at assessing ability and knowledge, but they also assess the ability of the individual to organise information on paper quickly. Revision must therefore involve storing information and learning how to retrieve it quickly.

Skill Development   Metacognitive awareness increases the efficiency of revision, and revision is best is it is **manageable**, **multisensory** and **memorable**.

Manageable   Revision should be targeted and systematic. It is made manageable by knowing what has to be done; course outlines are very helpful. Rating how well the

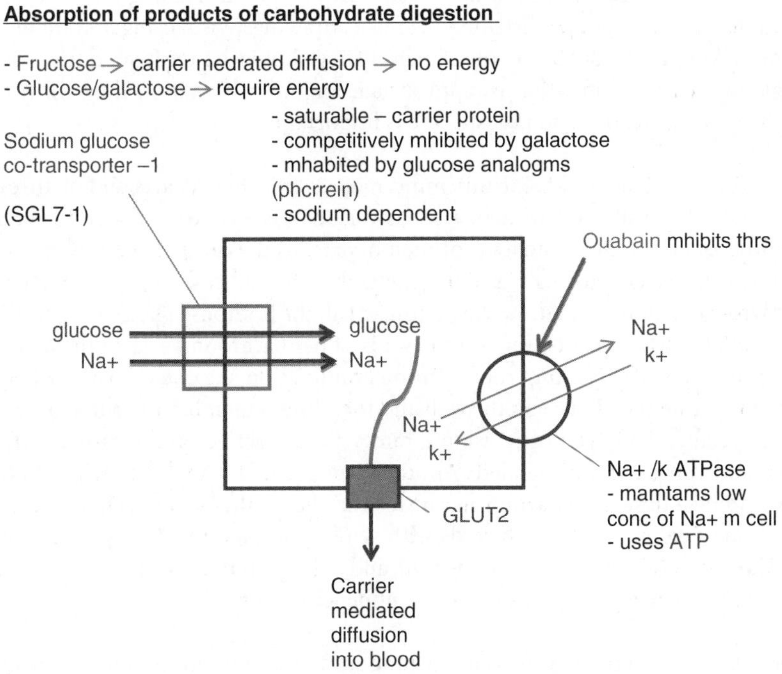
Absorption of products of carbohydrate digestion
- Fructose → carrier medrated diffusion → no energy
- Glucose/galactose → require energy
- saturable – carrier protein
- competitively mhibited by galactose
- mhabited by glucose analogms
(phcrrein)
- sodium dependent
Sodium glucose
co-transporter –1
(SGL7-1)
Ouabain mhibits thrs
glucose
Na+
glucose
Na+
Na+
k+
Na+
k+
Na+ /k ATPase
- mamtams low
conc of Na+ m cell
- uses ATP
GLUT2
Carrier
mediated
diffusion
into blood

Figure 7.2 Example of Revision Notes

information on a specific subject is known, and its relative importance for the examination is the next step. Planning a timetable and breaking it into manageable parts is essential. It is a more effective use of time if specific topics are targeted each day. The revision plan must, however, be flexible.

Revision should build on what is already known and a five minute brainstorming at the start of a session activates knowledge, giving a clear indication of gaps and therefore what needs to be revised. Likewise, at the end of a session, a quick mind map or notes outline can be a good self test of what has been revised and learned. Furthermore, it is a way of practising the retrieval of information at speed, an important part of the examination process. Reducing the amount of verbal material makes managing the information easier, summarising in keywords, pictures or symbols so that minimal cues will access material from long-term memory.

> I wanted to send some examples of my revision notes. I found it useful to see other students' work when I cam and I hope you may find it useful to show others. As you can see from the cards, I was having difficulty learning the subtle differences between similar conditions and had to try to find a way of making the differences memorably obvious. Friends were horrified that I cut up my expensive textbooks but if I never took them off the shelf to read and could never understand the text, they were not a lot of use to me even if they were shiny and expensive.

Multisensory   Making revision multisensory can include discussing information with a friend, using a dictaphone, listening to music, drawings, visualising and highlighting or note making using different colour pens. They should be creative, but ensure that strategies are task specific: that is, appropriate for the information they are trying to learn. Being very creative and task specific is important.

Memory Aids   Memory aids include mind maps, cards, flow charts and pictures. Displaying these on walls and whiteboards in various places means that information is frequently reviewed. A combination of memory aids is the most effective. One student, when trying to learn all the names of the plants that she had covered in her horticultural course wrote the names and drew the pictures of all the hothouse plants and put them in her kitchen; the water plants were on the walls of her bathroom, and all the cool plants were on the walls of the sitting room. In the examination she could visualise herself in each room, locate the picture on the wall and therefore remember the name of the plant and the spelling. This type of revision strategy is very active, multisensory, extremely creative and can be recommended. Another student had wallpaper strips round her wall providing a time line chart for her history studies. Other students have mind maps on their walls, colour coded flash cards with symbols to identify the day the lecture was given. Having a visible timetable on the wall, and ticking off the days and the information covered can also be a good memory and confidence booster.

Compensations   Compensations can include studying a minimum number of subjects in depth as, when preparing for examinations, focusing on a few topics rather than trying to acquire a widespread knowledge can make it easier to recall specific material.

Compensation can also come from recoding material and listening to it whilst engaged in other activities. Talking can be a very powerful way of learning, so revising with a fellow student or students can facilitate understanding and, therefore, recall.

Accommodations   Accommodations involve having regard for the fact that dyslexic people can easily become overloaded and have difficulty with the automatic retrieval of information in an examination setting. Modular courses, where examinations cover a small number of topics and are frequent, can suit a dyslexic. Multiple choice tests place fewer demands on automatic recall, although these do present other difficulties. The timetabling of examinations can also reduce the demands on the dyslexic person. There should be no more than one each day and there should also be a good time spacing between examinations.

Examinations

There are many reasons as to why dyslexic people find examinations demanding. Even the basic problem of being unable to write quickly can undermine the higher level processes required for a student to reflect their knowledge and understanding (Connelly et al., 2005). Examination techniques should also be part of a revision package and, for the dyslexic student, as much practice as possible is essential. At university and on professional training programmes, the culmination of a course is often a set of examinations for which they have had no previous practice. All students have to deal with an element of the unknown. Younger students will have had the discipline of facing school examinations and will have had practice, but not at a more advanced level. Mature students will not have had this experience and examinations can be daunting.

> Now that I understand why I find it difficult to face the ritual of examinations, I have taken practical steps towards making examinations less demanding. For example, I have arranged with my college to use a word processor rather than handwriting examination papers; I now also take additional time to sit each paper. But more importantly than this, because I am gradually developing an understanding of dyslexia and the problems it causes me, I appreciate my own effort all the more when I achieve a respectable result in an examination.

Familiarisation with the place where the examination is to be held as well as double-checking the timing of the session and how long it takes to get there can reduce stress. It is imperative that all the accommodations for the examination are in place well beforehand.

Skill Development   A dyslexic person can find that examinations tap all their weaknesses in that they require the automatic retrieval and organisation of information at speed. It is important for the dyslexic person to know that examinations require different skills than those needed for completing an assignment. They rely heavily on the recall of what they know and the effective use of information. They may only need to recall four or five important facts, as this may be sufficient as long as it can be demonstrated why these facts are the central issues and they know how to apply them.

Time management is one of the keys to success in examinations and many students run out of time even though they have been allowed extra. Many find that extra time is best spent reading the questions carefully and planning answers at the beginning rather than too much proofreading at the end. It is advisable for students to have a watch on their table so that they can monitor the time passing. Some students find it extremely helpful to try and allocate marks within their questions. Being able to do this comes from practice using past papers. It is very important that the dyslexic student knows the format of each examination, the kinds of questions to be asked and the equipment they need. They should have as much practice with planning answers as possible. Some examination papers are made up of a variety of question types – combining short answer and long answer questions. Others also include multiple choice questions. Some are prepared questions and some are open book. All these factors should impact on the revision strategy as well as the examination strategy.

Preparing an action plan for how the time is going to be divided up can help, as can deciding on an order in which to answer the questions. Highlighting the key part of the question and the process words can be essential in making sure it is answered appropriately. Answers should always be planned to help the person stay on track and remember the point of the question. It can be encouraging to tick off the questions as they are completed.

> Thinking more constructively about my skills and abilities has helped me to understand why I struggled in my formal school examinations and why I find sitting examinations for my current

degree studies so demanding. Under the intense pressure of examination conditions my ability to recall information – which dyslexia impairs anyway – becomes disengaged to an even greater extent; this and my slow rate of writing lead to my becoming frustrated with the entire process.

Compensation   This involves developing alternative skills such as competence in word processing, and taking examinations verbally.

Accommodations   Accommodations in examinations involve making special arrangements for dyslexic candidates. These should be evidence based and this is discussed in Chapter 10. They can, however, include:

1. Allowing extra time to take into account a number of factors such as the reduction of stress, slow rates of reading and writing, difficulties with comprehension, and the need for planning and proofreading.
2. Increasingly multiple choice formats (MCQ) are used in academic and processional examinations. Some dyslexic people like them, but some hate them. A common problem is locating the correct place on a score sheet. This can easily be accommodated by allowing the marking of responses on the questions booklet. Further, some dyslexic people find computer-based MCQ tests difficult. They should be offered the option of a pencil and paper version.
3. Allowing the use of a word processor where this has become the main way in which a student communicates in writing, and there is a discrepancy between their verbal ability and their written expression.
4. Where students have significant problems with reading, examinations could be presented on tape, or the student could be provided with a reader.
5. When a student has handwriting difficulties but does not have sufficient competence to use technology, they could be allowed to write out their examination paper and then dictate it for transcription.
6. A combination of written and verbal examinations would allow dyslexic candidates who have difficulties with written expression to demonstrate their knowledge and competence.
7. Duplicate copies of examination papers, which enable students to see both sides of the paper at once, can be very helpful.
8. Examination papers can be produced in large print and, sometimes, different colours where there is a sensitivity to colour and background.

Statistics

Many people entering higher education or undergoing professional training are required to complete courses in statistics. Some dyslexic people find this very difficult, as they have a poor background in maths, and because their weak memory creates problems in areas such as sequencing and recalling concepts. They will be expected to operate at an abstract level and learn new terminology which they have to remember. Recalling the difference between 'quantitative' and 'qualitative' can for example be difficult. Issues of confidence in their mathematical ability arise.

Skill Development   The teaching of statistics needs to be as concrete as possible, using practical examples. It is important to tap understanding and reasoning, rather than automatic recall. In particular, when learning the language of statistics, terminology such as 'data', 'mean' and so on needs to be explained in a concrete way, and with a rationale.

Dyslexic people can also be taught very specific strategies for recalling the operations involved in statistics. It is a subject that can be made very visual by the use of graphs and tables. Mnemonics can help in remembering sequential patterns, as can memory techniques that rely on making connections.

Compensation   The most obvious compensation is to use a computer to perform statistical operations. Dyslexic people will, however, need to understand the concepts if they are going to perform the correct operation. Using a computer or calculator is not, therefore, cheating. A 'self-prepared' manual containing basic concepts, definitions and formula can be a useful aid.

Accommodations   The most effective accommodation is relying on a statistician when needing to analyse and interpret data. It is probable that most people for whom statistics is not a daily task need to rely on others or go back to books and manuals, whether they are dyslexic or not. Providing simple guides with very clear instructions regarding the procedures which should be used can help.

Many dyslexic students can understand statistics at a conceptual level but find it difficult to deal with tests and examinations. If the purpose is to demonstrate understanding so as to ensure that students are able to interpret research material correctly, setting a project or open book type examination in which they can refer back to sources and do not have to rely on memory would be appropriate.

Presentations

For some dyslexic people presentations are the best possible way of displaying their knowledge and their abilities, as they are better at talking than writing. Others consider it a nightmare as they have trouble with word finding. Presentation skills should be developed for a variety of reasons. They are often used as a method of assessment. They can be an exercise in developing communication or life skills, or the starting point for discussion of a subject at university. Increasingly they are used in the workplace as a way of reporting to colleagues.

Skill Development   It is important to know the aim of the presentation, whom the audience is and the duration. If it is longer than 15 minutes it is important to break it up to maintain the audience's attention. The general principle should be clarifying the main aspects of the topic, and not being too ambitious about what is covered. In some cases the presentation will be very formal and questions will be taken at the end. In others there will be interaction with the audience. Planning, structure and confidence are key elements.

The principles of making tasks manageable, memorable and multisensory are useful. How the dyslexic person presents the information is again a question of personal style – some people like overheads, some computer software and others prefer cue cards. Illustrations and diagrams often make the points clearer and serve as a memory aid.

Dyslexic people need to know that there are three elements in the process of verbal communication: the words you use, the way they are said and body language. It can be reassuring for dyslexic people to know that it is not just the words that have impact and that anyone can make a mistake. The way in which the information is delivered must be considered, variation in tone and speed of delivery being important. Many people speak too quickly when they are nervous, and this is when the use of visual aids can help.

The dyslexic needs to feel in control of the presentation and it can be a good idea to have a contingency plan if things start to go wrong. They may also need to explain, without using the word 'dyslexia', that they have trouble with words when they are in a nervous or stressful situation. One person, for example, used it as an advantage as he warned the audience it would help to keep them on their toes and make them listen carefully to what he had to say. It is important that they know that they are allowed to say 'I have lost my place' or 'Now where was I?' and that this occurs when others deliver presentations.

Compensation   Making a video or using a computer package such as PowerPoint reduces the load on memory. This can be easier than trying to keep overheads in order and on the projector at the right time. It enables the presenter to focus on talking.

Accommodation   This can include having a colleague or fellow student to operate the equipment or write on a flipchart, thus the burden on the presenter is reduced.

Working in a Group

Working in a group can be advantageous for dyslexic students, but can also present significant problems. Many dyslexic people prefer to work on their own because they lack confidence when working with others. They prefer to work according to their own routines and in their own way. Many university and training courses, however, now have 'a working in a group' component, partly because it helps develop the ability to work in a team. It is also thought to help build self-confidence. For a dyslexic person it can be difficult because it might reveal their weaknesses, and they can feel that they are letting the group down if they cannot perform at an expected level. It also places demands on their time in that they have to be at meetings punctually and complete work to deadlines.

Some dyslexic people can be sensitive as they find it hard to follow a fast moving conversation so they can be somewhat defensive. This can lead to difficult working relationships. It is important for the dyslexic person to know that working in a group or a team can be difficult for anyone and the problems they may be experiencing might be the same for others but exaggerated. If the team is really not working well, it is essential for them to seek outside help from a tutor, rather than allow the situation to deteriorate too far.

> These old demons are still there. Several nights ago at the university someone had written 'your' instead of 'you're'. Another person turned to me and asked me if the original spelling was wrong. My reply was no, probably because 'your' is very similar to 'you're'. Nothing came of this incident, no one, apart from me, probably remembers it, it lasted about two seconds. Yet, the anxiety upon leaving myself open to petty ridicule was there, worse, someone could question my intellectual capabilities. I felt my confidence waver slightly, and although it only lasted a split second it was noticeable to me. That said, I know 'what the score is': why these things happen. Moreover, my ever-growing self confidence means I don't feel any need to 'prove' how clever I am and such events are rare and brief: I soon realise what is happening and take control of my reactions.

Skill Development   Dyslexic people are likely to encounter misunderstanding, so they need to be able to explain their situation and offer solutions for any potential difficulties to avoid conflict. It is an area in which they can do well as they often generate creative and original ideas, solve difficult problems and present information very effectively. They need to be able to say what they are good at and avoid situations where they may display their weaknesses. They might, for example, suggest that someone else takes the minutes, if they deliver the presentation. On some courses, documentation needs to be kept for each meeting. Using a proforma outlining who is present and key areas to be discussed, with a summary of the points covered during the meeting, can be a useful strategy.

Compensation   This can include using a dictaphone as a way of recording proceedings.

Accommodation   This can include having someone take notes of the meeting, and the delegation of specific tasks generally, each person taking on specific roles.

Tutorials

The tutorial is a key part of university life for students. It is a chance to gather information, develop ideas, focus their thinking and gain confidence. Tutorials also enable students to keep on track with their course. For many dyslexic students they are not as effective as they should be, and the success of the dyslexic student is dependent to some extent on the tutorial support that they are given. Unless they have had personal experience many tutors are unlikely to understand dyslexia. Some students report that their tutor has been very good, enabling them to access the information they need while not doing the work for them. Others have suggested that their tutor has tried to control the situation to the extent that the student did not feel they had ownership of the work that was presented in the end. Some students also report that their tutors try hard but do not understand, and tend to make things more difficult. A dyslexic student's confidence can easily be undermined.

The Role of the Tutor

It can be difficult for tutors to know exactly how much help should be given. Why, for example, should they direct a dyslexic student to a greater extent than one who has financial worries or other concerns? What are the criteria for support? Should one student be given extra time to complete the work because they are dyslexic and another not, even though the latter has pressing family concerns and can only work late at night? These are difficult issues and the students need to acknowledge this. Organisational policies help outline procedures. The experience the tutor has of dealing with dyslexic students in the past is a significant factor.

It is often successful dyslexic students who are best at developing the understanding of tutors and lecturers. Some tutors have reported that working with dyslexic students has improved their own teaching and professional development. Equally, they have found some of the strategies dyslexic students use helpful for themselves (Scott & Gregg, 2000). Certainly, it enables the lecturer to suggest specific study skills that will be relevant to the discipline. As one student said:

> My tutor is great, he has so much knowledge on the subject as it really interests him, but what he can also do is give me the key points. I then go away and think about it, and return to him with new ideas. We have some great discussions and I then find I can write down the outcome easily.

Sheridan (cited in Scott & Gregg, 2000) has suggested that, if attention to dyslexic students leads to heightened consciousness of the importance of skilful teaching, then the presence of these students on campuses will have made a significant contribution to the improvement of higher education.

Skill Development   The skills a tutor needs to develop when working with dyslexic students are to increase their understanding and to recognise that each individual is affected in a different way. Dyslexia is an information processing difficulty and it is important for the tutor to know that this sometimes creates a problem with verbal as well as written information. Some students leave tutorials feeling as confused or as uninformed as they were when they went in, because they have been too frightened to ask for clarification for fear of seeming stupid. The tutor needs to ask specific questions and clarify that the student has interpreted what is being said in the way that it was meant. Dyslexic students need positive feedback on their performance. Mistakes can be important learning tools and constructive criticism enables them to see how to improve. When returning essays, it is helpful if tutors give clear recommendations and suggestions about content and style and, if possible, talk it through with the student. Similarly, reviewing examination scripts can also significantly improve performance as often students don't know or remember what they have done wrong and are likely to repeat errors. Tutors can also help provide key points of information in areas around which the student needs to work. It is also helpful if students are allowed to present a first draft to ensure that they are on track. Tutors do need to remember that the amount of time and effort that may have gone into a first draft can be considerable, and that even rewriting can take a dyslexic much longer than expected.

Compensations   The tutor could allow tutorials to be recorded, and provide a summary of the key points at the end of the session, as well as a written list of suggestions for work that could be covered ahead of time.

Accommodations   These involve being flexible over deadlines, seeing more drafts and plans of assignments, and being in closer contact with the student.

The Role of the Student

The skills the student needs to develop are an understanding of the parameters of the tutorial. It is important for the student to be prepared, to know what the tutorial is going to be about and to know how to ask the right questions. They need to know how to frame what they are asking for. They are more likely to get a positive response if they ask a question such as, 'I thought X's discussion was excellent. I wonder if you could direct me to somebody with another point of view so I can clarify my ideas?' Students need to ask if they can take a recorder to sessions so they can concentrate on listening and understanding the content. A summary, either at the end of the session or shortly afterwards, can help recall the material.

The Keys to Success

The factors influencing success can be summarised as:

- Students feeling in control of their learning and the information that they have to deal with.
- Having a range of strategies to enable them to overcome some of the difficulties that they face.
- Support from their family and their friends.
- A stable environment in which to live and work.
- Sympathetic tutors and friends on the course with whom they can exchange ideas and notes.
- The appropriate choice of course and options.
- Having an interest in the subject they are studying.
- Feeling comfortable in their environment.
- Persistence, determination and hard work.
- Being able to talk to other dyslexic students, to share experiences and exchange strategies.

The Responsibilities of Colleges and Universities

Support for dyslexic students has improved significantly in recent years but much still needs to be done. Disability legislation requires colleges and universities to provide for dyslexic students but there is also a need for the following:

- There should be more awareness training for academic and administrative staff. Both groups need to recognise that to access some of the compensations and accommodations at university dyslexic students have to deal with paperwork they can find difficult.
- Greater awareness and understanding amongst tutors and lecturers would improve the teaching/learning process. If universities are institutions that foster independent learning, then they should be able to accommodate the dyslexic students' needs.
- There should be more practical and departmental support in terms of accessing knowledge, specialist support directed towards developing literacy and learning skills, and counselling support to help the dyslexic person overcome some of the affective issues that affect their learning.
- More self-help groups would help the dyslexic student feel less isolated.

Some mature students undertake pre university courses prior to attending university and these can be very helpful in developing the skills needed to embark on a career in higher education. The difference between the level of support provided during such courses and that available at university level is sometimes considerable. There is a need for a carefully planned transition process, directed at independent learning. This could greatly relieve the stress on the dyslexic student and reduce the demands on the tutors at university.

Although dyslexic people need individual support that addresses their specific needs it can be helpful to work within a structure, and courses are sometimes successfully conducted with small groups. A suggested programme for a Study Skills Course is as follows.

Study Skills Course Outline

Individual Learning Plan of Skills Development Strategies for Students with Specific Learning Difficulties

Student name:	Tutor:
Student no.:	Start date:
Goals set	Goals achieved

Initial consultation – planning long-term and short-term goals
1. **Self-understanding** – understanding dyslexia and its effects on the individual development of metacognitive skills

2. **Self-advocacy** – explaining the difficulties, identifying problems, providing solutions and taking control
3. **Personal and critical thinking skills** – developing understanding of individual skills and abilities, thinking skills, and learning and working style to facilitate improved performance
4. **Organisation of time** – developing awareness of time, how to use it effectively, prioritising work and setting goals. **Organisation of work** – creating filing and record-keeping systems. **Organisation of self**-developing strategies to integrate study, work and personal life
5. **Task analysis and self-reflective thinking skills** – developing global and specific task analysis skills; practising goal setting, previewing, monitoring and reviewing skills to make them more automatic
6. **Memory skills** – developing understanding of memory and the individual's memory strategies; developing visual and auditory memory skills; exploring the principles of making things manageable and multisensory and making use of memory aids
7. **Efficient reading strategies** – developing effective strategic reading skills through scanning, skimming and main idea approaches; practising reading critically and analytically; improving decoding and word recognition
8. **Research skills** – using the Internet to find information keywords – literature review skills
9. **Writing skills** – developing understanding of specifics of the writing task and different academic writing styles; developing planning skills, question analysis skills, critical analysis skills and structure of an argument; writing a dissertation; using different reference systems
10. **Writing tools** – developing the use of academic language; developing grammar knowledge including parts of speech, phrases and clauses, sentence structure and paragraphing; developing knowledge of the purpose and principles of punctuation
11. **Note-making and note-taking** – exploring the purpose of making notes and practising different recording strategies, e.g. flow diagrams, mapping and linear techniques
12. **Strategies for success in examinations** – developing revision techniques including managing time, practising and over-learning; understanding what the examiner is looking for; enhancing performance on the day; rehearsal and visualisation strategies; practising for different examination formats: written examinations, presentations, practical assignments, interviews and vivas
13. **Communication skills** – developing effective listening skills, concentration, awareness of non-verbal communication, and appropriate responses in various contexts; exploring team-working, handling difficult situations and self-presentation skills
14. **Managing stress and coping with change** – developing awareness of sources of stress for the individual and exploring solutions for different contexts
15. **IT skills** – providing top-up training and over-learning on assistive software
16. **Skills and strategies for dealing with number** – developing effective critical analysis, memory and over-learning techniques for maths and statistics modules
17. **Presentation skills** – planning – and preparation. Coping with different styles – PowerPoint – speaking from notes, having confidence
18. **Other individual skills**
19. **Career choices** – the importance of the goodness of fit
20. **Challenges in the workplace** – being in control

A Dyslexic Person's Perspective

Moving On

At school you were stupid, a bit of a fool.
Hit round the head; admonished, quite cruel.
You could think of the big things, argue and call, but ask you to write it, no . . . not at all.
Your spelling creative; your writing was poor. So they heaped on the scolding, you would always take more.

They said you were lazy, to buck up and work.
With more concentration, you'd get a perk.
You're friends thought you odd; to mix was a trial.
To talk to your fancy, took a great while.

To avoid humiliation, you'd sought to fail.
You weren't lazy or stupid, you tried and how.
But no matter what effort, the way always barred.
Your classmates progressed, while you stayed behind.

So what was the matter, were they all blind?
You could do better; you knew that for sure.
But who would listen, who would be kind?
You went with your feelings, they told you at last.

Confirmed your suspicions, that you are not daft.
A bit of a problem, inconvenient, but at last.
Yes they can help you, to attain what you seek.
But you surge with great anger, confused with relief.

So how did they miss it, why weren't you briefed?
Self-pity, annoyance a natural response, to wallow and grumble . . . is that what you want?
But what ever has happened cannot be changed. Remember, but don't be swallowed in pain.

You can sit in a circle, cry and complain. Demand restitution, seek money . . . personal gain?
Or you can accept what has happened, go out . . . prove they were wrong.
The question my friend, is can you be strong?
Put it behind you, look forward, make your own perks.
You can prove to that teacher that you weren't a berk.

Sample Assessment Report

This report is in two sections:

- The first section is the assessment report that identifies abilities and difficulties and provides the evidence for recommendations for adjustments in assessment settings. This section is required by examination boards.
- The second section is for the individual. It makes recommendations for strategy development and outlines ways in which STU can work more effectively.

Section 1

Summary of diagnostic assessment
The Diagnostic Assessment report
Background information
The assessment results
Conclusions and recommendations for assessment settings
Results appendix

Section 2

Consultancy Report
Impact of dyslexia
Recommendations for
   1.   Skills and strategy training
   2.   Technological solutions

Summary

STU is a student at a London University. He is experiencing difficulties with his course, particularly with keeping up with his reading and getting his assignments in on time. The purpose of this assessment was to determine the reason for his difficulties and make recommendations if appropriate.

This assessment revealed that:

- STU is a person of considerable ability. His verbal reasoning skills are in the high average range and his non-verbal reasoning abilities are all above average.
- There is evidence that he has problems with phonological processing. This is impacting on his working memory and affecting his literacy skills, which are not commensurate with his other abilities.
- He has developed his skills to a competent level but continues to have difficulties with reading speed, spelling and written expression. This would have contributed to his poor performance, having difficulty with reading and producing assignments to deadlines.
- Therefore the findings from this assessment confirm that STU is dyslexic.

Recommendations

On the basis of this assessment it would be appropriate for STU to have the following adjustments made for him when he is being assessed:

- Extra time to compensate for his slower rates of reading, and to enable him to proofread his work.
- If possible, being in a quiet room so that he is not distracted by extraneous noise.
- Being able to use a computer for the written aspect of the assessment where he will have access to the spell checker.

Section 1

Assessment Report

STU

Introduction   STU is in his 2nd year of his degree course at a London university. He is finding the demands of his course work overwhelming. He sought help from the learning support department, who referred him for an assessment to establish the nature of his difficulties.

Background   STU found school hard and his education was quite disrupted, he had speech therapy for a period in primary school and he was in a special class which he found embarrassing as he felt he did not fit in there. When he was at secondary school he focused on more practical subjects, avoiding literacy-based work. He left school when he was 16 years old having gained modest GCSEs in English and Maths and went to college where he gained an HND in Business Studies and Computer Science. He then had a variety of retail jobs before going to university.

STU said that he is determined to do well. He enjoys dealing with people. He likes problem-solving, he can work well in a team, but also likes to work independently. His IT skills are good, although if he does not use programmes regularly he gets 'a bit rusty'.

His general health is good, and there is no family history of dyslexia.

Outline of present difficulties   STU said his main problem was taking a long time to read everything and complete written tasks. He felt he could manage his assignments as he knew what to do but he was so slow. He said that his spelling was erratic especially when under pressure; he preferred to use a computer. He did not read much for pleasure as he had to reread material in order to absorb the information. He got people to proofread his work if he was concerned. His memory was good if he did something frequently but he did forget some things; he had developed a 'memory trigger' strategy to help him. He sometimes found map reading confusing. His spoken language skills were generally good, although he occasionally misinterpreted words so would clarify information. STU said he was becoming better organised but had always had to work on his time management.

Test conditions   STU was quite comfortable in the assessment setting at this office and concentrated well on all the tasks.

Assessment

Underlying Ability

The Wide Range Intelligence Test was administered. This test comprises of four sub-tests: Verbal Analogies and Vocabulary, which assess verbal ability, and Matrices and Diamonds, which assess ability in visual (perceptual) reasoning.

On the verbal items STU's score for Vocabulary, the definition of a word that is presented orally, was good, being at the 73rd centile. His performance on Verbal Analogies, the provision of a word orally to complete a sentence, e.g. 'Cat is to kitten as Dog is to . . .' was also in the high average range, being at 70th centile. This test has a general knowledge element to it.

The non-verbal/visual test also has two sections, Matrices and Diamonds. STU's performance on Matrices (non-verbal problem solving) was above average at the 83rd centile. He found Diamonds (visual / spatial skills) even easier; his score was at the 84th centile.

These results indicated that STU has considerable abilities both in verbal and non-verbal domains.

Cognitive Processing

Memory Skills

STU's auditory memory skills were assessed using the Digit Span Test (Turner, 2006). His score overall was at the 23rd centile, and inconsistent with his other abilities. His performance was much stronger on digits forward. It was evident that he used some strategies to help him.

Phonological Processing

STU's phonological processing skills were explored using the Comprehensive Test of Phonological Processing (CTOPP). This test is only normed for adults up to the age of 24.11 years but it is a useful indicator as these skills underpin the literacy processes. Taking STU's age into account his performance was still well below what would be expected. His performance on the tests of phonological awareness was very low, indicating that he has significant trouble manipulating sounds in words. STU's performance on the phonological memory task was better, being within the average range. This test measures the ability to recall information from working memory. Again it was evident that he used a visualisation and chunking strategy to help. His performance on tests of rapid naming was slow. This test measures the labelling and retrieval of information from long-term memory.

On a test of coding (Digit Symbol Modality) STU's performance was at the average level. This measures the efficient integration of verbal and perceptual and fine motor processes.

The Test of Word Reading Efficiency (TOWRE) was administered. This test measures the ability to recognise familiar words and the ability to sound out words quickly and accurately. Again this test is only normed for adults up to the age of 24.11 years but it is a useful indicator of underlying skills. STU's performance was accurate on the sight word sub-test, indicating that he has a good sight vocabulary. His performance on the phonemic decoding efficiency sub-test was much weaker. These results are consistent with the CTOPP scores and confirm that STU has a problem with phonological processing and he is likely to find decoding unfamiliar words hard.

Attainments in Literacy

Reading

STU's performance on the Wide Range Achievement single word reading test was at the 32nd centile, which is consistent with his performance on the earlier tests. His reading comprehension skills were assessed using the Spadafore Diagnostic Reading Test. He read quite fluently and accurately at the professional level (the highest level of reading) and indicated that he makes good use of context. On a test of silent reading comprehension STU scored at the professional level, reading slowly at a speed of 180 words per minute. He could answer 75% of the comprehension questions. His listening comprehension skills were good but he did need to clarify fine detail at times.

Writing and Spelling

STU was asked to write on a subject that was work related; he produced a short paragraph on working in a team. He wrote somewhat untidily at 17 words per minute. His sentence structure and punctuation was competent. However on a test of copying STU wrote quickly and more legibly at 26 words a minute. The difference between the two tasks are significant in that it demonstrates that when STU has to think about what he is writing he is slower at processing than would be expected. This is consistent with his performance on the rapid naming and the phonological awareness tasks.

STU's spelling skills were assessed using the Wide Range Achievement Test; his performance was at the 27th centile. He did not attempt to spell words he had not encountered before and most of his spelling errors were minimal and would be rectified by the use of a spellchecker.

Conclusion

This assessment confirms that STU is dyslexic. It reveals that he has good cognitive abilities, his non-verbal reasoning is particularly good; however he has a specific difficulty with phonological awareness and rapid naming. This is impacting on his literacy skills which are not commensurate with his other abilities. He has worked hard but continues to have considerable difficulty with reading speed, spelling and written expression.

STU is likely to be a big picture and strategic thinker and his performance in this assessment is consistent with him being good at logical problem solving. He may take longer to achieve things and this is a reflection of his different way of processing. He does need to develop some skills and strategies, but he has the abilities which would enable him to be successful.

Recommendations

On the basis of this assessment it would be appropriate for STU to have the following adjustments made for him in assessment settings:

- 25% extra time to compensate for his slow rates of reading.
- If possible, being in a quiet room so that he is not distracted by extraneous noise.
- Being able to use a computer for the written aspect of the assessment where he will have access to the spell checker.

Recommendations for further skill development are in the attached report.

Section 2

Consultancy Report

STU

Summary of Assessment   This assessment revealed that STU has good thinking abilities; his non-verbal reasoning is particularly good. However STU has problems with processing information in working memory; his phonological processing skills are weak and this is affecting his written language skills, therefore this assessment confirms STU is dyslexic.

Dyslexia is best recognised as an information processing difficulty; each dyslexic individual has their own pattern of skills and abilities. The cognitive difference can lead to difficulties with organisation, literacy, numeracy and some memory tasks. However these can be overcome with skill and strategy development, then dyslexic people are able to demonstrate their often considerable strengths and work at a high level. Dyslexia is hidden in nature and this can cause problems with confidence and misunderstanding; it is important that the individual knows how it affects them so they can ask for what will help them to work well.

Recommendations

STU would benefit from study skills support focusing on the areas outlined below.

Skill Development

Personal Skills

STU is aware about the way he works but he does not always know why he does things in certain ways. He places a lot of pressure on himself to perform well and he does not like to make mistakes. Therefore he would benefit from:

- Developing his understanding of dyslexia and its impact to increase his confidence.
- Increasing his awareness of skills and abilities, and how he learns and works best so that he can better advocate for what he needs to help him work effectively.

Memory Strategies

STU should take a multisensory approach to learning; he should also try and use a strategy that matches the task. It will help him to:

- Chunk or group information to make it more manageable.
- Use a colour code and symbols to organise and recall information.
- Use concept diagrams or mind maps.
- Have a note book to jot down key words, phrases and mnemonics.
- Preview information before lectures, as this will make a significant difference in his ability to take in and recall the information.
- Use revision techniques.

Planning and Organisation

STU likes to be organised but he would benefit from refining these skills to meet the present demands by:

- Developing routines and flexible structures.
- Spending a few minutes each day organising work, prioritising and estimating how long tasks may take.
- Deliberately using previewing, planning and reviewing skills to monitor his performance.
- Setting personal specific and achievable goals and reviewing the outcomes positively, which should help STU with concentration and confidence.

Literacy Skills

Reading

STU reads slowly therefore he would benefit from:

- Developing speed comprehension strategies which would enable him to retain information from text more easily, e.g. scanning and skimming techniques. This would give him an overview of what the text is about and would help him decode unfamiliar words. It would also enable him to predict what is coming, and help process the information.

- Monitoring his reading comprehension and check that he has not misread words, particularly with new and unfamiliar material.
- Working for short, focused periods when reading and making brief notes, which should help to anchor information.
- Critical reading techniques for his dissertation.
- Strategies for answering MCs, and for his examinations.

Written Work

STU finds producing and proofreading reports and case papers time consuming. He should:

- Develop his question analysis strategies for assignments.
- Explore strategies such as using Post-it notes as markers and checklists to help him collate all the information more easily.
- Develop planning strategies and use a structure when producing assignments.
- Develop his proofreading strategies. He should take a step by step approach and carry out his own error analysis.

Spelling

STU has a good sight vocabulary; however, he may benefit from utilising some strategies which would help him learn the words he most commonly uses. Visual analysis, syllabification and knowledge of prefixes and suffixes may help him.

Technological Aids

STU is keen on IT and he should keep up to date on developments that may help him as many free applications are now available on-line. However, the technology that would provide STU with immediate and long-term solutions for his course includes the following:

- STU may find using software packages such as **Texthelp Read and Write** very useful. It is a self learning package which helps with spelling and vocabulary, and would enable him to proofread his work more effectively.
- STU has used concept mapping software, such as **Inspiration, or Mind Manager** in the past and it will be useful for him now as it would enable him to link information and remember it better. It may also help him plan his written work.
- Because his spoken language is good, STU may find using **voice-recognition** the best way to produce written work. He can experiment with this if he has an iPhone as **Dragon Dictation** is a downloadable app.
- A dictaphone and/or a **live scribe** pen may help him in lectures and to make personal memos.

Recommendations for Adjustments in Assessment Settings

On the basis of this assessment it would be appropriate for STU to have the following adjustments made for him in assessment settings:

- Extra time to compensate for his slower rates of reading and to enable him to proofread his work.
- If possible, being in a quiet room so that he is not distracted by extraneous noise.
- Use of a laptop so that he can spell check his work.

The appendix contains the detailed tests results and an outline and references of tests used (not included here).

I would be happy to discuss the contents of this report.

Assessment Results – Page Format

Name: STU Date of birth:	Date seen:

General Cognitive Ability
Wide range Intelligence Test (General IQ)
Verbal

Verbal Analogy	Standard Score	Centile
Vocabulary	Standard Score	Centile

Non-verbal

Matrices	Standard Score	Centile
Diamonds	Standard Score	Centile

Tests of Memory

Memory for Digits (Turner)	Comp score	Centile
Symbol Digit Modalities Test	average	

Comprehensive Test of Phonological Processing

Phonological Awareness	Comp score	Centile
Phonological Memory	Comp score	Centile
Rapid Naming	Comp score	Centile
Rapid Object Naming		Centile

Test of Word Reading Efficiency (TOWRE) Form A

Sight word efficiency	Standard Score	Centile
Phonemic Decoding efficiency	Standard Score	Centile

Attainments in Literacy

Reading

Single word recognition (WRAT4, Green)	Standard Score	Centile
Spadafore Diagnostic Reading Test		
Prose reading accuracy		Level

Comprehension (Silent reading)		Level
Reading speed (Silent reading)		Words per min
Listening Comprehension		Level
Spelling (WRAT 4 Spelling Test, green)	Standard Score	Centile

Writing

Rate of Writing:	Free writing	Words per min
	Copying	Words per min
	Legibility	
Content		Satisfactory
Grammar and sentence structure		
Punctuation		

List of published tests used in assessment

Glutting, J., Adams, W. & Shaslow, D. (2000). *Wide Range Intelligence Test (WRIT)*. Detroit: Wide Range Inc.

Smith, A. (2002). 9th edition, *Symbol Digit Modalities Test*. Los Angeles, California: Western Psychological Services.

Spadafore, G.D. (1983). *Spadafore Diagnostic Reading Test*. Novato, California: Academic Therapy Publications.

Torgesen, J., Wagner, R. & Rashotte, C. (1999). *Test of Word Reading Efficiency* (TOWRE). Texas: Pro-Ed.

Wagner, R., Torgesen, J. & Rashotte, C. (1999). *Comprehensive Test of Phonological Processing* (CTOPP). Texas: Pro-Ed.

Wilkinson, G.S. (2006). *Wide Range Achievement Test (WRAT) 4*. Lutz, Florida: Psychological Assessment Resources Inc.

Appendix 1 – Extended reporting of WRIT scores

	Sum of scores	Underlying ability	Percentile	95% confidence interval
Verbal (crystallised)				
Visual (fluid)				

Summary

1. Higher and professional education presents dyslexic people with considerable challenges. Moving on to these levels of education and training represents a significant transition.

2. Successful adaptation at this level is heavily reliant on the development of a dyslexic person's metacognitive skills, as these enhance executive functioning.

3. The specific skills which should be addressed include reading and listening comprehension techniques, essay writing strategies, note taking, proofreading, as well as organisation.
4. At this level technology has a great deal to offer in terms of compensation.
5. Institutions, tutors and trainers can make reasonable and sensible adjustments that allow those undertaking courses of higher and professional education to show themselves at their best.

8

Career Development and Guidance

Synopsis. *This chapter describes the issues involved in providing career counselling for dyslexic people, as well as their continued career development. A decision-making model of career guidance is outlined.*

Introduction

Assisting with career development and the provision of suitable career counselling and guidance can be among the most important areas of professional work, but is the least resourced. Appropriate career guidance at school, as well as ongoing career counselling and development, especially at times of transition, are among the professional activities which can assist a dyslexic person to find their niche and achieve 'goodness of fit'.

> I was diagnosed last year just after turning 40 – so I have quite a lot of work to do in order to understand how this 'learning difference' has affected me throughout my life. For how much I have always loved and enjoyed reading and writing, I have mostly done it for pleasure and not in a 'structured' way, as I didn't apply to university after my A-levels – my excuse then was that I couldn't have afford it financially (student loans never existed in my country), but I can all too well recall the fear of failure that always accompanied me throughout my studies. Having said this, for most of my studies I was doing really well in all subjects – at least before some wrongly chosen A-levels left me struggling to cope, and giving up on the challenge of taking up a more suitable course of studies.

Peel (1992) suggests that the most useful definition of 'career' is the broadest and cites the *Shorter Oxford Dictionary* as defining 'career' as 'a person's course or progress through life'. He intends this to include paid and voluntary employment, both full and part-time, self-employment, domestic roles and periods out of paid employment.

The Dyslexic Adult: Interventions and Outcomes – An Evidence-based Approach, Second Edition.
David McLoughlin and Carol Leather.
© 2013 John Wiley & Sons, Ltd. Published 2013 by John Wiley & Sons, Ltd.

Approaches to Counselling and Development

There are essentially two views of career, the organisational and the individual, (McCormick & Ilgen, 1985). The former considers careers within the context of organisations whilst the latter considers the nature of the people involved for an explanation of career events. Although there are competing views, a common theme which runs throughout much career development is that, although the process of career development is similar for all students, many issues are unique to the individual, especially those with disabilities (Wehman, 1996). The view taken here therefore is that career development and counselling should be individualised to meet the unique needs of dyslexic people.

The individual view draws on the developmental changes that are part of the continual process of maturing and ageing. Maturation is usually broken down into stages, identified by dominant behaviour present at those periods in one's life. Levinson (1986, 1996) exemplifies the individual orientation towards careers. According to his theory, all of us mature and develop whilst passing through a sequence of eras, each lasting about 20 to 25 years. In particular, there are four significant eras or stages in each of our lives:

1. Pre-adulthood: age 0–22
2. Early adulthood: age 17–45
3. Middle adulthood: age 40–60
4. Late adulthood: age 60+

These should probably be revised to encompass the notion of emerging adulthood, but within the early adulthood stage Levinson included three sub-phases:

1. Entering the adult world.
2. Age 30 transition.
3. Settling down.

In the first the individual is faced with some major transitions. They begin by shifting from the role of a child in a family to becoming a 'novice adult', with responsibility for his or her own life. One of the major decisions with long-term implications at this time revolves round the choice of a career. Levenson argues that at this time it is necessary for the person to be able to explore alternatives which may be open to them and to try out some of the possible roles to see 'how they fit'. During the moves from one stage to another the transitions become important. These are major changes from what was done in the past and can take three to six years to complete. A major theme is the existence of the dream or vision of life's goals (Upton, 2011).

Being dyslexic has made me work very hard academically and it has also made me quite competitive. After leaving School with no qualifications, I was determined to prove myself and to others that I could succeed. I now have three Masters Degrees, two of which have a Merit grade and one with a Distinction, a PGCE teaching qualification and I am now also considering undertaking a Doctorate in Education. Dyslexia has also shaped the direction of my career. For instance, whilst working as a Lecturer in Film and Media, I discovered that my key strengths, talents and abilities lay in providing advice, support and guidance to the students on my course who were either struggling with their work, or who were identified as being dyslexic.

In addressing the issue of career development and transitions for people with learning difficulties, Wehman (1996) lists several key aspects of career development that need to be considered. These include:

1. Career development is a process that begins at birth and should continue throughout life.
2. Early career development is essential for making satisfactory choices later.
3. Significant gaps or periods of neglect in any area of basic human development can affect career development and the transition from one stage of life to another.
4. Career development is responsive to intervention and programming when the latter involves direct instructions for individual needs.

The first two of these in particular address the importance of adequate career counselling at school and college. There are various theories of career choice but Yost and Corbishley (1987) argued that, although there are contradictions between them, there are central themes which have implications for career counselling. These include the assumption that people make career decisions out of the context of a life-time of experiences; that people have strong expectations of work and, therefore, the exploration of intra-personal satisfaction they expect or derive from work is important; there is a need for skills specific to job selection, acquisition and retention which need to be assessed or taught; there are personal, social and environmental factors which need to be explored as these can be a barrier to deciding on or pursuing a particular career. On this basis and in the absence of a comprehensive career theory, they take a pragmatic view and argue for a decision-making model which acknowledges the influence of the central themes of the various theories. A decision-making model, they argue, has the advantages of focusing on the established core of career choice – that is, the centrality of decision making. It also has considerable face validity for clients and allows a good deal of flexibility. Their model, adapted for use with dyslexic people, is outlined below.

Career Guidance: A Decision Making Model

1. *Initial assessment*, the aim of which is to gather personal and employment information about the client and to arrive, in collaboration with them, at a feasible career counselling goal the client is motivated to pursue.

It is important to make dyslexic people aware of the difficulties that might arise and provide advice on how they might overcome these. Further, it is important to make them aware of the possibility of their dyslexia adding to normal occupational stress and fatigue. The teenager who wanted to become an air traffic controller, for example, need not have been dissuaded from pursuing this occupation despite the fact that she still had trouble with sequential tasks and with labelling, including naming right and left correctly. She could have used strategies to overcome such difficulties; however, it was pointed out that she would be putting more pressure on herself in an already stressful occupation, as some of the skills required would never come to her automatically.

It is also important that dyslexic people do not fall for stereotypes such as assuming that being dyslexic they will have good spatial abilities and should therefore enter into artistic endeavours or work with computers. In a study of high school students, Hearne et al. (1988) found that learning disabled students were no worse or better than their non-disabled peers in terms of an aptitude for working with computers.

2. *Self-understanding.* The client explores his or her values, interests, experience and abilities that relate to the present goal. In addition, assessment is made of psychological issues that may affect career counselling.

3. *Making sense of self-understanding data.* The information gathered in the previous stage is synthesised into a coherent set of statements which indicate the client's desired outcomes for a career choice. These will be used as a reference point in future stages. Personal and environmental barriers to success in pursuing the desired career are summarised.

4. *Generating alternatives.* Using the information acquired thus far, counsellor and client develop a list of possible career alternatives without making any judgement about the value of the options.

5. *Obtaining occupational information.* Learning as much about each option as is necessary to make an informed choice. The list of options is narrowed.

6. *Making the choice.* The client makes a choice among options – any psychological problems which arise should be dealt with at this stage.

7. *Making plans to reach the career choice goal.* Contingency plans are worked out to handle any setbacks which might arise.

8. *Implementing plans.* The client takes whatever action is necessary to achieve the selected career goal. This could include further training or education, learning how to present oneself on paper and in person to prospective employers and conducting a job search.

Career Guidance and the Dyslexic: A Model

Provided they have the necessary competencies, talents and abilities dyslexic people should not be excluded from particular occupations as they can develop strategies for dealing with literacy and memory tasks, as well as with organisation. Developing a list of unsuitable occupations similar to that which is prepared for people who are colour-blind would not be helpful.

1. Initial interview   The aim of this is to gather personal and employment information about the client. This should include the usual information about aptitudes and abilities. Careful thought should be given to the question of aptitude and ability testing. Pencil and paper and/or timed tests can be unsuitable as they often provide more information about the clients' dyslexia than they do about their abilities. Reid (1999) has, however, reported some success using the Morrisby Test with dyslexic adolescents, particularly in boosting confidence in their abilities. Being diagnosed as dyslexic will have involved an assessment process, including the administration of a comprehensive a wide-ranging intelligence test such as the Wechsler Scale. Further testing can therefore be redundant, particularly if the information from the assessment is interpreted correctly. A high verbal score would suggest that someone might do well in a job requiring good language skills. A high non-verbal score predicts that someone might be suited to a more practical role. In fact many of the abilities measured during the course of a diagnostic assessment have been shown to correlate with employment success including general intellectual functioning, memory and executive functions (Kalechstein et al., 2003).

Holland's Self-Directed Search is untimed and provides a self-rating with regard to interests, competencies and abilities which can be useful here. There is a FORM E which takes into account reading levels. Holland's theory of vocational education and planning emphasises the match between characteristics of the person and those of the environment. It is based on the assumption that we gravitate towards academic subjects and occupations we think we will find attractive and think we will succeed in (Holland, 1973, 1985). The Self-Directed Search was developed to assist individuals and counsellors to assess characteristics and provide information for improving career decisions.

Holland's theory assumes that most people can be classified into six general types which reflect their orientation towards careers and these are shown in Table 8.1. It should be remembered that, as with any labelling system, there is considerable variance. The types or categories only give a general impression, the exact mix varying from person to person. The specific descriptions within a category are not precise either; they are just meant to provide a general impression of the types of traits that make up the category. Holland's theory also assumes that some types of job environment match these person types. Given these two conditions, people and jobs, the final assumption is that people search their environment for jobs that allow them to use their skills and abilities, to express their attitudes and values and to perform work roles that agree with their general orientation towards work and people at work. Factor analytic studies have provided support for this theoretical model (Rachman et al., 1981).

Completion of the Self-Directed Search using FORM E leads to a two-letter code or summary score being provided. This combines the types and can be checked against a list of suitable occupations. The summary scores have been shown to correlate with self-efficacy expectations: that is, an individual's belief in their ability to successfully engage in specific work related tasks or activities (Feehan & Johnston, 1999).

Table 8.1   Holland's Classification of Person and Environment Characteristics

Type	Person characteristics	Environment characteristics
Realistic	Aggressive Mechanically orientated Practical minded Physically strong Conventionally masculine Acts out problems Avoids interpersonal tasks Prefers concrete to abstract tasks	Requires explicit, concrete, physical tasks Outdoors Needs immediate behaviour Needs immediate reinforcement Makes low interpersonal demands
Investigative	Thinks through problems Scientifically inclined Inventive Precise Achieving Shy Radical	Requires thought and creativity Task-idea orientated Makes minimum social demands Requires laboratory equipment but not high physical demands

Artistic	Original
	Asocial
	Dislikes structure
	More conventionally feminine
	Emotional
		Interprets and modifies human
		  behaviour
		Has ambiguous standards of excellence
		Requires intense involvement for long
		  periods of time
		Works in isolation

Social	Responsible
	Humanistic
	Accepting of conventionally
	  feminine impulses
	Interpersonally skilled
	Avoids intellectual problem solving
		Interprets as well as modifies human
		  behaviour
		Requires high communications
		Helps others
		Emphasises prestige
		Delays reinforcement

Enterprising	Verbally skilled Power and status oriented	Needs verbal responses Fulfils supervisory roles Needs persuasion Needs management behaviours
Conventional	Prefers structure High self-control Strong identification with power and status	Systematic, routine Concrete Makes minimal physical demands Indoors Makes low interpersonal demands

(Adapted from: McCormick & Ilgen, 1985).

Dyslexic people use the Self-Directed Search sensibly and answer it honestly. There are of course risks, mainly based on assumptions people might make about themselves. These include:

i.   The publicity given to gifted dyslexics, particularly those with very strong visual creative abilities, can result in dyslexic people agreeing with all items relating to abilities and career choices in those areas when this is unrealistic. Research has also suggested that dyslexic individuals can be attracted to people-orientated professions (Taylor & Walker, 2003). That is, there is a risk that they might adopt a 'should' rather than 'can' approach.

ii. Many dyslexic people underestimate their ability and can therefore be reluctant to check items for which they assume they would need more ability and competence than they have.

iii. The damage done to the self-esteem of some dyslexic people means that they will be 'trying to prove something' and only check items which lead them to making choices which are entirely unrealistic.

The use of the Self-Directed Search for people with learning difficulties has been systematically researched. Having considered this, Taymans (1991) makes the following recommendations:

1. One to one administration of the test is recommended. This has the advantage of enabling the test taker to ask questions about reading and understanding words which might be unfamiliar.
2. It is helpful to develop demonstration and practice items so that it can be ensured that the format and types of questions to be answered are understood.
3. A list of alternative words or phrases to help explain unclear items can be developed.
4. The administrator of the test should keep a record of any specific problems the test taker seemed to encounter.
5. Scoring should be undertaken by the administrator of the test with the client participating to verify agreement of scores and personal interests.
6. The Self-Directed Search is available in pencil and paper, personal computer and Internet formats. Whilst it might be easier to make adaptations for dyslexic people using the pencil and paper version, the three formats have been shown to be equivalent in terms of the scores achieved (Lumsden et al., 2004).

Helping dyslexics to identify their abilities and understand their inefficiencies seems to be an important part of vocational guidance work when dealing with those leaving school and for the career counsellor working with those who have reached a critical point in their working life. Buchanan and Wolf (1986) found evidence of the lack of ability to assess their own strengths and weaknesses amongst students with learning disabilities.

2. Self-understanding   The client explores his or her values, interests, experience and abilities that relate to the present goal. In addition, assessment is made of psychological issues that may affect career counselling. One important issue is personality and this is sometimes evaluated, both within organisations and by career counsellors, using the Myers–Briggs Type Indicator (Myers & McCaulley, 1985). Again this is based on type theory, Myers proposing 16 psychological types, each described in terms of four preferences. The concept of preference is important to the theory and in administering and interpreting the MBTI. Preference means 'feeling most comfortable and natural with'. The MBTI is designed to measure preferences rather than abilities, skills, or how well developed the preferences are. It is essentially a categorising measure, the scores achieved indicating the degree of confidence in the chosen preference, not the degree of development.

The type theory suggests four pairs of preferences:

Extraversion (E) and Introversion (I); Sensing (S) and Intuition (N); Thinking (T) and Feeling (F); and Judging (J) and Perceiving (P). 'E', 'I', 'J' and 'P' are called attitudes; 'S', 'N', 'T' and 'F' are called functions. A person's type is described in four letters, one from each pair of preferences.

Myers' theory assumes there is a 'true type' and people develop this 'normally' over a period of time. 'False type' development can result when there has been interference with normal development of true preferences. An example of someone who has developed a false type would be a person whose ideal self-concept includes a preference for thinking but neglects their true preference for feeling. According to type theory, such a person would be 'acting out of character'.

The general motives associated with each dominant function are shown in Table 8.2.

In terms of personality assessment, however, it might not be necessary to administer tests. As mentioned in Chapter 2, persistence and determination have been shown to be important factors in determining success. This will have been manifested during their academic and work careers. It can also be important to assess the extent to which their experiences at school and perhaps at work have affected confidence and self-esteem.

Assessing the extent to which dyslexia is still affecting literacy, memory and executive functioning is especially important. Persisting problems with literacy do of course make a difference. Even residual difficulties such as slow reading and writing would make some occupations onerous. Abilities such as verbal fluency would also be relevant as strengths in this area might compensate for weaker written language skills.

Table 8.2 Myers–Briggs Personality Types

Introverted Sensing (IS)	To work quietly and systematically on something practical or tangible
Extraverted Sensing (ES)	To work with machines or objects in an easygoing, sociable setting
Introverted Intuition (IN)	To develop new theories and ideas
Extraverted Intuition (EN)	To change the environment/situation
Introverted Thinking (IT)	To analyse and understand ideas
Extraverted Thinking (ET)	To organise and criticise the environment/situation
Introverted Feeling (IF)	To work quietly and individually on something which is highly valued
Extraverted Feeling (EF)	To help others

In helping people explore their values, interests, experience and abilities that relate to their goal, considering the extent to which they understand dyslexia and how it affects them would seem to be particularly important. Denial of their weaknesses or failure to recognise possible problems they might face could prevent them from achieving their goals.

Disclosure research shows that dyslexic adults sometimes deny that they have problems with literacy and learning. They perceive it as a school matter and now that they are leaving an academic environment they think it will no longer be a problem. Further, they have a realistic concern that people will focus on their weaknesses rather than what they can do. The importance of self-understanding has been a recurrent theme throughout this book. Many dyslexic people have been given a label but have never had a reason as to why they find certain tasks difficult. The following conversation is not uncommon:

Question: 'What does being dyslexic mean?'
Answer: 'That you have trouble with spelling'.

Question: 'Why do you have trouble with spelling?'
Answer: 'Because I am dyslexic'.

It is important that they understand why tasks are difficult if they are to make sensible career choices, as well as plan for transitions.

3. Making sense of self-understanding data   The information gathered is summarised into statements or goals which can be used as a reference point. For a dyslexic person, summarising the obstacles their dyslexia might present in pursuing their desired career, and the skills, compensations and accommodations they might need, would seem to be particularly important. At this stage a 'skills audit' in mind map or spreadsheet format can be helpful in identifying skills, abilities, interests and hobbies. This can address questions such as:

- What skills does the job require?
- What skills do I have?
- Where might the gaps be?
- How can I develop new skills?

4. Generating alternatives   Using the information acquired thus far, counsellor and client develop a list of possible career alternatives without making any judgement about the value of the options. This should not differ greatly to when working with non-dyslexics, but the options should be realistically based on the information provided from the previous stages.

5. Obtaining occupational information   Career-related knowledge has been identified as a factor in successful employment outcomes (Mathis, 2009). This involves learning as much about each option as is possible and narrowing the list of options. Again, for the dyslexic, considering the limits the syndrome might place on the client is important. The question 'What aspects of the job might make it unsuitable for me?' is particularly important. At the same time they should consider whether they have any transferable skills that might address these. Other issues at this stage might be the route to qualification for an occupation. In the United Kingdom, for example, a series of vocational qualifications or an apprenticeship would be an easier and more relevant pathway to a career than completing examinations at Grade 12. The extent to which allowances will be made for their dyslexia on particular courses of study or training is an important issue, as is the matter of how they will be evaluated. Many find that course work assessment suits them better than examinations.

Vocational guidance counsellors working with dyslexics might find themselves needing to encourage their clients to pursue courses of training for occupations they had ruled out because of their difficulties. Plata and Bone (1989) studied the way in which disabled adolescents viewed the importance of particular occupations. They found that students in their sample perceived skilled, semi-skilled and unskilled occupations as being more important than managerial and professional occupations, despite the fact that some were of well above average intelligence. It might therefore be that school experiences of some lead them to underestimate their capabilities and potential.

6. Making a choice   The client makes a choice amongst options based on all the above information. This is no different from the situation faced by non-dyslexic people, although they might have to consider alternative routes to the achievement of a goal.

7. Making plans   The purpose at this stage is to make plans to reach the career choice goal. Where the choice might be affected by the outcome of school or examination results contingency plans should be worked out. Alternative routes to the same career paths should be considered. A series of vocational qualifications might, for example, allow entry to a higher level qualification. This can also allow time to build up the skills necessary for studying and living independently.

8. Implementing plans   The client takes whatever action is necessary to achieve the selected career goal. This can involve:

i.   Pursuing further or higher education, or a course of vocational training.
ii. Developing the literacy and learning skills required for a course of training or a particular job. Gaining related work experience.
iii. Developing memory and organisational skills.
iv. Developing the use of compensations, including technology.
v.   Preparing a curriculum vitae, preferably with advice.
vi. Practising filling in application forms as it is often a requirement that these be prepared by hand. Typed applications are better than handwritten ones but if an employer insists that they should be completed in one's own handwriting, it could

be an important indicator that it is not going to be easy to achieve 'goodness of fit'. That is, an employer who insists on handwritten applications could be fussy about neatness, and if this does not come naturally, the dyslexic person will not fit in. They could of course insist on typing the application and add a note saying they are dyslexic.

vii.　As we have written elsewhere in this book dyslexic people need to consider the issue of 'disclosure' carefully, but it is worth reiterating here. It is a personal matter and there is no easy answer. They must, however, consider it so they can become clear in their own mind as how they might deal with it when it arises. If it is likely to become obvious immediately, disclosure is perhaps best. It is particularly important that dyslexic people focus on what they can do and what they need. This could include:

> You should know that I am dyslexic which means than I am inclined to be very thorough in the way I read and sometimes take more time.
>
> I am dyslexic, my reading is fine but I still have some trouble with spelling. Would it be OK to use my laptop computer at work?
>
> I am dyslexic but have sorted out my reading, writing and spelling, but sometimes can't see mistakes I make. Is there somebody who would be able to proof read my work for me?

That is, they should say that they are dyslexic but tell people how it affects them and what they need to do about it.

Hoffman et al. (1987) found that filling in application forms, as well as knowing where to find a job and how to get training, were major problems. One client sought help because preparing her application was proving difficult, despite the fact that she had a degree in Fine Art and a postgraduate diploma.

At stage 8 it can be useful to prepare a written action plan such as that shown in Table 8.3.

Table 8.3　Action Plan

Action Plan
1. My goal is:
2. My action steps are:
3. Number the action steps in a logical sequence.
4. Write down your plan:
– Over the next week I will
– Over the next month I will . . . .
– Over the next 3 months I will . . . .
– Over the next 6 months I will . . . .
5. Decide when you will review progress
My review date will be . . . .

(Adapted from Nathan & Hill, 1992).

Case Example

F.	27 years of age
Occupation:	Chef – holding Vocational Qualifications. He had worked in the Catering Industry since leaving school.

1. **Initial Assessment**

   Although F. was still interested in catering work and was competent he was feeling bored and could not see a future for himself while continuing to work as a chef.

   F. was also in the Territorial Army where he had gained Non-Commissioned Officer status. He enjoyed the structure and routine, as well as having a supervisory role.

2. **Self-Understanding**

   F. had been diagnosed as being dyslexic. Assessment showed him to be of above average intelligence but to have poor auditory memory.

   F's reading skills were at the professional level, but he read slowly and had difficulty with comprehension. His writing and spelling skills were limited.

   Although in many ways a confident young man, F. did have poor self-esteem with regard to his academic ability.

   Completion of the Self Directed Search suggested that he was an 'S.E' type person, S meaning social and E enterprising. This is consistent with him working in the Hotel and Catering Industry.

3. **Making Sense of Self-Assessment**

   On the positive side F. had good general ability as well as good practical skills. He had a knowledge of the catering industry and some experience of supervision through his work in the Army.

   On the negative side F. had low self-esteem regarding academic matters, as well as problems with literacy.

4. **Listing Alternatives**

   One of the main alternatives seemed to be in Hotel/Recreation Management.

5. **Occupational Information**

   Hotel and Catering Management courses were available at Further and Higher. Education level.

6. **Making a choice**

   F. decided that he would like to pursue a Hotel and Recreation Management course so that he could remain within the catering industry, but move up to management level.

7. **Making Plans**

   The timing of the interview was such that F. would not be able to begin a course immediately but he did agree to make enquiries about suitable ones. He thought that a Further Education programme might be preferable to Higher Education as this was more likely to be course work assessed.

8. **Implementing Plans**

F. formulated the following action plan.

Action Plan

My goal is: *To qualify and work in the management side of the Hotel/Recreation industry.*

1. My action steps are: *Gain admission to a course. Prepare for the course by developing my writing and spelling, learning to type, as well as learning how to study.*
2. Number the action steps in a logical sequence.
3. Write down your plan:
   - Over the next week I will *Find out about courses*
   - Over the next month I will *Start lessons with a tutor*
   - Over the next 3 months I will *Learn to type*
   - Over the next 6 months I will *Make sure that I have all the skills I need to complete a course*

My review date will be *in 2 months*

Career Development

Peel (1992) describes career development as the life-long process of fostering and cultivating the shape of the individual's working life so as to make the best use of inherent talents, skills, knowledge and interests for that person's and the employer's benefit. It should be forward looking and concerned with potential: that is, the potential of individuals and of the situation in which they are or may be in the future. It is at times of transition that dyslexic people need to consider career development carefully, particularly as they do not always follow the same linear pathway as others. It does not necessarily involve promotion and can mean making a present job situation more satisfying and enabling someone to be more effective for their employer. In assisting dyslexic people, organisations can access a number of resources including:

- further and higher education, as well as vocational training;
- human resource specialists within the organisation;
- government and private advisory agencies, including schemes designed to support disabilities such as Access to Work;
- literature and learning aids;
- any professional organisation an individual might belong to;
- managers and peer groups;
- the individual's abilities and personality.

Positive career development can benefit individuals in terms of them fulfilling their potential and the organisation itself in terms of the contribution that person will make.

As well as access to outside resources, organisations can support dyslexic people through coaching, tutoring and mentoring. Coaching largely refers to advice whilst on the job. As suggested in Chapter 2 it is usually an individual activity and focuses on the facilitation of skills a person needs to function more effectively. It has, for example, been shown to be effective in encouraging teachers to adopt evidence-based practices (Kretlow & Bartholomew, 2010). Tutoring is usually provided by subject experts; an example would be someone who needs to have a better knowledge of accountancy being tutored on an individual or group basis. Mentoring usually involves a more senior and experienced person helping an employee on a personal, one to one, and probably long-term basis. The assistance they offer is general rather than subject related. Mentoring can help in a number of ways, including overcoming problems with relationships, difficulties in studying, devising projects, offering new perspectives and insights, motivation and time management. Mentors can come from within or outside an organisation.

A Dyslexic's Perspective: Dyslexia and Journalism

As someone with dyslexia I often feel foolish, and no more so than in my choice of career. I am a journalist. This sometimes makes me feel not just a moron, but an oxymoron. Like a blind painter or a deaf musician, a dyslexic journalist just doesn't sound right. But although the rapid word-based nature of my work can make it very frustrating, it is also rewarding. And just occasionally the complex nature of the condition makes me feel that I can succeed as a reporter not in spite of dyslexia but because of it.

I've been a journalist for 15 years now. I am currently a news reporter for the Guardian. Not surprising you might think given the paper's reputation. Only the politically correct spelling mistake-riddled Grauniad could employ a dyslexic journalist. But my appointment was not an act of positive discrimination. When I was given the job nine years ago, the Guardian didn't know I was dyslexic. I didn't know myself until a year ago, and when I plucked up the courage to tell my employers they were surprised.

But I wasn't. Though I may have concealed it, I've always found reading and writing demanding. I struggled at school, but when I was written off by teachers this spurred me on to prove them wrong, and I managed to get into university by working hard. I did very well at university but only by putting in lots of hours of study each week and shunning the usual attractions of student life.

My tutors praised my writing style, which encouraged me into journalism. I started off on trade journals writing about housing and then architecture. Again I worked hard, often getting up early to part-write articles at home which was less distracting than the office.

I got a job at the Guardian when it was looking for a housing specialist. I was lucky that the role came up just after I had written a couple of pieces for the paper. Some years later, the paper decided it no longer needed to devote a specialist to this area, so I was redeployed as a general news reporter.

Again I felt fortunate because I've always struggled at work. After several years of huffing and puffing at journalism I thought it should be getting easier. But as it wasn't I had myself tested for dyslexia. I was told that I had a classic dyslexic profile – my abilities were held back by a poor working memory.

My initial reaction was to flee from journalism in despair and take up something less wordy. But as I couldn't afford to drop a well-paid job, I had to somehow deal with it.

In dyslexia counselling speak I wasn't stupid, I just had problems processing information. I was advised that there are ways around dyslexia and even ways of making it work to your advantage. I was sceptical at first but I have become more convinced that dyslexia isn't necessarily a problem even for a journalist.

First it was very helpful to have an explanation for my trouble at work. No wonder I had found shorthand so tricky, or that I missed out words in my copy, or found it hard to concentrate in an open-plan office. Once I had identified such difficulties as dyslexic problems rather than broader character flaws, solutions became more apparent.

I abandoned struggling with shorthand and no longer felt shame in using a dictaphone. I was more willing to slow people down if I hadn't understood an instruction. I have taken more trouble about proof reading and using text-to-speech software to spot errors. I also don't feel quite so anti-social now when I take myself off to quiet areas to work.

More importantly, the diagnosis helped me change my role at work. Unsurprisingly I found distilling lots of information into 600-word articles challenging, but also a frustrating way of conveying information.

Instead I have begun to develop a specialism in liveblogging big stories for the Guardian's website. The task involves posting regular updates on breaking stories, like the protests in Iran, the Copenhagen climate summit, or the earthquake in Haiti.

This may sound like an awkward task for someone with dyslexia, but I find it much easier to do than more conventional journalism. It involves writing short time-stamped updates rather than a long written-through piece. Over the course of the day of liveblogging I might write thousands of words. This is less daunting than it sounds because the task is broken up into chunks.

Whenever news develops, or I find some interesting comments or coverage elsewhere on the web, I will post an update. For me this sequential way of working in brief chronological chunks is more manageable than summarising more information in a single article.

With a breaking news story there is also more urgency. The adrenaline helps drown out the usual doubts I have about my writing ability.

But the best thing for a dyslexic person about blogging rather than conventional writing is that it is not just about words. One of the main tasks is to seek out the latest videos, audio clips and images on a particular story, and then embed those into a blog.

This multi-media dimension to news is becoming increasingly important with the rise of citizen journalism. Content from ordinary people using their mobile phones has become a key way of telling breaking news stories. People caught up in events capture them on their phones and video cameras before the news crews move in or are allowed to move in. So a story about the impact of a snow storm can be enhanced by listening to a man stranded in his car in a recording that he has posted on the internet, or by YouTube footage of people skiing to work.

I find seeking out such material enjoyable, and I've become good at sifting through it and picking out the best bits. And this is where dyslexia feels more like a help than a hindrance. Dyslexic people are supposed to be slow with words but quick with images. That seems to be true in my case, and being quick with images and other multi-media content is a great advantage.

And even when I'm working just with words, there are some dyslexic traits that seem to be useful. Dyslexic people are good at seeing the bigger picture, which can be helpful in spotting news angles and honing in on the essentials of a subject and not getting bogged down in detail. We are also supposed to be good lateral and creative thinkers. Again this is useful in looking for new angles and exploring new ways of telling stories.

The difficulty I have with words also makes me determined to ensure that my writing is easily understood. I'm constantly aware that understanding sentences can be hard, so I'm perhaps more conscious of trying to write clearly, even if I don't always succeed.

I don't want to overstate the case – journalism is a difficult job for someone with dyslexia. But sometimes I feel I can bring a different perspective and a set of skills that can be useful to a newsroom. Journalism still seems like a strange choice of career, but may be I am proving that dyslexic people can work well with words.

Summary

1. Career counselling is a professional activity which can assist dyslexic people to adapt positively to transitions.
2. A decision-making approach to career counselling can enable dyslexic people to make sensible and realistic choices, based on a knowledge of their strengths and weaknesses.
3. Preparation of an action plan can assist in the setting and achievement of realistic goals.
4. Dyslexic people may need continued support in the development of their careers through coaching, tutoring and mentoring.

9

Dyslexia At Work

Synopsis. *In this chapter the challenges facing both employers and employees are outlined. The skills, compensations and accommodations that address work-related tasks, and that can enable dyslexic people to work effectively, are described.*

Introduction

Internationally there has been little empirical research directed to the impact of disability legislation on outcomes for dyslexic people (Gerber et al., 2011), and that which has focused on disclosure rates has shown that there is still a reluctance amongst individuals to inform employers (Price et al., 2005; Martin & McLoughlin, 2012). Nevertheless, on the basis of our experience, we are in no doubt that in response to legislation many organisations have adopted a positive approach to supporting dyslexic employees. Others have made provision more cynically, fulfilling their statutory obligations by providing inappropriate nomothetic solutions, probably to their loss. Ajadi has written that the 'fixation on anti-discrimination exclusively becomes the equivalent of confusing auditing and fraud detection as the summary of a financial system, thereby ignoring processes such as budget setting or cash flow forecasting' (Ajadi, 2002: 264).

Being dyslexic is not necessarily a barrier to occupational success; there are too many dyslexic people in all occupations to refute this. Some jobs are more dyslexia-friendly than others, tapping the dyslexic person's strengths. There are undoubtedly dyslexic people who are in the wrong job: that is, they are in a situation where the demands of tasks they find difficult outweigh their competencies and strengths. The difficulties facing a dyslexic person at work can be exacerbated because the challenges they face are not obvious, being concerned with organisation, social skills and coping with transitions rather than the literacy problems usually associated with the syndrome. Many dyslexic people, having survived the traumas of the school system and leaving with few qualifications, find learning 'on the job' more effective. As they deal with the problems they face, they may

The Dyslexic Adult: Interventions and Outcomes – An Evidence-based Approach, Second Edition.
David McLoughlin and Carol Leather.
© 2013 John Wiley & Sons, Ltd. Published 2013 by John Wiley & Sons, Ltd.

learn to avoid situations involving literacy skills and become very well organised in work. They certainly may have more confidence than they had in school, being evaluated on their performance rather than through tests and examinations. This will however only be maintained if they have opportunities to continue developing the literacy, learning and technological skills they need. Like any employee, they also need to feel valued.

Walker recommended that organisations should value differences as an approach to affirmative action and equality of opportunity. Rather than allow differences to create discomfort and conflict, she suggests that they should be seen as something which can 'fuel creative energy and insight ... (as) points of tension that spark alternative viewpoints and ideas, and ignite the kindling process behind creativity and innovation' (Walker, 1994: 212).

Walker's Valuing Differences Model is based on four principles:

1. People work best when they feel valued.
2. People feel most valued when they believe that their individual and group differences have been taken into account.
3. The ability to learn from people regarded as different is the key to becoming fully empowered.
4. When people feel valued and empowered, they are able to build relationships in which they work together interdependently.

She suggests that valuing difference is a way of helping people think through their assumptions and beliefs about all kinds of differences, facilitating both individual personal growth and an organisation's productivity. Recognising and valuing the 'differences' manifested by dyslexic people will facilitate their success and contribute to that of the organisation. As Armstrong has written:

> Managing diversity is about ensuring that all people maximise their potential and their contribution to the organisation. It means valuing diversity, that is, valuing the differences between people and the different qualities they bring to their jobs which can lead to the development of a more rewarding and productive environment. (Armstrong,1999: 804)

Enabling dyslexic people to feel comfortable and allowing them to use their skills is a matter of establishing the 'Goodness of Fit' referred to in Chapter 2. It can be improved through encouraging a positive attitude towards dyslexic people. The ideal situation is one in which where there are three levels of input: the whole organisation, the managerial and trainer level, as well as an individual level – that is, when there is a good understanding of dyslexia and a network throughout the organisation to support the dyslexic employee. To use Gerber's terminology, well developed 'social ecologies' are essential.

The Whole Organisation: Awareness Training

As with any disability there should be a policy of awareness throughout the organisation. This can be achieved in a variety of ways: intranet, policy documents, network groups and

Figure 9.1 Organisational Departments

designated/bespoke awareness training presentations or briefings. Awareness training should be directed towards increasing everyone's understanding. During any employee's career in a large organisation they will probably come into contact with people from a large number of departments. This is illustrated in Figure 9.1. People from all these departments should be included in an awareness event, or at the very least be provided with informative literature.

Some departments require a special understanding. The IT department, for example, is often responsible for assistive technology solutions. Surprisingly sometimes occupational health departments and human resources departments have limited knowledge, and do not always recognise the impact dyslexia can have on an individual. For the dyslexic employee, knowing that people will have some understanding of their difficulties relieves pressure. Continually having to explain why they take much longer to learn new procedures and why they may not do things in the same way as other people can emphasise the difficulties and undermine an individual's confidence.

Awareness training should provide an opportunity for everyone to ask questions, raise their concerns and develop good communication platforms. It should include:

- An explanation of what dyslexia is and its impact on the individual in particular workplace settings.
- An outline of the skills and strengths of dyslexic people.
- A description of the profile of difficulties that can be experienced by an individual.
- Provision of a wide range of solutions for potential problems, based on the skills compensation and accommodation framework described in Chapter 2, including:

  i.   dyslexia specific strategy coaching and mentoring;
  ii.   IT solutions;
  iii. adjustments in assessment settings and to the workplace, such as extra time for training and learning new procedures. That these should be evidence based, and personal to the individual in a job context, must be emphasised.

Employers cannot be expected to be experts in disability, and given the complex nature of dyslexia it is sensible to seek specialist advice. It is also essential that the awareness training is bespoke and delivered by someone who has specific occupational knowledge. The impact of dyslexia in the emergency services, for example, can be very different from that in the banking or retail industries, as the demands of the job differ greatly.

The focus of awareness training should be on solutions rather than problems, and emphasise that many of the adjustments made for dyslexic people can improve the working environment for everyone. Some are already in place: for example, dual screens for a computer are widely used in the financial services industry, and for many dyslexic people who do not have them, they would improve their performance as not having to constantly switch between applications when analysing data relieves the demands on working memory.

There is a need for balance when delivering awareness training; it is easy to exaggerate the difficulties, portraying dyslexia as an insurmountable problem, when it doesn't have to be. At the same time by highlighting simple solutions the difficulties experienced by dyslexic people on a day to day basis can be underestimated.

I have been informed that after 12 years of schooling and 10 years of work that I have dyslexia. I still don't understand what it is and how it affects my daily life but the attitude of others does stand out when they get told.

Awareness training can be followed up by establishing support groups, intranet systems, identifying named staff in human resources or occupational health who can be contacted for advice, setting up a mentoring system and arranging specialist input when necessary. In general, there should be a coordination of and cooperation with staff responsible for human resources, equal opportunities, as well as in-house differentiation in selection, training and appraisal.

My employer has organised training and this has been pointing out issues and that my current operations are how people with my condition may deal with it. If it sounds like I have an illness.

Its because that is how I've felt since I have been told. My level of confusion has increased and no one seems to be able to help.

Employers do, however, need to take action through specific initiatives. Among the ten most successful of these described by Kandola and Fullerton (1994) which would be relevant to dyslexic people are: buying specialised equipment; employing helpers; and training trainers in equal opportunities. Employers should consider the 'reasonable adjustments' which can be made to allow dyslexic people to show themselves at their best. They need to be aware of their legal responsibilities, specifically meeting the requirements of disability legislation. Employers should be able to answer the following questions:

- Do you provide information to job applicants and employees about their rights?
- Have you informed supervisory staff of their responsibilities?
- Have you ensured your employment practices and procedures do not discriminate against applicants or employees who are dyslexic?
- Do you make adjustments for dyslexic applicants during the selection process and when employed by you?
- Can you identify the main skills involved in jobs, and do interview questions focus on whether an applicant has or can acquire these skills?

(Adapted from Wehman, 1996).

Employers should consider financial issues but often cost considerations are minimal. The two questions they really need to address are:

Can we alter the job?
- Restructure the job
- Extend a training period
- Provide alternative training
- Modify work schedules
- Reassign tasks
- Provide a mentor or coach

Can we alter the workplace?
- Change the work station
- Provide organisational aids
- Allow flexible working hours
- Provide appropriate technology

Legislation requires employers to make adjustments or accommodations to compensate for the individual's specific difficulties. These adjustments should be evidence based and often include:

- extra time in selection and promotion examinations, in training and to learn new procedures;
- adjusting the job role; for example, being exempt from taking minutes;

Table 9.1   Framework for Analysis at Transition

Job demands	Skills to be developed	IT solutions	How others can help	Adjust the job/the workplace
At recruitment				
In training				
General work tasks				
Promotion & assessment				

- making changes to the workplace – moving the desk, being exempt from hot desking;
- providing technological aids;
- providing skills and strategy coaching to explore personalised solutions.

Awareness of the nature of dyslexia is particularly important at certain times, particularly those representing transition, such as recruitment, training, promotion, changes in job roles and routines. Table 9.1 provides a framework for analysis for these periods.

Disclosure: To Tell or Not To Tell

To access resources and adjustments an individual must disclose that they are dyslexic. Research has revealed that many are reluctant to do so, fearing discrimination (Gerber & Price, 2003). This is discussed in more detail in Chapter 10, but it should be noted here that some of the reasons given reflect much misunderstanding surrounding dyslexia, both in terms of the stereotypes held by non-dyslexic people as well as the lack of understanding dyslexic people have of themselves.

It is important, therefore, that an organisation develops an environment of trust, by having an accessible policy and raising awareness through the dissemination of information via the intranet, help lines and support groups. The outcome of providing an environment where people feel valued is that it helps dyslexics feel more confident about disclosure. We have referred to this in other chapters, but reiterate that it is a personal decision, complex and made more so as dyslexia's hidden and diverse nature allows greater choice. One of the keys to gaining support at work is being able to 'disclose' in a constructive manner, providing solutions not problems and promoting their skills, reflecting self-awareness and the ability to define oneself as more than one's disability (Goldberg et al., 2003).

Goodness of Fit

The impact of dyslexia is contextual and can vary depending on the type of job a person is in, therefore the goodness of fit should be considered. Gerber and his colleagues (1994) found this to be a factor in the success of dyslexic people. In essence, this is people being in a job that taps a higher proportion of their skills than their weaknesses; being comfortable with the demands of the job role and having good support systems around them. Goodness of fit leads to feelings of greater 'self efficacy', a belief in one's ability to successfully complete a task in a particular situation and this in turn leads to increased motivation, greater commitment and perseverance when things are challenging (Bandura, 1997). Self-efficacy is also related to job satisfaction, a person who feels competent in their job being more likely to feel satisfied with it and therefore work more effectively.

Much has been written about dyslexic people choosing certain occupations: those that tap visual skills, for example, such as the arts, engineering and architecture. This is largely anecdotal and it is possible that the disclosure rate is higher amongst people who feel they have found their niche in life. Taylor and Walter (2003) did, however, find a sample surveyed revealed that the dyslexic people were 'predisposed towards people orientated professions', such as sales and nursing, and had avoided occupations that involve written work, management and finance. In our work we have met large numbers of dyslexic people working successfully in different occupations, having a good understanding of themselves, their skills and how to match these to job demands.

Whatever the choice of career it is important for dyslexic people to be aware that the demands of different jobs vary considerably. Some public service roles are very different from office-based work. There can be risk critical and public safety elements in a job. The role may require a rapid assessment of circumstances, clear communication at speed, great accuracy when recording information, the ability to respond to changing environments, as well as being able to produce reports or written documentation quickly. Some jobs may require considerable multitasking; contributing to telephone conference calls, helpline or call centre work are good examples. For some dyslexic people producing written work will be the only problem, being able to deal with and possibly thriving on rapidly changing situations within the context of their job. For others however the literacy demands are not a problem, but developing the multi-tasking aspects of the job to an automatic level are. Both the individual and the employer are more likely, therefore, to achieve 'goodness of fit' if the individual can predict what might be a challenge, and the organisation can offer solutions.

Recruitment and Selection

Recruitment

As we have written earlier dyslexia should not be a barrier to occupational success, provided people have the requisite skills and the time to develop strategies to help them solve any difficulties. Outlining the demands of the job clearly in an advertisement can help a dyslexic person to make an informed decision as to whether it is the correct one for them, and whether they have or can develop the skills required.

Many organisations do ask people to disclose if they have a disability on the application form so they can then make some adjustments, such as allowing extra time in entry tests.

Some dyslexic people take advantage of this; others do not. Fear of discrimination is always a concern at this level and anecdotal evidence would suggest it occurs.

Selection

It is important that entry tests reflect the job role as much as possible. They need to be valid and have predictive reliability. This enables informed decisions to be made, as it is important that the competencies required to do the job are achieved. Further, the integrity of the job and also of dyslexic people should not compromised. Extra time and the use of a computer are widely recommended as the adjustments for dyslexic people. Sometimes, if appropriate, scribes and readers can be used. Being allowed to make notes and/or take notes into interviews can also be reasonable. The interviewer understanding that dyslexic candidates might take longer to formulate an answer or need to clarify a supplementary question is also helpful. As with anyone anxiety at interviews can affect the recall of information – it may exacerbate the dyslexic individual's difficulties.

The Workplace Assessment/Consultation

In the United Kingdom employers and employees can seek support through the government scheme known as Access to Work. This is designed to provide help to overcome the barriers people with disabilities experience in the workplace. One of its functions is to provide a workplace assessment. This is sometimes confused with the diagnostic assessment. The latter described in Chapter 3 is usually carried out by a psychologist or a specialist assessor. It provides the formal evidence for dyslexia or other specific learning difficulty such as dyspraxia, by investigating cognitive processes and literacy attainments. The workplace assessment is, however, carried out by a dyslexia specialist or an employment needs assessor. Its purpose is to provide the employee and employer with evidence-based recommendations for adjustments within the context of a job. Knowing which kind of assessment is relevant can be quite confusing but the guide at the end of Chapter 3 should help.

The workplace assessment should look at the whole person, including their skills and abilities. It should be flexible, individualised and provide a wide variety of solutions, as well as suggestions for coaching and skill development. The resulting recommendations should facilitate progression and independence. Monitoring and evaluation of the recommendations, although rarely done, are an important part of this process, to ensure effectiveness. Further, if the job role changes the adjustments may need to be reviewed.

Office-based jobs that are likely to tap literacy and numeracy problems are relatively well understood, and in these situations technological aids are frequently recommended as the solution. Even then the different task demands should be considered; writing a policy document is very different from preparing a project management report. Some job roles do not require large amounts of writing and much of it can be completed by using templates. If an individual lacks confidence in their IT skills then specific technical literacy training might be more effective than using specialist software packages as the

Table 9.2 Framework for Workplace Assessment

The job	*The person*
• Main duties of the job	• Skills and abilities
• The context of the job role	• Personal strengths/attributes
• Competencies and skills required	• Transferable skills
• Outline of concerns	• Personality characteristics – levels of
• Indicators of performance levels	self understanding
• Percentage of tasks successful completed	• External constraint concerns
The environment	*The impact of dyslexia – difficulties with*
• Structure of the dept/team	• Literacy
• Features of the workplace	• Memory
• Social aspect – team work, colleagues,	• Organisation
managers' expectations	• Confidence
• Physical aspects – work station	• Specific work skills
• Technological assessment – where necessary	

(Adapted from Langton & Ramseur, 2001).

latter often demand considerable new learning. In fact, sometimes, the recommendation of the use of IT can undermine a person's performance and confidence, the 'solution' becoming a barrier to improved performance. General solutions are not the answer to very specific individual difficulties.

Table 9.2 outlines the areas that should be addressed in a workplace assessment. It should also include a cost analysis.

The workplace assessment report should be a summary of the information gathered and should be written in jargon free language. It should outline solutions based on the skills competencies required for the job. The employer and the dyslexic person should explore the recommendations in the workplace assessment report and discuss those that might fit best with the individual and the job role. Good communication between the manager and the dyslexic employee is essential. This can be fostered/facilitated by a specialist coach/trainer. Communication and trust has sometimes broken down and the trainer can provide a bridge towards greater understanding.

The Manager's Role

Managers often have a key role in enabling dyslexic people to work effectively. Managers need to be clear about what is required and consider what can be achieved through the correct adjustments. It should always be remembered that dyslexic people:

1. Process information differently.
2. Often perform less well in written tasks than is expected.
3. Can be defensive in new training situations because of their past experience.
4. Always need positive feedback.

5. Can lack confidence and be reluctant to ask questions.
6. Have skills and abilities they themselves do not recognise.

Dyslexic people are not unique in this of course, and many people are initially bewildered in a new job or when faced with change. Furthermore, management is part of many people's job description and it can be a confusing and challenging experience for them too. Managing a dyslexic employee can be quite simple and straightforward, but it can also be very demanding. Whilst there is increasing recognition that dyslexic people need support in the workplace, guidance is often not afforded to their managers. It is an area that requires consideration, particularly as managers can make a positive or negative difference to the way in which dyslexic people perform in their job role.

If an individual is struggling, they are likely to look to the manager for support. If they have known they are dyslexic for a while, or even if they have just discovered that it is the reason for their difficulties, they may expect employers and managers to address their needs and make adjustments to their workplace. These expectations may or may not be realistic within the context of the job, and this can present difficulties. Managers have their own pressures; they are likely to have high targets to achieve, deadlines to meet and increasing demands. They may be responsible for the smooth running of their team, and the supervision of many others' work. Other members of the team or work may be supportive or possibly resentful of the extra time or attention that a manager may give a dyslexic employee (Paetzold et al., 2008). Such difficulties can be addressed through awareness training and improving understanding. Many can be avoided by organisations being proactive rather than reactive in their provision of support.

The following are comments from managers of dyslexic people we have worked with:

1. I learnt so much about the job when working with John, because in order to help him I had to understand what I was asking of him.
2. I found that I learned much about the different ways people learn and work, and it helped me to manage other members in the team. I am much clearer when I am asking people to do things. I learned about new ways of working: mind mapping and coding. I now work much more efficiently too.
3. It took me a long time to reassure Sally that I was trying to help her – I had to work hard at it but it was worth it as we now get on well.
4. Pete was about to be dismissed when it all came out. It was a big learning curve for us all and we found it hard for a while, but things are good now – it is surprising how things can change.

The remainder of this chapter addresses many of the issues faced by the individual.

Challenges Facing Dyslexic People

The most common challenges facing a dyslexic person at work are in areas such as:

- Organisation;
- Time management and work prioritisation;

- Demands on written language abilities;
- Memory for procedures;
- Training situations;
- Carrying out instructions;
- Unsympathetic colleagues;
- Dealing with distractions of noise, people and place.

These issues can all have a negative influence on the performance of anyone at work, but they are more challenging for dyslexic people, affecting self-confidence. The negative feelings they experienced at school are rekindled. Their manager's confidence in their ability to do the job can also be undermined.

> There are people at work who undermine me but it has been covert and therefore it is difficult to put you finger on it. I was passed over from promotion but have since been moved to a new job and promoted to the same level on a temporary basis so I proved that I can do it. My confidence is very fragile. I don't think I have done much wrong, but I just want to make sure I get the procedures right because I know I can do what the job entails and somebody of my ability should be able to get a great deal further.

Unlike education which is linked to the goals of individuals, training is 'role specific'. It starts with the requirements of a particular organisation and, within that, of a given job (Miner, 1992).

Success at work depends on several factors, including:

1. Knowing one's own individual skills and abilities.
2. Knowing what the job demands are.
3. Feeling comfortable in the environment in which one works: that is, having the chance to use one's skills and knowing they are valued.
4. The ability to reflect on and evaluate one's own performance.
5. The 'social ecologies' or the support of other colleagues to help circumvent any problems that they might encounter.

The first four are metacognitive in nature. This has been discussed in previous chapters, but the development of metacognitive processes in the workplace is particularly important for dyslexic people. Its significance for learning and work situations is widely documented (Henk & Graaff, 2004; Kumar, 2010; Mosakowski & Earley, 2010; Pintrich, 1994; Schmidt, 2003; Swanson, 2000; Zimmerman, 1992). It is said to improve performance, irrespective of ability (Batha, 2007; Ruban, 2003; Swanson, 1990), and is not contingent on memory ability (Keleman et al., 2000; Schraw & Dennison 1994). Furthermore it increases self-efficacy (Bandura, 1996; Goldberg et al., 2003; Raskind et al., 1999). In their model of success for people with learning disabilities Gerber et al. (1992) identified the internal control factors such as self-understanding, planning and goal setting as being keys to some of the success. Metacognitive skills are also used by some dyslexic people as a possible compensatory strategy, enabling them to think more strategically and achieve comparable success with their peers (Ruban et al., 2003; Tranin & Swanson, 2005).

Metacognitive Skills at Work

Some dyslexic people use metacognitive skills but are not aware of it, and others need to develop them through coaching. Task analysis is an essential part of metacognitive thinking and effective performance at work. To do a job well one has to analyse what the demands are. These are often written in a job description, but it is important that the dyslexic person understands and interprets what is expected of them, as well as knowing what skills the job may require. They need to be encouraged to ask questions such as 'What does the job involve and what is the best way for me to tackle it?' The application of the Performance Improvement Strategy described in Chapter 5 can improve performance at work through strategy selection and monitoring. Some people make more than one plan when deciding what to do, always having a Plan B, and contingency plans are often a good way of maintaining a feeling of control over a situation.

Transfer of Skills

Understanding task demands and using a strategy employed successfully in a previous job situation but adapted for the current one can lead to efficient performance. Automatic strategy selection and generalisation are, however, contingent upon effective executive functioning and the use of the episodic buffer. To dyslexic people each situation can be a completely new one. They fail to transfer and generalise successful learning and working experiences to new situations. Graduates, for example, do not always use the skills they developed for planning essays while a student to report writing tasks: that is, they do not use the mind mapping techniques that helped in the past.

Evaluation and Reflection

Dyslexic people can also fail to change an inefficient method because they are so busy trying to keep up with current job demands. They do not have the time or confidence to think about changing something that will improve it. Often they will work in the way they have been told to work by a line manager and be too anxious and lacking in confidence to adapt and use their own strategies. Thus it is important that the individual is able to explain the rationale behind their ways of working. This goes back to the role of self-understanding.

Changes and Transitions at Work

Dyslexic people find adapting to change challenging, and one of the problems facing them is that there has been a great deal of change in the workplace in recent years. This is a continuing process, the rate of change being quite overwhelming. There are three areas of potential difficulty. Firstly, a change in job requirements places obvious demands as the person is likely to have to learn new skills. A very good playgroup leader, for example, found her job changed in that she was increasingly required to write reports and keep daily logs. This placed tremendous demands on her literacy skills which were very weak, and she was unable to develop them in the time required by her supervisors. She left her job, which was a great loss to the children she had worked with and those with whom she might have worked in the future.

Secondly, changes of personnel can also affect a dyslexic person's performance. They may have to display their weaknesses and difficulties to another person who has no understanding or interest. This can destroy their confidence in their work. It is often a change in management personnel which prompts people to seek help and advice, a lowering of self-confidence undermining performance in work rather than skill deficits. Changes in support staff can also affect performance; one highly successful man's personal assistant left, and was replaced by someone who was less organised. As a result he needed to spend more time sorting out problems, and his own work suffered. Getting used to new colleagues and different expectations can also create difficulties in social interaction.

Changes in procedures or the introduction of new IT systems which require new learning are also challenging for dyslexic people. Unlearning what has been harder to learn in the first place is challenging and learning the new systems can take considerably longer, particularly if it is a move towards computerisation.

Finally, changes in the environment can also affect performance. This is not usually a long-term problem, but it can take dyslexic people longer to settle into new surroundings. It is at such times that they should anticipate that it might take them longer to do their job than usual. They can also be distracted by noises around them. Certainly if they have moved into an open plan office, many dyslexic people find it extremely difficult to concentrate. Here it is external factors creating the problem and the solution lies in modifying the environment.

We have referred to significance of transitions earlier. These are not insurmountable and strategies such as temporary promotion, shadowing and mentoring can all be useful in helping people to understand the job demands, find solutions to the increased challenges and become familiar with new staff and environments.

Support in the Workplace

Tutoring Training, Coaching and Mentoring

As has been mentioned in Chapter 2 the words coaching, tutoring and mentoring are used synonymously, despite the fact that they mean something different. Tutoring usually describes help given to learners by subject experts, in the context of a specific course of study or in the acquisition of specific skills. Here tutoring refers to 'off the job' learning. Individual tutoring or tutor groups composed of students following the same course can be particularly helpful, offering as they do opportunities for exchanging views and

Table 9.3   Goal Focused Coaching

Problem	Reason	Solution	Refinement
Learning training notes	Poor memory Inefficient recall	3 Ms system Task specific revision strategies	Put chart on wall
Recall of procedures not used regularly	Not enough practice to develop automaticity	Self review – own learning, using e-learning and training	Involve others in team to remind and practise

experience, debate and general support. We have advocated elsewhere individual tuition, and if tutorial groups are to work, they need to be kept small. Ideally they should not be too demanding in terms of the need to attend, but should be regular.

Coaching can refer to 'on the job' advice, or to an activity that links on and off the job learning. It is a coaching model that is usually the most appropriate for the dyslexic specialist trainer to adopt. Individuals will have developed their own ways of working, be they effective or ineffective, and the coach should aim to refine and enhance their working and learning strategies. In addition the coaching should aim to provide a reason for the difficulty and a solution. It does, therefore, need to be provided by someone who has a full understanding of the nature of dyslexia and an andragogical approach to the learning process. The coaching session should be explicitly goal orientated. This is reflected in Table 9.3.

Both coaches and tutors need to have a good understanding of the nature of dyslexia in adulthood and within the work context. Specialist trainers who have only worked in higher education settings may have a limited, largely literacy focused view of dyslexia, and therefore the intervention may mean that less ineffective. Lengthy spelling programmes for many dyslexic people are inappropriate, especially if there are technological solutions available.

A Coaching Example

Jane was a 30-year-old project coordinator for a charity. It was her second job. She was diagnosed as dyslexic at school, received specialist tuition and her spelling skills improved. She has not wanted or received any help since then. She had gained an upper second class degree in graphics, and communicated well with people, articulating her ideas clearly. She liked to be organised and had been good at all aspects of her job. Recent changes meant she was tasked with taking helpline calls two days a week, whilst having to complete her administration tasks at the same time, if the phones were quiet. The multi-tasking involved in this undermined her confidence in her abilities, and her performance levels dropped rapidly.

Jane was referred for a work-based assessment. This revealed that she read slowly, her memory skills were weak, but her writing skills were competent. During the course of

Table 9.4 Evidence-based Adjustments

Problem	Reason/evidence	Adjustment Specialist coaching	Aims/goals	Review when/date
Poor performance two days per week on helpline calls	Low knowledge base	Speed comprehension strategies – note making	1. Build knowledge base	3 months or as confidence grows
Confidence in accurate financial advice	Reading speed Rapid naming	Buddy support Drop to one day per week	2. Develop strategies	
Impacting on other areas of work			3. Improve confidence	

the assessment it became obvious that Jane did not understand the impact of dyslexia, seeing it only as a spelling problem.

The programme devised for Jane included: developing her understanding of dyslexia; increasing her metacognitive awareness; an analysis of the tasks that were causing the problem, including identifying the hardest part and then discussing solutions; developing her reading skills and confidence. See Table 9.4.

Outcome

Jane completed ten hourly sessions; the first five were on a weekly basis, the remainder on a monthly basis. Over this period Jane's confidence in her ability, reading skills and knowledge base grew significantly. She is now managing the helpline on her own and coping with the other aspects of her job. She is also a lot less defensive about her dyslexia as she understands it better, feels more in control and can advocate for herself more effectively.

Programme Length

The length and frequency of any programme should be flexible and variable. In our experience most people benefit from one to two hours' coaching maximum in any session over a period of time. It is unlikely that any person who has been dyslexic all their lives is going to overcome their difficulties in three half-day training sessions. Spreading the training sessions over a longer period enables people to develop, practise, consolidate and refine their skills. Then mentoring can be a cost effective way for people to have continued support.

Mentoring

Mentoring involves making available an experienced person to help an employee or learner on a personal, long-term one to one basis, offering general rather than subject specialist help. Mentoring can help with overcoming relationship problems, difficulties in studying, the application of theoretical knowledge and devising projects. It can also bring perspectives and insights while facing personal problems associated with study, self-motivation and time management. Mentoring can be of value as part of an induction process, especially when an employee is 'different'. It can sometimes be sufficient support, but generally it can be a useful addition or follow-on from specialist coaching, as it provides more informal support over a longer period. It is often much more work and career focused.

Addressing Challenges
Organisation

> Dyslexic people ... may have to organise their lives differently from others, but that does not mean that they perform less well. Indeed, in many instances it will be found that the problems that they meet are little different from those met by everyone else – but they are exaggerated and made more obvious. (Hales, 2004: 62)

Organisation can cover several dimensions including time management, general organisation for work, personal organisation and organisation for learning and training. Some of these issues have already been addressed in earlier chapters, so there is inevitably a certain amount of repetition here.

As suggested in Chapter 1 the dyslexic person's weakness in terms of organisational skills is a direct result of their inefficient working memory, particularly its impact on executive functioning. Organisation involves sequencing information and behaviour, as well as keeping track of sets of instructions. A receptionist, for example, needs to be able to hold in memory a sequence of instructions or facts long enough to organise them on paper, or she will not be able to accurately record telephone messages. A secretary asked to file papers needs to be able to locate the correct file if she is to keep the files organised.

Organising one's work and workload is a commonly reported difficulty. If people have trouble organising themselves, being promoted to a managerial position could be stressful as they then have to organise others as well. At the same time this can act as a catalyst, leading to people becoming highly organised; some become so meticulous that every event is recorded in a diary and their determination to plan and organise activities results in them becoming very reliable. 'My friends think I have OCD' is an often made remark. Paradoxically, it is the fact that they are so well organised that indicates they have a fundamental weakness in organisational skills.

Dyslexic people can learn organisational skills, and it is often one of the areas requiring most attention. Becoming better organised involves:

Table 9.5 Developing Organisational Skills

Skill Development	Compensations	Accommodations
Organisation of Time	Mobile phone, electronic	Secretarial support
Concept of time	organisers	Friends, colleagues or
Estimation of time for task	Watches, alarm clocks	supervisors providing
Planning	Diaries, filofax	reminders
Previewing skills	Wall charts, planners	
Contingency planning	Time management software	
Organisation of Work or Dealing with Work Overload		
Planning	Urgent/important tray	Extra time with colleague
Prioritisation	Colour coding	to plan
Task analysis	Review list	Work prioritised with
Time management	Filing system	markers
Reviewing skills	Year planner	Checking with colleague
Goal setting	Monthly, weekly, daily	
Use of space	charts	
Filing		
Personal Organisation		
Daily chores plan	To do list	Family member to consult
Weekly timetables	Mobile phone	
Personal finance skills		
Improving Concentration and Attention		
Orientation to task	Ear plugs or headset to cut	Flexitime to check-ins with
Setting achievable goals	noise	colleagues
	Use answer phones or voice	Work when quiet
	mail to control phone	Change position of desk
	calls	Flexitime to work
	Working for short periods	A screen to block off

- understanding the nature of the task;
- goal setting (targets and priorities);
- planning time;
- monitoring;
- lists and classifications;
- filing.

It is not unusual to meet dyslexic people who have in fact become highly organised, and some of the skills and compensations they can develop, as well as the accommodations which can be made are shown in Table 9.5.

Time Management and Work Prioritisation

Skill Development Time management and being able to prioritise work are important in the workplace. The skills involved include developing an awareness of time, being able to estimate how long a task will take, and being able to allocate the appropriate amount of time to it. It also involves being able to determine which are the most urgent or important tasks, and being able to place them in an efficient order. This can be achieved by brainstorming and then ordering the tasks. It can be a good idea to consider potential pitfalls in the plan, and build in contingency time for tasks that take longer than expected or last minute demands from colleagues or supervisors. Setting targets, making plans, and monitoring progress are all important. Reviewing where time has gone is also essential. Telephone calls, for example, can take up much more time than anticipated, either because the conversation goes on longer than expected or because sometimes it can take several calls to actually make contact with the right person. Reading emails and listening to voice mail can also take much longer than planned for.

Another common problem with prioritising is that an employee can be instructed by several different people:

> Everyone always thinks their work is the most important – how do I know? My solution is to do the most recent one so I never seem to complete a task.

Many dyslexics do feel that their workload is too great. Discussing this with their line manager and establishing a system for allocation is important.

Compensations　　This mainly involves the use of mobile phones, electronic notebook organisers, watches with timers, filofaxes, diaries and time management computer software.

Accommodations　　These can include the use of secretarial support, line managers providing reminders and helping to plan work or assign specific tasks, as well as colleagues checking how the plan is going.

Organisation of Work and the Work Space

Skill Development　　Ideally the dyslexic person needs to develop their own system of organisation so that it is appropriate to them. Some prefer to be highly organised with everything filed away neatly and tidily in filing cabinets. Other people prefer boxes or piles of things. Some people need to have the 'work in progress' highly visible, as a memory aid.

The work space is an important consideration as it can be essential to looking and feeling in control. Keeping a tidy desk is something that can be important but difficult for a dyslexic person. Further, 'hot desking', where employees are expected to work at the desk available, has become increasingly popular as a way of maximising the use of office space. This can make the personalisation of desks and the development of individualised systems difficult. It is, however, best for a dyslexic employee to establish their own system, have their way of organising their desks and, if possible, establishing their position. What has to be done should be made as manageable as possible, and systems should be reviewed frequently to see if minor adjustments can be made.

Compensation   This involves the use of trays marked, 'Important', 'Urgent', on desks, as well as wallcharts and pinboards. Some dyslexic people find colour coding very helpful. Electronic memo devices/Mobile phones/Outlook and similar computer applications can be used to provide reminders.

Accommodation   To a large extent this just requires supervisors to provide the materials and equipment the dyslexic employee needs. Their contribution to finding sensible solutions, as well as enabling the employee to feel it is alright to 'do it their way' is, however, crucial. One solution to hot desking, where allowing an employee to have her own desk was impossible, was to allow her to move between just three desks rather than the 15 in the office.

Memory

Having an efficient memory or at least good strategies is essential for the workplace. This is possibly increasing, although arguably the type of memory people need is changing. Being able to remember where to find information and procedures when using computer systems is essential in the modern workplace. Similarly the number of training courses people are asked to attend or complete is on the increase. Some of these involve e-learning, which some dyslexic people like as they can go over it again and again. Others dislike it intensely, not being able to learn easily from a screen, especially as it is often word based.

We have written about memory strategies in earlier chapters, and the same principles apply here. People should have a range of strategies so they can use those that are task specific and relevant to what they are trying to learn or remember. Application of the 3M principles of making it manageable and multi sensory and using memory aids is appropriate. In a training situation the single most useful adjustment that can be made is for the individual to have the course material or at least an outline of what is going to be covered in advance. Allowing them to preview the information enables people to plan and prepare how best they can, and allows them to understand and retain the new information. This can also apply to practical situations. A despatch rider, for example, needs to be able to hold on to information about directions and routes. Knowing the area through looking at a map first will enable them to get to the destination more efficiently, if their GPS breaks down.

Reading at Work

People only need the reading skills that they need and reading tasks at work vary. Some occupations do not require much reading at all, and many dyslexics have managed with little or no literacy skills. People often have a technical sight vocabulary and they can deal with the demands of their job. Increasing demands for qualifications and the use of technology are placing much greater emphasis on literacy skills. When people once used the telephone it might now be expected that they use email. People, who can produce quite complex reports, can be flummoxed by a relatively simple email if the content is unfamiliar. The speed of email has meant that people often have less time to deal with the information and consider it before a response is required. This can increase stress and affect an individual's performance.

Many jobs now involve a large amount of reading: letters, reports, leaflets, minutes of meetings and so on. Comprehension and getting information from text are the most important skills in the workplace. Reading skill development has been discussed in Chapters 6 and 7, but it is important to note that people can meet the literacy demands of their jobs by specific strategy development, as well as with certain compensations and accommodations made available to them. The PASS strategy referred to earlier – that is, knowing the purpose of the text and the reason for reading it – can be instrumental in enabling a person to improve their skills.

There are occasions when people at work will be asked to read aloud. This might be just a social activity such as reading out an article from a newspaper or the horoscopes, but can also be work related, reading a letter or a report or briefing paper. Dyslexic people should be able to decline reading aloud without embarrassment. A simple 'I prefer not to read aloud' will often suffice. Alternatively, 'I am sure you will read aloud better than I can because I don't enjoy doing it' will do.

Reading for Information

Skill Development   Scanning, skimming and careful reading, as well as knowing when to apply them, are the most useful skills to develop for reading at work. It is also helpful to build up work or technologically specific vocabulary. In addition, for some critical review, analysis and research skills are important.

Compensation   This can include having somebody highlight the key points; reading aloud to a dictaphone and listening later; asking for an overview or an outline before reading a report. Equally, asking a colleague what they think about a report before actually reading it can give a great deal of information about the content and therefore make it easier to understand. Using a scanner and Text to Speech software can allow reading by listening.

Accommodation   This can include providing someone to highlight key points or record material. Some dyslexic people do not like reading from a computer screen and therefore emails are easier to deal with if they are printed. It can also help everyone in the office if the presentation of written work is considered. This includes fonts, as well as layout and colour. These all improve readability.

Reading Complex Material

A systematic approach such as a critical reading technique for workplace documents can improve comprehension. This involves:

- Reflecting on the reason for reading – what are you hoping to learn?
- Reflecting on the author's viewpoint – what is he/she trying to convey?

- Getting an overview from scanning the material for layout, length, organisation, tables.
- Skimming the headings.
- Reading the abstract, summary, conclusions or recommendations carefully.
- Recognising the style of certain sections or the whole document. Some will be descriptive or informative, others evaluative or discursive, some will be persuasive or promotional, some will be analytical.
- Carefully reading the important sections – this may be the whole document, which may require highlighting or noting key words to aid memory and comprehension. It may also mean that it should be undertaken in stages, or by taking breaks and allocating time for reflection on the text.
- Interacting with the text as it is being read can also help. Is the line of argument or reasoning clear? Does it make assumptions? What can be inferred from the text? What can be deduced? How else could it be interpreted? These are all questions that increase comprehension.

Dyslexic people have often not developed such an approach automatically but their application can make a significant difference to their performance.

Specific Visual Difficulties

As suggested in Chapter 1 visual difficulties can cause some people additional problems with reading. These should be investigated by a vision specialist, but can be compensated for and accommodated in a number of ways:

Compensations   These can include:

- changing the colour of the paper or the computer display background;
- using coloured overlays;
- changing the font on the computer;
- sub-vocalising to provide auditory feedback;
- using aids such as Text to Speech software.

Accommodations   These can include:

- providing a reader;
- ensuring that instructions are provided in pictorial or diagrammatic form or recorded;
- ensuring lighting is very good.

Performance Issues

Underlying performance at work are affective factors such as confidence and freedom from stress. These have been addressed in earlier chapters, but are summarised in Table 9.6, as well as ways of dealing with them.

Table 9.6 Performance Issues

Skill Development	Compensations	Accommodations
Stress	Increased technological	Take breaks
Relaxation techniques	support	Extra time
Identifying sources		Have job coach or mentor
		Decrease workload
		Extra supervision
Problems with Memory	Record	Instructions to be written
Learn memory strategies, e.g.		down
mindmapping, not taking notes		
Confidence	List of positive	Review with supervision
Set own goals	statements on walls	Mentor/coach
Review performance		
Self talk		

Written Work in the Office

The writing tasks in the office can range from notes and memos to recording telephone messages, taking minutes at meetings, letter writing and report writing. For many dyslexic people it is the written aspect of their work that is most challenging and causes them the most humiliation. With all written work it is important to know who it is being written for, and whether it will be proofread constructively. Some people have extremely helpful and supportive colleagues who will look over work and make helpful suggestions; others have to cope with managers who are overly critical. The dyslexic person needs to recognise that this may happen and try not to take it too personally.

Knowing to whom the written work is addressed is important, as when writing memos and emails to a colleague a casual and informal style is acceptable. The appropriate style needs to be chosen for the task. In general, most written tasks should be clear, structured and precise. Often bullet points will suffice. All written work should be planned. Planning written work has been addressed earlier, but the following principles apply. It involves knowing the nature of the communication, its audience, its purpose, gathering information, ordering it and then writing the document. A simple 'who, what, when, where, why and how' approach can clarify the ideas. Using proformas for memos and emails can help, but they all require the date, name of writer and recipient, as well as the subject matter. Writing business letters requires even more careful planning, and it is important to try and adopt the organisational format and language. Any letter to be sent out should of course be proofread, ideally by somebody else, as this is good practice for everyone. We all read what we think we have written.

Record Keeping

Many jobs now require that records and logs of all activities be made. This can include phone calls made or visits carried out. Developing proformas to provide a structure for the details is a solution and can speed up the process. The more the format is planned the easier it is for a dyslexic person to manage the information. They will then be more efficient in producing a written report when this is required.

Report Writing

Report writing is a skill that can be learned and developed. Reports can be lengthy and complex, so their production is daunting. It is essential, therefore, that they are made manageable by being broken into stages. Reports are structured and have a specific purpose so planning can be easier. They usually contain an introduction, main body, conclusion, often recommendations and sometimes appendices. They may have additional sections such as the background, a financial section and that containing research and results. The precise format of the report should be discussed with the line manager so that exactly what is required is known. Nearly all reports are drafted; the first draft can often be information gathering and an exploration of ideas, the end result being quite different. Often several people will collaborate on a report and this can cause difficulties for dyslexic people as they sometimes perceive the revision of a draft as criticism when it might not be. The editing process can be improved by the use of a checklist which includes questions such as: Are the introduction and conclusion appropriate? Is each section clear in its aim and expression? Is the style correct and not repetitive? Is there enough material or evidence? Are the important sections and the argument easy to follow?

It is not unusual for dyslexic people to have planning strategies for dealing with written work. Graduates for example are used to writing essays. Nevertheless, when they move on to work they do not apply the skills they have to new tasks. As has been said previously they often do not use flow charts or visual planning structures that they employed at college or university.

Skill Development　　Different occupations are likely to have specific formats or procedures for report writing, and often templates are available. General principles of writing in bullet points, keeping the sentences short and simple, as well as using summaries, will however always be applicable. Being able to extract the main idea and express it lucidly and cogently are skills that also need to be developed. The ability to gather and sift information, identify specific issues, edit, as well as structure and plan, are also important. Dyslexic people should be encouraged to develop an awareness of their own style, the emphasis being on communication, and adapt it as necessary to that required. It is not uncommon for dyslexic people to have difficulty varying their writing style – the difference between a briefing document and a policy document, for example. The subtleties of language are lost in the process of transcription; understanding that there is a difference in phraseology and the nuances of words such as 'should' and 'must' enables people to develop the appropriate writing style. Developing appropriate task specific planning strategies is essential as they make the whole process more manageable.

Compensation　　This involves the use of technology, including planning software, as well as having standard formats and proformas.

Accommodation   This involves providing the appropriate secretarial support and/or indeed delegation of the task. Many dyslexic people are extremely good at coming up with ideas, but are less good at recording them. One man, working for a media company, said that his department would always come to him for the ideas to go into a report but they sent him to somebody to dictate them to as, if they waited for him to write it down, he would miss every deadline. Furthermore, many dyslexic people are better at editing a report than starting from a blank page as it makes fewer demands on the working memory system. For some people, therefore, it would be helpful if a colleague drafted the report and the dyslexic person made better use of their time undertaking the editing.

Numeracy

Most occupations involve numeracy skills of some kind, even if this just relates to how much one earns and understanding a pay slip. The complexity of numeracy tasks will vary according to the demands of the job. 'Salespeople and cashiers need to know how to give correct change to customers, total sales for the day and balance the cash drawer. A person who works for a delivery service must be very skilful at knowing addresses, managing time, and maintaining a log' (Patton et al., 1997: 179).

As indicated in Chapters 1 and 6, dyslexic people do not usually have conceptual problems with numeracy. Readers should refer to the section on improving quantitative literacy in Chapter 6 as the suggestions made there are relevant to the workplace, although some of these are reiterated here.

Skill Development   There are those who have a very poor background in maths and will need to go over the basics. Essentially, helping a dyslexic person with maths problems should ensure that (i) they understand the language, and (ii) they have strategies for dealing with:

- symbols;
- sequences;
- calculations.

Maintaining the place when dealing with a series of numbers can often be a problem, and they do need to use a guide, such as a ruler. A multi-sensory approach can be adopted and this includes sub vocalisation when dealing with symbols and numbers.

Compensations   These can include very basic strategies, such as using fingers, but much will be resolved by the efficient use of an electronic calculator. When possible, a calculator that has a voice-chip in it so that auditory feedback is provided, can be particularly useful.

Accommodations   These can include delegation, reducing the demands in this regard and relying on an accountant.

Proofreading and Checking

It is often difficult for dyslexic people to check their own work. We reiterate that proof-reading one's own work is difficult because one anticipates what should be, rather than what actually is written.

Skill Development   Structured approaches to proofreading can include systems such as COPS (checking capitalisation of letters, examining the overall appearance, punctuation, checking spelling (Schumaker et al., 1981)). Other skills can include keeping a list of errors one consistently makes, as well as reading from right to left when checking for spelling, to prevent anticipation. It can often be best to leave proofreading until well after the document has been prepared, certainly at a time when one is not tired.

Compensations   Sometimes proofreading work can be more effective if the font on the computer is changed for the individual so that it looks like a new report. Equally, changing the colour on the background can make proofreading easier. Reading the letter or document into Speech to Text software so that proofreading can be undertaken by listening through the use of Text to Speech software can be effective. Using grammar checks can also be helpful but they do require some knowledge of grammatical structure.

Accommodation   The simplest accommodation is to have someone else proofread one's work.

Listening Skills at Work

Good listening skills are an essential part of success at work, but they place a heavy load on working memory. Remembering instructions, coping with telephone calls, minutes of meetings, and indeed meetings themselves, require effective listening skills. Hearing what is being said and remembering it at the same time places demands on dyslexic people and often requires some note taking. It is important for the person to think about what they are about to listen to. If, for example, it is a list of instructions, then they perhaps need to use some concrete aid such as their fingers, noting how many things they have to remember. If it is a telephone call, then a notepad and pen will help. Minutes in a meeting demand other strategies, as does listening to information delivered at meetings and presentations.

Listening and recording telephone messages can present dyslexic people with many difficulties as they often rely on visual clues to help them understand what is being said. Unfamiliar voices at the end of an anonymous telephone can present the dyslexic person with a panic situation. If they do not hear or process the information clearly, they often assume it is their fault rather than that of the person who is speaking. They do need to develop the confidence to ask people to slow down or repeat what they have just said. If necessary, they can blame a poor telephone line or distractions in the office. If a major part of the job is concerned with telephone messages, proformas can be developed to address the specific information that might arise during a phone call: the name of caller, time of call, aim of call, points 1, 2, 3, 4, action to be taken and how urgent or important the message is.

Skill Development   Effective listening and remembering for the dyslexic person depends on how much they can control the flow of information. When taking instructions or telephone messages they need to develop the skill of being able to slow down the rate at which information is being given. If, for example, it is an address or telephone number then they need to be able to say, 'Could you repeat that, or start with the 0207 . . .' which will automatically slow the speaker down. Instructions for work tasks can be repeated back. Learning to listen for signal words, the obvious ones being 'one, two and three', is also helpful. It is nearly always essential for the dyslexic person to make some form of note to help with the recall of the information that they have just heard. A list of instructions demands chronological note taking which can be in words or pictures.

Compensations   The simplest compensation involves the use of a recording device.

Accommodations   These can include the provision of information visually, as well as written instructions, and having the chairperson sum up as each point on the agenda is covered.

Minute and Note Taking

Taking notes or minutes can be a particularly difficult skill for a dyslexic person as it places a heavy load on working memory.

Skill Development   In general, dyslexic people should adopt a minimalist approach to this activity, focusing on listening and understanding. Too many people take notes at the expense of 'noting'. Similar strategies can include the use of mind maps, drawing pictures, noting key points and using abbreviations. It is first important to identify the purpose of taking notes, using the Agenda to provide a structure.

Compensation   This can include using a recorder as a back-up to minimalist strategy, as well as using a laptop computer in training sessions and meetings.

Accommodation   This should include relying on other people's notes, being provided with a note taker and ensuring that employees are given handouts.

Meetings

Listening to what is going on in meetings, formulating ideas and arguments, and then remembering what is being said as well as the action to be taken, can be a nightmare for some dyslexic people.

Skill Development   Coping with meetings, presentations and training courses can be made easier by using systematic approaches, including PQLR – tuning in, questioning, listening and reviewing. This suggests the participant tries to identify the position the speaker will be taking and listen for evidence of this; generates questions about the topic at the end of the session or meeting; and mentally reviews the material to ensure that important points are remembered. The dyslexic person should seek clarification, use cross questioning and seek an overview. It is important for the dyslexic person to be aware of how good they are at listening and how often they need to seek clarification. With different people they will need to seek different levels of clarification. They also need to have a list of phrases or ways of asking for clarification and repetition without causing irritation. Often it can be useful to make projections or predictions of what the meeting might cover. Some people find it extremely useful to draw a map of where the individual other members are sitting at the meeting, and attribute the information from the meeting to the place settings. Being well prepared prior to the meeting – having the agenda and spending just a few minutes planning and thinking about the content – memo mapping what needs to be said, enables people to contribute effectively.

Compensation   This can be taking a recorder to the meeting/presentation/training session, to allow the person to listen to and control the information more readily.

Accommodations   These can include providing overviews or diagrams, allowing recording, encouraging discussions and questions. It is important for the dyslexic person to know what they do remember following a meeting, and where the gaps are so they can ask specific questions. They do need to be reassured that it is all right to acknowledge that there is a gap. No one takes in all the information in a meeting.

The way in which skill development, compensation and accommodation can be applied to a variety of work related tasks is summarised in Table 9.7.

Working in a Team

Working in a team can cause a dyslexic person a great deal of difficulty but it can be a positive experience. In a good team a dyslexic person may be allowed to display their strengths, including their presentation and speaking skills, as well as creative and problem solving abilities. Teamwork can be good for a dyslexic person as it can enable them to focus on their talents while other people deal with the areas that present them with difficulty. Working in a team can, however, involve exposing areas of weakness to colleagues. As White (1992) has written:

> In the past it could be successfully argued that higher levels of basic skills would increase one's vocational chances. This may no longer be true. What is needed now and in the future is not simply more of the same basic academic skills that have been taught for 20 years: Adults are expected and will be expected to use these basic skills to solve problems and communicate with others; adults are expected and will be expected to listen to others, be able to negotiate, and work as team members. (White, 1992: 456)

Table 9.7 **Work Skills**

Skill Development	Compensations	Accommodations
Telephone Work		
Listening skills	Use dictaphone, answer phone,	Ask someone else
Note taking	voice mail	
Using proformas		
Clarification strategies		
Filing		
Sequencing skills	Colour coding	Administrative support
Verbal reinforcement	Highlighters	
Visual scanning	Technology	
Organised Desk		
Filing	In/Out trays	Secretary or PA
Daily organisation goal	Urgent or Important trays	
Planning use of space	Laptop	
Following Instructions		
Listening skills	On tape or diagram	Broken into small sections
Visualisation skills		
Notes		
Minute Taking		
Listening skills	Using proformas	Someone else to do it
Memory strategies	Dictaphone	
Note taking		
Meetings		
Preview meetings	Dictaphone	Collaborate with others
Prediction of outcome		
Note taking		
Memory strategies/place		
Data entry		
Sub vocalisation	Colour coding	Work for short periods
Task analysis	Post-its	
Goal setting	Checklists	
Presentations		
Speaking skills	Role rehearsal	Presentation software
Memory	Video	Presentation training
aids/mindmapping		
Key notes		
Report Writing		
Purpose	Software	Collaborate with others
Planning	Proformas	Dictate to another
Drafting	Dictaphone	
Editing		

Some team members might be unaware of difficulties with written language and, if the dyslexic person is unable to provide an explanation, their lack of performance can be misconstrued. This will undermine the performance of the team in general, as well as the confidence of the dyslexic individual. Some dyslexics find working with other people extremely difficult because they like to have control over their own work routines. It is for this reason that self-employment is sometimes a good option, provided they create an infrastructure which helps them deal with the tasks they find difficult.

Interviews

Although some dyslexic people are good at expressing themselves verbally, because of their information processing difficulty, interviews can be especially stressful. Their lack of confidence can undermine the way they present and, at times, exacerbate their difficulties in areas such as word finding and their clarity of expression. It is important for a dyslexic person to be able to answer the following questions about the job they are being interviewed for:

- What is the job description?
- What are the task demands?
- What do I have to do?
- What skills do I have?
- What skills do I need to develop?
- Can I transfer any skills from my previous experiences, either at work or home?
- What are the potential difficulties?
- What type of supervision and support systems are there?

At the interview it is important to try and 'get a feel' for the job and address the question 'is this job good enough for me?'

The issues of disclosure must be considered and this is raised again in Chapter 10. Dyslexic people do need to consider how they might answer some of the following questions:

- What does dyslexia mean?
- How exactly does it affect you?
- What problems will it present you in this job?
- What would you need to help solve these problems?
- How do you work best?
- Will being dyslexic interfere with your output?
- If we need to train you, how do you learn best?
- Can you work well in a team?
- Can you be given a lead role in a team?
- Why should I employ you when I can hire another person who does not have any difficulties?
- What are you good at?

Mind mapping the job competencies and also noting examples of their experience of these enables people to answer the interviewer's questions more easily. It can also be helpful for dyslexic people to role play an interview situation or to rehearse what they are going to say. Some people find that visualisation techniques can help them deal with a stressful situation. It can be useful, although somewhat painful, to have feedback on why the interview was not a success. Once again, being prepared is essential.

A Note on the Use of Technology

There is no doubt that the use of technology has made an enormous difference to the lives of dyslexic people. It does, however, demand people develop new skills, including typing, as well as the appropriate use of hardware and software. There has also been a reduction in the availability of secretarial support, leaving those who are able to rely on this vulnerable and exposed as they are responsible for all their own written work. Nevertheless, there is a wide range of technological aids available that many dyslexic people find useful, including Speech to Text and Text to Speech software, time management, planning and organisation packages. Many employers are happy to provide technological aids as a way of making adjustments, allowing the dyslexic person to compensate. This can be supported by government programmes, Access to Work, and an Assessment of Need being conducted to determine suitable provision. Perhaps the most important aspect is, however, ensuring that appropriate training in the use of technology is provided. An example of a workplace assessment reports follow.

Workplace Consultancy Report

Contents of Report

Purpose of consultation
Background information
Impact of dyslexia and recommendations for
  1. Skills and strategy training
  2. Technological solutions
  3. The working environment

Purpose of Consultation   C came to my office for a dyslexia consultation at the request of his managers. The purpose was:

• To discuss the impact dyslexia was having on his performance at work.
• To make recommendations for adjustments to enable C to further develop his skills, capitalise on his strengths and work effectively.

The report has been compiled from information gathered from discussion with C himself, and his dyslexia assessment report.

Dyslexia Consultancy Report

Introduction

C is an auditor (trainee). He is experiencing some difficulties at work. Recently the demands of his job have been increasing; he has to process large amounts of information as well as pay attention to detail; he has to write an increasing number of reports. This takes him longer and he has to work to deadlines, which has increased the pressure on him as he is no longer in control of his own time. This has been affecting his performance. As he is dyslexic, C's employers are keen to establish how best he can be helped so they sought this workplace consultation.

Background

C was first assessed as dyslexic when he was a child and he had specialist help and extra time during his education. He was successful, having found solutions to his difficulties; he gained a 2:1 in Finance and Accounting from Smithfield University. Like many dyslexic people, after achieving a good degree, C was not aware that dyslexia might impact on his performance at work; he knew that he might have to work longer to produce work of a high standard but was prepared to do this. He told his employers that he was dyslexic on entry and received extra time in his professional examinations.

C was last assessed as dyslexic when he was at university. The assessment revealed that he is a person of considerable ability; he has a sound general knowledge and very good verbal comprehension skills. His non-verbal reasoning skills are also good: he can see the big picture, analyse problems well from all angles and is likely to have good strategic thinking skills. However, he is dyslexic as he has difficulty processing information in working memory and this is affecting his literacy skills in that he reads and writes slowly and his spelling and proofreading are not commensurate with his other abilities.

The Impact of Dyslexia   C has a high level of metacognitive awareness and it is this, coupled with his intelligence, that has enabled him to succeed thus far. However, people not recognising that he might take longer to complete some tasks, especially when it involves new learning and having to work harder to achieve work of a good standard without understanding, will undermine his confidence in his ability and impact on his performance.

C said that he is self-motivated and determined. He was aware that he had to be organised; he preferred to deal with one task at a time; and that he needed to write the important things down. He knew he was better at both writing and speaking if he has the chance to reflect on what needed to be said. He took longer to assimilate information but then he could reproduce it in a clear and concise format.

C's job includes:

- assisting the team in gathering audit evidence
- preparing analysis of accounting data

- building client relationships, and managing the budget and timetable of an account
- participation in the process and finalisation of audit assignments
- ensuring compliance with internal and external requirements
- providing the initial solutions to client challenges

His work involves:

- gathering data from a variety of sources
- attending meetings with clients
- reading and analysing information
- writing reports – producing detailed and accurate paperwork
- accessing information from databases
- organising his time
- attending training courses
- taking professional examinations
- general administrative tasks – emails – taking phone calls

C enjoys his job and feels that so long as he has time to develop his skills and extra time to absorb information in the early stages, he will be successful. He said that he is good at problem solving; this is consistent with his dyslexia assessment report which stated that he is capable of working at a high level. C also said that he enjoys working in a team and the management and coaching role of his job and he likes the client facing focus of his work.

Recommendations for Skill Development, IT solutions and Adjustments

C has found many solutions and ways of working effectively. Furthermore many of the suggestions may well have been implemented as good management practice; however he would benefit from the following:

1. Organisational Strategies

These are the key skills for a dyslexic person. C has already developed some good strategies but he does need to continue to extend these as the demands of the job role increase. C could:

- Refine his task analysis skills – knowing exactly what needs to be done – knowing how best to approach it – what might be the barriers.
- Improve his time estimation and goal setting skills so that he can produce work more easily to deadline.
- Prioritisation skills – developing symbols or colour-coding techniques.

- Make better use of a calendar and task bar on Outlook or equivalent or use a diary to have an overall view of what needs to be done on a quarterly, monthly and weekly basis.

IT Solutions to be Considered

- a Blackberry that synchronises with the office diary;
- remote working access to the office systems.

Input from Others

- Overview of the project so that C can put the work in the context of the bigger picture.
- Clear instructions.
- Deadlines being given as soon as possible.
- Priority work being highlighted.
- Brief catch up meetings if required.

2. Paperwork

C has worked hard and his literacy skills are competent. However he has residual problems with reading, spelling and proofreading.

Reading – C reads slowly and it can take him a while to get the information he needs. He already uses strategies such as skimming and scanning to get the detail at speed but he would benefit from:

- Refining these skills and having more confidence.
- He should be more deliberate in seeking out the information, analysing the task before he begins – trying to identify what he is looking for before he reads – this will also help him focus his attention and aid concentration.
- Developing a systematic approach to record the information so he can use it more efficiently, i.e. using printouts and top copy summaries.

Written Work – C said generally his writing was competent but that sometimes found the translation of his ideas into words and onto paper difficult. He would benefit from developing the following skills:

- Exploring strategies such as using Post-it notes as markers and checklists to help him collate all the information more easily.
- Utilising a variety of planning strategies – e.g. mind mapping, flow charts, bullet points – depending on the task.
- Using templates and proformas – to develop a framework and structure to work from.
- Some coaching in sentence construction to help him express the information clearly.

- Developing proofreading strategies such as error analysis and his own glossary for homophones.

Technological Solutions

C has been recommended specialist software packages in the past but not found them helpful. However I would recommend that he explore what is available now; some of packages are available online now for him to trial.

The following may help him:

1. Voice recognition software: **Dragon Naturally Speaking** with appropriate headsets would help him get the information down more easily. There is also a read-back facility which would enable him to proofread more effectively. He can experiment with this if he has an **i-phone** as **Dragon Dictation** is a downloadable app.
2. A **dictaphone** that is compatible with the voice recognition software would help with note taking after meetings and personal memos.
3. Planning software such as **Mind Genius or Mind manager or Inspiration** which would help him structure his reports.
4. **Texthelp Gold** is a software package that helps with spelling and homophones, and proofreading.

Input from Others   C should be able to:

- Present a first draft.
- Ask people to proofread important documents for him before they are sent out, particularly if he is overloaded or it has been a very busy day.
- Be given extra time to produce new or complex written work.

3. Meetings and Presentations

To work effectively in meetings and give presentations, people have to be able to listen, process information and often take notes at the same time. This all places great demands on the working memory system; it requires good immediate and rapid recall and automatic literacy skills. C, like many dyslexic people, may find this challenging.

He would benefit from developing:

- Planning and reviewing skills, which should improve his confidence and performance.
- Minimalist note making techniques such as mind mapping.
- Strategies for clarification and the control of information.

Technological Solutions

1. The **Live scribe pen** may help him take notes in meetings although it does record speech and so it may not be possible to use on all occasions.

4. Input from Others

- Being given an overview as far in advance as possible.
- The opportunity to have a brief discussion prior to a particular meeting to confirm or clarify information.
- Clarification and summarising points in a meeting would enable him to make notes and write up minutes more easily.

5. Professional Examinations

C would benefit from refining his revision and examination strategies to enable him to recall the information more efficiently.

- 3 Ms
- Planning his revision and timing in the examination
- MCQ strategy practice
- Examination question analysis

6. The Work Environment

C works in an open plan office with people in quite close proximity, which can be distracting. It is not a problem at the moment and it is part of his job to be able to converse easily with other members of the team. However the following may be helpful.

- The location of his desk to the quietest place in the room – perhaps next to a wall – end of row away from people traffic
- Auditory distraction – ear plugs, i-Pods, noise cancelling head phones.
- Small/low screens to avoid distraction and give him somewhere to pin reminders.
- Flexitime to work when office less busy.
- Working from home.
- A quiet office where he can go when working on complex material. This would be particularly important if he is using Dragon Dictation software.

Coaching

C has developed many effective ways of working but he would benefit from some dyslexia specialist coaching; to increase his understanding of dyslexia and the ways in which he can transfer his skills; to explore the suggestions above and to enable him to make the best use of his skills and to work more efficiently. I would recommend up to six one-hour sessions. These can be provided at this Centre or at his place of work.

Mentoring

He may also benefit from having a mentor with whom he can discuss his performance and any concerns without being misunderstood.

Conclusion

Dyslexia is best understood as an information processing difference. It is hidden and complex; each dyslexic person has their own pattern of skills and abilities; these are shaped by their experience and their personality; and the impact of dyslexia varies according to circumstances. It is important that the individual knows how it may affect them and what they need to ask for to work well. In terms of career progression it is important that C is in a job that taps his skills as this will enable him to demonstrate his abilities.

Current research with dyslexic people indicates four factors that enable them to be successful: self understanding; being in a job that taps their strengths; making use of technological and creative solutions; and managers understanding the individual's dyslexia.

C is a man of considerable skills and ability; he has already achieved a great deal and, given time, he is capable of doing well. He will be best helped to achieve this by being able to refine his skills as the demands of his job increase and by an understanding that he may take a little longer at times and need to do things differently in the context of his job; this is not a reflection of his ability or competency, just a different way of processing information.

A Coaching Course Outline

Following the kind of evaluation described above a dyslexic person can embark on a course of training/coaching. The programme should be planned with the client, in discussion with their manager/supervisor, but should cover most of the following areas.

The programme should be formulated as a personal development plan and a suggested format is set out below.

Initial Consultation

This involves goal setting. Long-term goals are discussed and short-term aims are planned. Particular problems are raised and possible ways of solving them are considered. How the experience and the skills the person has can be built upon, and the compensations and accommodations that are available, are also considered.

Personal Development Modules

Understanding Dyslexia

This module focuses on the nature of the person's difficulties and how they affect them now, how they have affected them in the past, and what solutions they have found to help them. Having some understanding and an explanation for their difficulties helps the person feel in control, and can give them confidence.

Self Advocacy

Understanding their skills and abilities, their thinking skills, as well as their learning and working style enables a person to utilise their strengths more effectively. It is important they know how to explain the nature of the difficulties they have, what problems they encounter, and the solutions that they can offer. It is also important that they know how to promote their abilities.

Skill Development Modules

1. **Organisational Skills**
   These skills underpin success. Dyslexic people have to work hard at this as it is not automatic. This module includes:

   > Organisation of time – developing the awareness of time, the effective use of time, prioritising, goal setting.
   > Organisation of work – setting up an appropriate filing system and record keeping.
   > Personal organisation – organisation at home, coping with chores, and personal issues such as health, etc.

2. **Task Analysis and Metacognitive Skills**
   Analysing a task so they recognise the components enables a person to match their skills to the task with the right strategy. It enables them to improve their performance by developing previewing, monitoring and reviewing skills. It helps to focus concentration.

3. **Memory Skills**
   Understanding what memory is, how an individual remembers best, and developing visual and auditory memory skills, enables a person to feel more in control. A range of strategies such as visualisation, mnemonics and memory systems are looked at. The three principles that aid memory – making things manageable and multisensory and making use of memory aids – are discussed.

4. **Specific Work Training Skills**
   This module looks at the job description, the task demands of the job, and developing specific skills. It considers transferable skills, such as:
   - data entry, filing, recording information
   - coping with meetings
   - telephone skills
   - interview skills and presentation skills
   - working in a team
   - remembering instructions.

5. **Basic Literacy Skills**
   This module works on developing basic literacy skills. It also focuses on the skills for daily living, e.g. form filling, reading timetables.

6. **Reading Speed Comprehension Strategies**
   This module aims to develop the client's reading skills to enable them to extract information more quickly from text. Skimming, scanning and finding the main idea are covered. It can also cover critical and analytical reading. It is based on the four levels of reading: Functional, Vocational, Technical and Professional.

7. **Writing Skills**
   This module includes understanding the nature of the task, writing with a purpose, and looking at different styles of writing: descriptive, reports, memos, using bullet points, presentations, planning and editing written work, as well as proofreading.

8. **Spelling, Punctuation and Grammar**
   This is based on a diagnostic assessment with the focus being largely on learning strategies for specific, personal or technical spellings required by the individual. Some spelling rule instruction will be included.

9. **Numeracy**
   Training focuses on specific areas, with practical applications of maths. The first step is to establish whether the problem is conceptual or procedural, and the implications for training.

10. **Social Skills**
    This module covers effective communication skills, including listening skills, developing concentration, awareness, non-verbal communication, appropriate responses, controlling anger and frustration, and working in a team.

11. **Stress Free Strategies**
    The module explores a range of strategies which can be used to manage stress in the workplace. It includes identifying the source, relaxation techniques, dealing with motivation, and coping with panic and with change.

Summary

1. Dyslexic people can be successful in most, if not all occupations. This, however, is reliant on a combination of the support they receive at work as well as their own personal development.

2. A whole organisation approach to supporting dyslexic people can be the most effective way of ensuring that they are able to capitalise on their talents.

3. The problems they experience with literacy can continue to undermine a dyslexic person's performance at work, but difficulties in organisation, time management and coping with the work environment can also contribute to them performing less well than expected.

4. There are a whole range of skills and compensations dyslexic people can develop which will enhance their performance.

5. Relatively simple and cost effective adjustments can be made for dyslexic people and these ensure that they are able to fulfil their potential.

10

Advocacy

Synopsis. *This chapter focuses on the understanding of dyslexic people and the way in which this is fostered through the legislative framework. The role of advocacy and self advocacy groups is also described.*

Introduction

The preceding chapters have described the interventions that can enable dyslexic people to become successful. We reiterate that the underlying philosophy of this book is understanding. As well as evidence-based practice understanding is also fostered through advocacy, including legislative provision and self-advocacy.

Essential to the improvement of provision for dyslexic adults is the three 'U's. That is:

- Understanding – by parents and partners
- Understanding – by teachers/tutors and employers
- Understanding – dyslexic people's self-understanding.

The past 30 years has seen an increased interest in advocacy and self-advocacy. Advocacy for dyslexic people has been best represented by the work of organisations such as the British Dyslexia Association, the International Dyslexia Association, the European Dyslexia Association and the Learning Disabilities Association of America. Self advocacy is reflected in the work of adult support groups, often promoted by advocacy groups. The former have argued for help, support and equal opportunities. The latter have argued for rights and equity.

Organisations advocating in the interests of dyslexic people have been quite effective in promoting greater understanding, but without allowing for self-advocacy they can

The Dyslexic Adult: Interventions and Outcomes – An Evidence-based Approach, Second Edition.
David McLoughlin and Carol Leather.
© 2013 John Wiley & Sons, Ltd. Published 2013 by John Wiley & Sons, Ltd.

conflict with the very people they are trying to help. At the same time self-advocacy needs to be based in self-understanding and empathy. Otherwise those seeking their rights and greater equity can alienate those who are trying to help them. It should be recognised that rather than there being 'experts in dyslexia' there are a variety of people who have an expertise. There are professionals for example who know how to diagnose, advise and train dyslexic people. Dyslexic individuals do, however, have their own views and an understanding based on their personal experience. As we have written earlier we have learned a great deal from them. Nevertheless, we need to be careful about the use of alternative terminology. Neurodiversity, for example, has been applied to all the specific learning difficulties, including dyslexia, dyspraxia, Attention Deficit Disorder, Tourette's Syndrome, Autistic Spectrum Disorders and Anxiety disorders (Hendrickx, 2010; Pollack, 2009). The term was devised by the more articulate within the self-advocacy movement. It is doubtful that the 40-year-old who cannot read or write and is before a court, having signed a document they could not understand, would see himself as being neurodiverse rather than having a disability. Nor would the person who can't read the destination sign on the front of a bus quickly enough to signal it to stop.

The desire to be thought of as different rather than disabled is understandable, but the use of one term to replace another that some find unattractive does not, as has been suggested, reflect a paradigm shift, and as Kauffman (2008) has written, 'people soon figure out the euphemisms we use for the phenomena we call disabilities' and they 'fool no one for long, but they do confuse communication for a while and ultimately make whatever we are referring to appear more negative or less worthy of respect than the original term' (Kauffman, 2008: 246). Further, there is no legislative provision for neurodiversity, only for impairment or disability. How, therefore, do we decide on criteria for the allocation of resources? There are plenty of people who do things differently out of preference and habit. Are they entitled to accommodations for their diversity? New terminology is too easily adopted without clearly thinking through the implications.

The description of dyslexia provided in Chapter 1 has implications for the perception of dyslexia within the context of models of disability. Several authors have interpreted it within the social rather than medical model and those who promote the concept of neurodiversity adhere to the former (Herrington & Hunter-Carsch, 2001; Dudley-Marling, 2004; Macdonald, 2009), and some of our work has been interpreted to reflect this (Reid et al., 2008). There is no doubt that environmental factors play a part in determining outcomes and that the impact of dyslexia rather depends upon the development of people's lives and careers, as well as changes in their circumstances. Those who adhere to the social model assume inclusion will be achieved through accommodation or adjustment. Grant (2009) wrote that 'there is a societal obligation that others make suitable adjustments and accommodations to enable inherent potential to be fully realized' (Grant, 2009: 34). This will not, however, enable dyslexic people and can lead to learned helplessness. If demands continue to increase, so will the need to develop new skills and strategies; dyslexic people can do both. Adjustments provide a window during which they have time to put them in place.

Specific learning difficulties should be seen as neither medical nor social, and polarising them in this way is unhelpful. What is needed is a new model of disability appropriate for people with specific learning difficulties:

specific cognitive → *skill deficit*

This acknowledges that there are difficulties caused by neurological and consequent cognitive differences, but that these can be addressed by the individual and society working in partnership. Dyslexic people who understand and can advocate for themselves, and know how to develop new skills, as well as transfer those they have to varied situations will be able to meet new challenges independently, regardless of whether the latter result from increased intellectual or societal demands.

Advocacy and self-advocacy are fostered by relevant legislation. The legislative framework can underpin rights, equity and equal opportunities, although it does not always work to the advantage of the individual (Konur, 2007). The policy and practices of government departments will foster appropriate help and support.

The Legislative Framework

In the United Kingdom provision has been made under the terms of the Disability Discrimination Act, 1995 and more recently the Equality Act, 2010. In the United States provision is fostered by a variety of legislation, including the Americans with Disabilities Act, 1990. The United Kingdom Acts owe much to the latter, having been modelled on it. The Equality Act defines a disability as *a physical or mental impairment that has a substantial and long-term adverse effect on his or her ability to carry out normal day-to-day activities.* The American Act defines a disability as *a physical or mental impairment that limits a major life activity.* Although the focus here is on the Equality Act, our experience being with this, some of the issues it raises are central to both. The Guidance on matters to be taken into account under the terms of the Equality Act indicates that:

- The person must have an impairment that is either physical or mental.
- The impairment must have adverse effects which are substantial.
- The substantial effects must be long term.
- The long-term substantial adverse effects must be effects on normal day-to-day activities.

(Office for Disability Issues, 2011: 7)

Dyslexia as a Mental Impairment

Developmental disorders such as dyslexia, dyspraxia and Asperger's syndrome are now included as examples of an impairment. Further, although not specifically mentioned in the existing World Health Organisation International Classification of Diseases or the

Diagnostic and Statistical Manual, the behavioural characteristics of dyslexia are listed under headings such as Specific Reading Disorder. Dyslexia can, therefore, be considered to constitute a mental impairment and be covered by the Equality Act but other criteria have to be met.

Adverse Effects which are Substantial

Concerns have been expressed at the parameters recommended for considering adverse effects by the legislators. A substantial effect is one that is more than minor or trivial. Some of the examples given that might apply to dyslexia are that it would be reasonable to regard as a substantial effect:

- Persistent inability to remember the names of familiar people such as family or friends.
- Difficulty in adapting to minor changes in work routine.
- Difficulty understanding or following simple verbal instructions.
- Persistent and significant difficulty in reading or understanding written material.
- Persistent distractibility or difficulty concentrating.

It would not be reasonable to regard as a substantial effect:

- Occasionally forgetting the name of a familiar person such as a colleague.
- Inability to concentrate on a task requiring application over several hours.
- Inability to fill in a long, detailed technical document without assistance.
- Inability to read at speed under pressure.

Long-Term Substantial Effects

Establishing that effects are long term is quite simple. As we have seen in Chapter 1 dyslexia is usually genetic in origin. Even when formal diagnosis has been well into adulthood, the individual will have always been dyslexic and will continue to be so.

Normal Day-to-Day Effects

These are not defined and establishing that there are adverse effects on the ability to carry out normal day-to-day activities can be difficult. Dyslexia is not well understood as an information processing difficulty and employers, as well as lawyers, are likely to focus on literacy skills alone. If someone does have very basic reading, writing and spelling skills this inevitably has an effect on day-to-day functioning.

I find it really hard to express to people to what extent being dyslexic makes me the person I am, and how much it effects my confidence. The Majority of people may understand that it means I have poor reading and writing skills, but it has probably never occurred to them how much it effects my day to day living. The number of times reading and writing are involved in an average day. For example something as simple as the invention of the printed cheque has made shopping a lot easier, for I do not have to worry about spelling numbers incorrectly or feeling embarrassed if I have to ask for help. There are numerous times that I have got lost driving a car or gone the wrong direction on the tube.

Literate dyslexics are, however, in a more difficult position. Those supporting dyslexic people need to focus on the extent of the information processing problem, particularly the impact on memory and executive functioning. Someone who has good academic qualifications and advanced literacy skills but needs to get to work much earlier than everyone else, and leave later in order to complete all the tasks which would be required in a normal day, is being affected on a day to day basis. The time taken to carry out a normal day-to-day activity in comparison with others can be taken into account, as can the way in which they carry it out. A Company Director who is also a mature student commented:

My day to day experience as a dyslexic can be compared to a tangled ball of string. Some days I am able to unravel the ball of string. Those are the good days when I am able to find the correct words to articulate myself. On the other days the ball of string seems to stay tangled. On those days I am aware that I am not expressing myself as well. I also experience what I call 'one off' dyslexic encounters. The 'one off' experiences are usually mispronouncing a word or mixing up a group of words as I speak or stumbling over reading something out load. I become embarrassed and frustrated especially if what I have said or read out load creates laugher. I know people aren't really laughing at me because when I mix up words or mispronounce them they often do sound funny! I also find that on most days I need to read things several times in order to understand what I have read.

In the United Kingdom Employment Tribunals have accepted that 'normal day to day activities' do not include work of a particular form because no particular form of work is normal for most people. They have also taken into account the warning that disabled persons are likely habitually to play down the effect that their disabilities have.

The implications of the terms of legislation for practitioners working with dyslexic people are that:

1. They need to be very specific about the nature of dyslexia in its widest context if:
   (a) it is to be interpreted as a disability, and
   (b) day-to-day effects are to be established.
2. They need to make very specific recommendations about appropriate skill development training, compensations and adjustments.
3. It also demonstrates that dyslexic people must understand their needs if they are to advocate for themselves in employment settings.

Reasonable Adjustments

Under the legislation employers must not discriminate and are obliged to make reasonable adjustments to the job or the workplace to help a disabled person do a job, as well as in recruitment/selection.

Reasonable adjustment/accommodation has become a standard phrase when referring to supporting dyslexic people. What is meant are adjustments which are reasonable. We have suggested adjustments for different contexts in Chapters 7 and 9. They should always:

- be based on documented individual needs
- allow the most integrated experience possible
- not compromise the essential requirements of the job/course
- not impose an undue financial or administrative burden

(adapted from Scott, 1994)

Individual Needs

Recommendations for adjustments should be evidence based. The sources of evidence are shown in the graphic organiser in Figure 10.1.

Consistent with the pillars of evidence described in Chapter 1, general objective evidence is provided by theory, particularly that which comes from the kind of research outlined in the earlier chapters of this book. Individual objective evidence is provided by the assessment process, based on research and theory. Subjective evidence is provided by the individual's history, including what has worked in the past, as well as their own preferences. A combination of the objective and subjective should ensure that an individual's needs are identified and contribute to them being met.

Integrated Experience

The underlying philosophy of disability legislation is inclusion. Adjustments should allow an individual to be included, and there is a risk that too many adjustments can exclude and lead to learned helplessness. There are, for example, adults whose difficulties were identified early in their life and during their school years many adjustments have

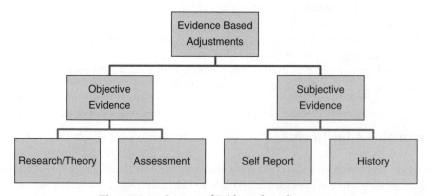

Figure 10.1   Sources of Evidence for Adjustment

been made for them. Their expectation on leaving school, therefore, is that this will also be the case in their working lives. They assume that they will be exempt from particular tasks required in a job, but this can mean that they feel excluded as they are not fully participating, and it can sometimes lead to resentment amongst their colleagues. This includes individuals who have, for example, been promoted without undertaking the usual evaluation process. Others can perceive this as being unfair, and the individual might always be left with doubts about their competence.

Essential Requirements of the Job/Course

It is assumed that when someone applies for and secures a job they will have most of the qualities and competencies required. Adjustments are intended to level the playing field and make it possible for individuals to demonstrate their competence without the difficulties stemming from dyslexia proving a major hindrance. The legislation is not designed to support people in job roles for which they have no aptitude and to which they are entirely unsuited.

An Undue Financial or Administrative Burden

In making adjustments financial and administrative constraints should be considered. Whilst, for example, it might be reasonable to provide an individual with specialist software it would be unreasonable to expect an organisation to spend a considerable amount of money modifying an integrated computer network in order that one person can take advantage of a specialist package. Further, as we have written earlier managers can make a significant difference to whether dyslexic individuals are successful in employment. Nevertheless, expecting them to devote an overwhelming amount of time to supporting one individual, particularly at the expense of their own work and the management of others, would not be reasonable.

Adjustments in Recruitment, Selection and Promotion

Another way in which employers are required to make adjustments is in the process of recruitment and selection. The Employers' Forum on Disability recommends flexibility, as often minor changes can make a significant difference, and a focus on 'what' is to be achieved in the job rather than 'how' it is to be achieved, allowing for a dyslexic person's different working style.

Usually the recruitment process begins with the completion of an application form. A simple format with a clear typeface, acceptance of emailed applications so that they can be typed and checked for spelling and perhaps the use of different coloured paper can all accommodate the needs of dyslexic people.

There have been particular concerns where psychometric tests measuring abilities and attainments are used. Dyslexia does affect performance in test situations, especially where there are time constraints, and dyslexic people might therefore be prevented

The Dyslexic Adult

from demonstrating their abilities. Someone could, for example, be very good at verbal reasoning but this is not reflected in their performance when they complete 'pencil and paper' tests. It is not unusual for dyslexics to gain lower scores on group administered tests of ability than those they achieve when tests are administered individually and verbally.

In making adjustments the key issue is to provide an accurate assessment of job-relevant abilities and aptitudes (Meehan et al., 1998). They should eliminate obstacles that are immaterial to what tests are intended to measure, and include changes in materials and procedures that enable an individual to participate in an assessment in such a way that allows them to demonstrate their knowledge and ability rather than their disability (Thurlow et al., 2009).

Types of Test Accommodations/Adjustments

Gregg (2009) provides a comprehensive guide to making adjustments evidence based, particularly in assessment settings. Whether for academic purposes, recruitment, selection or promotion these can include:

Test presentation – this provides access to content and can include:
- reader (human);
- Text to Speech software;
- consideration of print size and font, as well as colour.

Test response – this provides the opportunity to show knowledge/ability and can include:
- verbal test;
- Speech to Text software;
- scribe;
- word processor.

Test scheduling/timing – this addresses speed issues and can include:
- extra time;
- breaks.

Test setting – this reduces distractions and allows for verbalisation:
- private room;
- quiet room;
- small group.

Adjustments for dyslexic people during the selection process could include:

i. Applicants should be contacted to provide information about the assessment process and the different types of task involved. This would enable them to say if they are likely to have any difficulties and how these can best be overcome.
ii. Applicants should be encouraged to provide information about the ways in which they would normally deal with a 'pencil and paper' task.
iii. Test publishers should be contacted as they might have materials required in the format the candidate can use.

iv. Un-timed tests could be used or candidates could be given extra time. Changing time allowances can, however, create problems in interpretation, especially when speed is integral to the test. If speed is important then no-one should be provided with adjustments. Determining how much extra time should be allowed is difficult. Too little might not lessen the disadvantage; too much might increase it, fatigue being a factor (Nester, 1993). The purpose of selection/promotion and academic tests is not to measure speeded reading comprehension, and extra time is not a benefit if an individual does not know or understand the material.

v. How the person would use the skill being measured on the job and whether the adapted version of the test measures the same ability is a key consideration.

vi. A qualitative view should be taken in making decisions, integrating all the information about the candidate, including test scores, exercise results and ratings. The skills the candidate may have gained from just managing his or her disability should not be underestimated.

vii. Employers who use methodology such as an interview could allow dyslexic people to refer to notes.

We reiterate that adjustments should always be evidence based and an example of how this can be achieved is shown in the graphic organiser shown in Figure 10.2.

The failure to make adjustments evidence based, and reliance on the nomothetic rather than ideographic, is perhaps best illustrated by the case of a medical student who took legal action against the institution at which she was studying, because she argued that multiple choice test formats discriminate against dyslexic individuals, relying on recommendations made by advocacy groups. At an objective level, on the basis of a study

---

Difficulty: Poor examination performance
Adjustment: Use of scribe in examinations
Rationale: – slow writing
           – poor handwriting

Underlying abilities	*Objective evidence*
Verbal ability	WAIS (IV) – verbal tests
– vocabulary	WRIT – verbal tests
– fluency	
Underlying abilities	*Subjective evidence*
Verbal ability	Performance in interview
	Previous experience of dictation
Underlying deficits	*Objective evidence*
Slow processing speed (symbols)	Digit symbol modalities
	WAIS (V) Processing speed index
	DASH +17
Underlying deficits	*Subjective evidence*
Slow writing	History of poor exam performance
	Complaints of others about legibility of writing

Figure 10.2   Evidence for Use of Scribe in Examinations

of 900 medical students, Ricketts et al. (2009) conclude that properly designed multiple choice format tests of medical knowledge do not discriminate against those with specific learning difficulties. At a subjective level our experience is that some dyslexic people like them and others don't. At an individual level the student in question didn't like them and sought an alternative assessment process. The question of why she found them difficult was not addressed. Nevertheless, on the basis of her performance on a multiple choice reading comprehension test, low processing speed score and difficulty with a spatial span task it was possible to make very specific recommendations. These included allowing extra time proportionate to her speed of reading, and allowing her to mark her answers on the question booklet rather than needing to locate codes on a separate score sheet.

It is common practice to allow dyslexic people extra time to complete tests and examinations. This does not, however, mean that the matter is without controversy. There are two particular issues:

1. It has been suggested that dyslexic people are advantaged by being allowed extra time.
2. There is disagreement on the issue of how much extra time should be allowed.

With regard to the first issue, systematic studies have demonstrated that extra time appears to minimise the impact of being dyslexic rather than advantage dyslexics. Shaywitz (2003) wrote that 'dyslexia robs a person of time: accommodations return it' (p. 314). That is, it makes a considerable difference for students with learning difficulties, but little to those without (Kay Runyan, 1991; Alaster, 1997; Sirecci et al., 2005; Lesaux, Lipka & Siegel, 2006). Extra time is therefore thought to level the playing field. 'Given sufficient time, dyslexic college students can perform at levels comparable to their non-disabled peers...' (Mosberg & Johns, 1994: 134). Nevertheless, following a meta-analysis of the existing literature, Gregg and Nelson (2012) concluded that there are still more questions than answers.

The issue of how much extra time a dyslexic candidate should be granted is more difficult, figures being plucked out of the air rather than based on evidence. Studies have revealed considerable variation amongst students with regard to the amount of time they needed to complete tasks. Insufficient will not accommodate the difficulty. Too much might be fatiguing and accommodate other factors such as anxiety and poor test taking skills, not just slow reading or writing. It might also result in an inflated perception of an individual's abilities (Zurcher & Bryant, 2001). Ofiesh and Hughes (2004) and Ofiesh et al. (2005) have suggested the decision as to the amount of time allowed should be multifaceted and include:

- Awareness of the average amount of time students use.
- An understanding of the test characteristics.
- Information from diagnostic tests in targeted areas, e.g. reading fluency.
- An individual's functional limitations.

The first provides an argument for criterion-based testing. Knowing, for example, that the average reading speed for a particular task is 200 words per minute allows for a recommendation of 50 per cent extra time when a candidate's reading speed is only 100 words per minute. Comparison will, however, require a knowledge of the nature of the tests to be taken, including readability levels. Diagnostic testing and measurement of functional limitations will reflect the extent of the difficulty to be accommodated. Following such a process should lead to the granting of equitable solutions and it should be clear from the next section of this chapter that dyslexic people requesting accommodations are rarely seeking an advantage.

Disclosing Dyslexia

We have referred earlier to the importance of disclosure. It is when dyslexic people start applying for jobs that they need to consider the question of disclosure very carefully. One of the ways in which the success of disability legislation and the understanding of specific learning difficulties is reflected in society is the disclosure rate; that is, the extent to which individuals inform employers and colleagues that they have a learning difficulty. Research has suggested that individuals with learning difficulties are reluctant to disclose, despite the existence of legislation that is supposed to prevent discrimination. The authors found that the majority of adults in the samples of individuals interviewed did not ask for accommodations (adjustments) in the selection process, did not tell their employers during an interview and did not ask for adjustments in the job (Gerber & Price, 2003; Gerber et al., 2004; Gerber et al., 2005; Madaus et al., 2002; Martin & McLoughlin, 2012).

Some of the reasons given reflect much misunderstanding surrounding dyslexia, both in terms of the stereotypes held by non-dyslexic people as well as the lack of understanding dyslexic people have of themselves. These included:

- I never thought it would apply to work.
- I was afraid to be found out – they might have taken the job away.
- They would think I couldn't do the job.
- People would look down on you.
- I was embarrassed.
- I didn't think it was my place to ask for those things.
- I would feel like a burden if they gave me anything extra.

Gerber and Price (2008) point out that the hidden nature of dyslexia means that dyslexic people have greater choice over whether or not to disclose. Dyslexic people are often selective, choosing those to whom they disclose carefully, and weighing up the benefits (Morris & Turnbull, 2006). Part of the process of disclosure involves educating others. Dyslexia is a 'hidden disability' and this means that dyslexic people often have to advocate for themselves, their difficulties being less obvious and less well understood. Many struggle with the issue, but if they wish to access resources and be protected under the terms of legislation they must. There are three key issues they need to address: When to raise the matter; Whom to tell; and What to say.

When to Say Something

To some extent addressing this has been resolved by the greater awareness that has resulted from disability legislation. Application forms often contain questions asking about issues such as disability. In the main dyslexic people should not be afraid to 'tick the dyslexia box' as its existence suggests the organisation might already be dyslexia friendly. If a dyslexic person gets past the first stage, submitting an application which secures an interview, they might raise the issue when interviewed, a second interview being a particularly good time.

Whom to Tell

The work that advocacy organisations do to promote understanding has helped to reduce the stigma sometimes associated with specific learning difficulties. Many organisations will have within their Human Resources Department individuals who have knowledge of disability provision; they will also have occupational health teams. It is within the Human Resources Department that one is most likely to find someone who can treat the matter confidentially and advocate for a dyslexic person by accessing resources and assisting them with career development. At a less formal level one might advise a supportive line manager or colleague.

What to Say

Whilst there is likely to be some expertise within an organisation this does not mean that the syndrome is properly understood. The common understanding of dyslexia is a misunderstanding. It is evident, for example, from the research referred to above that many dyslexic people themselves still think of it as a reading and spelling problem or at least an educational matter. They have never been told that the processing problem that creates difficulties with literacy persists into the adult years, undermining performance as demands increase.

The greatest expert on the impact of an individual's dyslexia can be the dyslexic person themselves. They know how it affects them on a day-to-day basis and usually have a good idea of how they work best. It is unreasonable to expect businesses to be experts in dyslexia. Disclosure is an exercise in self-advocacy so people need to develop their understanding of themselves and how dyslexia affects them in the workplace. 'I am dyslexic' is not enough. They need to explain what it means to them and offer solutions.

- 'I read thoroughly so need more time' is better than 'I read slowly'.
- 'I prefer dictating so use voice recognition software' is better than 'I am poor at typing.'
- 'I am a bit of a perfectionist so like to have others check over my work' is better than 'I am not good at proofreading'.
- 'I like instructions in writing' is better than 'I can't remember instructions'.
- 'I never forget a face' is better 'than I can't remember names'.

In other words dyslexic people need to be positive and be able to explain how they work best and suggest adjustments that will facilitate this.

In our experience dyslexic people rarely seek to advantage themselves by requesting adjustments. All they are asking for is to be valued for their abilities, persistence and determination, and to be treated equally. Adjustments do not give extra knowledge, talent or abilities. They just allow dyslexic people to show that they can do the job. Having said that, it is essential that dyslexic people are realistic about what they can achieve. They do need to have most of the competencies required, otherwise no amount of adjustment can make up the difference. The underlying philosophy of disability legislation is integration. Too many adjustments can lead to isolation as well as a great deal of frustration and stress. As we have indicated in Chapter 2 research has suggested that 'goodness of fit' is essential to success (Gerber et al., 1992). Disclosure, although a complex issue and process, is fundamental to achieving this. When it is done positively it should ensure that employers are able to meet a dyslexic person's needs and enable them to become increasingly successful. Nevertheless, more work needs to be done in the area of disclosure so that we can know exactly what will facilitate the process.

To avoid discrimination, and ensure that they are properly understood, dyslexic people need to be able to explain what dyslexia is, how it affects them, the way in which they work best, and what an employer can do to assist them. This applies during the process of selection and whilst in the job. Positive re-framing has been referred to earlier. Whilst it is never easy to know how much to say or when to say it, dyslexic people must:

1. **Understand themselves**
   - *Know their strengths.* We all have talents and abilities, and dyslexic people need to know what theirs are and feel positive about them.
   - *Know their weaknesses.* We all have these and need to work around them. It is important to be realistic and know one's limitations.
   - *Know what adjustments enable them to do their best.* Employers and colleagues can only know what to do if they are aware exactly what is being asked for.
   - *Know what situations to avoid.* There are those which will present difficulties which cannot be overcome.

2. **Be specific**
   - *Dyslexic people should only tell what is necessary to those who need to know.* They should therefore be discreet and selective. There will be people who are not ready to hear what they have to say.
   - *They should talk about what they can do.* If they have particular needs, they should tell people what they need rather than what their problem is.
   - *Dyslexic people should try to give a complete picture,* and be able to describe the problem, the cause and the solution.

3. **Provide information**
   It can be helpful to others to provide information, both verbally and in written form. Authoritative handouts provided by appropriate organisations can add credibility. These can include articles and books or DVD's about dyslexia, and suitable adjustments.

Essentially dyslexic people will get what they need by telling people what they need not what their problem is.

Policy and Practice in Employment

Responsibility for supporting people who have disabilities at work lies within government departments responsible for employment. In the United Kingdom it is the Department for Work and Pensions. The main scheme is known as Access to Work and is designed to provide help for people with disabilities in securing and maintaining employment with practical support such as the provision of special equipment, including technology and adaptations to premises, support workers and other assistants in meeting personal needs. Policies and practices change, but advice on current schemes should be available through the websites for different government departments, as well from advocacy groups.

Legislation in Education and Training

Internationally the rights of dyslexic students are supported by a variety of Acts and policies. In the United Kingdom the Disability Discrimination Act did not originally outlaw discrimination on grounds of disability in education. However, as a result of the Act, further and higher education institutions did have to publish disability statements. Training providers were covered under services and therefore they were not able to discriminate against disabled people on their training schemes. The Special Educational Needs and Disability Bill strengthened the Act, placing anti-discrimination responsibilities on schools and colleges, as well as providers of further education.

Policy in Higher Education

In the United Kingdom students in Higher Education can apply for funding from the Disabled Students Allowance, and there are similar programmes elsewhere. The United Kingdom scheme consists of three major supplementary allowances that can be claimed by a full-time or part-time student. These are:

1. Special equipment allowance to cover the duration of the student's course. This will pay for technical support.
2. Non-medical helper's allowance to enable the student to hire the services of someone to assist their academic work, for example a Learning Support tutor. They could also employ proofreaders, and so on.
3. There is also a General Disabled Students Allowance to cover items which are not covered by the other two allowances.

Disabled Students Allowances are available to any student who can prove that they have a disability, but they require current documentary evidence.

Self-Help and Self-Help Groups

We have referred to the benefit of shared experience in Chapter 4. Self-help is an attempt by people with a mutual problem to take control over the circumstances of their lives. It is founded on the principle that people who share a disability have something to offer each other that a professional cannot provide. Self-help can take many forms including formal self-help groups. They are based on the independent living paradigm. A self-help agency's role is to empower its clients through the following related activities at three levels of organisation:

1. Individuals are directly provided or helped to gain access to resources and skills necessary to reach desired goals, and alternative models are provided to counter stigma.
2. Organisations are structured to give clients access to roles that permit them to take responsibility for and exercise discretion over policies that affect them, collectively within agencies.
3. Changes are sought in the larger society that both better the condition of people with disabilities and enable them to participate in making decisions concerning policies that affect them.

(Segal, Silverman & Temkin, 1993)

Self-help groups can represent a demanding challenge even to professionals who wish to establish cooperation with them. The reality is that they exist and professionals need to accept the challenge of relating to and cooperating with them. Self-help groups may be distinguished from individual self-help in that they represent a mutual helping process, with members supporting and helping others whilst at the same time helping themselves. The benefits of such groups have been referred to in Chapter 4.

Self-help groups are not an alternative to professional services. They aim at and represent something quite different, namely the support which an equal relationship can give and the personal development, following from the combination of giving and receiving support. Self-help groups show that resources for help may be found in people themselves, provided therefore that a framework and professional support is available. Clarification of professional and voluntary approaches can be expressed thus:

Lay Persons Use	*Professionals Use*
Feelings and experiences	Knowledge and insight from theory
Intuition and common sense	Systematic assessment and knowledge about interventions
Here and now perspective	Long-term perspective
Identification	Awareness

The factors which seem to hold professionals back from self-help groups are:

1. Firstly they may not be aware that groups sometimes need professional support because they often do not know how to ask for help without risking being overwhelmed by too much professional benevolence.
2. Secondly professionals frequently feel annoyed and provoked by the different values of self help groups and think that it may be irresponsible to send their clients to such groups.
3. Another excuse for not getting involved with self help groups is that they claim to want to be independent and often voice this by saying that they do not want professionals to help them. However helping does not have to mean intervening and many self help groups do need support.

(Habermann, 1990)

Dyslexia and Criminal Law

A good deal of publicity has been given to the possibility of there being a disproportionate number of dyslexic people in the prison population. Studies in the United Kingdom and abroad have suggested that the incidence could be up to as much as 50 per cent. For a review of the literature readers are referred to Reid and Kirk (2001). Suffice it to say here that the issue is controversial; systematic studies having been criticised on a number of counts, including the criteria used to define dyslexia and the assessment methodologies employed.

Dyslexia does not cause criminal behaviour and is never an excuse for it. It does, however, make sense to assume that where affective characteristics such as frustration have become marked, dyslexic people could 'go off the rails', and they might be a mitigating factor.

It is important that individuals who are likely to encounter dyslexic people in the course of their work, including lawyers and police officers, are aware of the nature of dyslexia and its impact on both verbal and written communication and the fact that difficulties in these areas can be exacerbated when someone is under stress. People with literacy difficulties will sign documents they have been unable to read and/or understand, even when they have had them read to them. The problems with verbal communication described earlier can affect the way someone performs in an interview.

Even if the incidence of dyslexic people amongst the prison population has been exaggerated by studies, one of the encouraging aspects is that they have led to the recommendation that awareness training be provided for lawyers, magistrates and probation officers. The British Dyslexia Association (2012) publishes a guide for professionals working within justice systems.

Summary

1. The emphasis of any intervention designed to support dyslexic people should be on enabling them to advocate for themselves.

2. There needs to be an effective partnership between advocacy and self-advocacy groups, as they are working towards a common goal.
3. The success of dyslexic people can be promoted through relevant legislation, policy and practice.
4. Whilst dyslexic people can be supported in many ways, ultimately they each have to advocate for themselves. Being able to do so requires that they understand themselves and know how to ask for what they need.
5. Self-help and support groups can facilitate understanding and advocacy.
6. Justice professionals involved with discrimination and criminal matters need to understand dyslexia in its broadest context if they are to act appropriately.

Epilogue

Over the past decade there has been considerable development in the understanding of and provision for dyslexic adults. There are also many more readily available solutions brought about by the technological revolution. Nevertheless, the promised brave new world which was to provide opportunities for dyslexic people to capitalise on their talents and to be more valued than ever before has yet to fully materialise.

What it has brought about is a great deal of rapid change, creating demands on newer literacy skills. The use of most technology requires some reading and might involve different sub-skills which we do not yet understand. At the same time as technology is providing answers it is also creating new questions.

We hope that the way in which we have described dyslexia and the interventions which can support dyslexic people facilitate the processes they need to go through to adapt to the changes and challenges they face. Many of the solutions might seem obvious, but that should not be construed as a simplification of what for many dyslexic people find complex.

We also hope that what we have written will contribute to all dyslexic people being better understood, valued for their abilities, as well as the persistence, determination and resilience they demonstrate when faced with tasks most of us take for granted.

The Dyslexic Adult: Interventions and Outcomes – An Evidence-based Approach, Second Edition.
David McLoughlin and Carol Leather.
© 2013 John Wiley & Sons, Ltd. Published 2013 by John Wiley & Sons, Ltd.

Appendix A

Sample Interview Schedule

Name	D.O.B.	
Address	Age	
Occupation		
Source of referral		
Reason for referral		

Have you ever been formally assessed before?	Yes	No
Do you know the outcome?		
Do you have a written report?	Yes	No

. . . .

Medical History

Is your general health good?
Have you ever had any problems with the following?

Vision
Hearing

Family History of Learning Difficulties

Has anyone in your family had difficulty with any of the following?

			Comment
Reading	Yes	No	
Writing	Yes	No	
Spelling	Yes	No	
Maths	Yes	No	
Memory	Yes	No	
Organisation	Yes	No	
Co-ordination	Yes	No	
Spoken language	Yes	No	

The Dyslexic Adult: Interventions and Outcomes – An Evidence-based Approach, Second Edition.
David McLoughlin and Carol Leather.
© 2013 John Wiley & Sons, Ltd. Published 2013 by John Wiley & Sons, Ltd.

Educational History

At what age did you leave school?
What were your school years like for you?
Was your schooling disrupted in any way?
What were you good at, at school?
What did you enjoy at school?
What did you find difficult?
Did you need/have extra help at school?
Did you work hard at school?
Do you have any qualifications from school? What are they?
Have you tried to learn other languages? Did you find it difficult?

Characteristics of a Learning Difficulty

Have you ever had a problem with:

			Comment**
Remembering people's names	Yes	No	
Using a dictionary?	Yes	No	
Using a telephone directory?	Yes	No	
Following directions?	Yes	No	
Using a street map?	Yes	No	
Time keeping?	Yes	No	
Organising yourself?	Yes	No	
Taking telephone messages?	Yes	No	
Writing letters or memos?	Yes	No	
Concentration?	Yes	No	
Dealing with money?	Yes	No	
Remembering your tables?	Yes	No	

** Have you any specific strategies for dealing with these tasks?

Communication Skills

Comment

Do you ever mispronounce or use the wrong words?
Do you have trouble finding the right word?
Do you often lose trace of what you want to say,
or what other people are saying?

Is English your first language? If not what language do you speak with family and friends?
When did you learn English? Do you have problems with reading and writing in your
first language?

Social Skills

What is your social life like?
Do you have any hobbies or interests?
Do you think you are a confident person?

In which situation are you most confident?
What situation do you avoid?
Do you think you know how you learn best?
Do you get on well with people?

Employment History and Experience

Do you have any professional/vocational qualifications? If so what?
What jobs have you held?

What difficulties did they present you with, if any?
What are your short-term employment goals?
What are your long-term employment goals?

Do you enjoy training courses?	Yes	No
At work have you had trouble with:		

Comment**

Remembering instructions/new information?	Yes	No
Taking notes?	Yes	No
Organising your work space?	Yes	No
Prioritising your workload?	Yes	No
Understanding what you have read?	Yes	No
Remembering what you have read?	Yes	No
Writing?	Yes	No
Proof reading?	Yes	No
Spelling?	Yes	No
Transferring information from one source to another?	Yes	No
Presenting your ideas?	Yes	No
Concentration?	Yes	No
Interference from background noise?	Yes	No

**Do you use any specific strategies for dealing with these tasks?

What are your technological skills like?

Do you enjoy team work?	Yes	No
Can you supervise others?	Yes	No

Coping with Pressure

Do you cope easily with:

Changing demands?	Yes	No
Meeting deadlines?	Yes	No
Alterations to routine?	Yes	No
Doing several things at once?	Yes	No

Appendix B

Useful Contact Addresses

The British Dyslexia Association

Unit 8 Bracknell Beeches
Old Bracknell Lane
Berkshire, RG12 7BW
tel. +44 (0) 845 251 9002 helpline
    +44 (0) 845 251 9003 admin
    +44 (0) 845 251 9005 fax
e-mail helpline@bdadyslexia.org.uk

European Dyslexia Association

e-mail contact-eda@eda-info.eu
http://www.eda-info.eu

The International Dyslexia Association

40 York Rd., 4th Floor
Baltimore, MD 21204
Voice: +1 (410) 296-0232
Fax: +1 (410) 321-5069
www.interdys.org

The Dyslexic Adult: Interventions and Outcomes – An Evidence-based Approach, Second Edition.
David McLoughlin and Carol Leather.
© 2013 John Wiley & Sons, Ltd. Published 2013 by John Wiley & Sons, Ltd.

Learning Disabilities Association of America

4156 Library Road
Pittsburgh, PA 15234-1349
Phone (412) 341-1515 | Fax (412) 344-0224
http://www.ldanatl.org

Dyslexia Foundation of New Zealand

P.O. Box: 16141 Hornby
Christchurch
New Zealand
http://www.dyslexiafoundation.org.nz
Fax: 03 349 6141

Australian Dyslexia Association

http://dyslexiaassociation.org.au
dyslexia.association@gmail.com

Assessment and Coaching

There are many Centres providing assessment, coaching teaching and training for dyslexic adults. Contact details can be provided by the advocacy organisations listed above. The authors of this book can be contacted at:

Independent Dyslexia Consultants
Second Floor
1–7 Woburn Walk
London WC1H 0JJ
Tel. +44 (0) 20 7388 8744
e-mail: info@dyslexia-idc.org
www.dyslexia-idc.org

References

Aaron, P.G. & Baker, C. (1991). *Reading disabilities in college and high school*. Penn: York Press.

Adelman, K.A. & Adelman, H.S. (1987). Rodin, Patton, Edison, Wilson, Einstein: Were they really learning disabled? *Journal of Learning Disabilities, 20*(5), 270–279.

Ajadi, A. (2002). Whole organisation equality and diversity intervention strategies in practice. In N. Cornelius (Ed.), *Building workplace equality: ethics, diversity and inclusion*. London: Thomson.

Alexander-Passe, N. (2006). How dyslexic teenagers cope: an investigation of self-esteem, coping and depression. *Dyslexia, 1*, 256–275.

Alexander-Passe, N. (2008). The sources and manifestations of stress amongst school-aged dyslexics, compared with sibling controls. *Dyslexia, 14*, 291–313.

Alster, E.H. (1997). The effects of extended time on algebra test scores for college students with and without learning disabilities. *Journal of Learning Disabilities, 30*(2), 222–227.

Altemeier, L., Abbott, R. & Berninger, V. (2008). Executive functions for reading and writing in typical literacy development and dyslexia. *Journal of Clinical and Experimental Neuropsychology, 30*, 588–606.

American Psychiatric Association (1994). *Diagnostic and statistical manual of mental disorders* (4th ed.) Washington, DC: APA.

Americans with Disabilities Act (ADA) of 1990, Public Law No 101–336, 42 USC.

Ando, J., Ono, Y. & Wright, M.J. (2002). Genetic structure of spatial and verbal working memory. *Behaviour Genetics, 31*, 615–624.

Armstrong, D. & Humphrey, N. (2009). Reactions to a diagnosis of dyslexia among students entering further education: development of the 'resistance–accommodation' model. *British Journal of Special Education, 36*: 95–102.

Armstrong, M. (1999). *A handbook of human resources management practice*. London: Kogan Page.

Arnett, J.J. (2004). *Emerging adulthood: The winding road from the late teens through to twenties*. New York: Oxford University Press.

Authier, J. (1977). The psychoeducation model: definition, contemporary roots and content. *Canadian Counsellor, 12*(1), 15–22.

Bacon, A.M., Handley, S.J. & McDonald, E.L. (2007). Reasoning and dyslexia: A spatial strategy may impede reasoning with visually rich information. *British Journal of Psychology, 98*, 79–92.

Baddeley, A. (2000). The episodic buffer: a new component of working memory? *Trends in Cognitive Sciences*, 4(11), 417–423.

Baddeley, A.D. (1986). *Working memory.* London: Oxford University Press.

Baddeley, A.D. (2007). *Working memory, thought and action.* New York: Oxford University Press.

Baddeley, A.D. & Hitch, G.J. (1974). *Working Memory.* In G. Bower (Ed.), *Recent Advances in Learning and Motivation.* Viii, 47–90. New York: Academic Press.

Baddeley, A.D. & Hitch, G.J. (2007). Working memory: Past, present … and future? In R.H. Logie, N. Osaka & M. D'Esposito (Eds.), *The cognitive neuroscience of working memory.* Oxford: Oxford University Press.

Baddeley, A.D. & Larsen, J.D. (2007). The phonological loop: Some answers and some questions. *The Quarterly Journal of Experimental Psychology*, 60(4), 512–518.

Baltes, P.B. & Freund, A.M. (2003). Human strengths as the orientation of wisdom and selection with compensation. In L.G. Aspinwall & U.M. Staudinger (Eds.), *A psychology of human strengths: Perspectives on an emerging field* (pp. 23–35). Washington, DC: American Psychological Association.

Baltes, P.B., Reese, H.W. & Lipsett, L.P. (1980). Life span developmental psychology. *Annual Review of Psychology*, 31, 65–100.

Banai, K. & Ahissar, M. (2010). On the importance of anchoring and the consequences of its impairment in dyslexia. *Dyslexia*, 16, 240–257.

Bandura, A. (1993). Perceived self-efficacy in cognitive development and functioning. *Educational Psychologist*, 28(2), 117–148.

Bandura, A. (1997). *Self-efficacy: The exercise of control.* New York: W.H. Freeman.

Bannatyne, A. (1974). Diagnosis: A note on recategorization of the WISC scaled scores. *Journal of Learning Disabilities*, 7, 272–274.

Barkley, R.A. (1997). Behavioural inhibition, sustained attention and executive functions: Constructing a unifying theory of ADHA. *Psychological Bulletin*, 121, 65–94.

Barkley, R.A. (2006). *Attention-deficit hyperactivity disorder: A handbook for diagnosis and treatment* (3rd ed.). New York: Guilford Press.

Barkely, R.A. (2011). Attention-deficit/hyperactivity disorder, self-regulation and executive functioning. In K.D. Vona & R.F. Baumeister (Eds.), *Handbook of self-regulation: Research theory and applications* (pp. 551–563). New York: Guildford Press.

Barnett, A., Henderson, S.E., Scheib, B. and Schulz, J. (2010). *Detailed Assessment of Speed of Handwriting (DASH 17+)* London: Pearson.

Baron-Cohen, S. (2003). *The essential difference.* London: Allen Lane.

Baron-Cohen, S. (2008). Theories of the autisic mind, *The Psychologist.*

Baron-Jeffrey, M.C., Vogel, S. & Baron-Jeffrey, A.C. (2003). Support groups for adults with learning disabilities in higher education. In S.A. Vogel, G. Vogel, V. Sharoni & O. Dahan (Eds.), *Learning disabilities in higher education and beyond: an international perspective* (pp. 229–258). Mayland: York Press.

Barton, R.S. & Fuhrmann, B.S. (1994). Counselling and psychotherapy for adults with learning disabilities (pp. 82–92). In P.J. Gerber & H.B. Reiff (Eds.), *Learning disabilities in adulthood.* Austin, Texas: Pro-Ed.

Battle, J. (1990). *Self-esteem: the new revolution.* Edmonton: James Battle & Assoc.

Battle, J. (1992). *Culture-free self-esteem inventories* (2nd ed.). Austin, Texas: Pro-Ed.

Bauer, R.M. (2007). Evidence-based practice in psychology: Implications for research and research training. *Journal of Clinical Psychology*, 63(7), 685–694.

Beaton, A., McDougall, S. & Singleton, C. (1997). Editorial: Humpty Dumpty grows up? – Diagnosing dyslexia in adulthood. *Journal of Reading Research, 20*(1), 1–12.

Beck, A.T. (1990). *Beck anxiety inventory.* London: Psychological Corporation.

Beck, A.T., Rush, A.J., Shaw, B.F. & Emery, G. (1979). *Cognitive Therapy of Depression.* New York: The Guildford Press.

Beck, J. (1995). *Cognitive behavioural therapy: Basics and beyond.* New York: The Guildford Press.

Belsky, J.K. (1990). *The psychology of aging theory, research, and interventions.* Pacific Grove, CA: Brooks/Cole.

Benich, M.T. (2010). *Cognitive Neuroscience,* International Edition. KY: Cengage Learning.

Bental, B. & Tirosh, E. (2007). The relationship between attention, executive functions and reading domain abilities in attention deficit hyperactivity disorder and reading disorder: A comparative study. *Journal of Child Psychology and Psychiatry, 48,* 455–463.

Bentall, R.P. (2010). *Doctoring the mind.* Penguin: London.

Beringer, V.W. & Richards, T.L. (2002). *Brain literacy for educators and psychologists.* San Diego, CA: Academic Press.

Best, M. & Demb, J.B. (1999). Normal planum temporale symmetry in dyslexics with magnocellular pathway deficit. *Neuroreport, 10,* 607–612.

Biemiller, A. (1977–78). Relationships between oral reading rates for letters, words, and simple text in the development of reading achievement. *Reading Research Quarterly, 2,* 223–253.

Bigler, E.D. (1996). The neurobiology and neuropsychology of adult learning disorders. In J.R. Patton & E.A. Polloway (Eds.), *Learning Disabilities: The Challenges of Adulthood.* Austen, TX: Pro-Ed.

Bishop, D.V.M. & Adams, C. (1990). A prospective study of the relationship between specific language impairment, phonological disorders and reading retardation. *Journal of Child Psychology and Psychiatry, 31,* 1027–1050.

Blackman, L. & Dixon, R.A. (1992). Psychological compensation: A theoretical framework. *Psychological Bulletin, 112,* 259–283.

Blair, C. & Ursache, A. (2011). A bidirectional model of executive functions and self-regulation (pp. 300–320). In K.D. Vohs & R.F. Baumeister (Eds.), *Handbook of self-regulation: Research, theory and applications* (2nd ed.). New York: Guildford Press.

Bodenham, D. (2000). The Dyslexia Adult Screening Test (DAST). *Journal of the Application of Occupational Psychology to Employment and Disability, 2*(2), 51–56.

Borokowski, J.G. & Burke, J.E. (1996). Theories, models and measurements of executive functioning (pp. 235–261). In G. Reid Lyon & N.A. Krasnegor (Eds.), *Attention, memory and executive function.* Baltimore: Brookes.

Borokowski, J.G. & Multlukrishan, N. (1992). Moving metacognition into the classroom: 'Working Models' and effective strategy teaching (pp. 477–501). In M. Pressley, K.R. Harris & J.T. Guthrie (Eds.), *Promoting academic literacy: Cognitive research and instructional innovation.* Orlando, FL: Academic Press.

Bowden, S.C., Fowler, K.S., Bell, R.C., Whelan, G., Clifford, C.C., Ritter, A.J., Long, C.L. (1998). The reliability and internal validity of the Wisconsin Card Sorting Test. *Neuropsychological Rehabilitation, 8*(3), 243–254.

Bowyer-Crane, C., Snowling, M.J., Duff, F.J., Fieldsend, E., Carroll, J.M., Miles, J., Götz, K. & Hulme, C. (2008). Improving early language and literacy skills: Differential effects of an oral language versus a phonology with reading intervention. *Journal of Child Psychology and Psychiatry, 49*: 422–432.

Boyle, J.R. (2005). Learning from lectures: The implications of note-taking for students with learning difficulties. *Journal of Learning Disabilities, 14*(2), 91–97.

Breznitz, Z. (2002). Asynchrony of visual-orthographic and auditory-phonological word recognition processed: An underlying factor in dyslexia, *Reading and Writing: An Interdisciplinary Journal, 15*, 15–42.

Breznitz, Z. (2008). The origin of dyslexia: The Asynchrony Phenomenom. In G. Reid, A. Fawcett, F. Manis & L. Siegel (Eds.), *The Sage handbook of dyslexia.* Washington, DC: Sage.

Brinckerhoff, L.C., Shaw, S.F., & McGuire, J.M. (1992). Promoting access, accommodations, and independence for college students with learning disabilities. *Journal of Learning Disabilities, 25*, 417–429.

British Dyslexia Association (2012). *Good Practice Guide for Justice Professionals.* Bracknell: BDA.

Brook, J. (2009). Building strong coaching partnerships. *Assessment and Development Matters, 1*(3), 4.

Brooks, P., Everatt, J. & Fidler, R. (2004). *Adult Reading Test (ART).* London: Pearson.

Brooks, R.B. (2001a). Fostering motivation, hope, and resilience in children with learning disorders. *Annals of Dyslexia, 51*, 9–20.

Bloom, B.S. (1956). *Taxonomy of educational objective, Handbook I: The cognitive domain.* New York: David McKay Co. Inc.

Brosnan, M., Demetre, J., Hamill, S., Robson, K., Shepherd, H. & Cody, G. (2001). Executive functioning in adults and children with developmental dyslexia. *Neuropsychologia, 40,* 2144–2155.

Brown, A.L. (1980). Metacognitive development and reading (pp. 453–481). In R.J. Spiro, B. Bruce & W.F. Brewer (Eds.), *Theoretical issues in reading comprehension.* Hillsdale, NJ: Lawrence Erlbaum.

Brown, J.I., Fishco, V.V. & Hanna, G. (1993). *The Nelson-Denny reading test.* Itasca, IL: The Riverside Publishing Company.

Brown, T.E. (2001). *Brown Attention Deficit Disorder Scales*. San Antonio, TX: Pearson.

Bryant, B.R., Patton, J.R. and Dunn, C. (1991). *Scholastic Abilities Test for adults.* Austin, TX: Pro-Ed.

Buchanan, M. & Wolf, J.S. (1986). A comprehensive study of learning disabled adults. *Journal of Learning Disabilities, 19*(1), 34–38.

Burden, R. (2008). Is dyslexia necessarily associated with negative feelings of self-worth? A review and implications for future research. *Dyslexia, 14*, 188–196.

Burden, R. (2008). Dyslexia and self-concept: A review of past research with implications for future action. In G. Reid, A. Fawcett, F. Manis & L. Siegel (Eds.), *The Sage handbook of dyslexia.* Washington, DC: Sage.

Burden, R. & Burdett, J. (2007). What's in a name? Students with dyslexia: Their use of metaphor in making sense of their disability. *British Journal of Special Education, 34*(2), 77–82.

Burgess, P.W. & Shallice, T. (1997). *The Hayling and Brixton Tests.* London: Pearson.

Burns, D. (1980). *Feeling good: The new mood therapy.* New York: New American Library.

Butler, D.L. (1995). Promoting strategic learning by postsecondary students with learning disabilities. *Journal of Learning Disabilities, 28*(3), 170–190.

Butler, D.L. (2004). Metacognition and learning disabilities. In Wong, B.Y.L (Ed.), *Learning about learning disabilities.* California: Elsevier Academic Press.

Butterworth, B. (1999). The mathematical brain. *British Journal of Psychology, 74,* 311–342.

Carey, S., Low, S. & Hansboro, J. (1997). *Adult literacy in Britain.* London: OCNS.

Carroll, J.M., Maughan, B., Goodman, R. & Meltzer, H. (2005). Literacy difficulties and psychiatric disorders: Evidence for comorbidity. *Journal of Child Psychology and Psychiatry, 46*, 524–532.

Carter, R. (1998). *Mapping the mind.* London: Weidenfield & Nicolson.

Cavalier, A.R., Ferretti, R.P. & Okolo, C.M. (1998). Technology and individual differences. *Journal of Special Education Technology,12,* 175–181.

Chimel, N. (1998). *Jobs, Technology and People,* London: Routledge.

Chinn, S. (2006). What dyslexia can tell us about dyscalculia. *Dyslexia Review, 18*(1), 15–17.

Chinn, S. (2009). Dyscalculia and learning difficulties in mathematics. In G. Reid (Ed.), *The Routledge companion to dyslexia.* Oxford: Routledge.

Chinn, S.J. (2000). *The Informal Assessment of Numeracy Skills.* Mark, Somerset: Markco Publishing.

Chinn, S.J. & Ashcroft, J.R. (1993). *Mathematics for dyslexics: A teaching handbook.* London: Whurr.

Cirino, P.T., Israelian, M.K., Morris, M.K. & Morris, R.D. (2005). Evaluation of the double-deficit hypothesis in college students referred for learning difficulties. *Journal of Learning Disabilities, 38*(1), 29–44.

Cohen, G., Kiss, G. & Le Voi, M. (1993). *Memory: Current issues* (2nd ed.). Buckingham, UK: Open University Press.

Cohn, P. (1998). Why does my stomach hurt? How individuals with learning disabilities can use cognitive strategies to reduce anxiety and stress and the college level. *Journal of Learning Disabilities, 31*(3), 514–516.

Collette, F. & Van der Linden, M. (2002). Brain imaging of the central executive component of working memory. *Neuroscience and Biobehavioral Reviews, 26,* 105–125.

Colley, H. (2007). Understanding time in learning transitions throughout the life course. *International Studies in Sociology of Education, 17*(4), 427–443.

Collins, F.L., Leffingwell, T.R. & Belar, C.D. (2007). Teaching evidence-based practice: Implications for psychology. *Journal of Clinical Psychology, 63,* 657–670.

Connelly, V., Docknell, I.G. & Barnett, J. (2005). The slow handwriting of undergraduate students constrains overall performance in exam essays. *Educational Psychology, 25*(1), 99–107.

Cooke, A. (2001). Critical response to dyslexia, literacy and psychological assessment. *Dyslexia, 7*(1), 47–52.

Coolidge, F.L., Thede, L.L. & Young, S.E. (2000). Heritability and the comorbidity of ADHS with behavioural disorders and executive function deficits: A preliminary investigation. *Developmental Neuropsychology, 17,* 273–287.

Cordoni, B.K. & O'Donnell, J.P. (1981). Wechsler Adult Intelligence Score patterns for learning disabled young adults. *Journal of Learning Disabilities, 14*(7), 404–407.

Cottrell, S. (1999). *The study skills handbook.* London: Macmillan.

Cousins, M. & Smyth, M.M. (2003). Developmental coordination impairments in adulthood. *Human Movement Science, 22,* 433–459.

Covey, S.R. (2004). *Seven habits of highly effective people.* London: Simon & Schuster.

Cowen, S.E. (1988). Coping strategies of university students with learning disabilities. *Journal of Learning Disabilities, 21*(3), 161–164.

Cox, E.O. (1991). Advocacy and empowerment. *Social Action in Group Work, 14,* 77–90.

Crawford, J.R. (1998). Introduction to the assessment of attention and executive functioning. *Neuropsychological Rehabilitation, 8*(3), 209–211.

Creasey, G.L. & Jarvis, P.A. (1987). Sensitivity to non-verbal communication among male learning disabled adolescents. *Perceptual & Motor Skills, 64,* 873–874.

Cummins, J. (1979). Cognitive/academic language proficiency, linguistic interdependence, the optimum age question and some other matters. *Working Papers on Bilingualism, 19,* 121–129.

Cummins, J. (1994). *Bilingualism and special education: Issues in assessment and pedagogy.* Clevedon, England: Multilingual Matters.

D'Eposito, M., Detre, J.A. & Alsop, D.C. (1995). The Newal basis of the central executive system of working memory. *Nature, 378,* 279–281.

Dal, M. (2008). Dyslexia and foreign language learning. In G. Reid, A. Fawcett, F. Manis & L. Siegel (Eds.), *The SAGE handbook of dyslexia.* Washington, DC: Sage.

Darling, S. (2000). Do delayed response type tasks in adult humans suggest segregation between different types of visuo-spatial working memory? *Paper presented to Annual Conference of the British Psychological Society,* April.

Davis, R.D. (1997). *The gift of dyslexia* (2nd ed.). London: Souvenir Press.

De Fries, J.C. (1991). Genetics and dyslexia: An overview. In M. Snowling & M. Thomson (Eds.), *Dyslexia: Integrating theory and practice.* London: Whurr.

De Fries, J.C., Alarcon, M. and Olson, R.K. (1997) Genetic of reading and spelling deficits: Developmental differences. In M. Snowling & C. Hulme (Eds.), *Dyslexia: Biology, cognition and intervention.* London: Whurr.

Demonet, J.F., Taylor, M.J. & Chaix, Y. (2004). Developmental dyslexia. *Lancet, 363,* 1451–1460.

Devine, T.G. (1981). *Teaching study skills: A guide for teachers.* Boston: Allyn and Bacon.

Dexter, D. (2010). Graphic organizers and their effectiveness. *Thalamus, 26*(1), 51–63.

Dexter, D.D. (2010). Graphic organisers and their effectiveness for students with learning disabilities. *Thalamus, 26*(1), 51–67.

Di Filippo, G., Zoccolotti, P. & Ziegler, J.C. (2008). Rapid naming deficits in dyslexia: A stumbling block for the perceptual anchor theory of dyslexia. *Developmental Science, 11*(6), 40–47.

Division of Educational and Child Psychology (1999). *Dyslexia, literacy and psychological assessment.* Leicester: British Psychological Society.

Doyle, B. (1995). *Disability, discrimination & equal opportunities.* London: Mansell.

DuBay, W.H. (2004). *The principles of readability.* Costa Mesa, CA: Impact Information.

Ducharme, M.J. (2004). The cognitive behavioural approach to executive coaching. *Consulting Psychology Journal: Practice and Research, 56,* 214–224.

Dunn, R., Dunn, K. & Price, G.E. (1996). *Learning styles inventory.* Lawrence, KA: Price Systems.

Eden, G.F., Jones, K.M., Cappell, K., Gareau, L., Wood, F.B., Zeiffiro, T.A., Dietz, N.A.E., Agnew, J.A. & Flowers, D.L. (2004). Neural changes following remediation in adult developmental dyslexia. *Neuron, 44*(3), 411–422.

Edhart, K. (2008). Dyslexia not disorder. *Dyslexia, 15*(4), 363–366.

Egan, G.E. (1994). *The skilled helper* (5th ed.). Monterey, CA: Brooks/Cole.

Elbeheri, G., Everatt, J., Knight, D. & Wearmouth, J. (2009). *The Routledge companion to dyslexia.* London: Routledge.

Elbeheri, G., Everatt, J., Reid, G. & Mannai, H.A. (2006). Dyslexia assessment in Arabic. *Journal of Research in Special Educational Needs, 6,* 143–152.

Elbro, C. (2010). Dyslexia as disability of handicap: When does vocabulary matter? *Journal of Learning Disabilities, 43*(5), 469–478.

Ellis, A. (1962). *Reason and emotion in psychotherapy.* NY: Lyle Stuart.

Ellis, E.S. (1993). Integrative strategy instruction: A potential model for teaching content area subjects to adolescents with learning disabilities. *Journal of learning Disabilities, 26*(6), 258–383.

Eslinger, P.J. (1996). Conceptualizing, describing and measuring components of executive function: A summary. In G. Reid Lyon & N.A. Krasnegor (Eds.), *Attention, memory and executive function.* Baltimore, MD: Paul H. Brookes.

Evans, B.J.W. (2001). *Dyslexia and vision.* London: Whurr.

Everatt, J. (2007) Research methods in dyslexia. *Dyslexia, 13,* 231–233.

Everatt, J. & Elbeheri, G. (2008). Dyslexia in different orthographies: Variability in transparency. In G. Reid, A. Fawcett, F. Manis & L. Siegel (Eds.), *The Sage handbook of dyslexia.* Washington, DC: Sage.

Everatt, J. & Reid, G. (2009). Dyslexia: An overview of recent research. In G. Reid (Ed.), *The Routledge companion to dyslexia.* London: Routledge.

Everatt, J. & Smythe, I. (2001). Checklist for dyslexic adults (pp. 73–78). *The dyslexia handbook.* Reading, Berks: BDA.

Everatt, J., Steffert, B. & Smythe, I. (1999). An eye for the unusual: Creative thinking in dyslexics. *Dyslexia, 5*(1), 28–46.

Everatt, J., Bradshaw, M.F. & Hibbard, P.B. (1999). Visual processing and dyslexia. *Perception, 28*(2), 243–254.

Faas, L.A. & D'Alonzo, B.J. (1990). WAIS-R scores as predictors of employment success and failure among adults with learning disabilities. *Journal of Learning Disabilities, 23*(5), 311–316.

Faust, M., Dimitrovsky, L. & Shact, T. (2003). Naming difficulties in children with dyslexia: Application of the tip-of-the tongue paradigm. *Journal of Learning Disabilities, 36*(3), 203–215.

Fawcett, A. (2003). Screening and support for dyslexia in adults in the United Kingdom (pp. 107–132). In S.A. Vogel, G. Vogel, V. Sharoni & O. Dahan (2003). *Learning disabilities in higher education and beyond: An international perspective.* Maryland: York Press.

Fawcett, A.J. & Nicolson, R.I. (1998). *Dyslexia Adult Screening Test,* London: The Psychological Corporation.

Fawcett, A.J. & Nicolson, R.I. (2008). Dyslexia and the cerebellum. In G. Reid, A. Fawcett, F. Manis and L. Siegel (Eds.), *The Sage handbook of dyslexia.* London: Sage Publications.

Fawcett, A., Nicholson, R.I. & Dean, P. (1999). Performance of dyslexic children on cerebellar and cognitive tests. *Journal of Motor behaviour, 31,* 68–78.

Feehan, P.F. & Johnston, J.A. (1999). The self-directed search and career self-efficacy. *Journal of Career Assessment, 7*(2), 145–159.

Fenton, M. & Hughes, P. (1989). *Passivity to empowerment.* London: RADAR.

Fernandez-Duque, D., Baird, J.A. & Posner, M.I. (2000). Executive attention and metacognitive regulation. *Consciousness and Cognition, 9,* 288–307.

Fidler, R. & Everatt, J. (2012). Reading comprehension in adult student with dyslexia (pp. 91–100). In N. Brunswick (Ed.), *Supporting dyslexic adults in higher education and the workplace.* Chichester: Wiley.

Fink, R.P. (1998). Literacy development in successful men and women with dyslexia. *Annals of Dyslexia, 48,* 311–343.

Fink, R.P. (2003). Mastering of literacy and life: Individual interests and literacy development in successful adults with dyslexia. (pp. 339–370). In S.A. Vogel, G. Vogel, V. Sharoni & O. Dahan (Eds.), *Learning disabilities in higher education and beyond: An international perspective.* Maryland: York Press.

Fisher, S., Marlower, A., Lambe, J., Maestrin, E., Williams, D., Ason, A., Weeks, D., Stein, J.F. & Monaco, A. (1999). A quantitative trait locus on chromosome 6 influences different aspects of development dyslexia. *American Journal of Human Genetics, 64,* 146–156.

Flanagan, D.P. & Alfonso, V.C. (2011). *Essentials of specific learning disability identification.* New Jersey: John Wiley & Sons.

Flavell, J.H. (1979). Metacognition and cognitive monitoring. *American Psychologist, 34*(10), 906–911.

Fletcher, J.M., Reid, G.L., Fuchs, L.S. & Barnes, M.A. (2007). *Learning disabilities from identification to intervention.* New York: Guilford Press.

Flowers, D.L. (1993). Brain basis for dyslexia: A summary of work in progress. *Journal Learning Disabilities, 26,* 575–582.

Forness, S.R. & Kavale, K.A. (1991). Social skills deficits as primary learning disabilities: A note on problems with the ICLD diagnostic criteria. *Learning Disabilities Research and Practice, 6,* 44–49.

Frauenheim, J.G. (1978). Academic achievement characteristics of adult males who were diagnosed as dyslexic in childhood. *Journal of Learning Disabilities, 11*(8), 21–28.

Frauenheim, J.G. & Heckerl, J. (1983). A longitudinal study of psychological and achievement test performance in severely dyslexic adults, *Journal of Learning Disabilities, 16*(6), 339–347.

Frederickson, N. (1999). The ACID test-or is it? *Educational Psychology in Practice, 15*(1), April.

Freeman, P. (2003). *The nature of 'good and bad days' in dyslexic adults.* Unpublished Master's Dissertation. Graduate School of Education, University of Bristol.

Frith, U. (1995). Dyslexia: Can we have a shared theoretical framework? *Educational and Child Psychology, 12*(1), 6–17.

Frith, U. (1999). Paradoxes in the definition of dyslexia. *Dyslexia, 5*(4), 192–214.

Galaburda, A.M. (1999). Developmental dyslexia: A multilevel syndrome. *Dyslexia, 5*(4), 183–191.

Galaburda, A.M., Sherman, G.F., Rosen, G.D., Aboitiz, F. & Geschwind, N. (1985). Developmental dyslexia: Four consecutive cases with cortical anomalies. *Annals of Neurology, 18,* 222–233.

Gardner, H. (1996). *Extraordinary minds.* London: Weidenfeld & Nicolson.

Gardner, H. (2000) 'Now that the Battle's Over…', Informal remarks by Howard Gardner on the occasion of his receipt of the Samuel T. Orton Award by the International Dyslexia Association. *Annals of Dyslexia, 50,* ix–xvi.

Garner, P. & Sandow, S. (1995). *Advocacy, self-advocacy and special needs,* London: Fulton.

Garnett, K. (1985). Learning disabilities come of age: Transitions in adulthood. *Rehabilitation World.* Spring.

Gathercole, S.E. (2004). Working memory and learning during the school years. *Proceedings of the British Academy, 125,* 365–380.

Gathercole, S.E. (2008). Working memory in the classroom, *The Psychologist* [online].

Gerber, P.J. (1994). Researching adults with learning disabilities from an adult development perspective. *Journal of Learning Disabilities, 27*(1), 6–9.

Gerber, P.J. (2006). Acceptable loss and potential gain: Self-disclosure and adults with learning disabilities. *Thalamus, 24*(1), 49–55.

Gerber, P.J. (2009). Impact of learning disabilities on adults. In J. Taymans (Ed.), *Learning to achieve: A review of the research literature on serving adults with learning disabilities,* Washington, DC: National Institute for Literacy.

Gerber, P.J. (2012). The impact of learning disabilities on adulthood: A review of the evidence-based literature for research and practice in adult education. *Journal of Learning Disabilities, 45*(1), 31–46.

Gerber, P.J. & Price, L.A. (2000). Self-disclosure and adults with learning disabilities: Practical ideas about a complex process. *Learning Disabilities, 15,* 21–24.

Gerber, P. & Price, L. (2003). Persons with learning disabilities in the workplace: What we know so far in the American with Disabilities Act era. *Learning Disabilities Research and Practice, 18*(2), 132–136.

Gerber, P.J. & Price, L.A. (2008). Self-disclosure and adults with learning disabilities: Practical ideas about a complex process. *Learning Disabilities, 15*(1), 21–23.

Gerber, P.J., Batalo, C.G. & Achola, E.O. (2011). Learning disabilities and employment before and in the Americans with Disabilities Act era: Progress or a bridge too far? *Learning Disabilities, 17*(3), 123–129.

Gerber, P.J., Ginsberg, R. & Reiff, H.B. (1992). Identifying alterable patterns in employment success for highly successful adults with learning disabilities. *Journal of Learning Disabilities, 25*(8), 475–487.

Gerber, P., Price, L., Mulligan, R., & Shessel, I. (2004). Beyond transition: A comparison of the employment experiences of American and Canadian adults with LD. *Journal of Learning Disabilities, 37*(4), 283–291.

Gerber, P.J., Reiff, H.B. & Ginsberg, R. (1996). Reframing the learning disabilities experience. *Journal of Learning Disabilities, 29*(1), 98–101.

Gerber, P.J., Schneiders, C.A., Paradise, L.V., Reiff, H.B., Ginsberg, R.J. & Popp, P.A. (1990). Persisting problems of adults with learning disabilities: Self-reported comparisons from their school-age and adult years. *Journal of Learning Disabilities, 23*(9), 570–573.

Gibbs, J., Appleton, J. & Appleton, R. (2007). Dyspraxia or developmental coordination disorder? Unravelling the enigma. *Archives of Disease in Childhood, 92*, 534–539.

Ginzberg, E. (1972). Towards a theory of occupational choice. *Vocational Guidance Quarterly, 20*(3), 169–176.

Gittelman, R. & Feingold, I. (1983). Children with reading disorders – I. Efficacy of reading remediation. *Journal of Child Psychology and Psychiatry, 24*, 167–191.

Glutting, J., Adams, W. & Sheslow, D.C. (2000). *Wide Range Intelligence Test.* Wilmington, DE: Wide Range Inc.

Goldberg, R., Higgins, E., Raskind, M. & Herman, K. (2003). Predictors of success in individuals with learning disabilities: A qualitative analysis of a 20-year longitudinal study. *Learning Disabilities Research & Practice, 18*(4), 222–236.

Gollwitzer, P.M. & Schaal, B. (1998). Metacognition in action: Importance of implementation intentions. *Personality and Social Psychology Review, 2*, 124–136.

Goulandris, N.K. & Snowling, M. (1991). Visual memory deficits: A plausible cause of developmental dyslexia? Evidence from a single case study. *Cognitive Neuropsychology, 8*, 127–154.

Govindji, R. & Linley, P.A. (2007). Strengths use, self-concordance and well-being: Implications for strengths coaching and coaching psychologists. *International Coaching Psychology Review, 2*(2), 143–153.

Grant, D. (2009). The psychological assessment of neurodiversity (pp. 33–62). In D. Pollak (Ed.), *Neurodiversity in Higher Education.* Chichester: John Wiley & Sons.

Gray, D.E. (2006). Executive coaching: Towards a dynamic alliance of psychotherapy and transformative learning processes. *Management and Learning, 37*(4), 475–497.

Gregg, N. (2009). *Adolescents and adults with learning disabilities and ADHD: Assessment and accommodation.* New York: Guilford Press.

Gregg, N. (2009). Accommodations: Evidence-based accommodation research specific to the adolescent and adult population with learning disabilities. In National Institute for Literacy, J. Taymans (Ed.), *Learning to achieve: A review of the research literature on serving adults with learning disabilities*, Washington, DC.

Gregg, N. (2012). Increasing access to learning for the adult basic education learner with learning disabilities: Evidence-based accommodation research. *Journal of Learning Disabilities, 45*(1), 47–63.

Gregg, N. & Nelson, J.M. (2012). Meta-analysis of the effectiveness of extra time as a test accommodation for transitioning adolescents with learning disabilities: More questions than answers. *Journal of Learning Disabilities, 45*(2), 128–138.

Gregg, N. & Scott, S. (2000). Definition and documentation: Theory, measurement, and the court. *Journal of Learning Disabilities, 33*, 5–13.

Gregory, S. (1997). The effect of generalized metacognitive knowledge on test performance and confidence judgments. *Journal of Experimental Education, 65*(2), 135.

Gregory, S. & Dennison, R.S. (1994). Assessing metacognitive awareness. *Contemporary Educational Psychology, 19,* 460–475.

Griffin, E. & Pollak, D. (2009). Student experiences of neurodiversity in higher education: Insights from the BRAINHE project. *Dyslexia, 15,* 23–41.

Griffiths, C.B.B. (2007). Pragmatic abilities in adults with and without dyslexia: A pilot study. *Dyslexia, 13,* 276–296.

Groopman, J. (2007). *How doctors think.* New York: Houghton-Mifflin.

Gunn, L. (2000). The Dyslexia Adult Screening Test (DAST): A review. *Journal of the Application of Occupational Psychology to Employment and Disability, 2*(2), 37–44.

Guyer, B.P. & Sabatino, D. (1989). The effectiveness of a multisensory alphabetic approach with college students who are learning disabled. *Journal of Learning Disabilities, 22*(7), 430–434.

Habermann, U. (1990). Self help groups: A minefield for professional. *Groupwork, 3*(3), 221–235.

Hale, J.B., Hoeppner, J.B. & Fiorello, C.A. (2002). Analysing digit span components for assessment of attention processes. *Journal of Psychoeducational Assessment, 20,* 128–143.

Hales, G. (2004). Stress factors in the workplace (pp. 46–62). In T.R. Miles (Ed.), *Dyslexia and stress.* London: Whurr.

Hansell, N.K., Wright, M.J., Smith, G.A., Geffen, G.M., Geffen, L.B. & Martin, N.G. (2001). Genetic influence on ERP slow wave measures of working memory. *Behaviour Genetics, 31,* 603–614.

Harrison, A.G., Edwards, M.J. & Parker, K.C.H. (2008). Identifying students feigning dyslexia: Preliminary findings and strategies for detection. *Dyslexia, 14,* 228–246.

Harrison, A. and Nichols, E. (2005). A validation of the Dyslexia Adult Screening Test (DAST) in a post-secondary population. *Journal of Research in Reading, 28*(4), 423–434.

Hart, B.B. & Hart, C. (1996). Managing examination anxiety. *Contemporary Hypnosis, 13*(2), 84–88.

Hatcher, J., Snowling, M.J. & Griffiths, Y.M. (2002). Cognitive assessment of dyslexia students in higher education. *British Journal of Educational Psychology, 72,* 119–133.

Hayles, G. (2004). Stress factors in the workplace. In T.R. Miles (Ed.), *Dyslexia and stress* (2nd ed.). London: Whurr.

Haynie, J.M. et al. (2010). A situated metacognitive model of the entrepreneurial mindset. *Journal of Business Venturing, 25*(2), 217–229.

Hearne, J.D., Poplin, M.S., Schoneman, C. & O'Shaughnessy, E. (1988). Computer aptitude: An investigation of differences among junior high students with learning disabilities and their non-disabled peers. *Journal of Learning Disabilities, 21*(8), 489–492.

Heaton, A.K., Chelune, G.J., Talley, J.L., Kay, G.C. & Curtis, G. (1993). *Wisconsin Card Sort Test (WCST) manual, revised and expanded.* Odessa, FL: Psychological Assessment Resourses.

Hedderly, R. (1996). Assessing pupils with specific learning difficulties for examination special arrangements at GCSE, 'A' level and degree level. *Educational Psychology in Practice, 12*(1), 36–44.

Hendrick, S. (2010). *The adolescent and adult neuro-diversity handbook.* London: Jessica Kingsley.

Henk, V. & Graaff de, E. (2004). Developing metacognition: A basis for active learning. *European Journal of Engineering Education, 29*(4), 543–548.

HMSO (1995). *The Disability Discrimination Act 1995,* Her Majesty's Stationery Office, London.

Hock, M. (2009). Teaching methods: Instructional methods and arrangements effective for adults with learning disabilities. In J. Taymans (Ed.), *Learning to achieve: A review of the research literature on serving adults with learning disabilities*, Washington, DC: National Institute for Literacy.

Hock, M. (2012). Effective literacy instruction for adults with specific learning disabilities: Implications for adult educators. *Journal of Learning Disabilities, 45*(1), 64–78.

Hoffman, F.J. et al. (1987). Needs of learning disabled adults. *Journal of Learning Disabilities, 20*(1), 43–48.

Hoffman, W., Schmeichel, B.J, Friese, M. & Baddeley, A.D. (2011). Working memory and self-regulation. (pp. 204–225). In K.D. Vohs & R.F. Baumeister (Eds.), *Handbook of self-regulation: Research, theory and applications* (2nd ed.). New York: Guildford Press.

Holland, J.L. (1959). A theory of vocational choice. *Journal of Counselling Psychology, 6*, 35–45.

Holland, J.L. (1973). *Making vocational choices.* Engelwood Cliffs, NJ: Prentice Hall.

Holland, J.L. (1985). *Making vocational choices: A theory of vocational personality and work environments.* NJ: Prentice-Hall.

Honey, P. & Mumford, A. (1986). *The manual of learning styles.* Maidenhead: Honey.

Hoover, J.J. (1989). Study skills and the education of students with learning disabilities, *Journal of Learning Disabilities, 22*(7), 452–454.

Hopson, B., Anderson, J. & Kibble, D. (1998). *Learn to Learn.* Leeds: Lifeskills Associates.

Horn, J.L. & Blankson, N. (2005). Foundations for a better understanding of cognitive abilities. In D.P. Flanagan & P.L. Harrison (eds). *Contemporary intellectual assessment.* New York: Guilford Press.

Hornby, G. (1990). A humanistic developmental model of counselling: A psychological approach. *Counselling Psychology Quarterly, 3*(2), 191–203.

Howard, J. & Howard, P. (2000). Human resource optimisation: Creating training and development that sticks. *Selection Development Review, 16*(6), 8–13.

Hughes, D.L. & Bryan, J. (2002). Adult age differences in strategy use during verbal fluency performance. *Journal of Clinical and Experimental Neuropsychology, 24*, 642–654.

Hughes, W. & Dawson, R. (1995). Memories of school: Adult dyslexics recall their school days. *Support for Learning, 10*, 181–184.

Hulme, C. (1986). Memory development: Interactions between theories in cognitive and developmental psychology. *Bulletin of the British Psychological Society, 39*, 247–250.

Humphrey, N. & Mullins, P. (2002). Self-concept and self-esteem in developmental dyslexia: Implications for theory and practice. *Journal of Research in Special Educational Needs, 2*, 1–13.

Hunter-Carsch, M. & Herrington, M. (2001). *Dyslexia and effective learning in secondary and higher education.* London: Whurr.

Hynd, G.W. & Hiemenz, J.R. (1997). Dyslexia and gyral morphology variation (pp. 38–58). In C. Hulme & M. Snowling (Eds.), *Dyslexia: Biology, cognition and Intervention.* London: Whurr.

Jacobson, J.M., Nielsen, N.P., Minthon, L. & Warkentin, S. (2004). Multiple rapid automatic naming measures of cognition: Normal performance and effects of ageing. *Perceptual and Motor Skills, 98* (3 part 1), 739–753.

Jackson, J.W., Foxx, R.M. & Mulick, J.A. (Eds.) (2005). *Controversial therapies for developmental disabilities.* Mahwah, NJ.

Jackson, M. (2004). Limitations in using the 'at risk' quotient of the dyslexia adult screening test: A technical note. *Journal of Occupational Psychology, Employment and Disability, 6*(1), 11–13.

Jaeggi, S.M., Buschkuehl, M. & Perring, W.J. (2008). Improving fluid intelligence with training on working memory. PNAS Early Edition: *The National Academy of Sciences of the USA, 105*(19), 6829–6833.

James, A. (2004). *An investigation of computer-based screening tests for dyslexia for use in FE and HE.* Sixth BDA International Conference. Warwick.

Johansson, B.B. (2006). Cultural and linguistic influence on brain organisation for language and possible consequences for dyslexia: A review. *Annals of Dyslexia*, 56(1), 13–50.

Kadosh, R.C., Kadosh, K.C., Schuhmann, T., Kass, A., Goebel, R., Honik, A. & Sack, A.T. (2007). Virtual dyscalculia induced by parietal-lobe TMA impairs automatic magnitude processing. *Current Biology*, 17(8), 689–693.

Kalechstein, A.D, Newton, T.F. & van Gorp, W.G. (2003). Neurocognitive functioning is associated with employment status: A quantitative review. *Journal of Clinical and Experimental Neuropsychology*, 25(8), 1186–1191.

Kandola, R. & Fullerton, J. (1994). *Managing the mosaic: Diversity in action*. London: Institute of Personnel and Development.

Katz, L., Goldstein, G., Rudshin, S. & Bailey, D. (1993). A neuropsychological approach to the Bannatyne recategorization of the Wechsler Intelligence Scales in adults with learning disabilities. *Journal of Learning Disabilities*, 26(1), 65–72.

Kauffman, J.M. (2008). Labels and nature of special education: We need to face realities. *Learning Disabilities*, 14(4), 245–248.

Kaufman, A.S. & Kaufman, N.L. (2004). *Kaufman Brief Intelligence Test Second Edition* (KBIT-2). London: Pearson.

Kaufman, A.S. & Lichtenberger, E.O. (1999). *Essentials of WAIS-III Assessment*. New York: Wiley.

Kay Runyan, M. (1991). The effect of extra time on reading comprehension scores for university students with and without learning disabilities. *Journal of Learning Disabilities*, 2, 104–107.

Kelemen, W.L., Frost, P.J. & Weaver, C.A. (2000). Individual differences in metacognition: Evidence against a general metacognitive ability. *Memory Cognition*, 28(1), 92–107.

Kephart, N.C. (1968). Let's not misunderstand dyslexia, *The Instructor*, Aug/Sept., 78, 62–63.

Kihl, P., Gregerson, K. & Sterum, N. (2000). Hans Christian Andersen's spelling and syntax: Allegations of specific dyslexia are unfounded. (J/al) *Journal of Learning Disabilities*, 33(6), 506–519.

Kitz, W.R. & Nash, R.T. (1992). Testing the effectiveness of the Project Success Programme for Adult Dyslexics. *Annals of Dyslexia*, 42, 3–42.

Kirby, A. (2011). Developmental co-ordination disorder and emerging adulthood: Not just a motor disorder. *Journal of Adult Development*, 18(3), 105–106.

Kirby, A. & Rosenblum, S. (2008). *The Adult Developmental Coordination/Dyspraxia Checklist for Further and Higher Education*. Available on line at www.newport.ac.uk/dyscoverycentre

Kirby, A., Edwards, L. & Sugden, D.A. (2011). Emerging adulthood and developmental co-ordination disorder. *Journal of Adult Development*, 18(3), 107–113.

Kirby, A., Edwards, L. & Sugden, D.A. (2011). Driving behaviour in young adults with Developmental Co-ordination Disorder. *Journal of Adult Development*, 18(3), 122–129.

Kirby, A., Sugden, D., Beveridge, S., Edwards, L. & Edwards, R. (2008). Dyslexia and developmental co-ordination disorder in further and higher education – similarities and differences. Does the 'label' influence the support given? *Dyslexia*, 14, 197–213.

Kirk, J. and Reid, G. (2003). Adult dyslexia checklist – Criteria and considerations. Reading: *BDA Handbook*, 79–84.

Klassen, R.M. (2002). A question of calibration: A review of the self-efficiency beliefs of students with learning difficulties. *Learning Disability Quarterly*, 25, 88–103.

Klingberg, T. (2009). *The overflowing brain: Information overload and the limits of working memory*. New York: Oxford University Press, Inc.

Knowles, M. (1990). *The adult learner: A neglected species*. Houston, TX: Coulf.

Kolb, D.A. (1984). *Experiential learning*. Englewood Cliffs, NJ: Prentice Hall.

Kominsky, L. (2003). Successful adjustment of individuals with learning disabilities (pp. 259–277). In S.A. Vogel et al., *Learning disabilities in higher education and beyond: International perspectives*. Baltimore, Maryland: York Press.

Konur, O. (2007). A judicial outcome analysis of the Disability Discrimination Act: A windfall for employers? *Disability and Society, 22*(2), 187–204.

Korkman, M., S. Barron-Linnankoski & P. Lahti-Nuttila (1999). Effects of age and duration of reading instruction on the development of phonological awareness, rapid naming, and verbal memory span. *Developmental Neuropsychology, 16*(3), 415–431.

Kovas, Y., Haworth, C.M.A., Harlaar, N., Petrill, S.A., Dale, P.S. & Plomin, R. (2007). Overlap and specificity of genetic and environmental influences on mathematics and reading disability in 10-year-old twins. *Journal of Child Psychology and Psychiatry and Allied Disciplines, 48*, 914–922.

Kreiner, D.S. & Gough, P.B. (1990). Two ideas about spelling: Rules and Word-Specific Memory. *Journal of Memory and Language, 29*, 103–118.

Kretlow, A.G. & Bartholomew, C.C. (2010). Using coaching to improve the fidelity of evidence-based practices: A review of studies. *Teacher Education and Special Education, 33*, 279–299.

Kriss, I. & Evans, B. (2005). The relationship between dyslexia and Meares-Irlen Syndrome. *Journal of Research in Reading, 28*, 350–364.

Kronick, D. (1983). *Social development of learning disabled persons*. Toronto: Jossey-Bass.

Krumboltz, J.D. (1976). A social learning theory of career selection. *The Counselling Psychologist, 6*(1), 71–81.

Kuhn, D. (2000). Metacognitive development. *Current Directions in Psychological Science, 9*(5), 178–181.

Kumar, A.E. (1998). *The influence of metacognition on managerial hiring decision making: Implications for management development*. Unpublished doctoral dissertation: Virginia Polytechnic Institute and State University.

Laasonen, M., Lehtinen, M., Leppamki, S. Tani, P. & Hokkanen, L. (2010). Project DyAdd: Phonological processing, reading, spelling and arithmetic in adults with dyslexia and ADHS. *Journal of Learning Disabilities, 43*(1), 3–14.

Landi, N., Einar, M., Stephen, J.F., Sandak, R. & Pugh, G.H. (2010). An FMRI study of mutimodal semantic and phonological processing in reading disabled adolescents. *Annals of Dyslexia, 60*, 102–121.

Langdon, D.W. & Warrington, G.K. (1995). *A Verbal and Spatial Reasoning Test (VESPAR)*. Hove, UK: LEA.

Langton, A.J. & Ramseur, H. (2001). Enhancing employment outcomes through job accommodation and assistive technology resources and services. *Journal of Vocational Rehabilitation, 16*(1), 27–37.

Lashley, C. (1995). *Improving study skills*. London: Cassell.

Latham, G. (2007). *Work motivation*. London: Sage Publications.

Leather, C.A. & Kirwan, B.K. (2012). Achieving success in the workplace (pp. 157–166). In N. Brunswick (Ed.), *Supporting dyslexic adults in higher education and the workplace*. Chichester: Wiley.

Leather, C.A., Hogh, H., Seiss, E. & Everatt, J. (2011). Cognitive functioning and work success in adults with dyslexia. *Dyslexia, 17*, 327–338.

Lefly, D.L. & Pennington, B.F. (1991). Spelling errors and reading fluency in compensated adult dyslexics. *Annals of Dyslexia, 41*, 143–162.

Lenkowsky, L.K. & Saposnek, D.T. (1978). Family consequences of parental dyslexia, *Journal of Learning Disabilities, 11*(1), 47–53.

Leonard, F.C. (1991). Using Wechsler data to predict success for learning disabled college students. *Learning Disabilities Research and Practice*, 6(1), 17–24.

Lervag, A. & Hulme, C. (2009). Rapid Automatized Naming (RAN) taps on mechanism that places constraints on the development of early reading fluency. *Psychological Science*, 20(8), 1040–1048.

Lesaux, N.K., Lipka, O. & Siegel, L.S. (2006). Investigating cognitive and linguistic abilities that influence the reading comprehension skills of children from diverse linguistic backgrounds. *Reading and Writing*, 19, 99–131.

Levine, M. (1990). *Keeping a head in school*. Toronto: Educators Publishing Service.

Levinson, D.J. (1986). *The seasons of a man's life*. New York: Alfred Knopf.

Levinson, D.J. (1996). *The seasons of a woman's life*. New York: Alfred Knopf.

Lewis, R.B. (1998). Assistive technology and learning disabilities: Today's realities and tomorrow's promises. (I/al) *Journal of Learning Disabilities*, 31(1), 16–26.

Li, H. & Hamel, C.M. (2003). Writing issues in college students with learning disabilities: A synthesis of the literature from 1990 to 2000. *Learning Disability Quarterly*, 26, 29–46.

Lichtenberger, E.O. & Kaufman, A.S. (2009). *Essentials of WAIS-IV Assessment*. New Jersey: John Wiley & Sons Inc.

Linley, P.A., Nielsen, K.M., Wood, A.M., Gillet, R. & Biswar-Diener, R. (2010). Using signature strengths in pursuit of goals: Effects on goal progress, need satisfaction, and well-being, and implications for coaching psychologists. *International Coaching Psychology Review*, 5(1), 6–15.

Logan, J. (2009). Dyslexic entrepreneurs: The incidence; their coping strategies and their business skills. *Dyslexia*, 15(4), 328–346.

Logie, R.H. (1999). Working memory. *The Psychologist*, 12(4), 174–178.

Logie, R.H. & Maylor, E.A. (2009). An internet study of prospective memory across adulthood. *Psychology and Aging*, 24(3), 767–774.

Lucid Research Ltd (2010). *LADS Plus*. Beverley: UK.

Lumsden, J.A., Sampson, J.P., Reardon, R.C. & Lenz, P. (2004). A comparison study of the paper, personal computer (PC) and internet version of Wolland's self-directed search. *Measurement and Education in Consulting and Development*, 37, 85–94 and 25, 5–13.

Lyon, G.R. (2003). Defining dyslexia, comorbidity, jealous knowledge of language and reading. *Annals of Dyslexia*, 52(1), 1–14.

Macdonald, S.J. (2009). Windows of reflection: Conceptualizing dyslexia using the social model of disability. *Dyslexia*, 15: 347–362.

Madaus, J.W., Faggella-Luby, M.N. & Dukes, L.C. (2010). The role of non-academic factors in the academic success of college students with learning difficulties. *Learning Difficulties*, 17(2), 77–82.

Madaus, J.W., Ruban, L.M., Foley, T.E, McGuire, J.M. & Ruban, L.M. (2002). Employment self-disclosure of postsecondary graduates with learning disabilities: Rates and rationales. *Journal of Learning Disabilities*, 5(4) July/August, 364–369.

Mahoney, A.M, Dalby, J.T. & King, M.C. (1998). Cognitive failures and stress. *Psychological Reports*, 82, 1432–1436.

Manzo, A.N. & Manzo, U.C. (1993). *Literacy disorders*. Orlando, FL: Holt, Rhineheart, Winston.

Marsiske, M., Lang, F.R., Baltes, P.B. & Baltes, M.M. (1995). Selective optimisation with compensation: Life-span perspectives on successful human development. In R.A. Dixon & L. Backman (Eds.), *Compensating for psychological deficits and declines*. Mahwah, NJ: Lawrence Erlbaum Assoc.

Martin, A.E. & McLoughlin, D. (2012). Disclosing dyslexia: An exercise in self-advocacy. In N. Brunswick (Ed.), *Supporting dyslexic adults in higher education and the workplace.* Chichester: Wiley, 125–135.

Masten, A.S. (2001). Ordinary magic: Resilience processes in development. *American Psychologist,* 56(3), 227–238.

Mathuranath, P.S., George, A., Cherian, P.J., Alexander, A., Sarma, S.G. & Sarma, P.S. (2003). Effects of age, education and gender on verbal fluency. *Journal of Clinical and Experimental Neuropsychology, 25,* 1057–1064.

Mather, N. (1998). Relinquishing aptitude – achievement discrepancy: The doctrine of misplaced precision. *Perspectives.* Winter, 4–7.

Mathis, L.M. (2009). *The relationship between career-related knowledge, self esteem, locus of control, gender, and employment outcomes among individuals with learning disabilities.* Unpublished Doctoral Thesis. University of Arkansas.

Maughan, B., Messer, J. Collishaw, Pickles, A., Snowling, M. Yule, W. & Rutter, M. (2009). Persistence of literary problems: Spelling in adolescence and at mid-life. *Journal of Child Psychology and Psychiatry, 50*(8), 893–901.

McArthur, G.M., Hogben, J.H., Edwards, V.T., Heath, S.M. and Mengler, E.D. (2000). On the 'specifics' of specific reading disability and specific language impairment. *Journal of Child Psychology and Psychiatry, 41,* 869–874.

McBride-Chang, C., Lam, F., Lam, C., Doo, S., Wong, S.W. & Chow, Y.Y. (2008). Word recognition and cognitive profiles of Chinese pre-school children at risk for dyslexia through language delay or familial history of dyslexia. *Journal of Child Psychology and Psychiatry, 49,* 211–218.

McCormick, E.J. & Ilgen, D. (1985). *Industrial and organisational psychology* (8th ed.). London: Allen and Unwin.

McCrory, E.J., Mechelli, A., Firth, U. & Price, C.J. (2005). More than words: A common neural basis for reading and naming deficits in developmental dyslexia? *Brain, 128,* 261–267.

McLoughlin, D. (2003). Assessing adults with dyslexia: Towards understanding. In M. Johnson & L. Peer (Eds.), *The Dyslexia Handbook 2003.* Reading: British Dyslexia Association.

McLoughlin, D. & Beard, J. (2000). Dyslexia support in a multilingual environment. In L. Peer & G. Reid (Eds.), *Multiligualism, literacy and dyslexia.* London: David Fulton Publishers.

McLoughlin, D. & Kirwan, B.M. (2007). Coaching and dyslexia in the work place. *Selection and Development Review, 23*(2), 3–7.

McLoughlin, D., Fitzgibbon, G. & Young, V. (1994). *Adult dyslexia: Assessment, counselling and training.* London: Whurr.

McLoughlin, D., Leather, C.A. & Stringer, P.E. (2002). *The adult dyslexic: Interventions and outcomes.* London: Whurr.

Meehan, M., Birkin, R. & Snodgrass, R. (1998). Employment assessment (EA): Issues surrounding the use of psychological assessment material with disabled people. *Selection Development Review, 14*(3), 3–9.

Mezulis, A.H. et al. (2004). Is there a universal positivity bias in attributions? A meta-analytic review of individual, developmental and cultural differences in the self-serving attributional bias, *Psychological Bulletin, 130,* 711–747.

Miyake, A., Emerson, M.J. & Friedman, N.P. (2000). Assessment of executive functions in clinical settings: Problems and recommendations. *Seminars in Speed and Language, 21*(2), 169–183.

Miles, T.M. (2007). Criteria for evaluating interventions. *Dyslexia, 13,* 253–256.

Miles, T.R. (1996). Do dyslexic children have IQs. *Dyslexia, 2*(3), 175–178.

Miles, T.R. (2004). *Dyslexia and stress* (2nd ed.). London: Whurr.

Miles, T.R. & Miles, E. (1990). *Dyslexia: A hundred years on.* Milton Keynes: Open University Press.

Miles,T.R., Haslum, M.N. & Wheeler, T.J. (1998). Gender ratio in dyslexia. *Annals of Dyslexia, 48,* 27–57.

Miles, T.R., Thierry, G., Roberts, J. & Schiffeldrin, J. (2006). Verbatim and gist recall of sentences by dyslexic and non-dyslexic adults. *Dyslexia, 12,* 177–194.

Miller, C.J., Miller, S.R., Bloom, J.S., Jones, L., Lindstrom, W. & Craggs, J., et al. (2006). Testing the double-deficit hypothesis in an adult sample. *Annals of Dyslexia, 56,* 83–102.

Miller-Shaul, S. (2005). The characteristics of young and adult dyslexics readers on reading and reading related cognitive tasks as compared to normal readers. *Dyslexia, 11,* 132–151.

Miner, J.B. (1992). *Industrial and organisational psychology.* Singapore: McGraw Hill.

Minskoff, E.H. & Sautter, S.W. (1987). Employer attitudes toward hiring the learning disabled. *Journal of Learning Disabilities, 20*(1), 53–57.

Miyake, A., Friedman, N.P., Emerson, M.J., Witzki, A.H. & Howerter, A. (2000). The unity and diversity of executive functions and their contributions to complex 'frontal lobe' tasks: A latent variable analysis. *Cognitive Psychology, 41,* 49–100.

Moran, S. & Gardner, H. (2007). "Hill, Skill and Will": Executive Functions from a Multiple – Inetelligences Perspective. In L. Meltzer (Ed.), *Executive function in education: From theory to practice* (pp. 19–38). New York: Guildford Press.

Morris, D. and Turnbell, P. (2006). A survey-based exploration of the impact of dyslexia on career progression of UK registered nurses. *Journal of Nursing Management, 15*(1), 97–106.

Morris, R.G., Craik, F.M. & Gick, M.L. (1990). Age differences in working memory tasks: The role of secondary memory and the central executive system. *Quarterly Journal of Experimental Psychology, 42A,* 67–86.

Mosakowski, E. & Earley, P.C. (2010). A situated metacognitive model of the entrepreneurial mindset. *Journal of Business Venturing, 25*(2), 217–229.

Mosberg, L. & Johns, D. (1994). Reading and listening comprehension in college students with developmental dyslexia. *Learning Disabilities, Research & Practice, 9*(3), 130–135.

Mortimer, T. (2003). *Dyslexia and learning styles.* London: Whurr.

Myers, I.B. & McCauleey, M.H. (1985). *Myers-Briggs Type Indicator.* California: Consulting Psychology Press.

Nalavany, B.A., Carawan, L. & Rennick, R. (2011). Psychosocial experiences associated with dyslexia: A participant-driven concept map of adult perspectives. *Journal of Learning Disabilities, 44*(1), 63–79.

Nathan, R. & Hill, L. (1992). *Career counselling.* London: Sage.

Quandt, I.J. (1977). *Teaching reading: a human process.* Chicago: Rand McNally.

Nelson, J.M. (2011). Learning disabilities and anxiety. *Journal of Learning Disabilities, 44*(1), 3–17.

Nelson, J.M. (2012). Meta-analysis on the effectiveness of extra time as a test accommodation for transitioning adolescents with learning disabilities. *Journal of Learning Disabilities, 45*(2), 128–138.

Nelson, T.O., Stuart, R.B., Howard, C. & Crowley, M. (1999). Metacognition and clinical psychology: A preliminary framework for research and practice. *Clinical Psychology & Psychotherapy, 6,* 73–79.

Nelson-Jones, R. (1995). *The theory and practice of counselling.* London: Cassell.

Nergard-Nilssen, T. (2006). Developmental dyslexia in Norwegian: Evidence from single-case studies. *Dyslexia, 12,* 30–50.

Nester, M.A. (1993). Psychometric testing and reasonable accommodations for persons with disabilities. *Rehabilitation Psychology, 38*(2), 75–85.

Nicolson, R.I. & Fawcett, A.J. (1995). Dyslexia is more than a phonological disability. *Dyslexia, 1,* 19–37.

Nicolson, R.I. & Fawcett, A.J. (1999). Developmental dyslexia: The role of the cerebellum. *Dyslexia, 5*(3), 155–177.

Nicolson, R.I. & Fawcett, A.J. (2001). Dyslexia as a learning disability. In A.J. Fawcett (Ed.), *Dyslexia: Theory and good practice.* London: Whurr.

Nicolson, R.I. & Fawcett, A.J. (2008). *Dyslexia, learning and the brain,* Cambridge, MA: MIT Press.

Office for Disability Issues (2010). *Equality Act 2012,* Office for Disability Issues, London.

Ofiesh, N., Hughes, C. & Scott, S. (2004). Extended test time and postsecondary students with learning disabilities: A model for decision making. *Learning Disabilities Research and Practice, 19*(1), 57–70.

Ofiesh, N., Mather, N. & Russell, A. (2005). Using speed cognitive, reading, and academic measures to determine the need for extended test time among university students with learning disabilities. *Journal of Psychoeducational Assessment, 25,* 35–52.

Paetzold, R.L., Garcia, M.F. & Collella, A. (2008). Peer perceptions of accommodation unfairness. *Journal of Occupational Psychology, Employment and Disability, 10,* 1(Spring).

Papagano, C., Valentine, T. & Baddeley, A.D. (1991). Phonological short term memory and foreign language vocabulary learning. *Journal of Memory and Language, 30,* 331–347.

Parsons, F. (1909). *Choosing a vocation.* Boston: Houghton-Mifflin.

Passmore, J. (2007). Using psychometrics and psychological tools in coaching. *Selection and Development Review, 23*(5), 3–6.

Patton, J.R. & Polloway, E.A. (1992). Learning disabilities: The challenges of adulthood. *Journal of Learning Disabilities, 25*(7), 410–415.

Patton, J.R., Cronin, M.E., Bassett, D.S. & Koppel, A.E. (1997). A life skill approach to mathematics instruction: Preparing students with learning disabilities for the real-life math demands of adulthood. *Journal of Learning Disabilities, 30*(2), 178–187.

Paulesu, E., Demonet, J.-F., Fazio, F., McCrory, E., Chanoine, V., Brunswick, N., Cappa, S.F., Cossu, G., Habib, M., Frith, C.D. & Frith, U. (2001). Dyselxia: Cultural diversity and biological unity. *Science, 291,* 2165–2167.

Peel, M. (1992). *Career development and planning.* Berks: McGraw-Hill.

Peer, L. (2009). Dyslexia and glue ear (pp. 33–42). In G. Reid (Ed.), *The Routledge companion to dyslexia.* London: Routledge.

Pennington, B.F. (1990). The genetics of dyslexia. *Journal of Child Psychology and Psychology, 31,* 193–201.

Pennington, B.F. (2009). *Diagnosing learning disorders* (2nd ed.). New York: Guildford Press.

Pennington, B.F. & Olson, R.K. (2005). Genetics of dyslexia (pp. 453–473). In M. Snowling & C. Hulme (Eds.), *The science of reading: A handbook.* Oxford: Blackwell.

Pennington, B.F., Bennetto, L., McAleer, O. & Roberts, R.J. (1996). Executive functions and working memory (pp. 327–348). In G. Reid Lyon & N.A. Krasnegor (Eds.), *Attention, memory and executive function.* Baltimore: Brookes.

Pintrich, P.R. et al. (1994). Individual differences in motivation and cognition in students with and without learning disabilities, *Journal of Learning Disabilities, 27*(6), 360–370.

Plata, M. & Bone, J. (1989). Perceived importance of occupations by adolescents with and without learning disabilities. *Journal of Learning Disabilities, 22*(1), 64–71.

Pollak, D. (Ed.) (2009). *Neurodiversity in higher education: Positive responses to specific learning differences.* Chichester: Wiley Blackwell.

Portwood, M. (2010). Co-morbidity: Dyslexia, dyspraxia, ASD and ADHD – the exception or the rule. *Assessment and Development Matters, 2*(3), 33–35.

Pressley, M. (1991). Can learning disabled children become good information processors? How can we find out? (pp. 137–162). In L. Feagans, E. Short & L. Meltzer (Eds.), *Subtypes of learning disabilities*. Hillsdale, NJ: Erlbaum.

Price, G. (2010). Dyscalculia in the workplace. In C.A. Leather & D. McLoughlin (Eds.), *Employment and dyslexia handbook*. Bracknell: BDA.

Price, L.A. & Patton, J.R. (2002). Reshuffling the puzzle pieces: Connecting adult developmental theory to learning disorders. *Career Planning and Adult Development Journal, 18*(1), 10–48.

Price, L.A. & Shaw, S.F. (2000). An instructional model for adults with learning disabilities. *Journal for Vocational Special Needs Education, 22*(3), 14–24.

Price, L.A., Gerber, P.J. & Mulligan, R. (2005). To be or not to be learning disabled: A preliminary report on self-disclosure in adults with learning disabilities. *Thalamus, 23*, 18–27.

Puolakanaho, A., Ahonen, T., Aro, M., Eklund, K., Leppnen, P. H, Poikkeus, A.-M., Tolvanen, A., Torppa, M. & Lyytinen, H. (2007). Very early phonological and language skills: Estimating individual risk of reading disability. *Journal of Child Psychology and Psychiatry, 48*, 923–931.

Rachman, D., Americ, J. & Aranya, N. (1981). A factor-analytic study of the construct validity of Holland's Self-Directed Search Test. *Educational and Psychological Measurement, 41*(2), 425–437.

Rack, J. (1997). Issues in the assessment of developmental dyslexia in adults: Theoretical and applied perspectives. *Journal of Research in Reading, 20*(1), 66–76.

Raitano, N.A., Pennington, B.F., Tunick, R.A., Boada, R. & Shriberg, L.D. (2004). Pre-literacy skills of subgroups of children with speech sound disorders. *Journal of Child Psychology and Psychiatry, 45*, 821–835.

Ramus, F. (2003). Developmental dyslexia: Specific phonological deficit of general sensorimotor dysfunction? *Current Opinion in Neurobiology, 13*, 212–218.

Ramus, F. (2004). Neurobiology of dyslexia: A reinterpretation of the data. *Trends in Neurosciences, 27*(12), 720–726.

Ramus, F. & Szenkovits, G. (2008). What phonological deficit? *Quarterly Journal of Experimental Psychology, 61*(1), 129–141.

Ramus, F., Rosen, S., Dakin, S.C., Day, B.L., Castellote, J.M., White, S. & Frith, U. (2003). Theories of developmental dyslexia: Insights from a multiple case study of dyslexic adults. *Brain, 126*, 1–25.

Raskind, M.H., Goldberg, R.J., Higgins, E.L. & Herman, K.L. (1999). Patterns of change and patterns of success in individuals with learning disabilities: Results from a twenty-year longitudinal study. *Journal of Learning Disabilities Research and Practice, 14*, 35–49.

Rauch, A. & Frese, M. (2000). Psychological approaches to entrepreneurial success: A general model and an overview of findings (pp. 101–142). In C.L. Copper & I.T. Robertson (Eds.), *International Review of Industrial and Organisational Psychology*. Chichester: Wiley.

Ray, N.S., Fowler, S. & Stein, J.F. (2005). Yellow filters can improve magnocellular function: Motion sensitivity convergence, accommodation and reading. *Annals of the New York Academy of Sciences, 1039*, 283–293.

Redish, J.C. & Selzer, J. (1985). The place of readability formulas in technical communication. *Technical Communication, 32*, 46–52.

Reid, G. & Kirk, J. (2001). *Dyslexia in adults: Education and employment*. Chichester: John Wiley & Sons.

Reid, G. & Strnadova, I. (2008). Dyslexia and learning styles: Overcoming barriers to learning. In G. Reid, A.J. Fawcett, F. Mains & L. Siegel (Eds.), *The Sage handbook of dyslexia*. London: Sage.

Reid, M. (1999). Career assessment: Choosing the right tools. *Dyslexia Handbook,* Reading: British Dyslexia Association.

Reiff, H.B., Gerber, P.J. & Ginsberg, R. (1993). Definitions of learning disabilities from adults with learning disabilities: The insiders' perspectives. *Learning Disability Quarterly, 16,* 114–125.

Rice, M. & Brooks, G. (2004). *Developmental dyslexia in adults: A research review.* London: National Research and Development Centre for Adult Literacy and Numeracy.

Ricker, T.J., Aubuchon, A.M. & Cowan, N. (2010). Working memory. *Cognitive Science, 1,* 573–585.

Ricketts, C., Brice, J. & Coombes, L. (2009). Are multiple choice tests fair to medical students with specific learning disabilities? *Advances in Health Sciences Education, 15*(2), 265–275.

Riddick, B. (1996). *Living with dyslexia,* London: RKP.

Riddick, B., Sterling, C., Farmer, M. & Morgan, S. (1999). Self-esteem and anxiety in the educational histories of adult dyslexic students. *Dyslexia, 5,* 227–248.

Rijsdijk, F.V., Vernon, P.A. & Boomsam, D.I. (2002). Application of hierarchical genetic models to raven and WAIS subtests: A Dutch twin study. *Behaviour and Genetics, 32,* 199–210.

Roberts, R. & Mather, N. (1997). Orthographic dyslexia: The neglected subtype. *Learning Disabilities Research and Practice, 12,* 236–250.

Rochelle, K.S.H. & Talcott, J.B. (2006). Impaired balance in developmental dyslexia? *Journal of Child Psychology and Psychiatry, 47*(11), 1159–1166.

Rodríguez-Aranda, C., Waterloo, K., Sparr, S. & Sundet, K. (2006). Age-related psychomotor slowing as an important component of verbal fluency: Evidence from healthy individuals and Alzheimer's patients. *Journal of Neurology, 253,* 1414–1427.

Rogan, L.L. & Hartman, L.D. (1990). Adult outcomes of learning disabled students ten years after initial follow-up. *Learning Disabilities Focus, 5,* 91–102.

Rogers, C. (1951). *Client-centered Therapy.* Boston: Houghton-Mifflin.

Rosenblum, L. (1987). An experiment in group therapy with learning disabled adults (pp. 233–237). In D. Johnson & J. Blalock (Eds.), *Adults with learning disabilities: Clinical studies,* Orlando, FL: Grune and Stratton.

Roth, A.D. & Fonagy, P. (1996). *What works for whom? A critical review of psychotherapy research.* New York: Guildford Press.

Ruban, L.M. et al. (2003). The differential impact of academic self-regulatory methods on academic achievement among university students with and without learning disabilities. *Journal of Learning Disabilities, 36*(3), 270–286.

Ruben, M. & Hewstone, M. (1998). Social identity theory's self-esteem hypothesis: A review and some suggestions for clarification, *Personality and Social Psychology Revue, 2,* 40–62.

Ryan, A.G. & Price, L. (1992). Adults with LD in the 1990's. *Intervention in School and Clinic, 28*(1), 6–20.

Salvia, J. & Gajar, A. (1988). A comparison of WAIS-R profiles of non-disabled college freshmen and college students with learning disabilities. *Journal of Learning Disabilities, 21*(10), 632–635.

Saunders, P. (1994). *First Steps in Counselling.* Manchester: PCCS Books.

Savage, R.S., Frederickson, N., Goodwin, R., Patini, U., Smith, N. & Tuersley, L. (2005). Relationships among rapid digit naming phonological processing, motor automaticity and speech perception in poor, average, and good readers and spellers. *Journal of Learning Disabilities, 38*(1), 12–28.

Schmidt, A.M. & Ford, J.K. (2003). Learning within a learner control training environment: The interactive effects of goal orientation and metacognitive instruction on learning outcomes. *Personnel Psychology, 56,* 405–429.

Schraw, G. & Dennison, R. (1994). Assessing metacognitive awareness. *Contemporary Educational Psychology, 19,* 460–475.

Schumaker, J.B., Deshler, D.D., Nolan, S., Clark, F.L., Alley, G.R & Warner, M.M. (1981). *Error monitoring: A learning strategy for improving academic performance of learning disabled adolescents.* Lawrence, KS: University of Kansas.

Schumaker, J.D. & Caplan, D. (2006) Cognition, emotion and the cerebellum. *Brain, 129*(2), 209–292.

Schwartz, R.L. (2006). A checklist for distinguishing learning disabilities from second language learning differences. *Learning Disabilities Association of America 43rd International Conference.* Jacksonville, Florida. February.

Schwartz, R.L. (2009). Issues in identifying learning disabilities for English language learners. In J.M. Taymans (Ed.), *Learning to achieve.* Washington: National Institute for Literacy.

Schunk, D.H. & Parajes, F. (2004). Competence perceptions and academic functioning (pp. 85–104). In A.J. Elliot & C.S. Dweck (Eds.), *Handbook of competence and motivation.* New York: Guildford Press.

Scott, M.J. & Dryden, W. (1996). The cognitive behavioural paradigm (pp. 156–179). In R. Wolfe & W. Dryden (Eds.), *Handbook of counselling psychology.* London: Sage.

Scott, R. (2004). *Dyslexia and counselling.* London: Whurr.

Scott, S.S. (1994). Determining reasonable academic adjustments for college students with learning disabilities. *Journal of Learning Disabilities, 27,* 403–412.

Scott, S.S. & Gregg, N. (2000). Meeting the evolving needs of faculty in providing access for college students with LD. *Journal of Learning Disabilities, 33*(2), 158–167.

Segal, S.P., Silverman, C. & Tembin, T. (1993). Empowerment and self-help agency practice for people with mental difficulties. *Social Work, 38*(6), 705–712.

Shaywitz, S.E. & Shaywitz, B.A. (2005). Dyslexia (Specific Reading Disability). *Biological Psychiatry, 57*(II), 1301–1309.

Shaywitz, S.E., Shaywitz, B.A., Fulbright, R.K., Skudlarski, P., Mencl, W.E., Constable, R.T., Pugh, K.R., Holahan, J.M., Marchione, K.E., Fletcher, J.M., Lyon, G.R. & Gore, J.C. (2003). Neural systems for compensation and persistence; young adult outcome of childhood reading disability. *Biological Psychiatry Volume, 54* (1), 25–33.

Sherin, J. & Caiger, L. (2004). Rational emotive behaviour therapy: A behavioural change model for executive coaching. *Counselling Psychology Journal: Practice and Research, 56,* 225–233.

Shimamura, A.P. (2000). Toward a cognitive neuroscience of metacognition. *Consciousness and Cognition, 9,* 313–323.

Siegel, L.S. (1992). An evaluation of the discrepancy definition of dyslexia. *Journal of Learning Disabilities, 25*(10), 618–629.

Siegel, L.S. (2003). IQ – discrepancy definitions and the diagnosis of LD: Introduction to the Special Issue. *Journal of Learning Disabilities, 36*(1), 2–3.

Siegel, L.S. & Smythe, I.S. (2005). Reflections on research on reading disability with special attention to gender issues. *Journal of Learning Disabilities, 38*(5), 473–477.

Siegel, L.S. & Smythe, I.S. (2006). Supporting dyslexic adults – a need for clarity (and more research): A critical review of the Rice Report 'Developmental dyslexia in adults: A research review'. *Dyslexia, 12,* 68–79.

Siegel, L.S. & Smythe, I.S. (2008). The importance of phonological processing rather than IQ discrepancy in understanding adults with reading disorders. In L.E. Wolf, H.E. Schreiber & J. Wassersdeux. *Adult learning disorders: Contemporary issues.* NY: Taylor Francis.

Silani, G., Frith, U., Demonet, J.F., Fazio, F., Perani, D., Price, C. & Pauleso, E. (2005). Brain abnormalities underlying altered activation in dyslexia: A voxel based morphometry study. *Brain, 128,* 2453–2461.

Simos, P.G., Fletcher, J.M., Bergman, E., Breier, J.I., Foorman, B.R., Castillo, E.M., Davis, R.N., Fitzgerald, M. & Papanicolaou, A.C. (2002). Dyslexic – specific brain activation profile becomes normal following successful remedial training. *Neurology, 58*(2), 1203–1213.

Singer, E. (2008). Coping with academic failure, a study of Dutch children with dyslexia. *Dyslexia, 14,* 314–333.

Sireci, S.G., Scarpati, S.E. & Li, S. (2005). Test accommodations for students with disabilities: An analysis of the interaction hypothesis. *Review of Educational Research, 71,* 457–490.

Skottun, B.C. & Parke, L.A. (1999). The possible relationship between visual deficits and dyslexia: Examination of a critical assumption. *Journal of Learning Difficulties, 32*(1), 2–5.

Skottun, B.C. & Skoyles, J. (2007). Yellow filters, magnocellular responses and reading. *International Journal of Neuroscience, 117,* 287–293.

Smiley, E. (2005). Epidemiology of mental health problems in adults with learning disability: An update. *Advances in psychiatric treatment, 11,* 214–222.

Smith, J.D. (1996). Adult development theories: An overview and reflection of their relevance for learning disabilities. In J.R. Patton & E.A. Polloway (Eds.), *Learning disabilities.* Austin TX: Pro-Ed.

Smith, M.L. & Glass, G.V. (1977). Meta-analysis of psychotherapy outcome studies. *American Psychologist, 32,* 752–760.

Smith, M.L., Glass, G.V. & Miller, T.I. (1980). *The benefits of psychotherapy.* Baltimore: Johns Hopkins University Press.

Smith-Spark, J.H. & Fisk, J.E. (2007). Working memory functioning in developmental dyslexia. *Memory, 15*(1), 34–56.

Smith-Spark, J.H. & Moore, V. (2009).The representation and processing of familiar faces in dyslexia: Differences in age of acquisition effects. *Dyslexia, 15,* 129–146.

Smith-Spark, J.H., Fisk, J.E., Fawcett, A.J. & Nicolson, R.I. (2003). *European Journal of Psychology, 15*(4), 567–587.

Smythe, I. & Everatt, J. (2001). The new dyslexia checklist for adults. *The Dyslexia Handbook.* Reading: British Dyslexia Association, pp. 73–77.

Snowling, M.J. (2001). From language to reading and dyslexia. *Dyslexia, 7*(1), 37–46.

Spekman, N.J., Goldberg, R.J. & Herman, K.L. (1992). Learning disabled children grow up: A search for factors related to success in the young adult years. *Learning Disabilities Research and Practice, 7,* 161–170.

Spring, B. (2007). Evidence-based practice in clinical psychology: What it is, why it matters; what you need to know. *Journal of Clinical Psychology, 63,* 611–631.

Stanovich, K.E. (1991). Discrepancy definitions of reading disability: Has intelligence led us astray? *Reading Research Quarterly, 26,* 1–29.

Stein, J.F. (2001). The magnocellular theory of developmental dyslexia. *Dyslexia, 7*(1), 12–36.

Stein, J.F. (2008). The neurobiological basis of syslexia. In G. Reid, A. Fawcett, F. Manis & L. Siegel (Eds.), *The Sage handbook of dyslexia.* London: Sage Publications.

Stein, J.F. & Talcott, J. (1999). Impaired neuronal timing in developmental dyslexia – the magnocellular hypothesis. *Dyslexia, 5,* 59–77.

Sterling, C., Farmer, F., Riddick, B, Morgan, S. & Matthews, C. (1997). Adult dyslexic writing. *Dyslexia, 4,* 1–15.

Sternberg, R.J. (2004). Intelligence, competence and expertise (pp. 15–30). In A.J. Elliot & C.S. Dweck (Eds.), *Handbook of competence and motivation.* New York: Guildford Press.

Stevenson, J. & Fredman, G. (1990). The social environmental correlates of reading ability. *Journal of Child Psychology and Psychiatry, 31,* 681–698.

Stanovich, K.E. (1996). Towards a more inclusive definition of dyslexia. *Dyslexia, 2,* 154–166.

Stanovich, K.E. & Siegel, L.S. (1994). Phenotypic performance profile of reading-disabled children: A regression-based test of the phonologicalcore variable-difference model. *Journal of Educational Psychology, 86,* 24–53.

Super, D.E. (1969). Vocational development theory: Persons, positions and processes. *Counselling Psychologist, 1,* 2–9.

Swanson, H.L. (1990). Influence of metacognitive knowledge and aptitude on problem solving. *Journal of Educational Psychology, 82*(2), 306–314.

Swanson, H.L. (1994). The role of working memory and dynamic assessment in the classification of children with learning disabilities. *Learning Disabilities Research and Practice, 9*(4), 190–202.

Swanson, H.L. (2009). Assessment of adults with learning disabilities: A quantitative synthesis of similarities and differences. In J. Tyamans (Ed.), *Learning to achieve: A review of the research literature on serving adults with learning disabilities.* Washington, DC: National Institute for Literacy.

Swanson, H.L. (2012). Adults with reading disabilities: Converting a meta-analysis to practice. *Journal of Learning Disabilities, 45*(1), 17–30.

Swanson, H.L. & Siegel, L. (2001). Learning disabilities as a working memory deficit. *Issues in Education: Contributions of Educational Psychology, 7*(1), 1–48.

Swanson, H. l., Cooney, J.B. & O'Shaughnessy, T.E. (1998). Learning disabilities and memory (pp. 107–162). In B.Y.L. Wong (Ed.), *Learning about Learning Disabilities* (2nd ed.). San Diego CA: Academic Press.

Spadafore, G.J. (1983). *Spadafore Diagnostic Reading Test.* Novato, CA: Academic Therapy Publications.

Tan, L.H., Laird, A.R, Li, K. & Fox, P.T. (2005). Neuroanatomical correlates of phonological processing of Chinese characters and alphabetic words: A meta-analysis. *Human Brain Mapping, 25,* 83–91.

Tanner, K. (2009). Student perspectives: Adult dyslexia and the 'conundrum of failure'. *Disability and Society, 24*(6), 785–797.

Tanners, A., McDougall, D., Skouge, J. & Narkon, D. (2012). Comprehension and time expended for a doctoral student with a learning disability when reading with and without an accommodation. *Learning Disabilities, 18*(1), 3–10.

Taylor, K.E. & Waler, J. (2003). Occupational choices of adults with and without symptoms or dyslexia. *Dyslexia, 9*(3), 177–185.

Taymans, J.M. (1991). The use of the self-directed search and the self directed search form e with people with learning disabilities. *Learning Disabilities Research and Practice, 6,* 5–58.

Terras, M.M., Thompson, L.C. & Minnis, H. (2009). Dyslexia and psycho-social functioning: An exploratory study of the role of self-esteem and understanding. *Dyslexia, 15,* 304–327.

Thiede, K.W., Anderson, M.C.M. & Thierriault, D. (2003). Accuracy of metacognitive monitoring affects learning of texts. *Journal of Educational Psychology, 95*(1), 66–73.

Thomas, M. (2000). Albert Einstein and LD: An evaluation of the evidence. *Journal of Learning Disabilities, 33*(2), 149–157.

Thomas, M. (2009). *The psychology of dyslexia.* London: Wiley-Blackwell.

Thorn, B.E. (2007). Evidence-based practice in psychology. *Journal of Clinical Psychology, 63*(7), 607–609.

Thurlow, M.L., Moen, R.E., Liu, K.K., Scullin, S., Hausmann, K.E. & Shyyan, V. (2009). *Disabilities and reading: Understanding the effects of disabilities and the relationship to reading instruction and assessment.* Minneapolis, MN: University of Minnesota, Partnership for Accessible Reading Assessment.

Tonnessen, F.E. (1997). How can we best define 'Dyslexia'? *Dyslexia, 3,* 78–92.

Torgenson, J.K. (1979). Performance of reading disabled children on serial memory tasks: A selective review of recent research. *Reading Research Quarterly, 14*, 57–87.

Torgenson, J.K. (1985). Memory processes in learning disabled children. *Journal of Learning Disabilities, 18*, 350–357.

Torgenson, J., Wagner, R. & Rashotte, C. (1999). *Test of word reading efficiency.* London: Pearson.

Trainin, G. & Swanson, H.L. (2005). Cognition, metacognition and achievement of college students with learning disabilities. *Learning Disabilities Quarterly, 28*(4), 261–272.

Turner, M. (1997). *Psychological assessment of dyslexia.* London: Whurr.

Undheim, A.M. (2009). A thirteen-year follow-up study of young Norwegian adults with dyslexia in childhood: Reading development and educational levels. *Dyslexia, 15*(4), 291–303.

Uppstad, P.H. & Tønnessen, F.E. (2007). The notion of 'phonology' in dyslexia research: Cognitivism – and beyond. *Dyslexia, 13*, 154–174.

Upton, P. (2011). *Developmental psychology.* Exeter, UK: Learning Matters.

Vanderiendonk, A. & Franssen, V. (2000). Cognitive deficits affecting time perception. *Paper presented to The British Psychological Society London Conference.* December.

Vellutino, F.R. (1980). Alternative conceptualization of dyslexia: Evidence support of a Verbal-Deficit hypothesis (pp. 567–587). In M. Wolf, M.K. McQuillan & E. Radison (Eds.), *Thought and language: Language and reading.* Cambridge, MA: Howard Educational Review.

Vellutino, F.R., Fletcher, J.M., Snowling, M.J. & Scanlon, D.M. (2004). Specific reading disability (dyslexia): What have we learned in the past four decades? *Journal of Child Psychology and Psychiatry, 45*(1), 2–40.

Venneri, A. (2000). Cognitive deficits affecting time perception. *Paper presented to The British Psychological Society London Conference.* December.

Vogel, S.A. & Forness, S. (1992). Social functioning in adults with Learning Disabilities. *School Psychology Review, 21*(3), 374–385.

Vogel, S.A., Vogel, G, Sharoni, V., & Dahan, O. (2003). *Learning disabilities in higher education and beyond: An international perspective.* Mayland: York Press.

Von Karolyi, C., Winner, E., Gray, W. & Sherman, G.F. (2003). Dyslexia linked to talent: Global visual-spatial ability. *Brain and Language, 85*(3), 427–431.

Vukovic, R.K., Wilson, A.M. & Nash, K.K. (2004). Naming speed deficits in adults with reading disabilities: A test of the double-deficit hypothesis. *Journal of Learning Disabilities, 37*(5), 440–450.

Wagner, R., Torgensen, J.K. & Rashotte, C.A. (1999). Comprehensive Test of Phonological processing (CTOPP). London: Pearson.

Walker, B.A. (1994). Valuing differences: The concept and a model (pp. 211–223). In C. Mabey & P. Iles (Eds.), *Managing learning.* London: Routledge.

Wampold, B.E. (2001). *The great psychotherapy debate: Models, methods and findings.* Mahwah, NJ: Laurence Erlbaum Associates.

Webster, R.E. (1997). *Learning Efficiency test II – Revised.* Novato, CA: Academic Therapy.

Wechsler, D. (1944). *The Measurement of Adult Intelligence* (3rd ed.). Baltimore: Williams & Wilkins.

Wechsler, D. (1976). *The Wechsler Intelligence Scale for Children.* Windsor: NFER.

Wechsler, D. (1981). *The Wechsler Adult Intelligence Scale (Revised).* NY: Psychological Corporation.

Wechsler, D. (2005) *Wechsler Individual Achievement Test, Second Edition (WIAT-II).* London: Pearson.

Wechsler, D. (2008). *Wechsler Adult Intelligence Scale – Fourth Edition.* San Antonio, TX: Pearson.

Wechsler, D. (2009). *Wechsler Memory Scales (Fourth Ed.).* San Antonio, TX: Pearson.

Wehman, P. (1996). *Life beyond the classroom.* Baltimore: Brookes.

Weisberg, D.S., Keil, F.C., Goodstein, J., Randson, E. & Caray, J.R. (2008). The seductive allure of neuroscience explanations. *Journal Cognitive Neuroscience, 20*(3), 430–477.

West, T.G. (1997). *In the mind's eye* (2nd ed.). Buffalo, NY: Prometheus Books.

White, W.J. (1992). The postschool adjustment of persons with learning disabilities: Current status and future projections. *Journal of Learning Disabilities, 25*(7), 448–456.

Wiederholt, J.L. & Blalock, G. (2000). *Gray Silent Reading Test*. London: Pearson.

Wiederholt, J.L. & Bryant, B.R. (2001). *Gray Oral Reading Test – Fourth Edition*. London: Pearson.

Wiederholt, J.L. & Bryant, B.R. (2011). *Gray Oral Reading Test – Fifth Edition*. London: Pearson.

Wiig, E.H., Nielsen, N.P. & Jacobson, J.J. (2007). A quick test of cognitive speed: Patterns of age groups 15–95 years. *Perceptual and Motor Speed, 104*(3), 1067–1075.

Wiig, E.H., Nielsen, N.P., Minthon, L. & Warkentin, S. (2002). *A quick test of cognitive speed*. San Antonio, TX: Pearson Assessment.

Wilkins, A. (1995). *Visual stress*. Oxford: Oxford University Press.

Wilkins, A.J. (2003). *Reading through colour*, Chichester, Sussex: Wiley.

Wilkins, A.J., Jeanes, R.K., Pumfrey, P.D. & Laskier, M. (1996). Rate of Reading Test: Its reliability and its validity in the assessment of the effects of coloured overlays. *Ophthalmic and Physiological Optics, 16*, 491–497.

Wilkinson, G.S. & Robertson, G.J. (2006). *Wide range achievement test (Fourth Ed.)*. Los Angeles: Western Psychological Services.

Williams, E.G. (1965). *Vocational counselling*. NY: McGraw-Hill.

Wilson, A.M. & Lesaux, N.K. (2001). Persistence of phonological processing deficits in college students with dyslexia who have age-appropriate reading skills. *Journal of Learning Disabilities, 34*(5), 394–400.

Wilson, B.A., Alderman, N., Burgess, P., Emslie, H. & Evans, J. (1996). *Behavioural assessment of the Dysexecutive Syndrome*. Bury St. Edmunds, Suffolk: Thames Valley Test Company.

Wing, A.M. & Baddeley, A.D. (1980). Spelling errors in handwriting: A corpus and distributional analysis. In U. Frith (Ed.), *Cognitive processes in spelling*. London: Academic Press.

Winner, E., von Karolyi, C., & Malinski, D. (2000). Dyslexia and visual-spatial talents: No clear link. *Perspectives, 26*(2), 26–29.

Winspear, D. (2008). Using CBT to improve mental health and employment outcomes for Incapacity Benefit Customers: Final Report. *Journal Occupational Psychology, Employment and Disability, 10*, 2 Autumn, pp. 91–104.

Wolf, M. (2008). *Proust and the squid*. Cambridge: Icon Books Ltd.

Wong, B.Y.L. (1986). Metacognition and special education: A review of a view. *Journal of Special Education, 20*, 19–29.

Woodcock, W.R. (2011). *Woodcock-Reading Mastery Tests* (3rd ed.). London: Pearson.

Woodcock, W.R., McGrew, K.S. & Mather, N. (2001). *Woodcock-Johnson III Tests of Achievement*. Itasca, IL: Riverside.

Wray, D. (1994). Comprehension monitoring, metacognition and other mysterious processes. *Support for Learning, 9*, 107–113.

Wilkinson, L.A. (2008). A childhood disorder grows up, *The Psychologist* [online].

Yost, E.B. & Corbishley, M.A. (1987). *Career counselling*. London: Jossey-Bass.

Zabell, C. & Everatt, J. (2002). Surface and phonological subtypes of adult developmental dyslexia. *Dyslexia, 8*(3), 160–177.

Zdzienski, D. (1997). *Study scan*. London: PICO Educational Systems Ltd.

Zeffiro, T.J. & Eden, G. (2000). The neural basis of developmental dyslexia. *Annals of Dyslexia, 50*, 1–30.

Zimmerman, B.J. (1992). Self-motivation for academic attainment: The role of self-efficacy beliefs and personal goal setting. *American Educational Research Journal, 29*(3), 663–676.

Zimmerman, B.J. (2002). Becoming a self-regulated learner: An overview. *Theory into Practice, 41*(2), 64–70.

Zurcher, R. & Bryant, D.P. (2001). The validity and comparability of entrance examination scores after accommodations are made for students with LD. *Journal of Learning Disabilities, 34*(5), 462–471.

Index

abbreviated scales, 67, 68
abilities and strengths of dyslexics, 116–23
academic and professional learning skills,
    162–4
  behavioural learning styles, 166, 167
    time management, 167
    work organisation, 167, 168
  cognitive learning differences, 166
  extended reporting of WRIT scores, 201,
    202
  keys to success in higher and professional
    education, 164
  learning and working styles, 166
  metacognition, 164
  perspective of dyslexic person, 192
    assessment report, 192–7
    consultancy report, 197–9
    recommendations, 200–201
    written work, 199
  reading, 168
  recommendations, 253
  responsibilities of colleges and universities,
    189, 190
  self-reflection attribution and self-efficacy,
    165, 166
  self-understanding and self-reflection, 164,
    165
  skill development, 168–70
    comprehending diagrammatic and
      tabular formats, 171
    critical reading skills, 170, 171

  essay writing, 172, 173
  examinations, 182–4
  grammar and punctuation, 175
  group working, 186, 187
  listening comprehension, 176, 177
  note making, 179
  note taking, 177–9
  presentations, 185, 186
  proofreading, 174, 175
  revision and memory skills, 179–82
  spelling, 175, 176
  statistics, 184, 185
  understanding tasks, 173, 174
  study skills course, 190, 191
  tutorials, 187
    keys to success, 189
    role of student, 189
    role of tutor, 187–9
accommodations and adjustments, 49, 50
ACID profile, 66
adjustment in adult years
  external factors, 40
  internal factors, 39, 40
  risk and resilience, 38, 39
Adult Checklist, 57
adult dyslexia, 1–5, 34
  characteristics, 10–14
  degrees of dyslexia, 32, 33
  evidence-based practice, 8–10
  history, 5, 6
  other syndromes, 28–32

The Dyslexic Adult: Interventions and Outcomes – An Evidence-based Approach, Second Edition.
David McLoughlin and Carol Leather.
© 2013 John Wiley & Sons, Ltd. Published 2013 by John Wiley & Sons, Ltd.

adult dyslexia (*Continued*)
  prevalence, 33, 34
  psychological development, 35–7
  terminology, 6, 7
  working memory model, 19–28
advocacy, 257–9, 272, 273
  disclosing dyslexia, 267
    circumstances, 268
    nature, 268–70
    who to disclose to, 268
  dyslexia and criminal law, 272
  dyslexia as mental impairment, 259, 260
    day-to-day effects, 260, 261
    substantial adverse effects, 260
    substantial long-term effects, 260
  employment policy and practice, 270
  higher education policy, 270, 271
  legislation in education and training, 270
  legislative framework, 259
  reasonable adjustments, 261, 262
    essential requirements of job/course, 263
    individual needs, 262
    integrated experience, 262, 263
    undue financial/administrative burden,
      263
  recruitment, selection and promotion
    adjustments, 263, 264
  self-help and self-help groups, 271, 272
  types of test accommodations/adjustments,
    264–7
affective characteristics of dyslexia, 12, 13
  working memory model, 26, 27
alternative interventions, 49–51
anger, 12
anxiety, 12
  measurement, 80, 81
articulatory control system, 22
Asperger's syndrome, 31, 32
  diagnosis, 85
assessment. *See* identification and assessment
  of dyslexia
asynchrony phenomenon, 17
attention deficit disorder/attention deficit
    hyperactivity disorder (ADD/ADHD),
    31
  diagnosis, 85
Autistic Spectrum Quotient (AQ), 85

automatic skills, 17–19
awareness training, 220–24

Behavioural Assessment of Dysexecutive
    Syndrome (BADS), 70
behavioural characteristics of dyslexia, 10, 11
  empirical evidence, 15
    biology and neurology, 15–17
    cognition, 17–19
    explaining characteristics, 15
behavioural learning styles, 166, 167
  time management, 167
  work organisation, 167, 168
biological basis of dyslexia, 15–17
brain hemispheres, 117, 118
brain imaging studies, 16, 17
  working memory model of dyslexia, 20, 21
Brixton Test, 71
Brown ADD Scales, 85

career development and guidance, 203
  approaches to counselling and
    development, 204, 205
  career development, 215, 216
    dyslexia and journalism, 216, 218
  decision making model, 205, 206
  guidance model, 206–13
    case example, 214, 215
case history, 138–40
Central Executive subsystem, 20, 21
cerebellar theory, 17–19
characteristics of dyslexia
  affective, 12, 13
  behavioural, 10, 11
    empirical evidence, 15–19
  positive, 13–15
checklists, 57
client feedback of assessment, 86, 87
Cloze decoding, 74, 75
coach, role of, 44–6
coaching, 42–4
  workplace course, 254–6
cognition and dyslexia, 17–19
Cognitive Behavioural Therapy (CBT), 107
cognitive distortions, 108
cognitive learning differences, 166
compensated dyslexic, 6

compensation, 47
  strategies and solutions, 48–9, 50
Comprehensive Test of Phonological
      Processing (CTOPP), 68, 69
computer-based tests, 58
confidence, 12
counselling, 41, 42, 100
  aims, 101
  approaches, 102
    empathy, 102
    exploration, intervention and
        empowering, 104–110
    genuineness, 103
    non-judgemental acceptance, 103
    psycho-education stages, 103–5
  couple counselling, 110
  issue for dyslexics, 101, 102
  referring on, 110, 111
creativity, 40
criminal law and dyslexia, 272

decision making model, 205, 206
decoding, 73, 74
deep breathing technique, 109
definitions of dyslexia, 3, 6, 7
  working memory model, 28
degrees of dyslexia, 32, 33
desire, 39
development in adulthood, 35–7
  learning, 40, 41
  successful adjustment, 38–40
  transitions, 37, 38
*Developmental dyslexia in adults: a research
    review*, 2
diagnosis of dyslexia, 61, 62
Diagnostic and Statistical Manual 5
    (DSM 5), 7
diagnostic evaluation example, 94
  behaviour in test setting, 94
  cognitive ability, 94, 95
  conclusion, 96
  literacy skills, 95, 96
  memory and processing ability, 95
diagrams, comprehending, 171
differential diagnosis, 52
Digit Symbol Modalities, 84
Disability Discrimination Act (1995), 4

disclosure at work, 224, 267
  circumstances, 268
  nature, 268–70
  who to disclose to, 268
document literacy, 142
dyscalculia diagnosis, 84, 85
DyscalculiUM screening test, 84
dysfunctional schemas, 108
dyslexia, 34
  adults, 1–5
  as mental impairment, 259, 260
    day-to-day effects, 260, 261
    substantial adverse effects, 260
    substantial long-term effects, 260
  characteristics, 10–14
  criminal law, 272
  definitions, 3, 6, 7, 28
  degrees of dyslexia, 32, 3
  evidence-based practice, 8–10
  history, 5, 6
  interpreting, 113–16
  orthographic, 17
  other syndromes, 28–32
  prevalence, 33, 34
  terminology, 6, 7
  working memory model, 19–28
Dyslexia Adult Screening Test (DAST), 60
dyspraxia, 29
  diagnosis, 84

employment issues, 4
English as a foreign language, 81–3
essay writing, 172, 173
evidence-based practice, 8–10
examinations, 182–4
executive functioning tests, 70
external factors of successful adult
      adjustment
  goodness of fit, 40
  learned creativity, 40
  persistence, 40
  social ecologies, 40

forethought phase of metacognition, 46
frustration, 12
full-scale IQ test, 64, 65
functional level literacy, 148

Gilliam Asperger's Disorder Scale, 85
goal setting, 39, 40
goodness of fit, 40, 224, 225
grading evidence from research, 9, 10
grammar, 175
group working skills, 186, 187

Hayling Test, 71
hedonic detector, 27
heritability of dyslexia
  phonological storage, 21
  twin studies, 15, 16
history of dyslexia, 5, 6
Holland's Self-Directed Search, 207–9

ideational dyspraxia, 29
identification and assessment of dyslexia, 41,
    52, 53
  affective characteristics, 80
    anxiety, 80, 81
    self-esteem, 80
  client feedback, 86, 87
  diagnostic evaluation example, 94
    behaviour in test setting, 94
    cognitive ability, 94, 95
    conclusion, 96
    literacy skills, 95, 96
    memory and processing ability, 95
  English as a foreign language, 81–3
  executive functioning, 70
  formal diagnosis, 61, 62
  guide to assessments, 97–9
  Hayling and Brixton Tests, 71
  individually administered tests for dyslexia,
    59
    Dyslexia Adult Screening Test (DAST),
      60
    Scholastic Abilities Test for Adults
      (SATA), 60, 61
    York Adult Assessment Battery, 59, 60
  information gathering, 53, 54
  intelligence testing (IQ), 62, 63
    abbreviated scales, 67, 68
    full-scale IQ test, 64, 65
    index scores, 65
    item level test and task cognitive
      capacities, 66, 67
    perceptual reasoning tests, 64

    processing speed, 64
    teachers' tests, 68
    verbal tests, 64
    WAIS-IV, 63
    WAIS-IV as an ipsative test, 65, 66
    working memory tests, 64
  interviews, 54–7
  literacy and numeracy achievements
    comprehension, 74, 75
    decoding, 73, 74
    listening comprehension, 75
    numeracy, 79, 80
    reading, 71
    reading assessment components, 73
    reading levels, 71, 72
    reading metacognition assessment, 76,
      77
    reading speed, 75, 76
    writing and spelling, 77–9
  memory ability, 69, 70
  other syndromes, 83, 84
    ADD/ADHD, 85
    Asperger's syndrome, 85
    dyscalculia, 84, 85
    dyspraxia, 84
    pretending to have a learning difficulty,
      86
    visual stress, 85, 86
  psychological testing, 68
    phonological processing and naming
      speed, 68, 69
  report writing, 87, 88
  screening, 57
    checklists, 57
    computer-based tests, 58
    LADS plus, 58
    StudyScan and QuickScan, 58, 59
Identifying and Teaching Children and Young
    People with Dyslexia and Literary
    Difficulties, 3
ideomotor dyspraxia, 29
idiographic approach, 8, 9
index scores, 65
individually administered tests for dyslexia, 59
  Dyslexia Adult Screening Test (DAST), 60
  Scholastic Abilities Test for Adults (SATA),
    60, 61
  York Adult Assessment Battery, 59, 60

information processing and literacy,
    145–7
intelligence (IQ) of dyslexics, 5, 6
    testing, 62, 63
        abbreviated scales, 67, 68
        full-scale IQ test, 64, 65
        index scores, 65
        item level test and task cognitive
            capacities, 66, 67
        perceptual reasoning tests, 64
        processing speed, 64
        teachers' tests, 68
        verbal tests, 64
        WAIS-IV, 63
        WAIS-IV as an ipsative test, 65, 66
        working memory tests, 64
internal attributions, 108
internal factors of successful adult adjustment
    desire, 39
    goal setting, 39, 40
    re-framing, 40
interventions, 35
    alternative interventions, 49–51
    integrated framework for development,
        47–9
    metacognitive skill development, 46, 47
    role of tutor/coach, 44–6
    types, 41
        assessment, 41
        counselling, 41, 42
        training, coaching and mentoring,
            42–4
interviews for jobs, 247, 248
item level test, 66, 67

journalism, 216–18

Kaufman Brief Intelligence Test (KBIT), 68

learned creativity, 40
learning and working styles, 166
learning difficulties, 6
    pretending to have, 86
learning disabilities, 5
learning in adulthood, 40, 41
Learning to Achieve report, 3
listening comprehension, 176, 177
    workplace, 243, 244

literacy, 10, 141, 142
    definition, 141
    dimensions
        document literacy, 142
        prose literacy, 142
        quantitative literacy, 142
    improving levels, 147
    improving quantitative literacy, 156
        accommodations, 157, 158
        compensations, 157
        skill development, 156, 157
    improving reading accuracy
        accommodations, 151
        compensations, 149–51
        skill development, 147–9
    improving reading comprehension
        accommodations, 153
        compensations, 152, 153
        pass reading strategy, 152
        skill development, 151
    improving spelling, 153
        accommodations, 154
        compensations, 154
        skill development, 153, 154
    improving writing, 154
        accommodations, 156
        compensations, 155, 156
        skill development, 154, 155
    information processing, 145–7
    lifelong learning, 142–4
    perspective of dyslexic person,
        158–60
    planning a programme, 144, 145
        sample learning contract, 146
    professional level writing, 147
    tasks in adulthood, 144
    workplace
        listening skills, 243, 244
        meetings, 244, 245
        note taking, 244
        numeracy, 242
        proofreading, 243
        reading, 237, 238
        reading complex material, 238–40
        record keeping, 240, 241
        report writing, 241
        skill development, 241, 242
        writing, 240

literate dyslexics, 6
Lucid Adult Dyslexia Screening—Plus
    Version (LADS plus), 58

magnocellular processing, 18, 19
Meares–Irlen Syndrome, 32
meetings at work, 244, 245
    recommendations, 252, 253
memory
    problems with, 10
    testing, 69, 70
    tip of the tongue memory, 18
    working memory model, 19–23
    workplace skills, 237
mentoring, 42–4
metacognition, 123
    importance in higher and professional
        education, 164
    importance in learning and working, 124,
        125
    skills involved, 46, 47, 126, 127
        workplace, 230
    technique, 127, 128
Miscue Analysis, 74, 75
Myers–Briggs Type Indicator (MBTI),
    209–11

negative beliefs associated with dyslexia, 108
neurological basis of dyslexia, 15–17
nomothetic approach, 8
note making, 179
note taking, 177–9
    workplace, 244
numeracy, 10
    workplace, 242

optimisation, 47
organisational skills, 37
    workplace, 234, 235
        time management and prioritisation,
            235, 236
        workspace, 236, 237
orthographical dyslexia, 17
over generalisations, 108

pass reading strategy, 152
perceptual reasoning tests, 64
perfectionism, 132

performance phase of metacognition, 46, 47
persistence, 40
Person Centred Therapy, 102
personal and family tasks, 143
personal development, 112
    abilities and strengths, 116–23
    interpreting dyslexia, 113–16
    issues, 128
        accommodation, 130
        compensation, 130
        goal setting, 130
        memory skills, 132, 133
        personal organisation, 129, 130
        prioritisation, 130–32
        self-advocacy, 129
        social skills, 133–5
    metacognition, 123
        importance in learning and working,
            124, 125
        skills involved, 126, 127
        technique, 127, 128
    nature of the difficulty, 113
    self-understanding, 112, 113
personal perspective of a dyslexic person,
    135–8
    case history, 138–40
personality, 118, 119
Phonological Loop subsystem, 20–22
phonological processing and naming speed
    tests, 68, 69
phonological processing difficulties, 17, 18
phonological storage, 22, 23
    heritability of, 21
planning checklist, 131
planum temporale symmetry, 16
positive characteristics of dyslexia, 13–15
    abilities and strengths, 116–23
    working memory model, 23–6
presentation skills, 185, 186
    recommendations, 252, 253
pretending to have a learning difficulty, 86
prevalence of dyslexia, 33, 4
prioritisation in the workplace, 235, 236
processing speed, 64
professional learning skills. *See* academic and
    professional learning skills
professional level literacy, 150
professional level writing, 147

progressive relaxation technique, 109
proofreading, 174, 175
   workplace, 243
prose literacy, 142
psycho-education stages, 103–5
psychological development in adult years,
   35–7
   learning, 40, 41
   successful adjustment, 38, 40
   transitions, 37, 38
psychological testing for dyslexia, 68
   phonological processing and naming
      speed, 68, 69
punctuation, 175

quantitative literacy, 142
QuickScan, 58, 59

rapid automatic naming, 18
Rational-Emotive Therapy, 106
recruitment for employment, 225, 226
   adjustments, 263, 264
   interviews, 247, 248
reframing, 40, 105, 106
report writing, 87, 88
   sample report, 89–93
research, grading of evidence obtained, 9, 10
revision skills, 179–82
Rose Report, 3, 32

Scholastic Abilities Test for Adults (SATA), 60,
   61
scotopic sensitivity, 32
screening for dyslexia, 57
   checklists, 57
   computer-based tests, 58
   LADS plus, 58
   StudyScan and QuickScan, 58, 59
selection for employment, 47, 226
   adjustments, 263, 264
self-defeating thought processes, 107
self-efficacy, 46
   academic and professional learning skills,
      165, 166
self-esteem, 12
   building up, 109, 110
   measurement, 80
self-help and self-help groups, 271, 272

self-reflection, 164, 165
   attribution, 165, 166
self-reflection phase of metacognition, 47
self-regulation, 23, 46
self-talk, 132
self-understanding, 112, 113, 164, 165
skill development, 47, 48, 50
social ecologies, 40
social interaction skills, 13
spoken language skills, 10
statistics skills, 184, 185
Stewart, Sir Jackie, 13
StudyScan, 58, 59
syndromes co-occurring, 28, 29
   ADD/ADHD, 31
   Asperger's syndrome, 31, 32
   dyscalculia, 30, 31
   dyspraxia, 29
   visual stress, 32

tables of data, comprehending, 171
task cognitive capacities, 66, 67
teachers' tests for intelligence, 68
teamwork, 245–7
technical level literacy, 150
terminology, 6, 7
therapies
   idiographic, 8, 9
   nomothetic, 8
three pillars of evidence, 8
time management, 167
   workplace, 235, 236
tip of the tongue memory, 18
training, 42–4
transitions in adult years, 37, 38
tutor, role of, 44–6
tutorials, 187
   keys to success, 189
   role of student, 189
   role of tutor, 187–9
twin studies, 15, 16

verbal tests, 64
visual processing difficulties, 17
visual stress, 32
   diagnosis, 85, 86
   workplace recommendations, 251, 252
visualisation technique, 109

Visual-spatial Sketchpad subsystem, 20, 21
vocational level literacy, 149

Walker's Valuing Differences Model, 220
Wechsler Adult Intelligence Scale – Fourth
    Edition (WAIS-IV)
  as a normative test, 63
  as an ipsative test, 65, 66
Wechsler Memory Scales – Fourth Edition
    (WMS-IV), 69, 70
Wide Range Intelligence Test (WRIT), 68
  extended reporting, 201, 202
Wilkins Rate of Reading Test, 85
Wisconsin Card Sort Test, 70
work and dyslexia, 219, 220, 254, 256
  addressing challenges
    organisation, 234, 235
    time management and prioritisation,
      235, 236
    workspace, 236, 237
  awareness training, 220–24
  challenges facing dyslexic people, 228–30
  changes and transitions, 230, 231
  coaching course, 254–6
  disclosure, 224, 267
    circumstances, 268
    nature, 268–70
    who to disclose to, 268
  dyslexia consultancy report, 249, 250
  employment policy and practice, 270
  evaluation and reflection, 230
  goodness of fit, 224, 225
  listening skills, 243, 244
  meetings, 244, 245
  memory, 237
  metacognitive skills, 230
  note taking, 244
  numeracy, 242
  performance issues, 240
  proofreading, 243
    reading, 237, 238
      complex material, 238–40
    recommendations, 250
      IT solutions, 251
      meetings and presentations, 252, 253
      organisational strategies, 250
      paperwork, 251
      professional examinations, 253
      visual stress, 251, 252
      working environment, 253
    record keeping, 240, 241
    recruitment, 225, 226
      adjustments, 263, 264
      interviews, 247, 248
    report writing, 241
    role of manager, 227, 228
    selection, 226
      adjustments, 263, 264
    skill development, 241, 242
    support at workplace
      coaching example, 232, 233
      mentoring, 234
      programme length, 233
      tutor training, coaching and mentoring,
        231, 232
    teamwork, 245–7
    transfer of skills, 230
    workplace assessment/consultation, 226,
      227
    workplace consultancy report, 248
    written work, 240
work organisation, 167, 168
working memory model of dyslexia, 19–23,
    114
  definition of dyslexia, 28
  explaining affective characteristics, 26, 27
  explaining positive characteristics, 23–6
working memory tests, 64

York Adult Assessment Battery, 59, 60

How to have
Healthy
Happy
Children

649.1

BBC Active, an imprint of Educational Publishers LLP, part of the
Pearson Education Group
Edinburgh Gate
Harlow
Essex CM20 2JE
England

This book was originally published in 2006 as *Honey We're Killing the Kids* to
accompany the BBC television series of the same name. This is a revised and
updated edition.

The advice given in this book is aimed at children over the age of two.

This edition first published 2007

ISBN: 978-1-406-63893-6

Commissioned by Emma Shackleton
Project Edited by Jeanette Payne
Edited by Sarah Sutton
Designed by Annette Peppis
Cover illustration by Chris Long
Commissioned photographs by Chris Capstick © BBC Active
Production Controller: Franco Forgione

Printed and bound in China

The Publisher's policy is to use paper manufactured from sustainable forests.